COLLECTED POEMS

STÉPHANE MALLARMÉ

translated and with a commentary by

Henry Weinfield

COLLECTED POEMS

UNIVERSITY OF CALIFORNIA PRESS

Berkeley Los Angeles London

University of California Press
Berkeley and Los Angeles, California

University of California Press
London, England

Library of Congress Cataloging-in-Publication Data

Mallarmé, Stéphane, 1842-1898.
[Poems. English & French]
Collected poems / Stéphane Mallarmé : translated and
with a commentary by Henry Weinfield.
p. cm.
Includes bibliographical references.
ISBN 0-520-08188-9
l. Mallarmé, Stéphane, 1842-1898—Translations into English.
I. Weinfield, Henry.
PQ2344.A286 1994
841'.8—dc20   94-26794
                                        CIP

Printed in the United States of America

1 2 3 4 5 6 7 8 9

This translation of the poetry of Stéphane Mallarmé

is inscribed

to

Allen Mandelbaum

For the Master has gone to draw tears from the Styx

CONTENTS

POÉSIES

POËMES EN PROSE

UN COUP DE DÉS

COMMENTARY

INTRODUCTION

One does not introduce, much less sum up, the poetry of Stéphane Mallarmé. Though the quantity of the work is small, it contains a world and it is a world. My only way of encompassing that work and that world has been to translate it, poem by poem, and to interpret it, poem by poem, in the hope that the accumulation would add up to something. The translation contained in these pages includes, with the French text *en face*, all of the poems that Mallarmé wished to preserve and a few additional poems that have come to be regarded as central to the canon: the *Poésies* (poems in traditional forms), the *Poëmes en Prose*, and *Un Coup de Dés Jamais N'Abolira le Hasard* (the great free-verse poem of his final period); only the juvenilia and the occasional verse have been omitted. The interpretation, besides what is contained in the translation itself, appears as a separate Commentary at the back of the volume.

Mallarmé is at once the most musical and the most philosophical of modern poets—if we may speak of "music" and of "philosophy" not as they exist in themselves but from the standpoint of a poetry that completely transforms them to its own requirements. I would say, speaking metaphorically, that my primary struggle in this translation has been to render the "music," or "musical essence," or "spiritual essence," of the poetry. We don't have a language in which to express these things with any clarity: they are finally ineffable; but this, in a sense, is to the point, for the poetry of Mallarmé presents itself as the most resonant site that modern literature provides for coming to terms, at least in some fashion, with these ineffabilities. What I *can* say, with absolute certainty, is that in translating the *Poésies* it has been essential to work in rhyme and meter, regardless of the semantic accommodations and technical problems this entailed. If we take rhyme away from Mallarmé, we take away the *poetry* of his poetry. "Because, to him who ponders well, / My rhymes more than their rhyming tell / Of things discovered in the deep, / Where only body's laid asleep": thus Yeats, who had learned an enormous amount from Mallarmé and whose work would have been impossible without him.

The music and the philosophy of Mallarmé's poetry are ultimately one and the same; yet in order to grasp this fundamental unity, one must come to see how the vectors of form and content are turned in what may initially appear to be antithetical directions. On the level of form, we must take account of how Mallarmé "cede[s] the initiative to words" themselves—as he insists the poet must do in "Crise de Vers," the great theoretical essay that he rewrote several times between 1886 and 1896. Consider, for example, Mallarmé's penchant for polysyllabic homonymic rhyme, a tendency that comes to fruition in "Prose (pour des Esseintes)," the *ars poetica* of 1885, which, from one point of view at least, is his most radical poem. When rhymes such as *désir, Idées,* and *des iridées* come together, as they do in that poem, it is clear that the neoclassical ideal, according to which "the sound must be an echo to the sense," no longer applies; rather, we seem to have a situation in which, ceding the initiative to words, the poet has become a kind of magician or alchemist of language (both of these are metaphors that Mallarmé himself applies), raising hitherto undiscovered meanings out of the alembic of his craft. From this point of view, poetry becomes oriented to *enchantment* or *incantation* (Mallarméan terms that bring together the senses of music and magic), and the poet, working not in the abstract but in the concrete medium of a specific language, assumes the responsibility of invoking and gathering the divine Irises that would otherwise be stillborn in the soil of desire and of the idea.

Paul Valéry, who composed some of the most luminous—and loving—pages of criticism ever written on Mallarmé, is especially fine on the sheer poetic power of the verse:

> This poet was the least *primitive* of all poets, yet it came about that by bringing words together in an unfamiliar, strangely melodious, and as it were stupefying chant—by the musical splendor of his verse as well as by its amazing richness—he restored the most powerful impression to be derived from primitive poetry: that of the *magical formula*. An exquisite analysis of his art must have led him toward a doctrine, and something like a synthesis, of incantation. (*Leonardo, Poe, Mallarmé,* 279)

"Everything that is sacred and that wishes to remain so must envelop itself in mystery" ("Hérésies Artistiques: L'Art pour Tous," *OC,* 257). That sentence was written when Mallarmé was twenty years old, but the hermetic attitude he was already cultivating was, if anything, deepened with the course of time. So it is not surprising that he should have been dogged during his lifetime by accusations of mystification and preciosity, and that accusations of this kind should continue to the present day. (He sometimes deflected them in the contempt he expressed—in the poems themselves—for the bourgeois reading public, which, in the "Tombeau d'Edgar Poe," for example, is likened to a many-headed hydra.) Mallarmé is often obscure, but he is no obscurantist; his obscurity and difficulty are organic to, necessary concomitants of, the demands of his artistry, on the one hand—what Valéry terms "the rigorousness of [his] refusals" (*Leonardo, Poe, Mallarmé,* 250)—and on the other, the philosophical vision, the actual content of his poetry: the quest for Beauty and for a transcendent Ideal and the tragic vision on which that quest is based.

Georges Poulet has drawn a distinction between "the act of Cartesian consciousness by means of which existence founds itself in thought and the properly Mallarméan act of consciousness by means of which thought creates existence" (*The Interior Distance,* 264). I would add that the dualism that obtains in Mallarmé's work is not so much that of mind and body as of poetry and prose, the former corresponding to an ideal realm of the spirit and the latter to the actual realm of material reality. This basic attitude informs Mallarmé's thought as a whole; it is stated very explicitly in a famous letter of April 1866 to his close friend Henri Cazalis, which was written when Mallarmé was twenty-four, teaching

English in a lycée at Tournon, and in the midst of a deep spiritual crisis (the so-called "Nuits de Tournon"):

> Yes, I *know*, we are merely empty forms of matter, but we are indeed sublime in having invented God and our soul. So sublime, my friend, that I want to gaze upon matter, fully conscious that it exists, and yet launching itself madly into Dream, despite its knowledge that Dream has no existence, extolling the Soul and all the divine impressions of that kind which have collected within us from the beginning of time and proclaiming, in the face of the Void which is truth, these glorious lies! (*Selected Letters*, 60)

And again, to choose a matching passage from the poetry, it is present, more or less explicitly, in the great sonnet, "Quand l'ombre menaça de la fatale loi" (see p. 66), an early draft of which was written around the same time as the letter.

The spiritual crisis that Mallarmé underwent in the 1866-1867 period (in my opinion, it is merely the culmination of an experience that was waiting to unfold in him from the beginning) is a reflection of a general religious crisis occuring in Europe during the nineteenth century, with roots that stretch back much earlier. The form/content paradox in Mallarmé, then, is that while he conceives of poetry as that which "must envelop itself in mystery," his confrontation with the religious crisis of his time is as immediate and profound as that of any writer. Thus, Mallarmé is a genuine spokesman for his age, although without having had the slightest desire to serve as one.

Poetry is implicated in the religious crisis in a double sense (and we should recall the title of the essay, "Crise de Vers," from which a passage was quoted earlier): first, because in responding to the religious crisis, poetry confronts and to some extent transforms its traditional modes and procedures; and secondly (and perhaps more importantly), because it is given to poetry to step into the breach of theological certainty. Matthew Arnold, certainly a more conservative thinker than Mallarmé, makes precisely this point in "The Study of Poetry," an essay originally published in 1880:

> There is not a creed which is not shaken, not an accredited dogma which is not shown to be questionable, not a received tradition which does not threaten to dissolve. Our religion has materialized itself in the fact, in the supposed fact; it has attached its emotion to the fact, and now the fact is failing it. But for poetry the idea is everything; the rest is a world of divine illusion. Poetry attaches its emotion to the idea; the idea *is* the fact. The strongest part of our religion today is its unconscious poetry.

Insofar as the European mind is not simply overwhelmed by the forces of materialism, poetry becomes increasingly central and increasingly crucial; at the same time, however, it becomes more difficult, more sealed off from the quotidian—in a word, more hermetic.

"Poetry," wrote Mallarmé, in reply to a request for a definition, "is the expression of the mysterious meaning of the aspects of existence through human language brought back to its essential rhythm: in this way it endows our sojourn with authenticity and constitutes the only spiritual task" (see Michaud, *Mallarmé*, 107). And again, in the autobiographical sketch that he prepared for Paul Verlaine, Mallarmé defines poetry in terms of "the Orphic explanation of the earth, which is the sole duty of the poet" (*OC*, 663). Poetry is thus not only the vehicle but the locus of the sacred for Mallarmé, and in a sense, he remains a religious poet even though he loses his belief. The sacred exists for Mallarmé, but only insofar as it can be experienced phenomenologically; it exists only as an experience, through the concrete medium of language, or, in other words, as Beauty.

It would not, however, be true to say that the realm of poetry, with its hidden depths, represents an escape from the prosaic world of empty matter for Mallarmé, or that poetry exists in default of that world. Not only is the charge of mystification unfounded but there is a sense in which Mallarmé is much more of a realist than we have been given to understand, and I would even argue that an essential aim of this poet is toward demystification. Mallarmé would have agreed with Walter Pater's dictum that music is "the art toward which all the others aspire," and music is always and everywhere the signifier in his work of a transcendental ideal; but at the same time poetry remains for him, as it does for Hegel, the supreme art form. The reason for this, I would suggest, is that while the language of music presents itself as an already given transcendence, the language of poetry is initially the language of ordinary communication; thus, the transformation of ordinary language into poetry makes poetry an allegory of the transformation of life itself. For this reason, the duality of our being is concretized in poetry in a more immediate way than is possible in music. In the Mallarméan universe one might say that the "prosaic" world gazes darkly at the "poetic" one, as through a window (and the reverse is also true), so that the actual poetic emotion is engendered not by the vision of the ideal taken in itself but by this tragic duality. "I look at myself and see myself as an angel," the poet writes in "Les Fenêtres," one of the greatest of his early poems. The abundance of images in his verse that are at once symbols of reflection and of a passage to another life—windows, mirrors, ice, glass, and water—affirms the extent to which the Mallarméan vision is grounded in a series of irreconcilable polarities—self and other, the prosaic and the poetic, the temporal and the eternal.

It is true that for Mallarmé, as he asserts in "Le Livre, Instrument Spirituel" (another one of the essays on poetry that verges on being prose-poetry), "everything in the world exists in order to end up [or culminate—"*aboutir*"] in a book" (*OC*, 378). If we hear, in that sentence, an echo of the gospels, where everything happens "in order that the Scriptures be fulfilled," this is because, in the Mallarméan scheme of things, it is only through poetry that the indeterminacy otherwise governing the universe can be overcome. An additional level of irony must be taken into account, however, for the tragic in Mallarmé is not only composed of an omnipresent duality but is itself dual, in the sense of being aimed not only at a transcendental ideal but (since the latter is grasped as static and hence indistinguishable from death) at the temporal ground of our being. In the famous Swan sonnet, for example (see p. 67), it is as if the eternal gazed down upon the temporal, lamenting its loss. If there can be a definition of humanity, for Mallarmé, it is that which is always to be conceived in terms of "memories of horizons" ("Toast Funèbre," pp. 44–45); thus, in the final analysis—contrary to our received assumptions about the ingrown aestheticism of this poet and notwithstanding his preoccupation with death and nothingness—it may be that the real emphasis of the work is simply on life—life itself, which, in its beauty and fragility, always exceeds our grasp.

Mallarmé's development as a poet and as a thinker on poetry was extraordinarily rapid and intense; it can be traced in a series of remarkable letters written mainly during the 1866-1867 period referred to earlier, letters that are to French poetry what those of Keats, written when he was roughly the same age, are to English. During this period, Mallarmé was at work on two major poems, *Hérodiade* and "L'Après-midi d'un Faune," and his letters read as a workshop of his reflections and his discoveries. All of the characteristic emphases that constitute what we can call the Mallarméan system emerge during these years; for although he remained in large measure an "occasional" poet, responding, especially in sonnets, to events and experiences as they unfolded in his own life, very early on Mallarmé conceived of his oeuvre as an integrated totality, in terms of which each poem would represent both a part of the whole and, like Leibniz's monads, a reflection of the whole.

In July 1866 he writes to Théodore Aubanel:

> For my part, I've worked harder this summer than in my entire life and I can say that I've worked *for* my entire life. I've laid the foundations of a magnificent work. . . . I have died and been born again with the gem-encrusted key to my final spiritual casket. It's up to me now to open it in the absence of all extraneous impressions and its mystery will emerge into a very beautiful sky. I'll need twenty years during which I'll remain cloistered within myself, renouncing all publicity other than readings to friends. I'm working on everything at once, or rather I mean that everything is so well ordered in my mind that, as a sensation reaches me now, it is transformed and automatically places itself in the right book or the right poem. When a poem is ripe, it will drop free. You can see that I'm imitating the laws of nature. (*Selected Letters*, 66)

The emphasis on poetic impersonality, which was to have such an important impact on Yeats, Eliot, and twentieth-century poetry in general, emerges in this letter, not as an idea but as an experience born out of the creative process. As an idea, it can be traced to Hegel's assertion in the *Aesthetics*, that "however intimately the insights and feelings which the poet describes as his own belong to him as a single individual, they must nevertheless possess a universal validity" (2: 1111). But Mallarmé goes much further than Hegel; and, in a subsequent letter written the following May to Cazalis, we can see how the metaphorical death he describes coincides with the religious struggle to which we have already referred:

> I've just spent a terrifying year: my Thought has thought itself and reached a pure Concept. All that my being has suffered as a result during that long death cannot be told, but, fortunately, I am utterly dead, and the least pure region where my Spirit can venture is Eternity. My Spirit, that recluse accustomed to dwelling in its own Purity, is no longer darkened even by the reflection of Time.
>
> Unfortunately, I've reached this point through a dreadful sensitivity. . . . But this was even more the case a few months ago, firstly in my terrible struggle with that old and evil plumage, which is now, happily, vanquished: God. But as that struggle had taken place on his bony wing which, in death throes more vigorous than I would have suspected him capable of, had carried me into the Shadows, I fell, victorious, desperately and infinitely—until at last I saw myself again in my Venetian mirror, such as I was when I forgot myself several months before.
>
> I confess, moreover, but to you alone, that the torments inflicted by my triumph were so great, I still need to look at myself in that mirror in order to think and that if it were not in front of this desk on which I'm writing to you, I would become the Void once again. That will let you know that I am now impersonal and no longer the Stéphane that you knew—but a capacity

possessed by the spiritual Universe to see itself and develop itself, through what was once me. (*Selected Letters*, 74)

In the same letter Mallarmé writes: "I have made a long enough descent into the Void to speak with certainty. There is nothing but Beauty—and Beauty has only one perfect expression, Poetry. All the rest is a lie" (75). By taking on the mantle of impersonality, so as to become a "capacity possessed by the spiritual Universe," Mallarmé makes poetry an instrument of the Absolute, removing it, as he will say to Villiers de L'Isle-Adam in a letter of September 1867, "from the realms of Dream and Chance" (*Selected Letters*, 81).

The trajectory of Mallarmé's poetic career, however, is much more complex and varied than a discussion of his most salient themes and emphases would allow us to infer or that can be encompassed in a short introduction. The earliest poems in the *Poésies* and many of those in the *Poëmes en Prose* date from 1862, when Mallarmé was in his twentieth year; the last poems, the *tombeau* on Verlaine and *Un Coup de Dés*, were published in 1897, the year before the poet's death. In the interim the work undergoes profound changes, of course, but the poems of the early 1860s are already mature and of a very high order of excellence. Mallarmé was an assiduous reviser and he often returned to poems written many years earlier; so the stylistic propensities of the early poems often reflect the poet's later development. The work is extraordinarily self-contained and in some ways more single-minded than that of any poet of equal stature. Unless we study Mallarmé's poetry as a whole, however, we are likely to see it as much more one-dimensional than it actually is. In early poems such

as "Le Guignon" and "Le Phénomène Futur," for example (poems that are not among Mallarmé's most famous, especially in the English-speaking world), what one might call the poet's historical imagination and his concern with social and political issues is very much in evidence. This is a very different Mallarmé from the one we are accustomed to contemplating.

Similarly, when we conceive of Mallarmé's work as a whole, we find that his relationship to poetic patrimony is a more complex matter than we might have assumed. Baudelaire and Poe occupy the foreground early on, as is well known; but those influences become less salient over time, and, among the poet's most immediate forbears, one could argue that the role of Gautier is of equal, or even greater, importance. Lucretius and Dante are very strong presences in the work, both in themselves and through the mediation of others, and the voices of Gray, Shelley, and Keats connect Mallarmé to a poetic tradition that the author of *Les Mots Anglais* dearly loved. The poetry of Mallarmé is synonymous with the power of condensation he was able to bring to bear on the language; consequently, it is not surprising that the intertextual meta-narrative contained in the work is as richly complex as it is, and that much of it still remains to be mined.

The portion of the story that I have been able to uncover—either on my own or through my gleanings of the labors of other Mallarmistes—is articulated in the Commentary, which can thus be read both in relation to individual poems and as a loosely structured essay. The Commentary was originally intended as a series of explanatory notes on the poems. As the work progressed, however, my approach became increasingly essayistic, and I eventually abandoned what had been a naive attempt to separate annotation from interpretation. Whatever lucidities I have to offer, I hope are not tainted by corresponding oversimplifications (always a danger with Mallarmé criticism); and if, "musing the obscure," as Wallace Stevens would say, I have further clouded what was already veiled in ambiguity, I can only ask the reader's indulgence. I have allowed myself to have my say, both in the Commentary and in the translations themselves; for otherwise (such are the paradoxical vicissitudes of poetic translation and interpretation), it would not have been possible to be *faithful* to Mallarmé; and I have wanted to be faithful—though in the same measure that I have wanted to express myself and to be true to my own sense of the language. Faithfulness, with regard to the translations themselves, has meant balancing the literary against the literal—although, in the case of Mallarmé, it is not always possible to ascertain the literal meaning of a passage. To translate is to carry across, and I have wanted to carry Mallarmé across to a poetic milieu whose values are in many ways antithetical to those espoused by the French poet.

"English and French are one language," wrote Stevens optimistically; and I am consoled also by Jacques Derrida's generous observation that "Mallarmé's language is always open to the influence of the English language, that there is a regular exchange between the two . . . [and that] 'Mallarmé' does not belong completely to French literature" (*Acts of Literature*, 125). Indeed, if the poems have come to exist for me simultaneously in English and in French, in the "original" and in "translation" (as we say in our inadequate language), this should be taken neither as an expression of immodesty nor as a sign of incipient madness—for I can hardly expect that the reader will have a similar experience; rather, it is the inevitable by-product of a five-year immersion in the work of one who is certainly among the greatest of all lyric poets—and in whom I discovered, if not exactly *myself* (for that would be too great an irony), then at least something that I could do and perhaps be, something I could call my own. I am sufficiently admonished, in any event, by the animadversions of those semioticians for whom poetry (much less the poetry of Stéphane Mallarmé!) is untranslatable. According to Michael Riffaterre, for instance, "poetry does not translate—not because of certain intangible, quintessential elements usually invoked, but because of a semiotic displacement quite accessible to description" (*Semiotics of Poetry*, ix). In some moods, and from a theoretical point of view, I am willing to agree—but I did it anyway.

I was not so foolhardy, of course, as to have actually *planned* a translation of Mallarmé. It happened to me gradually, in the way most things in life do. Five years ago, when I tried my hand at one of the poems (I believe it was "Les Fenêtres"), I had no intention of going further; but the poetry pulled me in and my friends encouraged me, and, as my involvement took hold, I found that I had a work of some kind. Of course, my love for this strange poet goes back many years earlier, even (I am tempted to believe) to my childhood, and I think it has something to do with Montreal, the place where I was born, and where, if it were not for politics, English and French really would be one language. "The imperfection of languages," wrote Mallarmé in "Crise de Vers," "consists in their plurality, the supreme one is lacking: thinking is writing without accessories or even whispering, the immortal word still remains silent; the diversity of idioms on earth prevents everybody from uttering the words which otherwise, at one single stroke, would materialize as truth." Walter

Benjamin makes this passage the centerpiece of his great essay, "The Task of the Translator" (*Illuminations*, 77; *OC*, 363–364), as Hannah Arendt notes ("Introduction," *Illuminations*, 50), and George Steiner follows Benjamin in doing the same in *After Babel*, his study of translation. But the passage from "Crise de Vers" ends on a note that to lovers of poetry, at least, will not seem unduly pessimistic.

After observing that the plurality of languages militates against the immediacy of spoken truth, Mallarmé concludes that if there were only one language, and if the truth could therefore be uttered immediately, then "poetry would not exist: supreme complement [or completion], it compensates philosophically for what all languages lack" (*OC*, 364).

I am extremely grateful to the friends and colleagues who have helped, goaded, and encouraged me in the years that I have been working on Mallarmé, and I have benefited in no small measure from the annotators, commentators, and translators mentioned in the Commentary and the Bibliography in this volume. Norman Finkelstein, Michael Heller, David Katz, and Michael Perkins, brother poets, helped keep me alert to poetic values and to the impact of the poems on the English language. William Bronk, master of the plain style, humored me in my aberrations and kept me honest. And Louise Chawla, always sensitive to the intimate connection between poetry and the environment, put me in touch, through her wonderful letters, with a sense of spaciousness that seems now all but lost.

In addition to these, there were other dear friends who pored over my labors: Daniel Feldman, Eric Levy, Laury Magnus and Boris Jakim, Dale Ramsey, David Wolinsky.

That Richard Wilbur should have countenanced my early efforts was of no small importance to me. And I am extremely grateful to the four distinguished reviewers of the manuscript for the University of California Press—Paul Auster, Germaine Brée, Richard Goodkin, and Michael Palmer—for their encouragement, for the insights they offered, and for the difficulties they diagnosed.

Edward Foster kindly included a number of the translations and a number of sections from the Commentary in successive issues of *Talisman: A Journal of Contemporary Poetry and Poetics*. I would like to take this occasion to thank him—along with Mark Rudman of *Pequod*, Burt Kimmelman of *Poetry New York* and Donald Revell of *Denver Quarterly*, who also published my work in their journals.

I am grateful to Aimée Brown Price for the light she shed on Mallarmé's relationship to the painter Puvis de Chavannes; and, at the University of Notre Dame, to Joanne Dellaneva, for help with a passage in Ronsard; to Alain Toumayan, for his elucidation of a thorny knot in the "Tomb of Baudelaire"; to Bernard Doering, for the suggestions he offered in regard to "The Afternoon of a Faun"; and to Kent Emery, for his help with theological issues pertaining to "Saint."

Stephen Fredman, also at Notre Dame, was an assiduous reader of my prose, and conversations with Catherine Perry enriched my knowledge of the milieu in which Mallarmé lived and wrote. My research assistant, Colette LaForce, was wonderfully helpful with the proofs and with many other aspects of the project. I owe a tremendous debt of gratitude to Stephen Fallon, who, even while serving as chairman of the Program of Liberal Studies, took time away from his work on Milton to read long sections of the Commentary with scrupulous care. And I would like to thank the Institute for Scholarship in the Liberal Arts at Notre Dame, which generously supported my efforts.

With Stanley Holwitz, Rebecca Frazier, Hayes McNeill, Michelle Ghaffari, and the other members of the University of California Press with whom I interacted, I always felt that I was treated as a friend. I am exceedingly grateful to have worked with people for whom bookmaking is both an art in itself and an extension of poetry.

Stuart Liebman's friendship and conversation have been a source of continuity in my life for many years; he and Lois Greenfield know how sustaining their presence has been to me—but let me thank them again.

My wife, Joyce, while pursuing a triple career as psychologist, teacher, and writer, and while raising two daughters and a stepson, has not only given me support and strength throughout this project but has been a trusted interlocutor. And my son, Paul, and daughters, Saralena and Vera, have kept me anchored in the poetry of the natural world.

Allen Mandelbaum, to whom this volume is inscribed, made two epic descents during the period in which I was at work on Mallarmé's poetry, producing beautiful translations of the *Odyssey* and the *Metamorphoses*. These, of course, were added to the *Aeneid* and the *Commedia*, his earlier contributions—not to mention his renderings of modern Italian poetry, the extraordinary essays, and the brilliant poems. He was involved with this project from its inception, and he has left his imprint upon it, as he has done with the work of so many others; his generosity knows no bounds. Let the line from Mallarmé's "Sonnet en-*yx*" that I have inscribed beneath his name—a line I regard as one of the most beautiful in all poetry—serve as a measure of the esteem in which I hold my teacher and friend.

Henry Weinfield
Notre Dame, Indiana

POÉSIES

SALUTATION

Nothing, this foam, virgin verse
Only to designate the cup:
Thus, far off, drowns a Siren troop;
Many, upended, are immersed.

We navigate, O my diverse
Friends, myself already on the poop,
You the sumptuous prow to cut
Through winter wave and lightning burst;

A lovely drunkenness enlists
Me to raise, though the vessel lists,
This toast on high and without fear

Solitude, rocky shoal, bright star
To whatsoever may be worth
Our sheet's white care in setting forth.

SALUT

Rien, cette écume, vierge vers
A ne désigner que la coupe;
Telle loin se noie une troupe
De sirènes mainte à l'envers.

Nous naviguons, ô mes divers
Amis, moi déjà sur la poupe
Vous l'avant fastueux qui coupe
Le flot de foudres et d'hivers;

Une ivresse belle m'engage
Sans craindre même son tangage
De porter debout ce salut

Solitude, récif, étoile
A n'importe ce qui valut
Le blanc souci de notre toile.

FIRST POEMS

THE JINX

Gleaming above the bewildered human herd,
Flaunting their uncouth manes and filthy rags,
Beggars of azure skipped into our road.

Black winds upon their march deployed as flags
Whipped them with cold unto the very flesh,
Hollowing furrows in their arms and legs.

Always in hopes of encountering afresh
The sea, they journeyed without bowls or bread,
Biting the lemon of some bitter wish.

Most in the narrow straits of night dropped dead,
Drunk on the joy of seeing their blood flow:
O Death, sole kiss for silent mouths unfed!

A powerful angel plots their overthrow,
And when he waves on high his naked sword,
Clots in the grateful bosom lay them low.

They suck upon their pain as heretofore
Upon their dreams, and watch their neighbors suck,
Kneeling before the mother they adore.

Some are consoled and rise up from the muck,
But drag a hundred brothers in their wake,
Derided martyrs to their mangled luck.

PREMIERS POËMES

LE GUIGNON

Au-dessus du bétail ahuri des humains
Bondissaient en clartés les sauvages crinières
Des mendieurs d'azur le pied dans nos chemins.

Un noir vent sur leur marche éployé pour bannières
La flagellait de froid tel jusque dans la chair,
Qu'il y creusait aussi d'irritables ornières.

Toujours avec l'espoir de rencontrer la mer,
Ils voyageaient sans pain, sans bâtons et sans urnes,
Mordant au citron d'or de l'idéal amer.

La plupart râla dans les défilés nocturnes,
S'enivrant du bonheur de voir couler son sang,
Ô Mort le seul baiser aux bouches taciturnes!

Leur défaite, c'est par un ange très puissant
Debout à l'horizon dans le nu de son glaive:
Une pourpre se caille au sein reconnaissant.

Ils tètent la douleur comme ils tétaient le rêve
Et quand ils vont rythmant des pleurs voluptueux
Le peuple s'agenouille et leur mère se lève.

Ceux-là sont consolés, sûrs et majestueux;
Mais traînent à leurs pas cent frères qu'on bafoue,
Dérisoires martyrs de hasards tortueux.

The same salt tears gnaw at their gentle cheek,
They chew on ashes with the same desire,
But fate humiliates them till they break.

They too might have awakened like a lyre
The servile pity of a dull-voiced race;
Prometheans, no vultures eat their liver!

Abject inhabitants of some desert place,
They flee the lash of that cruel overseer,
The Jinx, who spits his laughter in their face.

He leaps upon love's saddle to seize his share!
Then, once the torrent's crossed, he vents his scorn,
Plunging the pristine couple in the mire.

Thanks to him, if one should blow his flügelhorn,
Boys will convulse us in unseemly howls
As, fist to arse, they trumpet in their turn.

Or if on the withered breast of some dead soul
A rose should kindle it to life again,
Spittle will shine on it to make it foul.

And this dwarf skeleton, in feathered cap inane,
Whose armpits teem with worms instead of hair,
Evokes for them infinitudes of pain.

Le sel pareil des pleurs ronge leur douce joue,
Ils mangent de la cendre avec le même amour,
Mais vulgaire ou bouffon le destin qui les roue.

Ils pouvaient exciter aussi comme un tambour
La servile pitié des races à voix ternes,
Égaux de Prométhée à qui manque un vautour!

Non, vils et fréquentant les déserts sans citerne,
Ils courent sous le fouet d'un monarque rageur,
Le Guignon, dont le rire inouï les prosterne.

Amants, il saute en croupe à trois, le partageur!
Puis le torrent franchi, vous plonge en une mare
Et laisse un bloc boueux du blanc couple nageur.

Grâce à lui, si l'un souffle à son buccin bizarre,
Des enfants nous tordront en un rire obstiné
Qui, le poing à leur cul, singeront sa fanfare.

Grâce à lui, si l'urne orne à point un sein fané
Par une rose qui nubile le rallume,
De la bave luira sur son bouquet damné.

Et ce squelette nain, coiffé d'un feutre à plume
Et botté, dont l'aisselle a pour poils vrais des vers,
Est pour eux l'infini de la vaste amertume.

Enraged, they'd give the evil one the dare:
Their rapier grinds his corpse in fantasy
As beams of moonlight cleave the empty air.

Lacking the pride that crowns adversity,
And grieved at the constant pecking of their bones,
They stew in impotent malignity.

They are the butt of urchins and old crones,
Harlots and fiddlers, the ancient brood
Of dancing ragamuffins, drunken clowns.

Poets for alms or vengeance may be good,
But unaware of how these vanquished gods
Have suffered, think them tedious and crude.

"They might have fled and taken other roads,
As virgin chargers bolt a stormy fray,
Rather than hurl themselves at armored squads.

"We'll crown the conqueror in oak wreaths or bay,
But as for these buffoons, let's harness them
In scarlet rags that scream to keep away."

When all of us have spat out our disdain,
Reduced to nothing, their eclipse complete,
These ciphers call down thunderbolts—and then

Go hang themselves from lampposts in the street.

Vexés ne vont-ils pas provoquer le pervers,
Leur rapière grinçant suit le rayon de lune
Qui neige en sa carcasse et qui passe au travers.

Désolés sans l'orgueil qui sacre l'infortune,
Et tristes de venger leurs os de coups de bec,
Ils convoitent la haine, au lieu de la rancune.

Ils sont l'amusement des racleurs de rebec,
Des marmots, des putains et de la vieille engeance
Des loqueteux dansant quand le broc est à sec.

Les poëtes bons pour l'aumône ou la vengeance,
Ne connaissant le mal de ces dieux effacés,
Les disent ennuyeux et sans intelligence.

« Ils peuvent fuir ayant de chaque exploit assez,
» Comme un vierge cheval écume de tempête
» Plutôt que de partir en galops cuirassés.

» Nous soûlerons d'encens le vainqueur dans la fête:
» Mais eux, pourquoi n'endosser pas, ces baladins,
» D'écarlate haillon hurlant que l'on s'arrête!»

Quand en face tous leur ont craché les dédains,
Nuls et la barbe à mots bas priant le tonnerre,
Ces héros excédés de malaises badins

Vont ridiculement se pendre au réverbère.

APPARITION

The moon was grieving. Seraphim in tears,
Musing in the calm of vaporous flowers,
Were drawing, bow in hand, from sad violas
Sobbing glissandos over blue corollas.
—It was the blessèd day of your first kiss.
My reverie, enraptured by the abyss,
Imbibed its wisdom from the sad perfume
Which even the dreams we gather in full bloom
Distill within the heart that gathers them.
My eyes on the worn stones, I wandered then,
When suddenly you happened to appear,
Laughing, with evening sunlight in your hair;
And I thought I saw the fairy with the cap
Of light, who passed before my infant sleep,
Opening her hands to scatter through the years
Snowy bouquets of richly scented stars.

APPARITION

La lune s'attristait. Des séraphins en pleurs
Rêvant, l'archet aux doigts, dans le calme des fleurs
Vaporeuses, tiraient de mourantes violes
De blancs sanglots glissant sur l'azur des corolles.
—C'était le jour béni de ton premier baiser.
Ma songerie aimant à me martyriser
S'enivrait savamment du parfum de tristesse
Que même sans regret et sans déboire laisse
La cueillaison d'un Rêve au coeur qui l'a cueilli.
J'errais donc, l'œil rivé sur le pavé vieilli
Quand avec du soleil aux cheveux, dans la rue
Et dans le soir, tu m'es en riant apparue
Et j'ai cru voir la fée au chapeau de clarté
Qui jadis sur mes beaux sommeils d'enfant gâté
Passait, laissant toujours de ses mains mal fermées
Neiger de blancs bouquets d'étoiles parfumées.

FUTILE PETITION

Princess! in envy of the fate of a Hebe
Dawning on the Sèvres at the kiss of your lips,
I wear out my fires, discreet as an abbé,
And will not even figure naked on the cups.

Since I am not the lapdog you baby,
Your lozenge or rouge or a pose you design,
And knowing your glances are closed to me, lady,
Blonde one whose hair is adorned by divine

Goldsmiths! Name us . . . you whose honeyed peals
Of laughter are conjoined in a troop of bleating lambs,
Cropping in ecstasy the votive gifts we made;

Name us . . . so that Love, winged as with a fan,
Can paint me there with flute, lulling the flock to bed:
Princess, name us shepherd of your smiles.

PLACET FUTILE

Princesse! à jalouser le destin d'une Hébé
Qui poind sur cette tasse au baiser de vos lèvres,
J'use mes feux mais n'ai rang discret que d'abbé
Et ne figurerai même nu sur le Sèvres.

Comme je ne suis pas ton bichon embarbé,
Ni la pastille ni du rouge, ni jeux mièvres
Et que sur moi je sais ton regard clos tombé,
Blonde dont les coiffeurs divins sont des orfèvres!

Nommez-nous … toi de qui tant de ris framboisés
Se joignent en troupeau d'agneaux apprivoisés
Chez tous broutant les vœux et bêlant aux délires,

Nommez-nous … pour qu'Amour ailé d'un éventail
M'y peigne flûte aux doigts endormant ce bercail,
Princesse, nommez-nous berger de vos sourires.

THE CLOWN CHASTISED

Eyes, lakes with my simple lust to be reborn
Other than as the actor whose gesture like a plume
Evoked the filthy soot of stage lamps when they fume,
So in the canvas wall a window have I torn.

Limpid traitorous swimmer with arms and legs upborne
In multiple leaps, renouncing a tawdry Hamlet's gloom!
As if inside a wave I fashioned many a tomb
In which to disappear, virgin, and be gone.

Hilarious gold of the cymbal beaten as by fists,
All at once the sun strikes the nakedness
That purely is exhaled from my freshness—nacreous.

Rancid night of the skin when you passed over me,
Not knowing this disguise held all my sanctity,
This rouge drowned in the glacial waters of perfidy.

LE PITRE CHÂTIÉ

Yeux, lacs avec ma simple ivresse de renaître
Autre que l'histrion qui du geste évoquais
Comme plume la suie ignoble des quinquets,
J'ai troué dans le mur de toile une fenêtre.

De ma jambe et des bras limpide nageur traître,
A bonds multipliés, reniant le mauvais
Hamlet! c'est comme si dans l'onde j'innovais
Mille sépulcres pour y vierge disparaître.

Hilare or de cymbale à des poings irrité,
Tout à coup le soleil frappe la nudité
Qui pure s'exhala de ma fraîcheur de nacre,

Rance nuit de la peau quand sur moi vous passiez,
Ne sachant pas, ingrat! que c'était tout mon sacre,
Ce fard noyé dans l'eau perfide des glaciers.

FROM THE SATIRICAL PARNASSUS

A NEGRESS

A negress roused by demons is on fire
To taste a child saddened by the strange
Forbidden fruits beneath their torn attire;
This glutton slyly plots a little binge:

Unto her belly holds two happy dugs,
And thrusts so high that hands can't hope to seize her
The dark explosion of her booted legs,
Much like a tongue that is unskilled in pleasure.

Against the trembling nudity of a gazelle,
Upon her back, an elephant gone wild,
She waits, and gazing at herself with zeal,
Flashes ingenuous teeth upon the child;

And where between her legs the victim's laid,
Raising black skin open beneath the fell,
The palate of that strange mouth comes gaping wide,
Pale and rosy as an ocean shell.

DU PARNASSE SATYRIQUE

UNE NÉGRESSE...

Une négresse par le démon secouée
Veut goûter une enfant triste de fruits nouveaux
Et criminels aussi sous leur robe trouée,
Cette goinfre s'apprête à de rusés travaux:

A son ventre compare heureuses deux tétines
Et, si haut que la main ne le saura saisir,
Elle darde le choc obscur de ses bottines
Ainsi que quelque langue inhabile au plaisir.

Contre la nudité peureuse de gazelle
Qui tremble, sur le dos tel un fol éléphant
Renversée elle attend et s'admire avec zèle,
En riant de ses dents naïves à l'enfant;

Et, dans ses jambes où la victime se couche,
Levant une peau noire ouverte sous le crin,
Avance le palais de cette étrange bouche
Pâle et rose comme un coquillage marin.

10

FROM THE CONTEMPORARY PARNASSUS

THE WINDOWS

Tired of the sad hospital and the fetid smell
That rises from the banal whiteness of the drapes
Toward the large crucifix bored of the empty wall,
The dying man straightens his old back and creeps

Slyly from bed, less to warm his carcass
Than to see the sunlight on the stones,
To press his white hair and the bones of his thin face
Against the windows, which a lovely ray of light wishes
                                                to bronze.

And his mouth, feverish and starved for the clear
Blue air—just as, when young, it drank in the bliss
Of a virginal skin long ago—smears
The warm, golden panes with a long, bitter kiss.

Drunk, he lives! forgetting the horror of the holy oils,
The medicine, the clock, the obligatory bed,
The cough; and when the evening bleeds along the tiles,
His eye, on the horizon of light, is fed

With golden galleys, beautiful as swans,
Wafted on purple and perfumed streams,
The tawny, rich light of their sinuous lines
In a vast nonchalance charged with memories!

DU PARNASSE CONTEMPORAIN

LES FENÊTRES

Las du triste hôpital, et de l'encens fétide
Qui monte en la blancheur banale des rideaux
Vers le grand crucifix ennuyé du mur vide,
Le moribond sournois y redresse un vieux dos,

Se traîne et va, moins pour chauffer sa pourriture
Que pour voir du soleil sur les pierres, coller
Les poils blancs et les os de la maigre figure
Aux fenêtres qu'un beau rayon clair veut hâler.

Et la bouche, fiévreuse et d'azur bleu vorace,
Telle, jeune, elle alla respirer son trésor,
Une peau virginale et de jadis! encrasse
D'un long baiser amer les tièdes carreaux d'or.

Ivre, il vit, oubliant l'horreur des saintes huiles,
Les tisanes, l'horloge et le lit infligé,
La toux; et quand le soir saigne parmi les tuiles,
Son œil, à l'horizon de lumière gorgé,

Voit des galères d'or, belles comme des cygnes,
Sur un fleuve de pourpre et de parfums dormir
En berçant l'éclair fauve et riche de leurs lignes
Dans un grand nonchaloir chargé de souvenir!

11

Thus, seized with disgust for the man of hard heart,
Sprawled in the comforts on which his appetite feeds,
And stubbornly thrusting his nose in the dirt
He offers the female who suckles his kids,

I flee, clinging to all the window frames,
From where one can turn one's back on this shit;
And blessed in their glass, bathed in eternal rains,
In the chaste morning of the Infinite,

I look at myself and see myself as an angel! and I die,
                                        and I yearn
—Be the window pane art, be it mysticism—
To be reborn, bearing my dream for a diadem,
In the former sky where Beauty flourished.

But, alas! the Here-below is master: it sickens me
Even in this refuge where I shelter secure,
And the foul vomit of Stupidity
Forces me to hold my nose before the azure.

Is there a way, O Self, thou who hast known bitterness,
To burst the crystal that the monster has profaned,
And take flight, with my two featherless
Wings—at the risk of falling through eternity?

Ainsi, pris du dégoût de l'homme à l'âme dure
Vautré dans le bonheur, où ses seuls appétits
Mangent, et qui s'entête à chercher cette ordure
Pour l'offrir à la femme allaitant ses petits,

Je fuis et je m'accroche à toutes les croisées
D'où l'on tourne l'épaule à la vie, et, béni,
Dans leur verre, lavé d'éternelles rosées,
Que dore le matin chaste de l'Infini

Je me mire et me vois ange! et je meurs, et j'aime
— Que la vitre soit l'art, soit la mysticité—
A renaître, portant mon rêve en diadème,
Au ciel antérieur où fleurit la Beauté!

Mais, hélas! Ici-bas est maître: sa hantise
Vient m'écœurer parfois jusqu'en cet abri sûr,
Et le vomissement impur de la Bêtise
Me force à me boucher le nez devant l'azur.

Est-il moyen, ô Moi qui connais l'amertume,
D'enfoncer le cristal par le monstre insulté
Et de m'enfuir, avec mes deux ailes sans plume
— Au risque de tomber pendant l'éternité?

THE FLOWERS

From golden showers of the ancient skies,
On the first day, and the eternal snow of stars,
You once unfastened giant calyxes
For the young earth still innocent of scars:

Wild gladioli with the necks of swans,
Laurels divine, of exiled souls the dream,
Vermilion as the modesty of dawns
Trod by the footsteps of the seraphim;

The hyacinth, the myrtle gleaming bright,
And, like the flesh of woman, the cruel rose,
Hérodiade blooming in the garden light,
She that from wild and radiant blood arose!

And made the sobbing whiteness of the lily
That skims a sea of sighs, and as it wends
Through the blue incense of horizons, palely
Toward the weeping moon in dreams ascends!

Hosanna on the lute and in the censers,
Lady, and of our purgatorial groves!
Through heavenly evenings let the echoes answer,
Sparkling haloes, glances of rapturous love!

Mother, who in your strong and righteous bosom,
Formed calyxes balancing the future flask,
Capacious flowers with the deadly balsam
For the weary poet withering on the husk.

LES FLEURS

Des avalanches d'or du vieil azur, au jour
Premier et de la neige éternelle des astres
Jadis tu détachas les grands calices pour
La terre jeune encore et vierge de désastres,

Le glaïeul fauve, avec les cygnes au col fin,
Et ce divin laurier des âmes exilées
Vermeil comme le pur orteil du séraphin
Que rougit la pudeur des aurores foulées,

L'hyacinthe, le myrte à l'adorable éclair
Et, pareille à la chair de la femme, la rose
Cruelle, Hérodiade en fleur du jardin clair,
Celle qu'un sang farouche et radieux arrose!

Et tu fis la blancheur sanglotante des lys
Qui roulant sur des mers de soupirs qu'elle effleure
A travers l'encens bleu des horizons pâlis
Monte rêveusement vers la lune qui pleure!

Hosannah sur le cistre et dans les encensoirs,
Notre Dame, hosannah du jardin de nos limbes!
Et finisse l'écho par les célestes soirs,
Extase des regards, scintillement des nimbes!

Ô Mère qui créas en ton sein juste et fort,
Calices balançant la future fiole,
De grandes fleurs avec la balsamique Mort
Pour le poëte las que la vie étiole.

RENEWAL

Lucid winter, season of art serene,
Is sadly driven out by sickly spring,
And where dull blood presides within my being
Impotence stretches itself in a drawn-out yawn.

White twilights glow lukewarm beneath my skull
Squeezed by an iron band like an ancient tomb,
As, following a vague, sweet dream, I sadly roam
Through fields whose sap is flaunted to the full

—Then fall, enfeebled by the trees' perfume,
And hollowing with my face a grave for my own dream,
Biting warm earth in which the lilacs push,

I wait, engulfed in rising ennui . . .
—Meanwhile the Azure laughs on every bush
And wakened birds bloom twittering in the sun.

RENOUVEAU

Le printemps maladif a chassé tristement
L'hiver, saison de l'art serein, l'hiver lucide,
Et, dans mon être à qui le sang morne préside
L'impuissance s'étire en un long bâillement.

Des crépuscules blancs tiédissent sous mon crâne
Qu'un cercle de fer serre ainsi qu'un vieux tombeau
Et, triste, j'erre après un rêve vague et beau,
Par les champs où la sève immense se pavane

Puis je tombe énervé de parfums d'arbres, las,
Et creusant de ma face une fosse à mon rêve,
Mordant la terre chaude où poussent les lilas,

J'attends, en m'abîmant que mon ennui s'élève…
— Cependant l'Azur rit sur la haie et l'éveil
De tant d'oiseaux en fleur gazouillant au soleil.

ANGUISH

I come not to ravish your body, O beast,
In whom the transgressions of multitudes flow,
Nor to rouse a sad storm in your tresses unchaste,
By the incurable ennui my kisses bestow.

I ask but a dull dreamless sleep from your bed,
Swathed beneath curtains oblivious of remorse,
Which you who know more about nothingness than the dead
Can taste when your falsehoods have run their dark course.

For Vice, having gnawed at my innate nobility,
Has marked me like you with a sad sterility:
But while you with your stony breast are the frame

For a heart that the tooth of no crime wounds with shame,
Obsessed by my shroud, I flee, pale, undone,
Afraid of dying when I sleep alone.

ANGOISSE

Je ne viens pas ce soir vaincre ton corps, ô bête
En qui vont les péchés d'un peuple, ni creuser
Dans tes cheveux impurs une triste tempête
Sous l'incurable ennui que verse mon baiser:

Je demande à ton lit le lourd sommeil sans songes
Planant sous les rideaux inconnus du remords,
Et que tu peux goûter après tes noirs mensonges,
Toi qui sur le néant en sais plus que les morts.

Car le Vice, rongeant ma native noblesse
M'a comme toi marqué de sa stérilité,
Mais tandis que ton sein de pierre est habité

Par un cœur que la dent d'aucun crime ne blesse,
Je fuis, pâle, défait, hanté par mon linceul,
Ayant peur de mourir lorsque je couche seul.

WEARY OF BITTER SLEEP

Weary of bitter sleep in which my indolence
Offends a glory for which I once fled childhood's innocence
   Charmed by woods with roses beneath an artless sky,
And seven times more weary still of the harsh necessity
   Of hollowing a pit each evening once again
Out of the cold and avaricious soil of my own brain,
   Grave digger without pity for his own sterility—
What shall I tell this Dawn, O Dreams, when roses visit me,
   If, frightened of livid roses, the enormous burial ground
Should fill in all the empty holes till not a one be found?

I would forsake the ravenous Art of cruel lands,
And smiling at the obsolete reproaches of my friends,
   Forget about the past, bid genius goodbye,
And even put aside the lamp that knows my agony,
   To follow that Chinese of fine, transparent soul
For whom the purest ecstasy is painting on a bowl
   Fashioned out of snowflakes stolen from the moon
The end of some exotic flower that sheds its scent upon
   His lucent life, the flower he sensed in infancy
Grafting itself upon the spirit's blue-tinged filigree.
   And like to death itself in the sage's only dream,
Serene, I'll take unto myself a youthful pastoral scene
   Pensively to depict once more upon the cups.
A line of azure, thin and faint, could be a lake, perhaps,
   A lake amid the porcelain bareness of the sky;
A bright crescent swallowed up in a cloud's obscurity
   Calmly dips its horn in the icy pool that leads
To three large cilia nearby, of emerald color, reeds.

LAS DE L'AMER REPOS…

Las de l'amer repos où ma paresse offense
Une gloire pour qui jadis j'ai fui l'enfance
Adorable des bois de roses sous l'azur
Naturel, et plus las sept fois du pacte dur
De creuser par veillée une fosse nouvelle
Dans le terrain avare et froid de ma cervelle,
Fossoyeur sans pitié pour la stérilité,
   — Que dire à cette Aurore, ô Rêves, visité
Par les roses, quand, peur de ses roses livides,
Le vaste cimetière unira les trous vides ?—

Je veux délaisser l'Art vorace d'un pays
Cruel, et, souriant aux reproches vieillis
Que me font mes amis, le passé, le génie,
Et ma lampe qui sait pourtant mon agonie,
Imiter le Chinois au coeur limpide et fin
De qui l'extase pure est de peindre la fin
Sur ses tasses de neige à la lune ravie
D'une bizarre fleur qui parfume sa vie
Transparente, la fleur qu'il a sentie, enfant,
Au filigrane bleu de l'âme se greffant.
Et, la mort telle avec le seul rêve du sage,
Serein, je vais choisir un jeune paysage
Que je peindrais encor sur les tasses, distrait.
Une ligne d'azur mince et pâle serait
Un lac, parmi le ciel de porcelaine nue,
Un clair croissant perdu par une blanche nue
Trempe sa corne calme en la glace des eaux,
Non loin de trois grands cils d'émeraude, roseaux.

THE BELL-RINGER

While the bell awakens its voice clear and bright
To the pure deep air of the morning time,
Passing over a child who pours out in delight
An Angelus amid lavender and thyme,

The ringer, brushed by a bird brought to light,
Plods sadly and, mumbling a Latin rhyme
On the stone that stretches the old cord tight,
Hears only the tinkling of a far-off chime.

I myself am that man. For alas! when I pull
On anxious night's rope to sound the Ideal,
Cold sins flaunt their faithful plumes in disdain

And the voice comes only as a hollow moan!
But one day, sick from having pulled in vain,
I'll hang myself, Satan, removing the stone.

LE SONNEUR

Cependant que la cloche éveille sa voix claire
A l'air pur et limpide et profond du matin
Et passe sur l'enfant qui jette pour lui plaire
Un angélus parmi la lavande et le thym,

Le sonneur effleuré par l'oiseau qu'il éclaire,
Chevauchant tristement en geignant du latin
Sur la pierre qui tend la corde séculaire,
N'entend descendre à lui qu'un tintement lointain.

Je suis cet homme. Hélas! de la nuit désireuse,
J'ai beau tirer le câble à sonner l'Idéal,
De froids péchés s'ébat un plumage féal,

Et la voix ne me vient que par bribes et creuse!
Mais, un jour, fatigué d'avoir en vain tiré,
Ô Satan, j'ôterai la pierre et me pendrai.

SUMMER SADNESS

O wrestler, the sun on the sand as you sleep
Heats a languorous bath in the gold of your hair,
And burning up scent from your unyielding cheek
It mixes a potion of love with your tears.

Saddened (O my timid kisses) you speak
From this white blaze of immutable calm:
"We shall never be merged beneath the antique
Sands, a sole mummy amid the glad palms!"

But your hair's a warm river in which we can drown
The soul that obsesses us, and when it's gone
Discover a Void that you never have known!

I'll taste the black paint that your eyelids have wept
To see if it gives to the heart that you whipped
The indifference of the azure and of stone.

TRISTESSE D'ÉTÉ

Le soleil, sur le sable, ô lutteuse endormie,
En l'or de tes cheveux chauffe un bain langoureux
Et, consumant l'encens sur ta joue ennemie,
Il mêle avec les pleurs un breuvage amoureux.

De ce blanc flamboiement l'immuable accalmie
T'a fait dire, attristée, ô mes baisers peureux,
« Nous ne serons jamais une seule momie
Sous l'antique désert et les palmiers heureux!»

Mais ta chevelure est une rivière tiède,
Où noyer sans frissons l'âme qui nous obsède
Et trouver ce Néant que tu ne connais pas!

Je goûterai le fard pleuré par tes paupières,
Pour voir s'il sait donner au cœur que tu frappas
L'insensibilité de l'azur et des pierres.

THE AZURE

The serene irony of the eternal Sky
Depresses, with the indolence of flowers,
The impotent poet cursing poetry
Across a sterile waste of leaden Hours.

Fleeing, with eyes shut fast, I feel it blight
With all the intensity of crushing remorse
My empty soul. Where can I fly? What
                            haggard night
Can stifle this scornful torment at its source?

Roll in, you fogs, and pour out ashen haze
In tattered rags of mist traversing heaven;
Smother the livid swamp of autumn days
And roof them in a grand and silent haven!

And you, dear Boredom, rise from Lethean pools,
Dredging their shoals for pallid reeds and slime;
Block with unwearying hand the great blue holes
Malicious birds keep gouging time after time.

Still unremitting! let sad chimneys smoke,
And let the smothering soot, a wandering prison,
In blackening trains of horror rise and choke
The sun now fading yellow on the horizon!

L'AZUR

De l'éternel Azur la sereine ironie
Accable, belle indolemment comme les fleurs,
Le poëte impuissant qui maudit son génie
A travers un désert stérile de Douleurs.

Fuyant, les yeux fermés, je le sens qui regarde
Avec l'intensité d'un remords atterrant
Mon âme vide. Où fuir? Et quelle nuit hagarde
Jeter, lambeaux, jeter sur ce mépris navrant?

Brouillards, montez! Versez vos cendres monotones
Avec de longs haillons de brume dans les cieux
Que noiera le marais livide des automnes
Et bâtissez un grand plafond silencieux!

Et toi, sors des étangs léthéens et ramasse
En t'en venant la vase et les pâles roseaux,
Cher Ennui, pour boucher d'une main jamais lasse
Les grands trous bleus que font méchamment les oiseaux.

Encor! que sans répit les tristes cheminées
Fument, et que de suie une errante prison
Éteigne dans l'horreur de ses noires traînées
Le soleil se mourant jaunâtre à l'horizon!

—The Sky is dead.—Toward you I run!
        Bestow, O matter,
Forgetfulness of Sin and the cruel Ideal
Upon this martyr who comes to share the litter
Where the happy herd of men is made to kneel.

For there I long, because at last my brain,
Like an empty rouge-pot on a dressing stand,
Has lost the art of decking out its pain,
To yawn morosely toward a humble end . . .

In vain! The Azure triumphs. I hear it sing
In all the bells. The more to frighten us,
It rises in its wicked glorying
From living metal, a blue angelus.

It rolls in with the fog, and like a sword
It penetrates your inmost agony.
Revolt or flight is useless and absurd;
For I am haunted. The Sky! the Sky! the Sky!

— Le Ciel est mort.— Vers toi, j'accours! donne, ô matière,
L'oubli de l'Idéal cruel et du Péché
A ce martyr qui vient partager la litière
Où le bétail heureux des hommes est couché,

Car j'y veux, puisque enfin ma cervelle, vidée
Comme le pot de fard gisant au pied du mur,
N'a plus l'art d'attifer la sanglotante idée,
Lugubrement bâiller vers un trépas obscur…

En vain! l'Azur triomphe, et je l'entends qui chante
Dans les cloches. Mon âme, il se fait voix pour plus
Nous faire peur avec sa victoire méchante,
Et du métal vivant sort en bleus angélus!

Il roule par la brume, ancien et traverse
Ta native agonie ainsi qu'un glaive sûr;
Où fuir dans la révolte inutile et perverse?
Je suis hanté. L'Azur! l'Azur! l'Azur! l'Azur!

SEA BREEZE

The flesh is sad, alas, and there's nothing but words!
To take flight, far off! I sense that somewhere the birds
Are drunk to be amid strange spray and skies.
Nothing, not the old gardens reflected in the eyes,
Can now restrain this sea-drenched heart, O night,
Nor the lone splendor of my lamp on the white
Paper which the void leaves undefiled,
Nor the young mother suckling her child.
Steamer with gently swaying masts, depart!
Weigh anchor for a landscape of the heart!

Boredom made desolate by hope's cruel spells
Retains its faith in ultimate farewells!
And maybe the masts are such as are inclined
To shipwreck driven by tempestuous wind.
No fertile isle, no spar on which to cling . . .
But oh, my heart, listen to the sailors sing!

BRISE MARINE

La chair est triste, hélas! et j'ai lu tous les livres.
Fuir! là-bas fuir! Je sens que des oiseaux sont ivres
D'être parmi l'écume inconnue et les cieux!
Rien, ni les vieux jardins reflétés par les yeux
Ne retiendra ce coeur qui dans la mer se trempe,
Ô nuits! ni la clarté déserte de ma lampe
Sur le vide papier que la blancheur défend
Et ni la jeune femme allaitant son enfant.
Je partirai! Steamer balancant ta mâture,
Lève l'ancre pour une exotique nature!

Un Ennui, désolé par les cruels espoirs,
Croit encore à l'adieu suprême des mouchoirs!
Et, peut-être, les mâts, invitant les orages
Sont-ils de ceux qu'un vent penche sur les naufrages
Perdus, sans mâts, sans mâts, ni fertiles îlots...
Mais, ô mon coeur, entends le chant des matelots!

SIGH

My soul, calm sister, ascends toward your brow
Where an autumn that's scattered with russet dreams now,
And toward your angelic eye's wandering heaven
Ascends, as in a melancholy garden
A white jet of water faithfully sighs
Toward October's pure, pale, and compassionate skies
That mirror in pools their infinite languor
And, on dead water where anguished leaves wander
Driven by wind, furrowing a hollow,
Let the sun be drawn out in a long ray of yellow.

SOUPIR

Mon âme vers ton front où rêve, ô calme sœur,
Un automne jonché de taches de rousseur,
Et vers le ciel errant de ton œil angélique
Monte, comme dans un jardin mélancolique,
Fidèle, un blanc jet d'eau soupire vers l'Azur!
— Vers l'Azur attendri d'Octobre pâle et pur
Qui mire aux grands bassins sa langueur infinie
Et laisse, sur l'eau morte où la fauve agonie
Des feuilles erre au vent et creuse un froid sillon,
Se traîner le soleil jaune d'un long rayon.

ALMS

Take this purse, Beggar! you only whine,
Senile nursling of a stingy tit,
To strain your death knell from it coin by coin.

Draw from the precious metal some sin that's quite
As vast and bizarre as ourselves, a fistful; kiss it and blow
An ardent fanfare till it writhe in the night.

Let these dives be churches with incense, for lo
On their walls, as if cradling a rift in the sky,
Tobacco's orisons wordlessly rise and flow,

And powerful opium shatters the pharmacy!
Dresses and skin—you'd have their satin torn
And drink in the happy spittle of indolency

At princely cafes awaiting the morn?
To the beggar at the glass sometimes they throw
A feast, beneath ceilings veiled nymphs adorn.

And shivering, old god, in your rags, when you go,
The dawn is a lake of golden wine
And you swear there are stars in your gullet that glow!

Unable to count up the treasure you find,
You can deck yourself out in a plume, and at mass
Offer a taper to your saint divine.

Do not imagine that I'm just blowing gas.
Earth opens old to those hunger strikes dead.
I hate other alms; forget me as I pass.

And above all, brother, do not go to buy bread.

AUMÔNE

Prends ce sac, Mendiant! tu ne le cajolas
Sénile nourrisson d'une tétine avare
Afin de pièce à pièce en égoutter ton glas.

Tire du métal cher quelque péché bizarre
Et vaste comme nous, les poings pleins, le baisons
Souffles-y qu'il se torde! une ardente fanfare.

Église avec l'encens que toutes ces maisons
Sur les murs quand berceur d'une bleue éclaircie
Le tabac sans parler roule les oraisons,

Et l'opium puissant brise la pharmacie!
Robes et peau, veux-tu lacérer le satin
Et boire en la salive heureuse l'inertie,

Par les cafés princiers attendre le matin?
Les plafonds enrichis de nymphes et de voiles,
On jette, au mendiant de la vitre, un festin.

Et quand tu sors, vieux dieu, grelottant sous tes toiles
D'emballage, l'aurore est un lac de vin d'or
Et tu jures avoir au gosier les étoiles!

Faute de supputer l'éclat de ton trésor,
Tu peux du moins t'orner d'une plume, à complies
Servir un cierge au saint en qui tu crois encor.

Ne t'imagine pas que je dis des folies.
La terre s'ouvre vieille à qui crève la faim.
Je hais une autre aumône et veux que tu m'oublies

Et surtout ne va pas, frère, acheter du pain.

GIFT OF THE POEM

I bring you the child of an Idumaean night,
Black, and with featherless wings bled white:
Through the windows burnished with incense and gold,
The rimed panes mournful, alas, from the cold,
The Dawn spread her fingers upon the angelic
Lamp, and when she had offered this relic
To the father smiling in spite of his qualms,
The sterile, blue silence was wafted by palms!
O mother cradling your infant daughter,
Welcome the birth of this untimely monster!
And with your voice like viol and harpsichord, O singer,
Will you press upon your breast a faded finger,
Through which in sibylline whiteness woman flows
For lips starved from the air the virginal azure blows?

DON DU POËME

Je t'apporte l'enfant d'une nuit d'Idumée!
Noire, à l'aile saignante et pâle, déplumée,
Par le verre brûlé d'aromates et d'or,
Par les carreaux glacés, hélas! mornes encor,
L'aurore se jeta sur la lampe angélique.
Palmes! et quand elle a montré cette relique
A ce père essayant un sourire ennemi,
La solitude bleue et stérile a frémi.
Ô la berceuse, avec ta fille et l'innocence
De vos pieds froids, accueille une horrible naissance:
Et ta voix rappelant viole et clavecin,
Avec le doigt fané presseras-tu le sein
Par qui coule en blancheur sibylline la femme
Pour les lèvres que l'air du vierge azur affame?

OTHER POEMS

HÉRODIADE

I. ANCIENT OVERTURE OF HÉRODIADE

THE NURSE

(Incantation)

Abolished, and her frightful wing in the tears
Of the basin, abolished, that mirrors forth our fears,
The naked golds lashing the crimson space,
An Aurora—heraldic plumage—has chosen to embrace
Our cinerary tower of sacrifice,
Heavy tomb that a songbird has fled, lone caprice
Of a dawn vainly decked out in ebony plumes…
Ah, mansion this sad, fallen country assumes!
No splashing! the gloomy water, standing still,
No longer visited by snowy quill
Or fabled swan, reflects the bereaving
Of autumn extinguished by its own unleaving,
Of the swan when amidst the cold white tomb
Of its feathers, it buried its head, undone
By the pure diamond of a star, but one
Of long ago, which never even shone.

Crime! torture! ancient dawn! bright pyre!
Empurpled sky, complicit in the mire,
And stained-glass windows opening red on carnage.

The strange chamber, framed in all the baggage
Of a warlike age, its goldwork dull and faint,
Has yesteryear's snows instead of its ancient tint;

AUTRES POËMES

HÉRODIADE

I. OVERTURE ANCIENNE D'HÉRODIADE

LA NOURRICE

(Incantation)

Abolie, et son aile affreuse dans les larmes
Du bassin, aboli, qui mire les alarmes,
Des ors nus fustigeant l'espace cramoisi,
Une Aurore a, plumage héraldique, choisi
Notre tour cinéraire et sacrificatrice,
Lourde tombe qu'a fuie un bel oiseau, caprice
Solitaire d'aurore au vain plumage noir…
Ah! des pays déchus et tristes le manoir!
Pas de clapotement! L'eau morne se résigne,
Que ne visite plus la plume ni le cygne
Inoubliable: l'eau reflète l'abandon
De l'automne éteignant en elle son brandon:
Du cygne quand parmi le pâle mausolée
Ou la plume plongea la tête, désolée
Par le diamant pur de quelque étoile, mais
Antérieure, qui ne scintilla jamais.

Crime! bûcher! aurore ancienne! supplice!
Pourpre d'un ciel! Étang de la pourpre complice!
Et sur les incarnats, grand ouvert, ce vitrail.

La chambre singulière en un cadre, attirail
De siècle belliqueux, orfèvrerie éteinte,
A le neigeux jadis pour ancienne teinte,

And its pearl-gray tapestry, useless creases
With the buried eyes of prophetesses
Offering Magi withered fingers. One,
With floral past enwoven on my gown
Bleached in an ivory chest and with a sky
Bestrewn with birds amidst the embroidery
Of tarnished silver, seems a phantom risen,
An aroma, roses, rising from the hidden
Couch, now void, the snuffed-out candle shrouds,
An aroma, over the sachet, of frozen golds,
A drift of flowers unfaithful to the moon
(Though the taper's quenched, petals still fall from one),
Flowers whose long regrets and stems appear
Drenched in a lonely vase to languish there…
An Aurora dragged her wings in the basin's tears!

Magical shadow with symbolic powers!
A voice from the distant past, an evocation,
Is it not mine prepared for incantation?
In the yellow folds of thought, still unexhumed,
Lingering, and like an antique cloth perfumed,
Spread on a pile of holy relics cold,
Through ancient hollows and through stiffened folds
Pierced in the rhythm of the pure lace shroud
Through which the old veiled brightness is allowed
To mount, in desperation, shall arise
(But oh, the distance hidden in those cries!)
The old veiled brightness of a strange gilt-silver,
Of the languishing voice, estranged and unfamiliar:
Will it scatter its gold in an ultimate splendor,
And, in the hour of its agony, render
Itself as the anthem for psalms of petition?
For all are alike in being brought to perdition
By the power of old silence and deepening gloom,
Fated, monotonous, vanquished, undone,
Like the sluggish waters of an ancient pond.

Et sa tapisserie, au lustre nacré, plis
Inutiles avec les yeux ensevelis
De sibylles offrant leur ongle vieil aux Mages.
Une d'elles, avec un passé de ramages
Sur ma robe blanchie en l'ivoire fermé
Au ciel d'oiseaux parmi l'argent noir parsemé,
Semble, de vols partis costumée et fantôme,
Un arôme qui porte, ô roses! un arôme,
Loin du lit vide qu'un cierge soufflé cachait,
Un arôme d'ors froids rôdant sur le sachet,
Une touffe de fleurs parjures à la lune
(A la cire expirée encor s'effeuille l'une),
De qui le long regret et les tiges de qui
Trempent en un seul verre à l'éclat alangui…
Une Aurore traînait ses ailes dans les larmes!

Ombre magicienne aux symboliques charmes!
Une voix, du passé longue évocation,
Est-ce la mienne prête à l'incantation?
Encore dans les plis jaunes de la pensée
Traînant, antique, ainsi qu'une toile encensée
Sur un confus amas d'ostensoirs refroidis,
Par les trous anciens et par les plis roidis
Percés selon le rythme et les dentelles pures
Du suaire laissant par ses belles guipures
Désespéré monter le vieil éclat voilé
S'élève: (ô quel lointain en ces appels celé!)
Le vieil éclat voilé du vermeil insolite,
De la voix languissant, nulle, sans acolyte,
Jettera-t-il son or par dernières splendeurs,
Elle, encore, l'antienne aux versets demandeurs,
A l'heure d'agonie et de luttes funèbres!
Et, force du silence et des noires ténèbres
Tout rentre également en l'ancien passé,
Fatidique, vaincu, monotone, lassé,
Comme l'eau des bassins anciens se résigne.

Sometimes she sang an incoherent song.
Lamentable sign!
                    the bed of vellum sheets,
Useless and closed—not linen!—vainly waits,
Bereft now of the cherished grammary
That spelled the figured folds of reverie,
The silken tent that harbored memory,
The fragrance of sleeping hair. Were these its treasure?
Cold child, she held within her subtle pleasure,
Shivering with flowers in her walks at dawn,
Or when the pomegranate's flesh is torn
By wicked night! Alone, the crescent moon
On the iron clockface is a pendulum
Suspending Lucifer: the clepsydra pours
Dark drops in grief upon the stricken hours
As, wounded, each one wanders a dim shade
On undeciphered paths without a guide!
All this the king knows not, whose salary
Has fed so long this agèd breast now dry.
Her father knows it no more than the cruel
Glacier mirroring his arms of steel,
When sprawled on a pile of corpses without coffins
Smelling obscurely of resin, he deafens
With dark silver trumpets the ancient pines!
Will he ever come back from the Cisalpines?
Soon enough! for all is bad dream and foreboding!
On the fingernail raised in the stained glass, according
To the memory of the trumpets, the old sky burns,
And to an envious candle it turns
A finger. And soon, when the sad sun sinks,
It shall pierce through the body of wax till it shrinks!
No sunset, but the red awakening
Of the last day concluding everything
Struggles so sadly that time disappears,
The redness of apocalypse, whose tears
Fall on the child, exiled to her own proud
Heart, as the swan makes its plumage a shroud

Elle a chanté, parfois incohérente, signe
Lamentable!
                    le lit aux pages de vélin,
Tel, inutile et si claustral, n'est pas le lin!
Qui des rêves par plis n'a plus le cher grimoire,
Ni le dais sépulcral à la déserte moire,
Le parfum des cheveux endormis. L'avait-il?
Froide enfant, de garder en son plaisir subtil
Au matin grelottant de fleurs, ses promenades,
Et quand le soir méchant a coupé les grenades!
Le croissant, oui le seul est au cadran de fer
De l'horloge, pour poids suspendant Lucifer,
Toujours blesse, toujours une nouvelle heurée,
Par la clepsydre à la goutte obscure pleurée,
Que, délaissée, elle erre, et sur son ombre pas
Un ange accompagnant son indicible pas!
Il ne sait pas cela, le roi qui salarie
Depuis longtemps la gorge ancienne et tarie.
Son père ne sait pas cela, ni le glacier
Farouche reflétant de ses armes l'acier,
Quand sur un tas gisant de cadavres sans coffre
Odorant de résine, énigmatique, il offre
Ses trompettes d'argent obscur aux vieux sapins!
Reviendra-t-il un jour des pays cisalpins!
Assez tôt? Car tout est présage et mauvais rêve!
A l'ongle qui parmi le vitrage s'élève
Selon le souvenir des trompettes, le vieux
Ciel brûle, et change un doigt en un cierge envieux
Et bientôt sa rougeur de triste crépuscule
Pénétrera du corps la cire qui recule!
De crépuscule, non, mais de rouge lever,
Lever du jour dernier qui vient tout achever,
Si triste se débat, que l'on ne sait plus l'heure
La rougeur de ce temps prophétique qui pleure
Sur l'enfant, exilée en son cœur précieux
Comme un cygne cachant en sa plume ses yeux,
Comme les mit le vieux cygne en sa plume, allée

For its eyes, the old swan, and is carried away
From the plumage of grief to the eternal highway
Of its hopes, where it looks on the diamonds divine
Of a moribund star, which never more shall shine!

De la plume détresse, en l'éternelle allée
De ses espoirs, pour voir les diamants élus
D'une étoile mourante, et qui ne brille plus.

II. SCENE

THE NURSE—HÉRODIADE

NURSE

Are you a living princess or her shadow?
Let me kiss your fingers and their rings, and bid you
Walk no longer in an unknown age . . .

HÉRODIADE
                              Forbear.
The blond torrent of immaculate hair
Bathing my lonely body, freezes it
With horror, and my tresses laced with light
Are deathless. A kiss would kill me, woman,
If beauty were not death . . .
                         By what attraction
Am I drawn, what morn forgotten by the prophets
That pours on the dying distance its sad rites?
How should I know? You've seen me, nurse of winter,
In a massive stone and iron prison enter
Where the savage era of my lions clings:
In the desert perfume of those ancient kings,
I pondered doom, my hands inviolate:
But have you seen the things that caused my fright?
Dreaming of banishment, I stop and peel,
As if beside a fountain's welcoming pool,
Petals within myself of lilies pale:
The fascinated lions watch the pile
Of fragments floating through my reverie,
And gaze on feet that would have calmed the sea
When they have swept aside my indolent dress.
Then calm the shuddering of your senile flesh,
And come, because my tresses now resemble
The manes of savage beasts that make you tremble:

II. SCÈNE

LA NOURRICE — HÉRODIADE

N.

Tu vis! ou vois-je ici l'ombre d'une princesse?
A mes lèvres tes doigts et leurs bagues et cesse
De marcher dans un âge ignoré…

H.
                              Reculez.
Le blond torrent de mes cheveux immaculés
Quand il baigne mon corps solitaire le glace
D'horreur, et mes cheveux que la lumière enlace
Sont immortels. O femme, un baiser me tûrait
Si la beauté n'était la mort…
                         Par quel attrait
Menée et quel matin oublié des prophètes
Verse, sur les lointains mourants, ses tristes fêtes,
Le sais-je? tu m'as vue, ô nourrice d'hiver,
Sous la lourde prison de pierres et de fer
Où de mes vieux lions traînent les siècles fauves
Entrer, et je marchais, fatale, les mains sauves,
Dans le parfum désert de ces anciens rois:
Mais encore as-tu vu quels furent mes effrois?
Je m'arrête rêvant aux exils, et j'effeuille,
Comme près d'un bassin dont le jet d'eau m'accueille,
Les pâles lys qui sont en moi, tandis qu'épris
De suivre du regard les languides débris
Descendre, à travers ma rêverie, en silence,
Les lions, de ma robe écartent l'indolence
Et regardent mes pieds qui calmeraient la mer.
Calme, toi, les frissons de ta sénile chair,
Viens et ma chevelure imitant les manières
Trop farouches qui font votre peur des crinières,

Help me to comb these plaits you dare not see,
Languid before a mirror listlessly.

NURSE

If not gay myrrh the phial's glass encloses,
Then ravished essences of withered roses:
Will you not sample their funereal charm?

HÉRODIADE

Away with those perfumes that do me harm!
I hate them, nurse, and would you have me feel
Their drunken vapors make my senses reel?
I want my tresses, since they are not flowers
Pouring oblivion on human sorrows,
But gold, forever pure of aromatics
In their dull pallor or their cruel prismatics,
To keep the cold sterility of metal,
Reflecting the jewels of my walls ancestral,
The armored halls of childhood's sad domain.

NURSE

Age had erased your prohibition, queen,
From my dull brain, as from a faded book.
Pardon . . .

HÉRODIADE

Hush! Hold this glass that I may look.
Mirror, cold water frozen in your frame
Through ennui, how many times I came,
Desolate from dreams and seeking memories
Like leaves beneath your chill profundities,
A far-off shadow to appear in you:
But, oh! Some evenings in your austere pool,

Aide-moi, puisqu'ainsi tu n'oses plus me voir,
A me peigner nonchalamment dans un miroir.

N.

Sinon la myrrhe gaie en ses bouteilles closes,
De l'essence ravie aux vieillesses de roses,
Voulez-vous, mon enfant, essayer la vertu
Funèbre?

H.

Laisse là ces parfums! ne sais-tu
Que je les hais, nourrice, et veux-tu que je sente
Leur ivresse noyer ma tête languissante?
Je veux que mes cheveux qui ne sont pas des fleurs
A répandre l'oubli des humaines douleurs,
Mais de l'or, à jamais vierge des aromates,
Dans leurs éclairs cruels et dans leurs pâleurs mates,
Observent la froideur stérile du métal,
Vous ayant reflétés, joyaux du mur natal,
Armes, vases depuis ma solitaire enfance.

N.

Pardon! l'âge effaçait, reine, votre défense
De mon esprit pâli comme un vieux livre ou noir...

H.

Assez! Tiens devant moi ce miroir.
                                    Ô miroir!
Eau froide par l'ennui dans ton cadre gelée
Que de fois et pendant des heures, désolée
Des songes et cherchant mes souvenirs qui sont
Comme des feuilles sous ta glace au trou profond,
Je m'apparus en toi comme une ombre lointaine,

I've glimpsed the Ideal in all its nakedness!

Nurse, am I fair?

NURSE

       A star, in truthfulness;
But this tress falls . . .

HÉRODIADE

       Cease and desist from your crime
Which chills my blood unto its source, and tame
That infamous gesture, impious and lewd:
What demon instills you with this sinister mood?
These kisses and offerings of perfume and
—Shall I say it, O heart?—this still profaned hand,
For you wanted to touch me—are signs of an hour
That shall not conclude without suffering on the tower . . .
O hour that Hérodiade looks on with dread!

NURSE

Heaven defend you! These are strange times, indeed.
A solitary shade or new fury, you wander,
Gazing at yourself, precocious in terror,
But always as adorable as any immortal,
So beautiful, my child, in your beauty so dreadful
That . . .

HÉRODIADE

Were you not going to touch me?

NURSE
       . . . I'd willingly serve

Mais, horreur! des soirs, dans ta sévère fontaine,
J'ai de mon rêve épars connu la nudité!

Nourrice, suis-je belle?

N.

       Un astre, en vérité
Mais cette tresse tombe…

H.

       Arrête dans ton crime
Qui refroidit mon sang vers sa source, et réprime
Ce geste, impiété fameuse: ah! conte-moi
Quel sûr démon te jette en le sinistre émoi,
Ce baiser, ces parfums offerts et, le dirai-je?
O mon cœur, cette main encore sacrilège,
Car tu voulais, je crois, me toucher, sont un jour
Qui ne finira pas sans malheur sur la tour…
Ô jour qu'Hérodiade avec effroi regarde!

N.

Temps bizarre, en effet, de quoi le ciel vous garde!
Vous errez, ombre seule et nouvelle fureur,
Et regardant en vous précoce avec terreur;
Mais toujours adorable autant qu'une immortelle,
Ô mon enfant, et belle affreusement et telle
Que…

H

Mais n'allais-tu pas me toucher?

N.
       …J'aimerais

The one for whom fate has chosen to reserve
Your secrets.

HÉRODIADE

Be silent!

NURSE

Will he come?

HÉRODIADE
                                O, you pure
Stars, do not listen!

NURSE
                                How, save through obscure
Terrors, imagine more implacable still
And as a suppliant the god who some day will
Receive the gift of your grace! and for whom,
Devoured by anguish, do you keep the unknown
Splendor and mystery of your being?

HÉRODIADE
                                For none
But myself.

NURSE

Sad flower that grows all alone
And, seeing its shadow reflected in a pool,
                feels nothing but anomie.

Être à qui le destin réserve vos secrets.

H.

Oh! tais-toi!

N.

Viendra-t-il parfois?

H.
                                Étoiles pures,
N'entendez pas!

N.
                                Comment, sinon parmi d'obscures
Épouvantes, songer plus implacable encor
Et comme suppliant le dieu que le trésor
De votre grâce attend! et pour qui, dévorée
D'angoisses, gardez-vous la splendeur ignorée
Et le mystère vain de votre être?

H.
                                Pour moi.

N.

Triste fleur qui croît seule et n'a pas d'autre émoi
Que son ombre dans l'eau vue avec atonie.

HÉRODIADE

Go, spare me your pity as well as your irony.

NURSE

Still, tell me … ah! no, some day it will wane,
Child that you are, this triumphant disdain.

HÉRODIADE

But who would dare touch one the lions left alone?
I want nothing human; and if, some day, a stone
Statue you find me, my eyes lost in bliss,
It's when I remember the milk of your breasts.

NURSE

Lamentable victim offered to her doom!

HÉRODIADE

Yes, it's for me, myself, that deserted I bloom!
You know this, gardens of amethyst, deep
In the dazzling, unfathomable caves where you sleep;
Hidden gold hoarding your antique light
Beneath the dark slumbers of primordial night;
You stones, like the purest of gems, whence my eyes
Borrow melodious clarities;
And metals that give to my youthful hair
Its fatal splendor and massive allure.
But you who were born in an age malign
For the evil of caverns sibylline,
Who speak of a mortal! and according to whom,
From the calyxes of my robes shall come,
Aroma of fierce delights, the shimmer
Of my nude, white body: prophesy that if summer,

H.

Va, garde ta pitié comme ton ironie.

N.

Toutefois expliquez: oh! non, naïve enfant,
Décroîtra, quelque jour, ce dédain triomphant.

H.

Mais qui me toucherait, des lions respectée?
Du reste, je ne veux rien d'humain et, sculptée,
Si tu me vois les yeux perdus au paradis,
C'est quand je me souviens de ton lait bu jadis.

N.

Victime lamentable à son destin offerte!

H.

Oui, c'est pour moi, pour moi, que je fleuris, déserte!
Vous le savez, jardins d'améthyste, enfouis
Sans fin dans de savants abîmes éblouis,
Ors ignorés, gardant votre antique lumière
Sous le sombre sommeil d'une terre première,
Vous, pierres où mes yeux comme de purs bijoux
Empruntent leur clarté mélodieuse, et vous
Métaux qui donnez à ma jeune chevelure
Une splendeur fatale et sa massive allure!
Quant à toi, femme née en des siècles malins
Pour la méchanceté des antres sibyllins,
Qui parles d'un mortel! selon qui, des calices
De mes robes, arôme aux farouches délices,
Sortirait le frisson blanc de ma nudité,
Prophétise que si le tiède azur d'été,

Before which instinctively woman goes bare,
Sees me in my modesty trembling like a star,
I die!

      I love the horror of virginity,
The dread my tresses give me when I lie
Retired at night, reptilian on my couch,
My useless flesh inviolate to the touch,
Feeling cold sparks from your lucidity,
You who die, you who burn with chastity,
White night of icicles and cruel snow!
And your solitary sister, O mine forever now,
My dream shall rise toward you: already such,
Rare clarity of a heart desiring it so much,
I am alone in my monotonous country,
While all those around me live in the idolatry
Of a mirror reflecting in its depths serene
Hérodiade, whose gaze is diamond keen …
O final enchantment! yes, I sense it, I am alone.

Will you die, then, Madam?

HÉRODIADE

         No, poor ancient one;
Be calm, and pardon this embittered heart,
Drawing the shutters tight as you depart:
Seraphic through the windows smiles the sky,
The radiant sky that I detest!

         The sea
Is lulled, and in the distance is no clime
Where the sinister heavens countenance the crime
Of Venus at evening smouldering in the leaves:
There would I go.

Vers lui nativement la femme se dévoile,
Me voit dans ma pudeur grelottante d'étoile,
Je meurs!

      J'aime l'horreur d'être vierge et je veux
Vivre parmi l'effroi que me font mes cheveux
Pour, le soir, retirée en ma couche, reptile
Inviolé sentir en la chair inutile
Le froid scintillement de ta pâle clarté
Toi qui te meurs, toi qui brûles de chasteté,
Nuit blanche de glaçons et de neige cruelle!
Et ta sœur solitaire, ô ma sœur éternelle
Mon rêve montera vers toi: telle déjà,
Rare limpidité d'un cœur qui le songea,
Je me crois seule en ma monotone patrie
Et tout, autour de moi, vit dans l'idolâtrie
D'un miroir qui reflète en son calme dormant
Hérodiade au clair regard de diamant…
Ô charme dernier, oui! je le sens, je suis seule.

N.

Madame, allez-vous donc mourir?

H.

         Non, pauvre aïeule,
Sois calme et, t'éloignant, pardonne à ce cœur dur,
Mais avant, si tu veux, clos les volets: l'azur
Séraphique sourit dans les vitres profondes,
Et je déteste, moi, le bel azur!

         Des ondes
Se bercent et, là-bas, sais-tu pas un pays
Où le sinistre ciel ait les regards haïs
De Vénus qui, le soir, brûle dans le feuillage:
J'y partirais.

Then, childish though it may be,
Kindle the lamps and let the wax drop tears
Once more upon their useless golden biers
And . . .

NURSE

Now?

HÉRODIADE

Farewell.
          Nude flower of my lips, you lie!
I wait, but do not know for what or why—
Or perhaps you are uttering the last bruised sighs,
Ignorant of the mystery and of your cries,
Of a childhood feeling its frozen gems
Being broken off at last amidst its dreams.

Allume encore, enfantillage
Dis-tu, ces flambeaux où la cire au feu léger
Pleure parmi l'or vain quelque pleur étranger
Et …

N.

Maintenant?

H.

Adieu.
          Vous mentez, ô fleur nue
De mes lèvres.
          J'attends une chose inconnue
Ou peut-être, ignorant le mystère et vos cris,
Jetez-vous les sanglots suprêmes et meurtris
D'une enfance sentant parmi les rêveries
Se séparer enfin ses froides pierreries.

III. CANTICLE OF SAINT JOHN

The sun as it's halted
Miraculously exalted
Resumes its descent
    Incandescent

I feel in my sinews
The spreading of shadows
Converging together
    With a shiver

And in solitary vigil
After flights triumphal
My head rise
    From this scythe

Through a clean rupture
That serves to dissever
The ancient disharmony
    With the body

As drunk from fasting
It persists in following
With a haggard bound
    Its gaze profound

Up where the frozen
Absolute has chosen
That nothing shall measure
    Its vastness, O glacier

III. CANTIQUE DE SAINT JEAN

Le soleil que sa halte
Surnaturelle exalte
Aussitôt redescend
    Incandescent

Je sens comme aux vertèbres
S'éployer des ténèbres
Toutes dans un frisson
    A l'unisson

Et ma tête surgie
Solitaire vigie
Dans les vols triomphaux
    De cette faux

Comme rupture franche
Plutôt refoule ou tranche
Les anciens désaccords
    Avec le corps

Qu'elle de jeûnes ivre
S'opiniâtre à suivre
En quelque bond hagard
    Son pur regard

Là-haut où la froidure
Éternelle n'endure
Que vous le surpassiez
    Tous ô glaciers

But according to a ritual
Illumined by the principle
That chose my consecration
    It extends a salutation.

Mais selon un baptême
Illuminée au même
Principe qui m'élut
    Penche un salut.

THE AFTERNOON OF A FAUN

ECLOGUE

THE FAUN

These nymphs that I would perpetuate:
                          so clear
And light, their carnation, that it floats in the air
Heavy with leafy slumbers.

                    Did I love a dream?
My doubt, night's ancient hoard, pursues its theme
In branching labyrinths, which, being still
The veritable woods themselves, alas, reveal
My triumph as the ideal fault of roses.
Consider . . .

          if the women of your glosses
Are phantoms of your fabulous desires!
Faun, the illusion flees from the cold, blue eyes
Of the chaster nymph like a fountain gushing tears;
But the other, all in sighs, you say, compares
To a hot wind through the fleece that blows at noon?
No! through the motionless and weary swoon
Of stifling heat that suffocates the morning,
Save from my flute, no waters murmuring
In harmony flow out into the groves;
And the only wind on the horizon no ripple moves,
Exhaled from my twin pipes and swift to drain
The melody in arid drifts of rain,
Is the visible, serene and fictive air
Of inspiration rising as if in prayer.

RELATE, Sicilian shores, whose tranquil fens
My vanity disturbs as do the suns,

L'APRÈS-MIDI D'UN FAUNE

ÉGLOGUE

LE FAUNE

Ces nymphes, je les veux perpétuer.
                          Si clair,
Leur incarnat léger, qu'il voltige dans l'air
Assoupi de sommeils touffus.

                    Aimai-je un rêve?
Mon doute, amas de nuit ancienne, s'achève
En maint rameau subtil, qui, demeuré les vrais
Bois mêmes, prouve, hélas! que bien seul je m'offrais
Pour triomphe la faute idéale de roses.
Réfléchissons…

         ou si les femmes dont tu gloses
Figurent un souhait de tes sens fabuleux!
Faune, l'illusion s'échappe des yeux bleus
Et froids, comme une source en pleurs, de la plus chaste:
Mais, l'autre tout soupirs, dis-tu qu'elle contraste
Comme brise du jour chaude dans ta toison?
Que non! par l'immobile et lasse pâmoison
Suffoquant de chaleurs le matin frais s'il lutte,
Ne murmure point d'eau que ne verse ma flûte
Au bosquet arrosé d'accords; et le seul vent
Hors des deux tuyaux prompt à s'exhaler avant
Qu'il disperse le son dans une pluie aride,
C'est, à l'horizon pas remué d'une ride,
Le visible et serein souffle artificiel
De l'inspiration, qui regagne le ciel.

Ô bords siciliens d'un calme marécage
Qu'à l'envi de soleils ma vanité saccage,

Silent beneath the brilliant flowers of flame:
"That cutting hollow reeds my art would tame,
I saw far off, against the glaucous gold
Of foliage twined to where the springs run cold,
An animal whiteness languorously swaying;
To the slow prelude that the pipes were playing,
This flight of swans—no! naiads—rose in a shower
Of spray . . ."

       Day burns inert in the tawny hour
And excess of hymen is escaped away—
Without a sign, from one who pined for the primal *A:*
And so, beneath a flood of antique light,
As innocent as are the lilies white,
To my first ardors I awake alone.

Besides sweet nothings by their lips made known,
Kisses that only mark their perfidy,
My chest reveals an unsolved mystery . . .
The toothmarks of some strange, majestic creature:
Enough! Arcana such as these disclose their nature
Only through vast twin reeds played to the skies,
That, turning to music all that clouds the eyes,
Dream, in a long solo, that we amused
The beauty all around us by confused
Equations with our credulous melody;
And dream that the song can make love soar so high
That, purged of all ordinary fantasies
Of back or breast—incessant shapes that rise
In blindness—it distills sonorities
From every empty and monotonous line.

Then, instrument of flights, Syrinx malign,
At lakes where you attend me, bloom once more!
Long shall my discourse from the echoing shore
Depict those goddesses: by masquerades,
I'll strip the veils that sanctify their shades;

Tacite sous les fleurs d'étincelles, CONTEZ
« Que je coupais ici les creux roseaux domptés
» Par le talent; quand, sur l'or glauque de lointaines
» Verdures dédiant leur vigne à des fontaines,
» Ondoie une blancheur animale au repos:
» Et qu'au prélude lent où naissent les pipeaux
» Ce vol de cygnes, non! de naïades se sauve
» Ou plonge... »

       Inerte, tout brûle dans l'heure fauve
Sans marquer par quel art ensemble détala
Trop d'hymen souhaité de qui cherche le *la:*
Alors m'éveillerai-je à la ferveur première,
Droit et seul, sous un flot antique de lumière,
Lys! et l'un de vous tous pour l'ingénuité.

Autre que ce doux rien par leur lèvre ébruité,
Le baiser, qui tout bas des perfides assure,
Mon sein, vierge de preuve, atteste une morsure
Mystérieuse, due à quelque auguste dent;
Mais, bast! arcane tel élut pour confident
Le jonc vaste et jumeau dont sous l'azur on joue:
Qui, détournant à soi le trouble de la joue,
Rêve, dans un solo long, que nous amusions
La beauté d'alentour par des confusions
Fausses entre elle-même et notre chant crédule;
Et de faire aussi haut que l'amour se module
Évanouir du songe ordinaire de dos
Ou de flanc pur suivis avec mes regards clos,
Une sonore, vaine et monotone ligne.

Tâche donc, instrument des fuites, ô maligne
Syrinx, de refleurir aux lacs où tu m'attends!
Moi, de ma rumeur fier, je vais parler longtemps
Des déesses; et par d'idolâtres peintures,
A leur ombre enlever encore des ceintures:
Ainsi, quand des raisins j'ai sucé la clarté,

And when I've sucked the brightness out of grapes,
To quell the flood of sorrow that escapes,
I'll lift the empty cluster to the sky,
Avidly drunk till evening has drawn nigh,
And blow in laughter through the luminous skins.

Let us inflate our MEMORIES, O nymphs.
"*Piercing the reeds, my darting eyes transfix,*
Plunged in the cooling waves, immortal necks,
And cries of fury echo through the air;
Splendid cascades of tresses disappear
In shimmering jewels. Pursuing them, I find
There, at my feet, two sleepers intertwined,
Bruised in the languor of duality,
Their arms about each other heedlessly.
I bear them, still entangled, to a height
Where frivolous shadow never mocks the light
And dying roses yield the sun their scent,
That with the day our passions might be spent."
I adore you, wrath of virgins—fierce delight
Of the sacred burden's writhing naked flight
From the fiery lightning of my lips that flash
With the secret terror of the thirsting flesh:
From the cruel one's feet to the heart of the shy,
Whom innocence abandons suddenly,
Watered in frenzied or less woeful tears.
"*Gay with the conquest of those traitorous fears,*
I sinned when I divided the dishevelled
Tuft of kisses that the gods had ravelled.
For hardly had I hidden an ardent moan
Deep in the joyous recesses of one
(Holding by a finger, that her swanlike pallor
From her sister's passion might be tinged with color,
The little one, unblushingly demure),
When from my arms, loosened by death obscure,
This prey, ungrateful to the end, breaks free,
Spurning the sobs that still transported me."

Pour bannir un regret par ma feinte écarté,
Rieur, j'élève au ciel d'été la grappe vide
Et, soufflant dans ses peaux lumineuses, avide
D'ivresse, jusqu'au soir je regarde au travers.

Ô nymphes, regonflons des SOUVENIRS divers.
« *Mon œil, trouant les joncs, dardait chaque encolure*
» *Immortelle, qui noie en l'onde sa brûlure*
» *Avec un cri de rage au ciel de la forêt;*
» *Et le splendide bain de cheveux disparaît*
» *Dans les clartés et les frissons, ô pierreries!*
» *J'accours; quand, à mes pieds, s'entrejoignent (meurtries*
» *De la langueur goûtée à ce mal d'être deux)*
» *Des dormeuses parmi leurs seuls bras hasardeux;*
» *Je les ravis, sans les désenlacer, et vole*
» *A ce massif, haï par l'ombrage frivole,*
» *De roses tarissant tout parfum au soleil,*
» *Où notre ébat au jour consumé soit pareil.*»
Je t'adore, courroux des vierges, ô délice
Farouche du sacré fardeau nu qui se glisse
Pour fuir ma lèvre en feu buvant, comme un éclair
Tressaille! la frayeur secrète de la chair:
Des pieds de l'inhumaine au cœur de la timide
Que délaisse à la fois une innocence, humide
De larmes folles ou de moins tristes vapeurs.
« *Mon crime, c'est d'avoir, gai de vaincre ces peurs*
» *Traîtresses, divisé la touffe échevelée*
» *De baisers que les dieux gardaient si bien mêlée:*
» *Car, à peine j'allais cacher un rire ardent*
» *Sous les replis heureux d'une seule (gardant*
» *Par un doigt simple, afin que sa candeur de plume*
» *Se teignît à l'émoi de sa sœur qui s'allume,*
» *La petite, naïve et ne rougissant pas:)*
» *Que de mes bras, défaits par de vagues trépas,*
» *Cette proie, à jamais ingrate se délivre*
» *Sans pitié du sanglot dont j'étais encore ivre.* »

Others will lead me on to happiness,
Their tresses knotted round my horns, I guess.
You know, my passion, that, crimson with ripe seeds,
Pomegranates burst in a murmur of bees,
And that our blood, seized by each passing form,
Flows toward desire's everlasting swarm.
In the time when the forest turns ashen and gold
And the summer's demise in the leaves is extolled,
Etna! when Venus visits her retreat,
Treading your lava with innocent feet,
Though a sad sleep thunders and the flame burns cold,
I hold the queen!

       Sure punishment . . .
                     No, but the soul,
Weighed down by the body, wordless, struck dumb,
To noon's proud silence must at last succumb:
And so, let me sleep, oblivious of sin,
Stretched out on the thirsty sand, drinking in
The bountiful rays of the wine-growing star!

Couple, farewell; I'll see the shade that now you are.

Tant pis! vers le bonheur d'autres m'entraîneront
Par leur tresse nouée aux cornes de mon front:
Tu sais, ma passion, que, pourpre et déjà mûre,
Chaque grenade éclate et d'abeilles murmure;
Et notre sang, épris de qui le va saisir,
Coule pour tout l'essaim éternel du désir.
A l'heure où ce bois d'or et de cendres se teinte
Une fête s'exalte en la feuillée éteinte:
Etna! c'est parmi toi visité de Vénus
Sur ta lave posant ses talons ingénus,
Quand tonne un somme triste ou s'épuise la flamme.
Je tiens la reine!

       Ô sûr châtiment…
                     Non, mais l'âme
De paroles vacante et ce corps alourdi
Tard succombent au fier silence de midi:
Sans plus il faut dormir en l'oubli du blasphème,
Sur le sable altéré gisant et comme j'aime
Ouvrir ma bouche à l'astre efficace des vins!

Couple, adieu; je vais voir l'ombre que tu devins.

THE FLIGHT OF FLAMING HAIR

The flight of flaming hair at the extreme
West of desires unfurling it forth
Comes to rest (as it were a dying diadem)
On the crowned brow its ancient hearth

Then sigh for no gold but this cloud that lives
The kindling of an always interior flame
Originally the only one it gives
To the truthful or laughing eye its gleam

The tender nudity of heroes demeans
The one on whose fingers no stars wave or fires
Whose dazzling head is the only means
By which woman simplified with glory conspires

To sow with rubies the doubt she would scorch
In the manner of a joyous and tutelary torch.

LA CHEVELURE...

La chevelure vol d'une flamme à l'extrême
Occident de désirs pour la tout déployer
Se pose (je dirais mourir un diadème)
Vers le front couronné son ancien foyer

Mais sans or soupirer que cette vive nue
L'ignition du feu toujours intérieur
Originellement la seule continue
Dans le joyau de l'œil véridique ou rieur

Une nudité de héros tendre diffame
Celle qui ne mouvant astre ni feux au doigt
Rien qu'à simplifier avec gloire la femme
Accomplit par son chef fulgurante l'exploit

De semer de rubis le doute qu'elle écorche
Ainsi qu'une joyeuse et tutélaire torche.

SAINT

At the window frame concealing
The viol old and destitute
Whose gilded sandalwood, now peeling,
Once shone with mandolin or flute,

Is the Saint, pale, unfolding
The old, worn missal, a divine
Magnificat in rivers flowing
Once at vespers and compline:

At the glass of this monstrance, vessel
Touched by a harp that took its shape
From the evening flight of an Angel
For the delicate fingertip

Which, without the old, worn missal
Or sandalwood, she balances
On the plumage instrumental,
Musician of silences.

SAINTE

A la fenêtre recelant
Le santal vieux qui se dédore
De sa viole étincelant
Jadis avec flûte ou mandore,

Est la Sainte pâle, étalant
Le livre vieux qui se déplie
Du Magnificat ruisselant
Jadis selon vêpre et complie:

A ce vitrage d'ostensoir
Que frôle une harpe par l'Ange
Formée avec son vol du soir
Pour la délicate phalange

Du doigt que, sans le vieux santal
Ni le vieux livre, elle balance
Sur le plumage instrumental,
Musicienne du silence.

FUNEREAL TOAST

O fatal emblem, thou, of all our happiness!

Dementia's grisly offering of liquid sacrifice:
Not to the magic hope of the corridor do I hold
My empty cup aloft where a monster writhes in gold!
Nor can your apparition ever suffice for me:
For I myself have placed you in a bed of porphyry.
The rite exists for hands to obliterate the flame
Against the massive iron portals of the tomb,
And we who have been chosen guardians of the word
Are simply called upon to sing the absence of the bard,
Whom this fine monument encloses now indeed.
If this is but the ardent glorying of the trade
Even in the common hour when the pyre's flames are spent,
Through the windowpane illumined by the evening's proud
                                                    descent
Return toward the fires of the pure mortal sun!

Magnificent, complete within itself alone,
It stands as an admonition to the foolish pride of men.
This haggard crowd announces: We are nothing, then,
Save for the sad opaqueness of the future ghosts we bear.
But I have scorned the lucid horror of a tear,
The regalia of mourning emblazoned on an empty wall,
When, deaf even to my sacred verses, which frighten him not
                                                    at all,
One of these blind men passing, mute, puffed-up with pride,
The inmate of his winding-sheet, should be transmogrified
Into the virgin hero of posthumous unveiling.
Vast abyss transported to the gathered mists prevailing,
By the irascible wind of words that he did not say,
Nothingness to this Man, abolished yesterday:
"Memories of horizons, O thou, what is the Earth?"

TOAST FUNÈBRE

O de notre bonheur, toi, le fatal emblème!

Salut de la démence et libation blême,
Ne crois pas qu'au magique espoir du corridor
J'offre ma coupe vide où souffre un monstre d'or!
Ton apparition ne va pas me suffire:
Car je t'ai mis, moi-même, en un lieu de porphyre.
Le rite est pour les mains d'éteindre le flambeau
Contre le fer épais des portes du tombeau:
Et l'on ignore mal, élu pour notre fête
Très simple de chanter l'absence du poëte,
Que ce beau monument l'enferme tout entier.
Si ce n'est que la gloire ardente du métier,
Jusqu'à l'heure commune et vile de la cendre,
Par le carreau qu'allume un soir fier d'y
                                        descendre,
Retourne vers les feux du pur soleil mortel!

Magnifique, total et solitaire, tel
Tremble de s'exhaler le faux orgueil des hommes.
Cette foule hagarde! elle annonce: Nous sommes
La triste opacité de nos spectres futurs.
Mais le blason des deuils épars sur de vains murs
J'ai méprisé l'horreur lucide d'une larme,
Quand, sourd même à mon vers sacré qui ne
                                        l'alarme,
Quelqu'un de ces passants, fier, aveugle et muet,
Hôte de son linceul vague, se transmuait
En le vierge héros de l'attente posthume.
Vaste gouffre apporté dans l'amas de la brume
Par l'irascible vent des mots qu'il n'a pas dits,
Le néant à cet Homme aboli de jadis:
« Souvenirs d'horizons, qu'est-ce, ô toi, que la Terre?»

Howls this dream; with a voice that can barely issue forth,
Space as a joke returns this cry: "I do not know!"

The Master's piercing eye, wherever he would go,
Has calmed the unquiet marvels of Eden's wild delights,
Of which the final spasm, in his lone voice, excites
For the Lily and the Rose the mystery of a name.
And is there, of this destiny, nothing that will remain?
O all you gathered here, forget that gloomy creed:
The splendid, the eternal genius has no shade.
And I would have survive, in deference to your will,
For one who now has vanished into the ideal
Duty we are given by the gardens of that star,
A solemn agitation of language in the air,
In commemoration of a calm catastrophe,
Vast translucent calyx and purple ecstasy
That, diamond and rain, with gaze forever clear
Remaining on those flowers, of which none disappear,
Isolates in the hour and radiance of the day!

We dwell in those true groves, where, having marked our way,
With large and humble gesture the pure poet must
Stand guard against the dream as enemy to his trust:
So that upon the morning of his high repose,
When the task of ancient death for Gautier is to close
His sacred eyes and keep his secrets, shall appear,
As tributary ornament of the corridor,
The solid sepulcher where all things harmful lie,
And avaricious silence and night's immensity.

Hurle ce songe; et, voix dont la clarté s'altère,
L'espace a pour jouet le cri: « Je ne sais pas!»

Le Maître, par un œil profond, a, sur ses pas,
Apaisé de l'éden l'inquiète merveille
Dont le frisson final, dans sa voix seule, éveille
Pour la Rose et le Lys le mystère d'un nom.
Est-il de ce destin rien qui demeure, non?
Ô vous tous, oubliez une croyance sombre.
Le splendide génie éternel n'a pas d'ombre.
Moi, de votre désir soucieux, je veux voir,
A qui s'évanouit, hier, dans le devoir
Idéal que nous font les jardins de cet astre,
Survivre pour l'honneur du tranquille désastre
Une agitation solennelle par l'air
De paroles, pourpre ivre et grand calice clair,
Que, pluie et diamant, le regard diaphane
Resté là sur ces fleurs dont nulle ne se fane,
Isole parmi l'heure et le rayon du jour!

C'est de nos vrais bosquets déjà tout le séjour,
Où le poëte pur a pour geste humble et large
De l'interdire au rêve, ennemi de sa charge:
Afin que le matin de son repos altier,
Quand la mort ancienne est comme pour Gautier
De n'ouvrir pas les yeux sacrés et de se taire,
Surgisse, de l'allée ornement tributaire,
Le sépulcre solide où gît tout ce qui nuit,
Et l'avare silence et la massive nuit.

PROSE

for des Esseintes

Hyperbole! can you not rise
In triumph from my memory,
A modern magic spell devise
As from an ironbound grammary:

For I inaugurate through science
The hymn of all hearts spiritual
In the labor of my patience,
Atlas, herbal, ritual.

Our wandering eyes took in the forms
(For we were two, as I divine)
Of the landscape's myriad charms,
O sister, likening them to thine.

The age of certainty wears thin
When, without reason, it is stated
Of this southland which our twin
Unconsciousness has penetrated

That, soil of an iris bed, its site,
They know if it was really born:
It bears no name that one could cite,
Sounded by Summer's golden horn.

Yes, on an isle the air had charged
Not with visions but with sight,
The flowers displayed themselves enlarged
Without our ever mentioning it;

PROSE

pour des Esseintes

Hyperbole! de ma mémoire
Triomphalement ne sais-tu
Te lever, aujourd'hui grimoire
Dans un livre de fer vêtu:

Car j'installe, par la science,
L'hymne des cœurs spirituels
En l'œuvre de ma patience,
Atlas, herbiers et rituels.

Nous promenions notre visage
(Nous fûmes deux, je le maintiens)
Sur maints charmes de paysage,
Ô sœur, y comparant les tiens.

L'ère d'autorité se trouble
Lorsque, sans nul motif, on dit
De ce midi que notre double
Inconscience approfondit

Que, sol des cent iris, son site,
Ils savent s'il a bien été,
Ne porte pas de nom que cite
L'or de la trompette d'Été.

Oui, dans une île que l'air charge
De vue et non de visions
Toute fleur s'étalait plus large
Sans que nous en devisions.

And so immense, each burgeoning shape,
It was habitually adorned
In such clear outline that a gap
Between it and the gardens formed.

Glory of long ideal desire
In exultation rose in me
To see the irises aspire
To this responsibility;

But that sister, wise and tender,
Went no further than to smile,
And that I might comprehend her
I cultivate my ancient skill.

O Spirit of litigation, know,
When we keep silent in this season,
The stem of multiple lilies grew
Too large to be contained by reason

And not as weeps the mundane shore,
When its monotonous pastime lies
In wishing plenitude should pour
Upon my juvenile surprise

At hearing the heavens and the map
Endlessly in my walks attested,
Even by the wave as it falls back,
That this country never existed.

Telles, immenses, que chacune
Ordinairement se para
D'un lucide contour, lacune
Qui des jardins la sépara.

Gloire du long désir, Idées
Tout en moi s'exaltait de voir
La famille des iridées
Surgir à ce nouveau devoir,

Mais cette sœur sensée et tendre
Ne porta son regard plus loin
Que sourire et, comme à l'entendre
J'occupe mon antique soin.

Oh! sache l'Esprit de litige,
A cette heure où nous nous taisons,
Que de lis multiples la tige
Grandissait trop pour nos raisons

Et non comme pleure la rive,
Quand son jeu monotone ment
A vouloir que l'ampleur arrive
Parmi mon jeune étonnement

D'ouïr tout le ciel et la carte
Sans fin attestés sur mes pas,
Par le flot même qui s'écarte,
Que ce pays n'exista pas.

The child resigns her ecstasy,
Already mastering the steps,
And "Anastasius!" says she,
Born for eternal manuscripts,

Lest at a tomb her ancestor
In any clime should laugh to bear
This sacred name: "Pulcheria!"
Hidden by the too large lily flower.

L'enfant abdique son extase
Et docte déjà par chemins
Elle dit le mot: Anastase!
Né pour d'éternels parchemins,

Avant qu'un sépulcre ne rie
Sous aucun climat, son aïeul,
De porter ce nom: Pulchérie!
Caché par le trop grand glaïeul.

A FAN

of Madame Mallarmé

With nothing else for speech
Than a pulsing in the skies
Our future verse shall rise
From a precious lodging—rich

Messenger winging low
This fan if it's the same
Through which behind you some
Mirror has clearly shone

(Where invisible ash pursued
In every tiny grain
Is going to fall again;
Hence my disquietude)

May it always thus appear
In your busy hands, my dear.

ÉVENTAIL

de Madame Mallarmé

Avec comme pour langage
Rien qu'un battement aux cieux
Le futur vers se dégage
Du logis très précieux

Aile tout bas la courrière
Cet éventail si c'est lui
Le même par qui derrière
Toi quelque miroir a lui

Limpide (où va redescendre
Pourchassée en chaque grain
Un peu d'invisible cendre
Seule à me rendre chagrin)

Toujours tel il apparaisse
Entre tes mains sans paresse.

ANOTHER FAN

of Mademoiselle Mallarmé

O dreamer, that I might
Plunge into pure delight,
Learn through a subtle stratagem
How to guard my fragile wing in your hand.

Crepuscular breezes blow
Their freshness out to you
As lightly each imprisoned stroke
Presses the whole horizon back.

Vertigo! see how space
Shimmers in one vast kiss
That, born for no one, hence deranged,
Cannot gush forth or be assuaged.

Do you sense how a primal Eden
Like laughter barely hidden
From the corner of your mouth has flowed
To the depths of the unanimous fold!

The scepter of rosy shores
Stagnant on golden twilight hours
Is this white closed-up wing you set
Against the fire of a bracelet.

AUTRE ÉVENTAIL

de Mademoiselle Mallarmé

O rêveuse, pour que je plonge
Au pur délice sans chemin,
Sache, par un subtil mensonge,
Garder mon aile dans ta main.

Une fraîcheur de crépuscule
Te vient à chaque battement
Dont le coup prisonnier recule
L'horizon délicatement.

Vertige! voici que frissonne
L'espace comme un grand baiser
Qui, fou de naître pour personne,
Ne peut jaillir ni s'apaiser.

Sens-tu le paradis farouche
Ainsi qu'un rire enseveli
Se couler du coin de ta bouche
Au fond de l'unanime pli!

Le sceptre des rivages roses
Stagnants sur les soirs d'or, ce l'est,
Ce blanc vol fermé que tu poses
Contre le feu d'un bracelet.

A FAN

Frigid roses to survive
In unison will interrupt
With a calyx white and prompt
Your icy breath when frosts arrive

But if my ardent strokes contrive
By a deep shock to free the tuft
The cold will soon be melted up
In the laughter of flowers that drunkenly thrive

Which shows you're better suited than
A perfume vial—and like a fan—
At focusing fragments of the sky

Nothing enclosing with emery
Can hold without losing or violating the
Aroma emitted from Méry.

ÉVENTAIL

De frigides roses pour vivre
Toutes la même interrompront
Avec un blanc calice prompt
Votre souffle devenu givre

Mais que mon battement délivre
La touffe par un choc profond
Cette frigidité se fond
En du rire de fleurir ivre

A jeter le ciel en détail
Voilà comme bon éventail
Tu conviens mieux qu'une fiole

Nul n'enfermant à l'émeri
Sans qu'il y perde ou le viole
L'arôme émané de Méry.

ALBUM LEAVES

ALBUM LEAF

Suddenly and as in play
Mademoiselle who said she would
Listen awhile to the display
Of diverse flutes within my wood

This performance I extended
In so picturesque a place
Seems good in that I chose to end it
So as to look you in the face

Yes, this vain breath that I exclude
Unto the furthest limit set
With crippled fingers forced and crude
Lacks the means to imitate

Your very natural and clear
Childish laugh that charms the air.

FEUILLETS D'ALBUM

FEUILLET D'ALBUM

Tout à coup et comme par jeu
Mademoiselle qui voulûtes
Ouïr se révéler un peu
Le bois de mes diverses flûtes

Il me semble que cet essai
Tenté devant un paysage
A du bon quand je le cessai
Pour vous regarder au visage

Oui ce vain souffle que j'exclus
Jusqu'à la dernière limite
Selon mes quelques doigts perclus
Manque de moyens s'il imite

Votre très naturel et clair
Rire d'enfant qui charme l'air.

REMEMBRANCE OF BELGIAN FRIENDS

At certain hours when barely a breeze has blown
The entire ruin etched in frankincense
As furtively and visibly I sense
Fold upon fold of it stripped to widowed stone

Floats or bears in itself no evidence
Except in pouring out as ancient balm
The time we immemorial ones had known
Such gladness in a friendship just commenced

Dear friends encountered in the never banal
Bruges where dawn in the defunct canal
Is multiplied in passages of swans

When solemnly that city taught me whom
Another flight marks out among its sons
To light the wingèd spirit to its home.

REMÉMORATION D'AMIS BELGES

A des heures et sans que tel souffle l'émeuve
Toute la vétusté presque couleur encens
Comme furtive d'elle et visible je sens
Que se dévêt pli selon pli la pierre veuve

Flotte ou semble par soi n'apporter une preuve
Sinon d'épandre pour baume antique le temps
Nous immémoriaux quelques-uns si contents
Sur la soudaineté de notre amitié neuve

Ô très chers rencontrés en le jamais banal
Bruges multipliant l'aube au défunt canal
Avec la promenade éparse de maint cygne

Quand solennellement cette cité m'apprit
Lesquels entre ses fils un autre vol désigne
A prompte irradier ainsi qu'aile l'esprit.

SONNET

Lady
      who burns without being burnt or trying
The rose that cruel or torn and weary even
Of its white gown unlaces it with crimson
To hear in its own flesh the diamond crying

Yes, without dewy crises and, gently complying,
Winds, though they make the storms pass from our heaven,
Jealous to furnish us some spacious haven
For the simple day, the veritable day of feeling:

Doesn't it seem to you that every year,
Whose grace renews your brow spontaneously,
Suffices whatever semblance it may bear

As a cool fan's astonished to revive
With the little emotion that it needs to thrive
Our whole unvarying, natural intimacy.

SONNET

Dame
      sans trop d'ardeur à la fois enflammant
La rose qui cruelle ou déchirée et lasse
Même du blanc habit de pourpre le délace
Pour ouïr dans sa chair pleurer le diamant

Oui sans ces crises de rosée et gentiment
Ni brise quoique, avec, le ciel orageux passe
Jalouse d'apporter je ne sais quel espace
Au simple jour le jour très vrai du sentiment,

Ne te semble-t-il pas, disons, que chaque année
Dont sur ton front renaît la grâce spontanée
Suffise selon quelque apparence et pour moi

Comme un éventail frais dans la chambre s'étonne
A raviver du peu qu'il faut ici d'émoi
Toute notre native amitié monotone.

SONNET

So dear from far and near and white, and so
Deliciously yourself, Méry, that I
Dream of rare balms oozed out in fantasy
From any vase of crystal in shadow.

You know that always, since years ago
Your dazzling smile has prolonged for me
The rose that plunges with its fair sea-
son
      into the past and the future also.

My heart in the night that would seek to be heard
Or to call you with what tender, ultimate word
Rejoices in none but the whisper of *sister*

Were it not, vast treasure and head so petite,
That you teach me another fragrance so sweet,
Spoken so softly by the kiss in your hair.

SONNET

O si chère de loin et proche et blanche, si
Délicieusement toi, Méry, que je songe
A quelque baume rare émané par mensonge
Sur aucun bouquetier de cristal obscurci

Le sais-tu, oui ! pour moi voici des ans, voici
Toujours que ton sourire éblouissant prolonge
La même rose avec son bel été qui plonge
Dans autrefois et puis dans le futur aussi.

Mon cœur qui dans les nuits parfois cherche à s'entendre
Ou de quel dernier mot t'appeler le plus tendre
S'exalte en celui rien que chuchoté de sœur

N'était, très grand trésor et tête si petite,
Que tu m'enseignes bien toute une autre douceur
Tout bas par le baiser seul dans tes cheveux dite.

RONDELS

I

Nothing you have when you awake
Not envisaged with a pout
Worse if a fit of laughter shake
Your wing on the pillows—sleep without

Fear that a breath's avowal wreak
Havoc—sleep the whole night out
Nothing you have when you awake
Not envisaged with a pout

All the astonished dreams can make
When this beauty knocks them about
Not one flower upon the cheek
Jewels in the eye pay not a groat
Nothing you have when you awake.

RONDELS

I

Rien au réveil que vous n'ayez
Envisagé de quelque moue
Pire si le rire secoue
Votre aile sur les oreillers

Indifféremment sommeillez
Sans crainte qu'une haleine avoue
Rien au réveil que vous n'ayez
Envisagé de quelque moue

Tous les rêves émerveillés
Quand cette beauté les déjoue
Ne produisent fleur sur la joue
Dans l'œil diamants impayés
Rien au réveil que vous n'ayez.

II

We'll love each other if you choose
With speechless lips a little while
Do not interrupt this rose
Or worse silences shall spill

Never yet from song arose
The radiance of a sudden smile
We'll love each other if you choose
With speechless lips a little while

Softly, sylph, between the rounds
In purple robes go softly still
A flaming kiss torn off shall rouse
The very wing tips with a thrill
We'll love each other if you choose.

II

Si tu veux nous nous aimerons
Avec tes lèvres sans le dire
Cette rose ne l'interromps
Qu'à verser un silence pire

Jamais de chants ne lancent prompts
Le scintillement du sourire
Si tu veux nous nous aimerons
Avec tes lèvres sans le dire

Muet muet entre les ronds
Sylphe dans la pourpre d'empire
Un baiser flambant se déchire
Jusqu'aux pointes des ailerons
Si tu veux nous nous aimerons.

STREET SONGS

I

THE SHOEMAKER

Without the wax, what can one do?
The lily's white from birth; its smell
To me is preferable to
This good cobbler, truth to tell.

He's going to add leather to my pair,
More than I ever had, which entails
Driving to acute despair
An indigence of naked heels.

His never-deviating hammer
Fastens longing on the sole
With nails that keep a steady banter
Always to be elsewhere—on the go.

The shoes that he would recreate,
If that was what you wanted, feet!

CHANSONS BAS

I

LE SAVETIER

Hors de la poix rien à faire,
Le lys naît blanc, comme odeur
Simplement je le préfère
A ce bon raccommodeur.

Il va de cuir à ma paire
Adjoindre plus que je n'eus
Jamais, cela désespère
Un besoin de talons nus.

Son marteau qui ne dévie
Fixe de clous gouailleurs
Sur la semelle l'envie
Toujours conduisant ailleurs.

Il recréerait des souliers,
Ô pieds! si vous le vouliez!

II

THE WOMAN SELLING
AROMATIC HERBS

Don't think I'm willing to pay cash
For the lavender straw of azure hue
You sell by flaunting a daring lash
As if for the devious hypocrite to

Hang discreetly upon the walls
Of the most fundamental stations
For the stomach that jeers and growls
At being reborn to blue sensations.

Better to pin it up aloft
Amid an overgrown tuft of hair
So that the wholesome stalk may waft
You as a zephyr, Pamela, or

Bear to the husband you entice
The very first fruits of your lice.

II

LA MARCHANDE
D'HERBS AROMATIQUES

Ta paille azur de lavandes,
Ne crois pas avec ce cil
Osé que tu me la vendes
Comme à l'hypocrite s'il

En tapisse la muraille
De lieux les absolus lieux
Pour le ventre qui se raille
Renaître aux sentiments bleus.

Mieux entre une envahissante
Chevelure ici mets-la
Que le brin salubre y sente,
Zéphirine, Paméla

Ou conduise vers l'époux
Les prémices de tes poux.

59

III

THE ROADMENDER

You break pebbles for your sins,
And as a troubadour
I too must open a cube of brains
Each day and year by year.

IV

THE SELLER OF
GARLIC AND ONIONS

The boredom of paying a call
With garlic we forestall;
The tearful dirge won't wait
If onions I should grate.

V

THE WORKMAN'S WIFE

Wife and child and soup being brought
To the working man where the stone
  is quarried
Congratulate him that he's cut
Into the habit of being married.

III

LE CANTONNIER

Ces cailloux, tu les nivelles
Et c'est, comme troubadour,
Un cube aussi de cervelles
Qu'il me faut ouvrir par jour.

IV

LE MARCHAND
D'AIL ET D'OIGNONS

L'ennui d'aller en visite
Avec l'ail nous l'éloignons.
L'élégie au pleur hésite
Peu si je fends des oignons.

V

LA FEMME DE L'OUVRIER

La femme, l'enfant, la soupe
En chemin pour le carrier
Le complimentent qu'il coupe
Dans l'us de se marier.

VI

THE GLAZIER

The pure sun—throwing off
Too much brightness to measure—
Dazzled, contrives to doff
Its shirt on the back of the glazier.

VII

THE NEWSPAPER VENDOR

Always, whatever the title,
Without even catching cold when it thaws,
We hear this gay half-pint's recital
Of the early edition news.

VIII

THE OLD-CLOTHES WOMAN

The piercing eye with which you see
What they contain essentially
Separates my rags from me
And naked I go as a deity.

VI

LE VITRIER

Le pur soleil qui remise
Trop d'éclat pour l'y trier
Ote ébloui sa chemise
Sur le dos du vitrier.

VII

LE CRIEUR D'IMPRIMÉS

Toujours, n'importe le titre,
Sans même s'enrhumer au
Dégel, ce gai siffle-litre
Crie un premier numéro.

VIII

LA MARCHANDE D'HABITS

Le vif œil dont tu regardes
Jusques à leur contenu
Me sépare de mes hardes
Et comme un dieu je vais nu.

NOTE TO WHISTLER

Not gusts of wind that hold the streets
Always without the slightest reason
Subject to dark flights of hats;
But a dancing girl arisen

As a muslin whirlwind or
Fury scattered in the spume
Which she raises up with her
Knee, that girl we lived for, to

Blast with her tutu all but him,
All platitudes that we despise,
Rapt motionless in her own dream
Without being angry otherwise

Except in joking that the air
From her skirt might fan Whistler.

BILLET A WHISTLER

Pas les rafales à propos
De rien comme occuper la rue
Sujette au noir vol de chapeaux;
Mais une danseuse apparue

Tourbillon de mousseline ou
Fureur éparses en écumes
Que soulève par son genou
Celle même dont nous vécûmes

Pour tout, hormis lui, rebattu
Spirituelle, ivre, immobile
Foudroyer avec le tutu,
Sans se faire autrement de bile

Sinon rieur que puisse l'air
De sa jupe éventer Whistler.

LITTLE AIR

I

Some sort of solitude
With neither swan nor dock
Mirrors its desuetude
In my abdicated look

Here from a realm too high
And glorious to hold
In which so many a radiant sky
Bedecks itself in sunset's gold

But languorously glides
Like linen floating down
Some passing bird if there beside
Plunge in exultation

Into the wave yourself your own
Naked jubilation grown.

PETIT AIR

I

Quelconque une solitude
Sans le cygne ni le quai
Mire sa désuétude
Au regard que j'abdiquai

Ici de la gloriole
Haute à ne la pas toucher
Dont maint ciel se bariole
Avec les ors de coucher

Mais langoureusement longe
Comme de blanc linge ôté
Tel fugace oiseau si plonge
Exultatrice à côté

Dans l'onde toi devenue
Ta jubilation nue.

LITTLE AIR

II

Indomitably must
Like my hopes flung after it
Have burst in ether and been lost
With the fury and silence of its flight:

Voice foreign to the wood
Or else unechoed, bird
That in a single lifetime could
Never more than once be heard.

The haggard musician,
It still expires in doubt
If not from his breast but my own
More grievous sobs came gushing out:

Tattered but entire, may
He still pursue some chosen way!

PETIT AIR

II

Indomptablement a dû
Comme mon espoir s'y lance
Éclater là-haut perdu
Avec furie et silence,

Voix étrangère au bosquet
Ou par nul écho suivie,
L'oiseau qu'on n'ouït jamais
Une autre fois en la vie.

Le hagard musicien,
Cela dans le doute expire
Si de mon sein pas du sien
A jailli le sanglot pire

Déchiré va-t-il entier
Rester sur quelque sentier!

LITTLE AIR

(Martial)

It suits me not to hold my peace
That from the fireplace I sense
A military trouser spread
Upon my thigh in bright blood-red

I lie in wait for the invasion
With the virgin indignation
Of the cudgel of command
In the soldier's white-gloved hand

Naked or holding to its bark
Not to beat the Teuton back
But as another threat for the
Task that is imposed on me

Of cutting off the festering weeds
That wild emotion rankly breeds.

PETIT AIR

(Guerrier)

Ce me va hormis l'y taire
Que je sente du foyer
Un pantalon militaire
A ma jambe rougeoyer

L'invasion je la guette
Avec le vierge courroux
Tout juste de la baguette
Au gant blanc des tourlourous

Nue ou d'écorce tenace
Pas pour battre le Teuton
Mais comme une autre menace
A la fin que me veut-on

De trancher ras cette ortie
Folle de la sympathie.

SEVERAL SONNETS

I

When the shadow menaced with its fatal law
That old Dream, desire and pain of my spine,
Grieved at being swallowed in night's black maw
It folded within me its indubitable wing.

O deluxe, ebony hall, where, to beguile a king,
Celebrated garlands are twisted in death:
You are but a proud lie composed of nothing
In the eyes of the solitary dazzled by his faith.

Yes, I know that the Earth, far off from this night,
Casts the radiant mystery of unprecedented light
Which the hideous centuries can never obscure.

Space, unaltered, if it grow or decrease,
Rolls in that boredom vile fires as witness
That genius has been kindled by a festive star.

PLUSIEURS SONNETS

I

Quand l'ombre menaça de la fatale loi
Tel vieux Rêve, désir et mal de mes vertèbres,
Affligé de périr sous les plafonds funèbres
Il a ployé son aile indubitable en moi.

Luxe, ô salle d'ébène où, pour séduire un roi,
Se tordent dans leur mort des guirlandes célèbres,
Vous n'êtes qu'un orgueil menti par les ténèbres
Aux yeux du solitaire ébloui de sa foi.

Oui, je sais qu'au lointain de cette nuit, la Terre
Jette d'un grand éclat l'insolite mystère
Sous les siècles hideux qui l'obscurcissent moins.

L'espace à soi pareil qu'il s'accroisse ou se nie
Roule dans cet ennui des feux vils pour témoins
Que s'est d'un astre en fête allumé le génie.

II

The virginal, vibrant, and beautiful dawn,
Will a beat of its drunken wing not suffice
To rend this hard lake haunted beneath the ice
By the transparent glacier of flights never flown?

A swan of former times remembers it's the one
Magnificent but hopelessly struggling to resist
For never having sung of a land in which to exist
When the boredom of the sterile winter has shone.

Though its quivering neck will shake free of the agonies
Inflicted on the bird by the space it denies,
The horror of the earth will remain where it lies.

Phantom whose pure brightness assigns it this domain,
It stiffens in the cold dream of disdain
That clothes the useless exile of the Swan.

II

Le vierge, le vivace et le bel aujourd'hui
Va-t-il nous déchirer avec un coup d'aile ivre
Ce lac dur oublié que hante sous le givre
Le transparent glacier des vols qui n'ont pas fui!

Un cygne d'autrefois se souvient que c'est lui
Magnifique mais qui sans espoir se délivre
Pour n'avoir pas chanté la région où vivre
Quand du stérile hiver a resplendi l'ennui.

Tout son col secouera cette blanche agonie
Par l'espace infligée à l'oiseau qui le nie,
Mais non l'horreur du sol où le plumage est pris.

Fantôme qu'à ce lieu son pur éclat assigne,
Il s'immobilise au songe froid de mépris
Que vêt parmi l'exil inutile le Cygne.

III

The beautiful suicide victoriously fled,
Firebrand of glory, bloody mist, gold, spume!
What irony if, beyond, the purple is spread
Regally to drape the absence of my tomb!

Of all that splendor, there remains not a shred,
Now that it's midnight, in the shade of our room,
Save that the presumptuous treasure of a head
Is languorously spun out like gold from a loom.

Yours always the delight! yes, yours the domain
In which alone the vanished heavens retain
Some vestige of triumph by dressing your hair

With radiance, when on the cushions you lie,
Like a young empress with helmet held high,
From which would fall roses—the emblem you bear.

III

Victorieusement fui le suicide beau
Tison de gloire, sang par écume, or, tempête!
Ô rire si là-bas une pourpre s'apprête
A ne tendre royal que mon absent tombeau.

Quoi! de tout cet éclat pas même le lambeau
S'attarde, il est minuit, à l'ombre qui nous fête
Excepté qu'un trésor présomptueux de tête
Verse son caressé nonchaloir sans flambeau,

La tienne si toujours le délice! la tienne
Oui seule qui du ciel évanoui retienne
Un peu de puéril triomphe en t'en coiffant

Avec clarté quand sur les coussins tu la poses
Comme un casque guerrier d'impératrice enfant
Dont pour te figurer il tomberait des roses.

IV

Her pure nails on high displaying their onyx,
The lampbearer, Anguish, at midnight sustains
Those vesperal dreams that are burnt by the Phœnix
And which no funeral amphora contains

On the credenzas in the empty room: no ptyx,
Abolished shell whose resonance remains
(For the Master has gone to draw tears from the Styx
With this sole object that Nothingness attains).

But in the vacant north, adjacent to the window panes,
A dying shaft of gold illumines as it wanes
A nix sheathed in sparks that a unicorn kicks.

Though she in the oblivion that the mirror frames
Lies nude and defunct, there rains
The scintillations of the one-and-six.

IV

Ses purs ongles très haut dédiant leur onyx,
L'Angoisse, ce minuit, soutient, lampadophore,
Maint rêve vespéral brûlé par le Phénix
Que ne recueille pas de cinéraire amphore

Sur les crédences, au salon vide: nul ptyx,
Aboli bibelot d'inanité sonore,
(Car le Maître est allé puiser des pleurs au Styx
Avec ce seul objet dont le Néant s'honore).

Mais proche la croisée au nord vacante, un or
Agonise selon peut-être le décor
Des licornes ruant du feu contre une nixe,

Elle, défunte nue en le miroir, encor
Que, dans l'oubli fermé par le cadre, se fixe
De scintillations sitôt le septuor.

HOMAGES AND TOMBS

SONNET

(For your dear departed one, her friend)
November 2, 1877

—"In the forgotten woods, when somber winter glowers,
You complain, O solitary captive of the sill,
That this double sepulcher, which is ours to fill,
Is burdened with the weight of absent flowers.

Heedless of Midnight, which vainly tolls the hours,
A vigil exalts you to keep watch until
My Shade at length is rendered visible
By the last embers that the dark devours.

Whoever would receive the Silent Ones
Should lay no weight of flowers on the stones
They struggle wearily to cast aside.

The trembling soul that hovers at the flame
Needs but the breath, to be revivified,
With which all evening you have called my name."

HOMMAGES ET TOMBEAUX

SONNET

(Pour votre chère morte, son ami)
2 novembre 1877

— « Sur les bois oubliés quand passe l'hiver sombre
Tu te plains, ô captif solitaire du seuil,
Que ce sépulcre à deux qui fera notre orgueil
Hélas! du manque seul des lourds bouquets s'encombre.

Sans écouter Minuit qui jeta son vain nombre,
Une veille t'exalte à ne pas fermer l'œil
Avant que dans les bras de l'ancien fauteuil
Le suprême tison n'ait éclairé mon Ombre.

Qui veut souvent avoir la Visite ne doit
Par trop de fleurs charger la pierre que mon doigt
Soulève avec l'ennui d'une force défunte.

Âme au si clair foyer tremblante de m'asseoir,
Pour revivre il suffit qu'à tes lèvres j'emprunte
Le souffle de mon nom murmuré tout un soir.»

THE TOMB OF EDGAR POE

As to Himself at last eternity changes him
The Poet reawakens with a naked sword
His century appalled at never having heard
That in this voice triumphant death had sung its hymn.

They, like a writhing hydra, hearing seraphim
Bestow a purer sense on the language of the horde,
Loudly proclaimed that the magic potion had been poured
From the dregs of some dishonored mixture of foul slime.

From the war between earth and heaven, what grief!
If understanding cannot sculpt a bas-relief
To ornament the dazzling tomb of Poe:

Calm block here fallen from obscure disaster,
Let this granite at least mark the boundaries evermore
To the dark flights of Blasphemy hurled to the future.

LE TOMBEAU D'EDGAR POE

Tel qu'en Lui-même enfin l'éternité le change,
Le Poëte suscite avec un glaive nu
Son siècle épouvanté de n'avoir pas connu
Que la mort triomphait dans cette voix étrange!

Eux, comme un vil sursaut d'hydre oyant jadis l'ange
Donner un sens plus pur aux mots de la tribu
Proclamèrent très haut le sortilège bu
Dans le flot sans honneur de quelque noir mélange.

Du sol et de la nue hostiles, ô grief!
Si notre idée avec ne sculpte un bas-relief
Dont la tombe de Poe éblouissante s'orne,

Calme bloc ici-bas chu d'un désastre obscur,
Que ce granit du moins montre à jamais sa borne
Aux noirs vols du Blasphème épars dans le futur.

THE TOMB OF CHARLES BAUDELAIRE

The buried temple empties through its bowels,
Sepulchral sewer spewing mud and rubies,
Abominably some idol of Anubis,
Its muzzle all aflame with savage howls.

Or if the recent gas the wick befouls
That bears so many insults, it illumines
In haggard outline an immortal pubis
Flying along the streetlamps on its prowls.

What wreaths dried out in cities without prayer
Of night could bless like that which settles down
Vainly against the marble of Baudelaire

In the fluttering veil that girds her absence round,
A tutelary poison, his own Wraith,
We breathe in always though it bring us death.

LE TOMBEAU DE CHARLES BAUDELAIRE

Le temple enseveli divulgue par la bouche
Sépulcrale d'égout bavant boue et rubis
Abominablement quelque idole Anubis
Tout le museau flambé comme un aboi farouche

Ou que le gaz récent torde la mèche louche
Essuyeuse on le sait des opprobres subis
Il allume hagard un immortel pubis
Dont le vol selon le réverbère découche

Quel feuillage séché dans les cités sans soir
Votif pourra bénir comme elle se rasseoir
Contre le marbre vainement de Baudelaire

Au voile qui la ceint absente avec frissons
Celle son Ombre même un poison tutélaire
Toujours à respirer si nous en périssons.

TOMB

Anniversary—January 1897

The black rock raging that the wind has rolled
It
    won't be stayed even for pious hands
Feeling its likeness to the woes of man
As if to bless in it some fatal mould.

Here often if the ringdove's tale be told
This cloudy grief in nubile folds descends
Upon the ripened star the future sends
Whose scintillations silvercoat the crowd.

Who seeks, pursuing the reclusive bound
Till now external of our vagabond—
Verlaine? He's hidden in the woolly sward

Only to find naively in accord
His lip not drinking there or bating breath
A shallow stream calumniated death.

TOMBEAU

Anniversaire—Janvier 1897

Le noir roc courroucé que la bise le roule
Ne s'arrêtera ni sous de pieuses mains
Tâtant sa ressemblance avec les maux humains
Comme pour en bénir quelque funeste moule.

Ici presque toujours si le ramier roucoule
Cet immatériel deuil opprime de maints
Nubiles plis l'astre mûri des lendemains
Dont un scintillement argentera la foule.

Qui cherche, parcourant le solitaire bond
Tantôt extérieur de notre vagabond—
Verlaine? Il est caché parmi l'herbe, Verlaine

A ne surprendre que naïvement d'accord
La lèvre sans y boire ou tarir son haleine
Un peu profond ruisseau calomnié la mort.

HOMAGE

The silence already funereal spreads a pall
With more than a single fold upon the props
Which with the column's imminent collapse
Must be hurled down without memorial.

Our old triumphal grammary of spells,
Hieroglyphs by which exultant mobs
Extend their wings with sentimental throbs!
Let some dark closet give it burial.

From the original smiling fracas hated among
Themselves by master clarities has sprung
Unto a parvis born for their simulacrum,

Golden trumpets swooning aloud on the vellum,
The god Richard Wagner making the sacred shine,
Unmuted even by the ink in sobbings sibylline.

HOMMAGE

Le silence déjà funèbre d'une moire
Dispose plus qu'un pli seul sur le mobilier
Que doit un tassement du principal pilier
Précipiter avec le manque de mémoire.

Notre si vieil ébat triomphal du grimoire,
Hiéroglyphes dont s'exalte le millier
A propager de l'aile un frisson familier!
Enfouissez-le-moi plutôt dans une armoire.

Du souriant fracas originel haï
Entre elles de clartés maîtresses a jailli
Jusque vers un parvis né pour leur simulacre,

Trompettes tout haut d'or pâmé sur les vélins,
Le dieu Richard Wagner irradiant un sacre
Mal tu par l'encre même en sanglots sibyllins.

HOMAGE

Even a Dawn too numb
To clench dark fingers and thumb
Against the azure trum-
pets
      she sounds though deaf and dumb

Has the shepherd with the gourd
To a divining rod secured
Till his future path is explored
And a copious fountain has soared

Thus you come before the van
O solitary Puvis de Chavannes
      never alone

Leading your time its thirst to slake
Before the unveiled nymph who makes
      your Glory known.

HOMMAGE

Toute Aurore même gourde
A crisper un poing obscur
Contre des clairons d'azur
Embouchés par cette sourde

A le pâtre avec la gourde
Jointe au bâton frappant dur
Le long de son pas futur
Tant que la source ample sourde

Par avance ainsi tu vis
Ô solitaire Puvis
De Chavannes
      jamais seul

De conduire le temps boire
A la nymphe sans linceul
Que lui découvre ta Gloire.

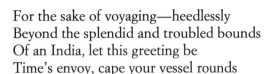

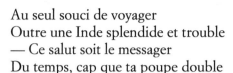

For the sake of voyaging—heedlessly
Beyond the splendid and troubled bounds
Of an India, let this greeting be
Time's envoy, cape your vessel rounds

As upon some yardarm low
Plunging with the caravel
A bird announcing tidings new
Gaily skimmed the foaming swell

And though the tiller never varied
Forever wailed in piercing tones
Of a motherlode deep buried
Night, despair and precious stones

Reflected by its song unto
The smile of some forsaken Vasco.

Au seul souci de voyager
Outre une Inde splendide et trouble
— Ce salut soit le messager
Du temps, cap que ta poupe double

Comme sur quelque vergue bas
Plongeante avec la caravelle
Écumait toujours en ébats
Un oiseau d'annonce nouvelle

Qui criait monotonement
Sans que la barre ne varie
Un inutile gisement
Nuit, désespoir et pierrerie

Par son chant reflété jusqu'au
Sourire du pâle Vasco.

The entire soul evoked
When slowly we expel it
In many a ring of smoke
Till other rings annul it

Attests that a cigar
Burns true to the extent
That out of its kiss of fire
It sheds the ash when it's spent

Should choirs of romance
Thus rise up to your lips
Exclude if you commence
The real in its vile shapes

Too fixed a sense erases
Your art in its faint traces.

Toute l'âme résumée
Quand lente nous l'expirons
Dans plusieurs ronds de fumée
Abolis en autres ronds

Atteste quelque cigare
Brûlant savamment pour peu
Que la cendre se sépare
De son clair baiser de feu

Ainsi le chœur des romances
A la lèvre vole-t-il
Exclus-en si tu commences
Le réel parce que vil

Le sens trop précis rature
Ta vague littérature.

OTHER POEMS AND SONNETS

I

Does Pride at evening always fume,
Torch snuffed out by a sudden stirring
Without the immortal gust deferring
The abandonment about to come!

The heir apparent's ancient room,
Rich though fallen trophies bearing,
Would still be cold if he came faring
Through passageways back through the gloom.

Inevitable death throes of the past
As with talons gripping fast
Disavowal's sepulcher:

Beneath the marble it isolates
No other fire fulminates
Than the console glittering there.

AUTRES POËMES ET SONNETS

I

Tout Orgueil fume-t-il du soir,
Torche dans un branle étouffée
Sans que l'immortelle bouffée
Ne puisse à l'abandon surseoir!

La chambre ancienne de l'hoir
De maint riche mais chu trophée
Ne serait pas même chauffée
S'il survenait par le couloir.

Affres du passé nécessaires
Agrippant comme avec des serres
Le sépulcre de désaveu,

Sous un marbre lourd qu'elle isole
Ne s'allume pas d'autre feu
Que la fulgurante console.

II

Sprung from the croup and the flight
Of an ephemeral vase,
The neck, stopped short and forgotten, must pause
Without flowering the long, bitter night.

I think that two mouths in delight
Never drank where the same phantom flows,
Neither my mother nor the lover she chose,
I, sylph of this ceiling's cold height!

Pure vessel of no liquor brewed
Save the bottomless widowhood
Dies slowly but does not consent,

Funereal kiss naive!
To breathe out any hint
That a rose in the darkness should live.

II

Surgi de la croupe et du bond
D'une verrerie éphémère
Sans fleurir la veillée amère
Le col ignoré s'interrompt.

Je crois bien que deux bouches n'ont
Bu, ni son amant ni ma mère,
Jamais à la même Chimère,
Moi, sylphe de ce froid plafond!

Le pur vase d'aucun breuvage
Que l'inexhaustible veuvage
Agonise mais ne consent,

Naïf baiser des plus funèbres!
A rien expirer annonçant
Une rose dans les ténèbres.

III

Lace sweeps itself aside
In the doubt of the ultimate Game
Only to expose profane-
ly
    eternal absence of bed.

This white and undivid-
ed
    garland's struggle with the same
Blown against the ghostly pane
Floats more than it would hide.

But where the dream would shine within
Sadly sleeps a mandolin,
The hollow core's musician

Such that toward some window, one
Through no belly but its own,
Filial, might have been born.

III

Une dentelle s'abolit
Dans le doute du Jeu suprême
A n'entr'ouvrir comme un blasphème
Qu'absence éternelle de lit.

Cet unanime blanc conflit
D'une guirlande avec la même,
Enfui contre la vitre blême
Flotte plus qu'il n'ensevelit.

Mais, chez qui du rêve se dore
Tristement dort une mandore
Au creux néant musicien

Telle que vers quelque fenêtre
Selon nul ventre que le sien,
Filial on aurait pu naître.

What silk steeped in the balms of time
Where writhes an old and worn Chimera
Can match the native cloud you twine
In wreaths stretched out beyond your mirror!

The holes of pensive flags may climb
Our avenue in proud bravura:
Me, your naked hair is mine,
And there my contented eyes can burrow.

No! The mouth will not be sure
Of tasting anything if your
Princely lover does not make

The cry expire like a gem
In the considerable brake,
The cry of Glories he would stem.

Quelle soie aux baumes de temps
Où la Chimère s'exténue
Vaut la torse et native nue
Que, hors de ton miroir, tu tends!

Les trous de drapeaux méditants
S'exaltent dans notre avenue:
Moi, j'ai ta chevelure nue
Pour enfouir mes yeux contents.

Non! La bouche ne sera sûre
De rien goûter à sa morsure,
S'il ne fait, ton princier amant,

Dans la considérable touffe
Expirer, comme un diamant,
Le cri des Gloires qu'il étouffe.

To insert myself into your story
Is as a hero shocked if he'll
Have barely touched with naked heel
Some grass plot of that territory

What peccadillo minatory
To glacial ridges could prevail
Against your efforts to have it fail
And loudly vaunt its conquering glory

Tell me if I am not happy
Thunder at the hubs and rubies
To see in air that fire has pierced

With kingdoms shattered and dispersed
The wheel as if in purple dying
Of my sole chariot of evening.

M'introduire dans ton histoire
C'est en héros effarouché
S'il a du talon nu touché
Quelque gazon de territoire

A des glaciers attentatoire
Je ne sais le naïf péché
Que tu n'auras pas empêché
De rire très haut sa victoire

Dis si je ne suis pas joyeux
Tonnerre et rubis aux moyeux
De voir en l'air que ce feu troue

Avec des royaumes épars
Comme mourir pourpre la roue
Du seul vespéral de mes chars.

Hushed to the crushing cloud
Basalt and lava its form
Even to echoes subdued
By an ineffectual horn

What shipwreck sepulchral has bowed
(You know this, but slobber on, foam)
The mast, supreme in a crowd
Of flotsam and jetsam, though torn

Or will that which in fury defaulted
From some perdition exalted
(The vain abyss outspread)

Have stingily drowned in the swirl
Of a white hair's trailing thread
The flank of a young Siren girl.

A la nue accablante tu
Basse de basalte et de laves
A même les échos esclaves
Par une trompe sans vertu

Quel sépulcral naufrage (tu
Le sais, écume, mais y baves)
Suprême une entre les épaves
Abolit le mât dévêtu

Ou cela que furibond faute
De quelque perdition haute
Tout l'abîme vain éployé

Dans le si blanc cheveu qui traîne
Avarement aura noyé
Le flanc enfant d'une sirène.

My old books closed upon Paphos's name,
I delight to return in my mind alone
To a ruin, hallowed by wind and foam,
Distant, beneath the hyacinth of the days of its fame.

Let the cold with its sickle of silence maim:
I shall not howl an empty moan
If this white frolic on the ground disown
All landscapes of the fictions they would claim.

On no fruits here does my hunger feast,
But finds in their learnèd lack the self-same taste:
Let one of them burst forth fragrant in human flesh!

My foot on some wyvern where love stirs our flames,
I brood on that other, distracted by dreams
Of an ancient amazon with cauterized breast.

Mes bouquins refermés sur le nom de Paphos,
Il m'amuse d'élire avec le seul génie
Une ruine, par mille écumes bénie
Sous l'hyacinthe, au loin, de ses jours triomphaux.

Coure le froid avec ses silences de faux,
Je n'y hululerai pas de vide nénie
Si ce très blanc ébat au ras du sol dénie
A tout site l'honneur du paysage faux.

Ma faim qui d'aucuns fruits ici ne se régale
Trouve en leur docte manque une saveur égale:
Qu'un éclate de chair humain et parfumant!

Le pied sur quelque guivre où notre amour tisonne,
Je pense plus longtemps peut-être éperdument
A l'autre, au sein brûlé d'une antique amazone.

POËMES EN PROSE

A PHENOMENON OF THE FUTURE

A pale sky, hovering over a world that is dying of its own decrepitude, is perhaps going to depart with the clouds: the shreds of worn-out purple sunsets fade in a river lying dormant on an horizon submerged in sunbeams and water. The trees are wearied and, beneath their whitened foliage (from the dust of time rather than from that of the roads), rises the tent of the Showman of things Past: many a streetlamp awaits the twilight and reanimates the faces of an unhappy crowd, vanquished by the immortal malady and the sin of the centuries, men accompanied by their wretched accomplices pregnant with the miserable fruits by which the earth will perish. In the troubled silence of all those eyes supplicating the far-off sun plunging beneath the water with the despair of a cry, here is the gist of his claptrap: "No sign regales you to the spectacle inside, for there is now no painter capable of rendering even a sad semblance of its existence. I present, living (and preserved through all the ages by sovereign science), a Woman of a former time. Some primordial and ingenuous madness, an ecstasy of gold, I don't know what! which she calls her hair, is folded with the grace of silk around a face lit up by the blood-red nakedness of her lips. In lieu of vain apparel, she has a body; and her eyes, though they resemble precious stones, are not equal to the expression that springs from her happy flesh: from breasts raised as if they were full of eternal milk, tipped toward the sky, to glistening legs that retain the salt of the primeval sea." Recalling their poor spouses, bald, morbid, and full of horror, the husbands squeeze forward: their melancholy wives, driven by curiosity, also want to see.

LE PHÉNOMÈNE FUTUR

Un ciel pâle, sur le monde qui finit de décrépitude, va peut-être partir avec les nuages: les lambeaux de la pourpre usée des couchants déteignent dans une rivière dormant à l'horizon submergé de rayons et d'eau. Les arbres s'ennuient et, sous leur feuillage blanchi (de la poussière du temps plutôt que celle des chemins), monte la maison en toile du Montreur de choses Passées: maint réverbère attend le crépuscule et ravive les visages d'une malheureuse foule, vaincue par la maladie immortelle et le péché des siècles, d'hommes près de leurs chétives complices enceintes des fruits misérables avec lesquels périra la terre. Dans le silence inquiet de tous les yeux suppliant là-bas le soleil qui, sous l'eau, s'enfonce avec le désespoir d'un cri, voici le simple boniment: « Nulle enseigne ne vous régale du spectacle intérieur, car il n'est pas maintenant un peintre capable d'en donner une ombre triste. J'apporte, vivante (et préservée à travers les ans par la science souveraine) une Femme d'autrefois. Quelque folie, originelle et naïve, une extase d'or, je ne sais quoi! par elle nommé sa chevelure, se ploie avec la grâce des étoffes autour d'un visage qu'éclaire la nudité sanglante de ses lèvres. A la place du vêtement vain, elle a un corps; et les yeux, semblables aux pierres rares, ne valent pas ce regard qui sort de sa chair heureuse: des seins levés comme s'ils étaient pleins d'un lait éternel, la pointe vers le ciel, aux jambes lisses qui gardent le sel de la mer première. » Se rappelant leurs pauvres épouses, chauves, morbides et pleines d'horreur, les maris se pressent: elles aussi par curiosité, mélancoliques, veulent voir.

When they have all gazed upon the noble creature, the vestige of an age already accursed, some, indifferent (for they will not have had the capacity to understand), but others, brokenhearted and with eyelids wet with resigned tears, will look at one another; while the poets of those times, feeling their dull eyes lighting up once again, will make their way toward their lamps, their brains momentarily drunk with an obscure glory, haunted by a Rhythm and forgetting that they exist in an age that has outlived beauty.

Quand tous auront contemplé la noble créature, vestige de quelque époque déjà maudite, les uns indifférents, car ils n'auront pas eu la force de comprendre, mais d'autres navrés et la paupière humide de larmes résignées se regarderont; tandis que les poëtes de ces temps, sentant se rallumer leurs yeux éteints, s'achemineront vers leur lampe, le cerveau ivre un instant d'une gloire confuse, hantés du Rythme et dans l'oubli d'exister à une époque qui survit à la beauté.

Since Maria left me to go to another star—which was it: Orion, Altair, or you, green Venus?—I have always cherished solitude. What long days I have passed alone with my cat. By *alone* I mean without a material being and my cat is a mystic companion, a spirit. I can therefore say that I have passed long days alone with my cat, and alone also with one of the last authors of the Latin decadence; for since that white creature has been no more, I have loved, strangely and especially, all that can be summed up in the word *fall*. Thus, during the year my favorite season is the last, languid stretch of summer immediately before autumn, and during the day, the hour when I go for a walk is when the sun rests just before vanishing, with sunbeams of copper yellow on the gray walls and copper red on the panes. Similarly, the literature to which my spirit turns for delight is the moribund poetry of the last days of Rome, so long, however, as it exudes nothing of the rejuvenating approach of the Barbarians and does not stammer the infantile Latin of the first Christian hymns.

So I was reading one of those beloved poems (whose artificial coloring has more charm for me than the rosiness of youth) and had plunged a hand into pure animal fur, when a hurdy-gurdy began to drone with languorous melancholy beneath my window. It was playing in the broad avenue of poplars whose leaves seem mournful to me now even in spring, since Maria has passed by them with candles for the last time. The instrument of sad souls, yes, surely: the piano sparkles, the violin gives light to torn fibres, but the hurdy-gurdy, in the twilight of memory, made me dream despairingly. Now it was murmuring one of

Depuis que Maria m'a quitté pour aller dans une autre étoile—laquelle, Orion, Altaïr, et toi, verte Vénus?—j'ai toujours chéri la solitude. Que de longues journées j'ai passées seul avec mon chat. Par *seul*, j'entends sans un être matériel et mon chat est un compagnon mystique, un esprit. Je puis donc dire que j'ai passé de longues journées seul avec mon chat, et seul, avec un des derniers auteurs de la décadence latine; car depuis que la blanche créature n'est plus, étrangement et singulièrement j'ai aimé tout ce qui se résumait en ce mot: chute. Ainsi, dans l'année, ma saison favorite, ce sont les derniers jours alanguis de l'été, qui précèdent immédiatement l'automne et, dans la journée, l'heure où je me promène est quand le soleil se repose avant de s'évanouir, avec des rayons de cuivre jaune sur les murs gris et de cuivre rouge sur les carreaux. De même la littérature à laquelle mon esprit demande une volupté sera la poésie agonisante des derniers moments de Rome, tant, cependant, qu'elle ne respire aucunement l'approche rajeunissante des Barbares et ne bégaie point le latin enfantin des premières proses chrétiennes.

Je lisais donc un de ces chers poëmes (dont les plaques de fard ont plus de charme sur moi que l'incarnat de la jeunesse) et plongeais une main dans la fourrure du pur animal, quand un orgue de Barbarie chanta languissamment et mélancoliquement sous ma fenêtre. Il jouait dans la grande allée des peupliers dont les feuilles me paraissent mornes même au printemps, depuis que Maria a passé là avec des cierges, une dernière fois. L'instrument des tristes, oui, vraiment: le piano scintille, le violon donne aux fibres déchirées la lumière, mais l'orgue de Barbarie,

those joyously common tunes that spread gaiety in the heart of the suburbs, an old-fashioned, banal tune: how is it that its refrain went straight to my soul and made me weep like a romantic ballad? I savored it slowly and threw not a single penny out the window, for fear of making myself miserable and perceiving that the instrument was not singing alone.

dans le crépuscule du souvenir, m'a fait désespérément rêver. Maintenant qu'il murmurait un air joyeusement vulgaire et qui mit la gaîté au cœur des faubourgs, un air suranné, banal: d'où vient que sa ritournelle m'allait à l'âme et me faisait pleurer comme une ballade romantique? Je la savourai lentement et je ne lançai pas un sou par la fenêtre de peur de me déranger et de m'apercevoir que l'instrument ne chantait pas seul.

That Dresden clock, which runs slow and strikes thirteen hours amid its flowers and its gods: to whom did it belong? To think that it came from Saxony by the slow stagecoaches of former years.

(Curious shadows hang from the worn-out panes.)

And your Venetian mirror, deep as a cold fountain, framed by a strand of wyverns that have lost their gilding: who has been reflected in it? Ah! I am sure that more than one woman has bathed the sin of her beauty in that water; and perhaps I could see a nude phantom if I gazed for a long time.

—Naughty boy, often you say such wicked things.

(I see spiderwebs on top of the high casements.)

Our chest of drawers is also very old: see how the fire reddens its sad wood; the dulled curtains are the same age, and the armchair upholstery denuded of color, and the old engravings on the walls, and all our ancient things? Doesn't it seem to you that even the wax birds and the blue bird are faded with time?

(Don't daydream about spiderwebs quivering on top of the high casements.)

You love all that, and that is why I can live beside you. Did you not desire, sister with the look of olden times, that in one of my poems these words should appear: "the grace of faded things?" Objects that are new displease you; they even frighten you with their discordant impudence; they make you feel as if you

Cette pendule de Saxe, qui retarde et sonne treize heures parmi ses fleurs et ses dieux, à qui a-t-elle été? Pense qu'elle est venue de Saxe par les longues diligences d'autrefois.

(De singulières ombres pendent aux vitres usées.)

Et ta glace de Venise, profonde comme une froide fontaine, en un rivage de guivres dédorées, qui s'y est miré? Ah! je suis sûr que plus d'une femme a baigné dans cette eau le péché de sa beauté; et peut-être verrais-je un fantôme nu si je regardais longtemps.

— Vilain, tu dis souvent de méchantes choses.

(Je vois des toiles d'araignées au haut des grandes croisées.)

Notre bahut encore est très vieux: contemple comme ce feu rougit son triste bois; les rideaux amortis ont son âge, et la tapisserie des fauteuils dénués de fard, et les anciennes gravures des murs, et toutes nos vieilleries? Est-ce qu'il ne te semble pas, même, que les bengalis et l'oiseau bleu ont déteint avec le temps?

(Ne songe pas aux toiles d'araignées qui tremblent au haut des grandes croisées.)

Tu aimes tout cela et voilà pourquoi je puis vivre auprès de toi. N'as-tu pas désiré, ma soeur au regard de jadis, qu'en un de mes poëmes apparussent ces mots « la grâce des choses fanées »? Les objets neufs te déplaisent; à toi aussi, ils font peur avec leur

have to wear them out, which is extremely difficult for those who have no taste for action.

Come, close your old German almanac, which you read with such attention, although it appeared more than a hundred years ago and the kings it mentions are all dead, and, stretched out on the old rug with my head propped upon your benevolent knees, in that dress of yours now grown pale, I shall speak to you, calm child, for hours; there no longer are any fields and the streets are all empty, I shall speak to you of the things that are our own . . . Is your mind wandering?

(These spiderwebs are shivering on top of the high casements.)

hardiesse criarde, et tu te sentirais le besoin de les user, ce qui est bien difficile à faire pour ceux qui ne goûtent pas l'action.

Viens, ferme ton vieil almanach allemand, que tu lis avec attention, bien qu'il ait paru il y a plus de cent ans et que les rois qu'il annonce soient tous morts, et, sur l'antique tapis couché, la tête appuyée parmi tes genoux charitables dans ta robe pâlie, ô calme enfant, je te parlerai pendant des heures; il n'y a plus de champs et les rues sont vides, je te parlerai de nos meubles . . . Tu es distraite ?

(Ces toiles d'araignées grelottent au haut des grandes croisées.)

Have unknown words ever sung on your lips, the damned fragments of a meaningless phrase?

I left my room with the precise sensation of a wing gliding over the strings of an instrument, languid and light, which was replaced by a voice pronouncing these words in a falling tone: "La Pénultième est morte"—such that

La Pénultième

ended the verse and

Est morte

                      detached itself from the fateful suspension, trailing uselessly off into the void of signification. I stepped into the street and recognized in the sound *nul* the taut string of the musical instrument which had been forgotten and which glorious Memory had just now surely visited with her wing or with a palm, and, with my finger on the mystery, I smiled and prayed with intellectual vows for a different order of speculation. The phrase returned, in all of its essence, released from the anterior fall of feather or branch, henceforth heard through the voice, until at last it articulated itself alone, alive in its own personality. I went along (no longer satisfied with a mere perception) reciting it as if it were the end of a line of verse, and, having once adapted it as an experiment to my voice, soon pronounced it with a pause after "Pénultième," discovering therein a painful joy: "La Pénultième"—then the string of the instrument, which had been stretched so tightly in oblivion over the sound *nul*, no doubt broke and I added as a kind of prayer: "Est morte."

Des paroles inconnues chantèrent-elles sur vos lèvres, lambeaux maudits d'une phrase absurde?

Je sortis de mon appartement avec la sensation propre d'une aile glissant sur les cordes d'un instrument, traînante et légère, que remplaça une voix prononçant les mots sur un ton descendant: « La Pénultième est morte », de façon que

La Pénultième

finit le vers et

Est morte

                      se détacha de la suspension fatidique plus inutilement en le vide de signification. Je fis des pas dans la rue et reconnus en le son *nul* la corde tendue de l'instrument de musique, qui était oublié et que le glorieux Souvenir certainement venait de visiter de son aile ou d'une palme et, le doigt sur l'artifice du mystère, je souris et implorai de voeux intellectuels une spéculation différente. La phrase revint, virtuelle, dégagée d'une chute antérieure de plume ou de rameau dorénavant à travers la voix entendue, jusqu'à ce qu'enfin elle s'articula seule, vivant de sa personnalité. J'allais (ne me contentant plus d'une perception) la lisant en fin de vers, et, une fois, comme un essai, l'adaptant à mon parler; bientôt la prononçant avec un silence après « Pénultième » dans lequel je trouvais une pénible jouissance: « La Pénultième » puis la corde de l'instrument, si tendue en l'oubli sur le son *nul*, cassait sans doute et j'ajoutais en manière d'oraison: « Est morte. » Je ne discontinuai pas de tenter un retour à des pensées de prédilection, alléguant, pour me

I kept trying to bring back more pleasant thoughts, rationalizing, to calm myself, that, indeed, "penultimate" is the lexical term signifying the next-to-last syllable of an utterance and that its apparition was the imperfectly abandoned residue of a linguistic labor on account of which my noble poetical faculty daily sobs at being interrupted; but the very sonority of that facile affirmation, and the air of falsehood assumed by my haste to arrive at it, were themselves a cause of torment. Harried, I resolved to let those words, by their nature so sad, wander on my lips of their own accord, and I went on murmuring in piteous tones: "La Pénultième est morte, elle est morte, bien morte, la désespérée Pénultième"—thinking that in this way I could quell my anxiety, and not without the secret hope of engulfing it in the amplification of a psalm, when, to my horror!—by an easily deducible and nervous magic—with my hand reflected in a shop window and making therein the gesture of a caress that descends over something—I sensed that I possessed the voice itself (the original one, which undoubtedly had been the only one).

But the irrefutable intervention of the supernatural, and the beginnings of that anguish tormenting my formerly masterful spirit—these were established at the moment I saw, raising my eyes, in the street of antique shops I had instinctively taken, that I was in front of a lute maker's shop, with old instruments hung on the wall, and, on the ground, yellow palms and ancient birds, their wings shrouded in shadow. I fled, bizarre person that I am, probably condemned to bear the grief of the inexplicable Penultimate.

calmer, que, certes, pénultième est le terme du lexique qui signifie l'avant-dernière syllabe des vocables, et son apparition, le reste mal abjuré d'un labeur de linguistique par lequel quotidiennement sanglote de s'interrompre ma noble faculté poétique: la sonorité même et l'air de mensonge assumé par la hâte de la facile affirmation étaient une cause de tourment. Harcelé, je résolus de laisser les mots de triste nature errer eux-mêmes sur ma bouche, et j'allai murmurant avec l'intonation susceptible de condoléance: « La Pénultième est morte, elle est morte, bien morte, la désespérée Pénultième, » croyant par là satisfaire l'inquiétude, et non sans le secret espoir de l'ensevelir en l'amplification de la psalmodie quand, effroi!—d'une magie aisément déductible et nerveuse—je sentis que j'avais, ma main réfléchie par un vitrage de boutique y faisant le geste d'une caresse qui descend sur quelque chose, la voix même (la première, qui indubitablement avait été l'unique).

Mais où s'installe l'irrécusable intervention du surnaturel, et le commencement de l'angoisse sous laquelle agonise mon esprit naguère seigneur c'est quand je vis, levant les yeux, dans la rue des antiquaires instinctivement suivie, que j'étais devant la boutique d'un luthier vendeur de vieux instruments pendus au mur, et, à terre, des palmes jaunes et les ailes enfouies en l'ombre, d'oiseaux anciens. Je m'enfuis, bizarre, personne condamnée à porter probablement le deuil de l'inexplicable Pénultième.

POOR PALE CHILD

Poor pale child, why do you bawl out your sharp, cheeky songs, in the street at the top of your lungs, since they fade among the cats, those lords of the rooftops? They will not reach beyond the first-floor shutters, and behind hang the heavy curtains of rose-tinted silk of which you have no knowledge.

Yet inevitably you sing, fatally, with the tenacious assurance of a little man who makes his way through life alone and, counting on no one, works for himself. Have you ever had a father? You don't even have an old woman to make you forget your hunger by beating you when you return without a penny.

But you work for yourself: standing in the streets, covered with faded clothes like those of a man, prematurely thin and too tall for your age, you sing for your supper, relentlessly, without lowering your malicious eyes toward the other kids playing on the pavement.

And your lament is so high, so high, that your bare head rising in the air as your voice rises seems to want to separate from your narrow shoulders.

Little man, who knows if it won't come off one day, when, having cried out for a long time in the cities, you have committed a crime; a crime is not hard to commit, believe me, it requires only that courage follow desire, and some who . . . Your little face is energetic.

Not a penny falls into the wicker basket that your thin hand holds balanced hopelessly over your pants:

PAUVRE ENFANT PÂLE

Pauvre enfant pâle, pourquoi crier à tue-tête dans la rue ta chanson aiguë et insolente, qui se perd parmi les chats, seigneurs des toits? car elle ne traversera pas les volets des premiers étages, derrière lesquels tu ignores de lourds rideaux de soie incarnadine.

Cependant tu chantes fatalement, avec l'assurance tenace d'un petit homme qui s'en va seul par la vie et, ne comptant sur personne, travaille pour soi. As-tu jamais eu un père? Tu n'as pas même une vieille qui te fasse oublier la faim en te battant, quand tu rentres sans un sou.

Mais tu travailles pour toi: debout dans les rues, couvert de vêtements déteints faits comme ceux d'un homme, une maigreur prématurée et trop grand à ton âge, tu chantes pour manger, avec acharnement, sans abaisser tes yeux méchants vers les autres enfants jouant sur le pavé.

Et ta complainte est si haute, si haute, que ta tête nue qui se lève en l'air à mesure que ta voix monte, semble vouloir partir de tes petites épaules.

Petit homme, qui sait si elle ne s'en ira pas un jour, quand, après avoir crié longtemps dans les villes, tu auras fait un crime? un crime n'est pas bien difficile à faire, va, il suffit d'avoir du courage après le désir, et tels qui… Ta petite figure est énergique.

Pas un sou ne descend dans le panier d'osier que tient ta longue main pendue sans espoir sur ton pantalon: on te rendra mauvais et un jour tu commettras un crime.

they will make you wicked and one day you will commit a crime.

Your head straightens up continually and wants to leave you, as if it knew in advance, while you sing with an air that becomes menacing.

When you pay for me, for those who are worth less than me, it will bid you adieu. That's probably why you came into the world and you are fasting from now on, we shall see you in the papers.

Oh! poor little head!

Ta tête se dresse toujours et veut te quitter, comme si d'avance elle savait, pendant que tu chantes d'un air qui devient menaçant.

Elle te dira adieu quand tu paieras pour moi, pour ceux qui valent moins que moi. Tu vins probablement au monde vers cela et tu jeûnes dès maintenant, nous te verrons dans les journaux.

Oh! pauvre petite tête!

THE PIPE

Yesterday I found my pipe while pondering a long evening of work, of fine winter work. Thrown aside were my cigarettes, with all the childish joys of summer, into the past which the leaves shining blue in the sun, the muslins, illuminate, and taken up once again was the grave pipe of a serious man who wants to smoke for a long while without being disturbed, so as better to work: but I was not prepared for the surprise that this abandoned object had in store for me; for hardly had I drawn the first puff when I forgot the grand books I was planning to write, and, amazed, moved to a feeling of tenderness, I breathed in the air of the previous winter which was now coming back to me. I had not been in contact with my faithful sweetheart since returning to France, and now all of London, London as I had lived it a year ago entirely alone, appeared before my eyes: first the dear fogs that muffle one's brains and have an odor of their own there when they penetrate beneath the case-ments. My tobacco had the scent of a somber room with leather furniture sprinkled by coal dust, on which the thin black cat would curl and stretch; the big fires! and the maid with red arms pouring coals, and the noise of those coals falling from the sheet-iron bucket into the iron scuttle in the morning—when the postman gave the solemn double knock that kept me alive! Once again I saw through the windows those sickly trees of the deserted square—I saw the open sea, crossed so often that winter, shivering on the deck of the steamer wet with drizzle and blackened from the fumes—with my poor wan-dering beloved, decked out in traveller's clothes, a long dress, dull as the dust of the roads, a coat clinging damply to her cold shoulders, one of those

LA PIPE

Hier, j'ai trouvé ma pipe en rêvant une longue soirée de travail, de beau travail d'hiver. Jetées les cigarettes avec toutes les joies enfantines de l'été dans le passé qu'illuminent les feuilles bleues de soleil, les mousselines et reprise ma grave pipe par un homme sérieux qui veut fumer longtemps sans se déranger, afin de mieux travailler: mais je ne m'attendais pas à la surprise que préparait cette délaissée, à peine eus-je tiré la première bouffée, j'oubliai mes grands livres à faire, émerveillé, attendri, je respirai l'hiver dernier qui revenait. Je n'avais pas touché à la fidèle amie depuis ma rentrée en France, et tout Londres, Londres tel que je le vécus en entier à moi seul, il y a un an, est apparu; d'abord les chers brouillards qui emmitouflent nos cervelles et ont, là-bas, une odeur à eux, quand ils pénètrent sous la croisée. Mon tabac sentait une chambre sombre aux meubles de cuir saupoudrés par la poussière du charbon sur lesquels se roulait le maigre chat noir; les grands feux! et la bonne aux bras rouges versant les charbons, et le bruit de ces charbons tombant du seau de tôle dans la corbeille de fer, le matin—alors que le facteur frappait le double coup solennel, qui me faisait vivre! J'ai revu par les fenêtres ces arbres malades du square désert—j'ai vu le large, si souvent traversé cet hiver-là, grelottant sur le pont du steamer mouillé de bruine et noirci de fumée—avec ma pauvre bien-aimée errante, en habits de voyageuse, une longue robe terne couleur de la poussière des routes, un manteau qui collait humide à ses épaules froides, un de ces chapeaux de paille sans plume et presque sans rubans, que les riches dames jettent en arrivant, tant ils sont déchiquetés par l'air de la mer et que les pauvres bien-aimées regarnissent pour bien des saisons encore. Autour de

straw hats with no feather and hardly any ribbons that wealthy ladies throw away upon arrival, mangled as they are by the sea, and that poor loved ones refurbish for many another season. Around her neck was wound the terrible handkerchief that one waves when saying goodbye forever.

son cou s'enroulait le terrible mouchoir qu'on agite en se disant adieu pour toujours.

How far civilization is from procuring the enjoyments attributable to that state! For example, it is astonishing that there exists no association of dreamers in every large town to support a journal that takes notice of events in the light peculiar to dreams. *Reality* is but an artifice, good only for stabilizing the average intellect amid the mirages of a fact; but, through this in itself, it rests on some universal understanding: let us see, then, if there is not, ideally, some quality—necessary, evident, simple—that can serve as a type. I want, for my own satisfaction, to write down a certain Anecdote, as it struck the gaze of a poet, before it is divulged by the *reporters* set up by the crowd to assign each thing a common character.

The little theater of the PRODIGALITIES adds the exhibition of a living cousin of Atta Troll or of Martin to its classic fairy tale, *The Beast and the Genius*; to acknowledge the invitation to a double-bill that had yesterday made its way to my home, I had placed my hat in the vacant stall by my side, a friend's absence bearing witness to the general distaste of the public for childish entertainments of this kind. What was happening in front of me? Nothing, except: from the evasive pallor of muslins taking refuge on twenty pedestals constructed in the Baghdad manner, there came a smile and open arms to the sad heaviness of the bear: while the hero, the evoker and guardian of those sylphs, a clown, in his lofty silvery nakedness, was taunting the animal with our superiority. To revel, like the crowd, in a myth enclosed in every banality: what relaxation, and, without neighbors or any outpouring of reflections, to behold the ordinary and splendid vigil discovered at the footlights by my

Que la civilisation est loin de procurer les jouissances attribuables à cet état! on doit par exemple s'étonner qu'une association entre les rêveurs, y séjournant, n'existe pas, dans toute grande ville, pour subvenir à un journal qui remarque les événements sous le jour propre au rêve. Artifice que la *réalité*, bon à fixer l'intellect moyen entre les mirages d'un fait; mais elle repose par cela même sur quelque universelle entente: voyons donc s'il n'est pas, dans l'idéal, un aspect nécessaire, évident, simple, qui serve de type. Je veux, en vue de moi seul, écrire comme elle frappa mon regard de poëte, telle Anecdote, avant que la divulguent des *reporters* par la foule dressés à assigner à chaque chose son caractère commun.

Le petit théâtre des PRODIGALITÉS adjoint l'exhibition d'un vivant cousin d'Atta Troll ou de Martin à sa féerie classique *la Bête et le Génie*; j'avais, pour reconnaître l'invitation du billet double hier égaré chez moi, posé mon chapeau dans la stalle vacante à mes côtés, une absence d'ami y témoignait du goût général à esquiver ce naïf spectacle. Que se passait-il devant moi? rien, sauf que: de pâleurs évasives de mousseline se réfugiant sur vingt piédestaux en architecture de Bagdad, sortaient un sourire et des bras ouverts à la lourdeur triste de l'ours: tandis que le héros, de ces sylphides évocateur et leur gardien, un clown, dans sa haute nudité d'argent, raillait l'animal par notre supériorité. Jouir comme la foule du mythe inclus dans toute banalité, quel repos et, sans voisins où verser des réflexions, voir l'ordinaire et splendide veille trouvée à la rampe par ma recherche assoupie d'imaginations ou de symboles. Étranger à mainte réminiscence de pareilles

quest appeased with imaginings or symbols. The most novel occurrence! foreign to the many recollections I had of similar evenings, aroused my attention: one of the numerous salvos of applause, bestowed in accordance with the enthusiasm for Man's incontestable privilege now being illustrated on the stage, had just now—broken by what?—come to a complete stop at its very apex, with the steady din of glorying unable to spread. All ears, it was necessary to be all eyes. From the puppet's gesture, a clenched fist opening its five fingers in the air, I understood that he, the ingenious one! had captured the sympathies of the crowd by the appearance of catching something in flight, an image (and that is all) of the facility with which an idea is taken up by everyone; and that moved by the slight breeze, the bear, rising rhythmically and gently, was interrogating this exploit, one claw posed upon the ribbons of the human shoulder. There was no one who did not gasp for breath, so grave were the consequences that this situation bore for the honor of the race: what was going to happen? The other paw tumbled down, supple, upon an arm hanging against the tights; and one saw (couple united in a secret *rapprochement*), as it were a man, inferior, squat and kind, standing on two spread-out furry legs, embrace, in order to grasp the practices of genius, and his skull with the black muzzle only half reaching it, the bust of his brilliant and supernatural brother: but as for him! he himself was raising, his mouth crazed with vagueness, a frightful head shaking by a thread visible in the horror the veritable denegations of a paper and gold fly. Luminous spectacle, vaster than the stage, with this gift, pertaining to art, of lasting for a long time: to render it complete, without being shocked by the probably fatal attitude taken on by the mime, that depository of our pride, I allowed the discourse forbidden to

soirées, l'accident le plus neuf! suscita mon attention: une des nombreuses salves d'applaudissements décernés selon l'enthousiasme à l'illustration sur la scène du privilège authentique de l'Homme, venait, brisée par quoi? de cesser net, avec un fixe fracas de gloire à l'apogée, inhabile à se répandre. Tout oreilles, il fallut être tout yeux. Au geste du pantin, une paume crispée dans l'air ouvrant les cinq doigts, je compris, qu'il avait, l'ingénieux! capté les sympathies par la mine d'attraper au vol quelque chose, figure (et c'est tout) de la facilité dont est par chacun prise une idée: et qu'ému au léger vent, l'ours rythmiquement et doucement levé interrogeait cet exploit, une griffe posée sur les rubans de l'épaule humaine. Personne qui ne haletât, tant cette situation portait de conséquences graves pour l'honneur de la race: qu'allait-il arriver? L'autre patte s'abattit, souple, contre un bras longeant le maillot; et l'on vit, couple uni dans un secret rapprochement, comme un homme inférieur, trapu, bon, debout sur l'écartement de deux jambes de poil, étreindre pour y apprendre les pratiques du génie, et son crâne au noir museau ne l'atteignant qu'à la moitié, le buste de son frère brillant et surnaturel: mais qui, lui! exhaussait, la bouche folle de vague, un chef affreux remuant par un fil visible dans l'horreur les dénégations véritables d'une mouche de papier et d'or. Spectacle clair, plus que les tréteaux vaste, avec ce don, propre à l'art, de durer longtemps: pour le parfaire je laissai, sans que m'offusquât l'attitude probablement fatale prise par le mime dépositaire de notre orgueil, jaillir tacitement le discours interdit au rejeton des sites arctiques: « Sois bon (c'était le sens), et plutôt que de manquer à la charité, explique-moi la vertu de cette atmosphère de splendeur, de poussière et de voix, où tu m'appris à me mouvoir. Ma requête, pressante, est juste, que tu ne sembles pas, en une angoisse qui n'est que

that scion of arctic sites to gush forth tacitly: "Be so kind (that was the meaning), and rather than lack charity, explain to me the virtue of this atmosphere of splendor, of dust and voices, in which you have taught me to move. My request—a pressing one—which you do not seem, in an anguish that is only a ruse, not to know how to answer, is just, launched into the regions of wisdom, subtle elder! toward myself, in order to make you free, still garbed in the shapeless habitation of the caves in which, in the night of humble epochs, I have once more plunged my latent force. Let us authenticate, by this tight embrace, before the multitude assembled for that purpose, the pact of our reconciliation." The absence of any breath united to space, in which absolute site I was living, one of the dramas of astral history, which had chosen, in order to produce itself there, this modest theater! The crowd gave way, utterly effaced, magnifying the stage as the emblem of its spiritual situation: modern dispenser of ecstasy, alone, with the impartiality of something elemental, the gas, in the heights of the hall, maintained a luminous noise of expectancy.

The spell was broken: that was when a piece of flesh, naked, brutal, guided from the gap between the stage settings, crossed my vision, a few seconds in advance of the mysterious reward that ordinarily occurs after these performances. A bloody rag of meat was substituted alongside the bear, who, having rediscovered the instincts he possessed prior to the higher curiosity with which the theatrical radiance had endowed him, fell back on his four paws and, as if bearing the Silence away with him, plodded off with the muted step of the species, to sniff this prey in order to apply his teeth to it. A sigh, almost free of disappointment, incomprehensibly relieved the as-

feinte, répondre ne savoir, élancé aux régions de la sagesse, aîné subtil! à moi, pour te faire libre, vêtu encore du séjour informe des cavernes où je replongeai, dans la nuit d'époques humbles ma force latente. Authentiquons, par cette embrassade étroite, devant la multitude siégeant à cette fin, le pacte de notre réconciliation. » L'absence d'aucun souffle unie à l'espace, dans quel lieu absolu vivais-je, un des drames de l'histoire astrale élisant, pour s'y produire, ce modeste théâtre! La foule s'effaçait, toute, en l'emblème de sa situation spirituelle magnifiant la scène: dispensateur moderne de l'extase, seul, avec l'impartialité d'une chose élémentaire, le gaz, dans les hauteurs de la salle, continuait un bruit lumineux d'attente.

Le charme se rompit: c'est quand un morceau de chair, nu, brutal, traversa ma vision dirigé de l'intervalle des décors, en avance de quelques instants sur la récompense, mystérieuse d'ordinaire après ces représentations. Loque substituée saignant auprès de l'ours qui, ses instincts retrouvés antérieurement à une curiosité plus haute dont le dotait le rayonnement théâtral, retomba à quatre pattes et, comme emportant parmi soi le Silence, alla de la marche étouffée de l'espèce, flairer, pour y appliquer les dents, cette proie. Un soupir, exempt presque de déception, soulagea incompréhen-siblement l'assemblée: dont les lorgnettes, par rangs, cherchèrent, allumant la netteté de leurs verres, le jeu du splendide imbécile évaporé dans sa peur; mais virent un repas abject préféré peut-être par l'animal à la même chose qu'il lui eût fallu d'abord faire de *notre image,* pour y goûter. La toile, hésitant jusque-là à accroître le danger ou l'émotion, abattit subitement son journal de tarifs et de lieux communs. Je me levai comme tout le monde, pour aller respirer au dehors, étonné de

sembly: whose opera glasses, row upon row, lighting up the clarity of their lenses, sought out the play-acting of that splendid imbecile evaporated in his fear; but saw an abject meal preferred perhaps by the animal to the same thing that he would first have had to make of *our image* in order to enjoy it. The curtain, hesitating until then to increase the danger or the emotion, suddenly lowered its announcements of prices and commonplaces. I got up, like everyone else, to take a breath of air, astonished at not having felt, once again, the same kind of impression as my fellows, but serene: for my way of seeing, after all, had been superior, and even the true one.

n'avoir pas senti, cette fois encore, le même genre d'impression que mes semblables, mais serein: car ma façon de voir, après tout, avait été supérieure, et même la vraie.

Orphan, I was wandering in black and with an eye vacant of family: at the quincunx, the tents of a fair were unfolded; did I experience the future and that I would take this form? I loved the odor of the vagabonds, and was drawn toward them, forgetting my comrades. No cry of a chorus clamoring through the canvas rift, nor distant tirade, the drama requiring the holy hour of the footlights, I wanted to speak with an urchin too unsteady in his wavering to figure forth among his people, in a nightcap cut like Dante's hood—who was already returning to himself, in the guise of a slice of bread and soft cheese, the snow of mountain peaks, the lily, or some other whiteness constitutive of internal wings: I would have begged him to admit me to his superior meal, which was quickly shared with some illustrious older boy who had sprung up against a nearby tent and was engaged in feats of strength and banalities consistent with the day. Naked, he pirouetted in what seemed to me the surprising nimbleness of his tights and moreover began: "Your parents? — I have none. — Go on, if you knew what a farce that is, a father . . . even the other week when he was off his soup, he still made faces as funny as ever, when the boss was flinging out smacks and kicks. My dear fellow!" and triumphantly raising a leg toward me with glorious ease, "Papa astounds us"; then, biting into the little one's chaste meal: "Your mama, maybe you don't have one, maybe you're alone? Mine eats rope and everyone claps his hands. You have no idea what funny people parents are, how they make you laugh." The show was heating up, he left: myself, I sighed, suddenly dismayed at not having parents.

Orphelin, j'errais en noir et l'oeil vacant de famille: au quinconce se déplièrent des tentes de fête, éprouvai-je le futur et que je serais ainsi, j'aimais le parfum des vagabonds, vers eux à oublier mes camarades. Aucun cri de chœurs par la déchirure, ni tirade loin, le drame requérant l'heure sainte des quinquets, je souhaitais de parler avec un môme trop vacillant pour figurer parmi sa race, au bonnet de nuit taillé comme le chaperon de Dante; qui rentrait en soi, sous l'aspect d'une tartine de fromage mou, déjà la neige des cimes, le lys ou autre blancheur constitutive d'ailes au-dedans: je l'eusse prié de m'admettre à son repas supérieur, partagé vite avec quelque aîné fameux jailli contre une proche toile en train des tours de force et banalités alliables au jour. Nu, de pirouetter dans sa prestesse de maillot à mon avis surprenante, lui, qui d'ailleurs commença: « Tes parents?— Je n'en ai pas. —Allons, si tu savais comme c'est farce, un père . . . même l'autre semaine que bouda la soupe, il faisait des grimaces aussi belles, quand le maître lançait les claques et les coups de pied. Mon cher! » et de triompher en élevant à moi la jambe avec aisance glorieuse, « il nous épate, papa », puis de mordre au régal chaste du très jeune: « Ta maman, tu n'en as pas, peut-être, que tu es seul ? la mienne mange de la filasse et le monde bat des mains. Tu ne sais rien, des parents sont des gens drôles, qui font rire. » La parade s'exaltait, il partit: moi, je soupirai, déçu tout à coup de n'avoir pas de parents.

THE DECLARATION AT A FAIR

Ah, Silence! It is certain that stretched out beside me, as in a dream, the rocking of the journey from beneath the wheels lulling the flowers that have interjected themselves, every woman, and I know of one who sees clearly in this respect, would excuse me from the effort of uttering a single syllable: to compliment her aloud on some interrogatory costume, almost offering itself to the man in whose favor the afternoon draws to a close, being unable, contrary to all this fortuitous conjunction of circumstances, to suggest more than the distance which on her features ends in the dimple of an intelligent smile. But reality does not consent that it should be so; for, pitilessly, beyond the sunbeam which one sensed expiring luxuriously on the glossy finish of the landau, amid too much silent felicity for a nightfall on the outskirts of town, there was a kind of outcry, with the storm, everywhere at once and without cause, of the ordinary strident laughter of things and their triumphal brassy chorus: in a word, a cacophony to the ears of anyone who, having turned aside for a moment, not to melt into his idea but to draw close to it, remains sensitive to the obsessive hauntings of existence.

"The festival of…" and I don't know what suburban meeting-place! called out the little girl who had been conveyed to my distraction, her voice clear of any hint of ennui; I obeyed and ordered a halt.

With no more compensation for that shock than the need it occasioned to construct a figurative explanation plausible to the mind, in the way that lamps symmetrically arranged in garlands and emblems are illuminated little by little, I decided, having lost my

LA DÉCLARATION FORAINE

Le Silence! il est certain qu'à mon côté, ainsi que songes, étendue dans un bercement de promenade sous les roues assoupissant l'interjection de fleurs, toute femme, et j'en sais une qui voit clair ici, m'exempte de l'effort à proférer un vocable: la complimenter haut de quelque interrogatrice toilette, offre de soi presque à l'homme en faveur de qui s'achève l'après-midi, ne pouvant à l'encontre de tout ce rapprochement fortuit, que suggérer la distance sur ses traits aboutie à une fossette de spirituel sourire. Ainsi ne consent la réalité; car ce fut impitoyablement, hors du rayon qu'on sentait avec luxe expirer aux vernis du landau, comme une vocifération, parmi trop de tacite félicité pour une tombée de jour sur la banlieue, avec orage, dans tous sens à la fois et sans motif, du rire strident ordinaire des choses et de leur cuivrerie triomphale: au fait, la cacophonie à l'ouïe de quiconque, un instant écarté, plutôt qu'il ne s'y fond, auprès de son idée, reste à vif devant la hantise de l'existence.

« La fête de… » et je ne sais quel rendez-vous suburbain! nomma l'enfant voiturée dans mes distractions, la voix claire d'aucun ennui; j'obéis et fis arrêter.

Sans compensation à cette secousse qu'un besoin d'explication figurative plausible pour mes esprits, comme symétriquement s'ordonnent des verres d'illumination peu à peu éclairés en guirlandes et attributs, je décidai, la solitude manquée, de m'enfoncer même avec bravoure en ce déchaînement exprès et haïssable de tout ce que j'avais naguères fui dans une gracieuse compagnie: prête et ne témoignant

solitude, to plunge, with bravura even, into this explicit and hateful unleashing of everything from which I had formerly fled in gracious company: prepared and displaying no surprise at the change in our plans, she leans an ingenuous arm upon me as we make our way down, our eyes on the rows, through the lane of confusion that divides the fairground into an echo of the same noise and permits the crowd to enclose the universe for a time therein. Subsequent to the onslaughts of a mediocre licentiousness, in view of whatever might divert our stagnation amused by the sunset, a poignant human spectacle, equal to the fiery cloud in the background, strange and purple, detained us: a hut, apparently empty, repudiated by its garishly painted frame or by the inscription in capital letters.

To whomever this mattress belonged, ripped open as it was in order to improvise, here, like the veils in all times and temples, the Arcanum! its frequentation during his fast had not excited in its possessor, before he unrolled it as a banner of joyous hopes, the hallucination of a marvel to be displayed (except for the inanity of his famished nightmare); and yet, moved by the fraternal character of exception to quotidinal misery, which a meadow, when established by the mysterious word "festival," derives from numerous shoes trampling upon it (in function of which some singular whim of a hard penny emerging for the sole purpose of being spent dawns in the depths of clothes), he too! anyone at all, stripped of everything except the notion that he had grounds to be one of the elect, if not to sell, then at least to show, but what? had yielded to the summons of the beneficent rendezvous. Or, in plain prose, perhaps the trained rat, unless he himself, this beggar, counting on the athletic vigor of his muscles to induce the

de surprise à la modification dans notre programme, du bras ingénu elle s'en repose sur moi, tandis que nous allons parcourir, les yeux sur l'enfilade, l'allée d'ahurissement qui divise en écho du même tapage les foires et permet à la foule d'y renfermer pour un temps l'univers. Subséquemment aux assauts d'un médiocre dévergondage en vue de quoi que ce soit qui détourne notre stagnation amusée par le crépuscule, au fond, bizarre et pourpre, nous retint à l'égal de la nue incendiaire un humain spectacle, poignant: reniée du châssis peinturluré ou de l'inscription en capitales une baraque, apparemment vide.

A qui ce matelas décousu pour improviser ici, comme les voiles dans tous les temps et les temples, l'arcane! appartînt, sa fréquentation durant le jeûne n'avait pas chez son possesseur excité avant qu'il le déroulât comme le gonfalon d'espoirs en liesse, l'hallucination d'une merveille à montrer (que l'inanité de son famélique cauchemar); et pourtant, mû par le caractère frérial d'exception à la misère quotidienne qu'un pré, quand l'institue le mot mystérieux de fête, tient des souliers nombreux y piétinant (en raison de cela poind aux profondeurs des vêtements quelque unique velléité du dur sou à sortir à seule fin de se dépenser), lui aussi! n'importe qui de tout dénué sauf de la notion qu'il y avait lieu pour être un des élus, sinon de vendre, de faire voir, mais quoi, avait cédé à la convocation du bienfaisant rendez-vous. Ou, très prosaïquement, peut-être le rat éduqué à moins que, lui-même, ce mendiant sur l'athlétique vigueur de ses muscles comptât, pour décider l'engouement populaire, faisait défaut, à l'instant précis, comme cela résulte souvent de la mise en demeure de l'homme par les circonstances générales.

populace to infatuation, was absent, at that precise instant, as so often results from the way in which human beings are compelled by general circumstances.

"Bang the drum!" declared Madame loftily . . . "you alone know Who". . . pointing to an old-fashioned tambour from which arose, his arms uncrossed in order to indicate the uselessness of approaching his theater lacking in marvels, an old man whom this companionship with an instrument of clamor and summoning had perhaps seduced to her inscrutable design; then, as if from what could all at once be here envisaged as most beautiful, the enigma glittered, a jewel clasping the fashionable one like the lack of an answer at her throat! and behold her swallowed up, to the surprise of the dumb clown I felt myself to be, before the halting of a public caught by the call of the drum's ruff-and-rum muffling my unvarying and at first even to me obscure pitch: "Enter, everyone, it's only a penny, it will be refunded to whoever is not satisfied with the show." The straw halo emptied into the gratitude joining two senile palms, I wave its colors, as a signal, from afar, and cover my head, ready to cut through the crowd standing in the secret of what the initiative of a contemporary of our evenings had known to make of this place so lacking in dreams.

Knee high, on a table, she was emerging from a hundred heads.

Clear as the beam that, having strayed from somewhere, was flashing her forth electrically, this reckoning burst upon me, that with everything lacking, she, in accordance with the instantiation of her beauty by fashion, fantasy, or the whim of the heavens, was amply paying the crowd, without the supplement of

« Battez la caisse! » proposa en altesse Madame . . . seule tu sais Qui, marquant un suranné tambour duquel se levait, les bras décroisés afin de signifier inutile l'approche de son théâtre sans prestige, un vieillard que cette camaraderie avec un instrument de rumeur et d'appel, peut-être, séduisit à son vacant dessein; puis comme si, de ce que tout de suite on pût, ici, envisager de plus beau, l'énigme, par un bijou fermant la mondaine, en tant qu'à sa gorge le manque de réponse, scintillait! la voici engouffrée, à ma surprise de pitre coi devant une halte du public qu'empaume l'éveil des ra et des fla assourdissant mon invariable et obscur pour moi-même d'abord. « Entrez, tout le monde, ce n'est qu'un sou, on le rend à qui n'est pas satisfait de la représentation. » Le nimbe en paillasson dans le remerciement joignant deux paumes séniles vidé, j'en agite les couleurs, en signal, de loin, et me coiffai, prêt à fendre la masse debout en le secret de ce qu'avait su faire avec ce lieu sans rêve l'initiative d'une contemporaine de nos soirs.

A hauteur du genou, elle émergeait, sur une table, des cent têtes.

Net ainsi qu'un jet égaré d'autre part la dardait électriquement, éclate pour moi ce calcul qu'à défaut de tout, elle, selon que la mode, une fantaisie ou l'humeur du ciel circonstanciaient sa beauté, sans supplément de danse ou de chant, pour la cohue amplement payait l'aumône exigée en faveur d'un quelconque; et du même trait je comprends mon devoir en le péril de la subtile exhibition, ou qu'il n'y avait au monde pour conjurer la défection dans les curiosités que de recourir à quelque puissance absolue, comme d'une Métaphore. Vite, dégoiser jusqu'à l'éclaircissement, sur maintes physionomies, de leur

dance or song, for the alms exacted in favor of whoever it might have been; and in the same stroke I understood my duty in the peril of that subtle exhibition, or that there was no earthly way of averting the defection of Beauty to mere curiosity save through some absolute power, such as Metaphor. Quick, rattle on until the elucidation, on many physiognomies, of a lack of apprehensiveness which, not grasping everything at once, surrenders, however arduously, to the evidence implied in the word and consents to exchanging its coppers for exact and superior presumptions, in short, the certainty for everyone of not being cheated.

A glance, the last one, at a lock of hair on which the paleness of a crêpe hat the same shade as the statuesque dress rising over one foot hydrangea-colored like the rest, and advancing toward the spectators, smokes and then lights up with the pomp of gardens.

Then:

The flight of flaming hair at the extreme
West of desires unfurling it forth
Comes to rest (as it were a dying diadem)
On the crowned brow its ancient hearth

Then sigh for no gold but this cloud that lives
The kindling of an always interior flame
Originally the only one it gives
To the truthful or laughing eye its gleam

The tender nudity of heroes demeans
The one on whose fingers no stars wave or fires
Whose dazzling head is the only means

By which woman simplified with glory conspires
To sow with rubies the doubt she would scorch
In the manner of a joyous and tutelary torch

sécurité qui, ne saisissant tout du coup, se rend à l'évidence, même ardue, impliquée en la parole et consent à échanger son billon contre des présomptions exactes et supérieures, bref, la certitude pour chacun de n'être pas refait.

Un coup d'œil, le dernier, à une chevelure où fume puis éclaire de fastes de jardins le pâlissement du chapeau en crêpe de même ton que la statuaire robe se relevant, avance au spectateur, sur un pied comme le reste hortensia.

Alors:

La chevelure vol d'une flamme à l'extrême
Occident de désirs pour la tout déployer
Se pose (je dirais mourir un diadème)
Vers le front couronné son ancien foyer

Mais sans or soupirer que cette vive nue
L'ignition du feu toujours intérieur
Originellement la seule continue
Dans le joyau de l'œil véridique ou rieur

Une nudité de héros tendre diffame
Celle qui ne mouvant astre ni feux au doigt
Rien qu'à simplifier avec gloire la femme
Accomplit par son chef fulgurante l'exploit

De semer de rubis le doute qu'elle écorche
Ainsi qu'une joyeuse et tutélaire torche

Mon aide à la taille de la vivante allégorie qui déjà résignait sa faction, peut-être faute chez moi de faconde ultérieure, afin d'en assoupir l'élan gentiment à terre: « Je vous ferai observer, ajoutai-je, maintenant de plain-pied avec l'entendement des visiteurs, coupant court à leur ébahissement devant ce congé

Supporting the waist of the living allegory, in order gracefully to cushion her descent to earth—for she was already resigning her post, perhaps because of a failure on my part to emit any further stream of words, "I would have you note, Ladies and Gentlemen," I added, now on a level with the understanding of the visitors, cutting short their astonishment at this dismissal by pretending to return to the authenticity of the performance, "that the person who has had the honor of submitting herself to your judgment requires no costume or any of the usual theatrical accessories to convey a sense of her charm to you. This naturalness is accommodated by the perfect allusion which dress always supplies to one of woman's primordial motives and, as your sympathetic approval convinces me, suffices." An appreciative silence, punctuated with outbursts of "Certainly!" or "That's right!" and "Yes" from a few gullets and with *bravos* bestowed by several generous pairs of hands, conducted the crowd with which we were going to mingle to an exit that gave upon a vacancy of trees and night—were it not that a soldier boy in white gloves, who was dreaming of unstiffening them at the appraisal of a haughty garter, was still waiting.

—Thank you, agreed the dear one, a drunken gust from a constellation or from leaves blown straight at her as if to find in it, if not the recovery of her serenity—for she had never doubted success—then at least the habitual cool of her voice: I have in mind the memory of things which are unforgettable.

—Oh! nothing but the commonplace of an aesthetic . . .

—Which you would not perhaps have introduced, who knows? my friend, the pretext of thus formulat-

par une affectation de retour à l'authenticité du spectacle, Messieurs et Dames, que la personne qui a eu l'honneur de se soumettre à votre jugement, ne requiert pour vous communiquer le sens de son charme, un costume ou aucun accessoire usuel de théâtre. Ce naturel s'accommode de l'allusion parfaite que fournit la toilette toujours à l'un des motifs primordiaux de la femme, et suffit, ainsi que votre sympathique approbation m'en convainc. » Un suspens de marque appréciative sauf quelques confondants « Bien sûr! » ou « C'est cela! » et « Oui » par les gosiers comme plusieurs bravos prêtés par des paires de mains généreuses, conduisit jusqu'à la sortie sur une vacance d'arbres et de nuit la foule où nous allions nous mêler, n'était l'attente en gants blancs encore d'un enfantin tourlourou qui les rêvait dégourdir à l'estimation d'une jarretière hautaine.

—Merci, consentit la chère, une bouffée droit à elle d'une constellation ou des feuilles bue comme pour y trouver sinon le rassérènement, elle n'avait douté d'un succès, du moins l'habitude frigide de sa voix: j'ai dans l'esprit le souvenir de choses qui ne s'oublient.

—Oh! rien que lieu commun d'une esthétique…

—Que vous n'auriez peut-être pas introduit, qui sait? mon ami, le prétexte de formuler ainsi devant moi au conjoint isolement par exemple de notre voiture—où est-elle—regagnons-la:—mais ceci jaillit, forcé, sous le coup de poing brutal à l'estomac, que cause une impatience de gens auxquels coûte que coûte et soudain il faut proclamer quelque chose fût-ce la rêverie…

—Qui s'ignore et se lance nue de peur, en travers

ing before me in the conjoined isolation, for example, of our carriage—where is it—let's get back to it:— but this gushed forth, forced out by the brutal blow in the stomach caused by the impatience of people to whom at any cost and spontaneously one must proclaim something, even if only daydreams . . .

—Which are unaware of themselves and hurl themselves naked from fear across the public; it's true. As you, Madame, I wager, would not have grasped so definitively that claptrap of mine corresponding to an early form of the sonnet,* despite its reduplication of a rhyme on the final stroke, if each term had not been echoed to you from various drums, to charm a sensibility open to the multiplicities of comprehension.

—Perhaps! agreed our identical thought in the playfulness of a nocturnal breeze.

du public; c'est vrai. Comme vous, Madame, ne l'auriez entendu si irréfutablement, malgré sa réduplication sur une rime du trait final, mon boniment d'après un mode primitif du sonnet*, je le gage, si chaque terme ne s'en était répercuté jusqu'à vous par de variés tympans, pour charmer un esprit ouvert à la compréhension multiple.

—Peut-être! accepta notre pensée dans un enjouement de souffle nocturne la même.

* In use in the English Renaissance.

* Usité à la Renaissance anglaise.

I had rowed for a long time, with a clean, sweeping, drowsy motion, my eyes turned inward in utter forgetfulness of the passage, as the laughter of the hour flowed round about. So much motionlessness idled away the time that, brushed by a dull sound into which my boat half slid, I was only able to determine that it had come to a halt by the steady glittering of initials on the bared oars, which recalled me to my worldly identity.

What was happening? where was I?

To see clearly into my adventure, I had to call to mind my early departure, on this flaming July day, through the lively opening, banked by dormant foliage, of an always narrow and meandering stream, in search of water flowers and with the intention of reconnoitering an estate belonging to the friend of a friend, to whom I might pay my respects on the spur of the moment. Without having been detained by any strip of grass before one landscape more than another, each being borne away with its reflection in the water by the same impartial movement of the oars, I had just run aground in a clump of reeds, the mysterious end of my voyage, in the middle of the river where, suddenly widened to a fluvial grove, it displays the indifference of a pool rippling with the hesitations of a well spring about to depart.

A detailed inspection revealed that this obstacle of tapering verdure in the current masked the single arch of a bridge that was extended on land, on both sides, by a hedge enclosing a series of lawns. Then I

J'avais beaucoup ramé, d'un grand geste net assoupi, les yeux au-dedans fixés sur l'entier oubli d'aller, comme le rire de l'heure coulait alentour. Tant d'immobilité paressait que frôlé d'un bruit inerte où fila jusqu'à moitié la yole, je ne vérifiai l'arrêt qu'à l'étincellement stable d'initiales sur les avirons mis à nu, ce qui me rappela à mon identité mondaine.

Qu'arrivait-il, où étais-je?

Il fallut, pour voir clair en l'aventure, me remémorer mon départ tôt, ce juillet de flamme, sur l'intervalle vif entre ses végétations dormantes d'un toujours étroit et distrait ruisseau, en quête des floraisons d'eau et avec un dessein de reconnaître l'emplacement occupé par la propriété de l'amie d'une amie, à qui je devais improviser un bonjour. Sans que le ruban d'aucune herbe me retînt devant un paysage plus que l'autre chassé avec son reflet en l'onde par le même impartial coup de rame, je venais échouer dans quelque touffe de roseaux, terme mystérieux de ma course, au milieu de la rivière: où tout de suite élargie en fluvial bosquet, elle étale un nonchaloir d'étang plissé des hésitations à partir qu'a une source.

L'inspection détaillée m'apprit que cet obstacle de verdure en pointe sur le courant, masquait l'arche unique d'un pont prolongé, à terre, d'ici et de là, par une haie clôturant des pelouses. Je me rendis compte. Simplement le parc de Madame..., l'inconnue à saluer.

Un joli voisinage, pendant la saison, la nature d'une personne qui s'est choisi retraite aussi

understood: this was simply the estate of Madame…
the unknown lady I was to greet.

A pretty spot during the season: the nature of a
person who had chosen so watery and impenetrable
a retreat for herself could only be in harmony with my
own inclinations. Surely she had formed from this
crystal an interior mirror to shelter her from the
brilliant indiscretion of the afternoon; she would
come there and the silvery mist glazing the willows
would soon be no more than the limpidity of her gaze
familiar with every leaf.

Completely lustral did I conjure her.

Leaning forward in the agile posture in which
curiosity held me, as if beneath the spacious silence in
which the stranger would announce herself, I smiled
at this commencement of a bondage released by a
feminine possibility: which the thongs attaching the
rower's shoes to the wood of the boat symbolized
quite adequately, for we are always at one with the
instruments of our magic spells.

"—Probably just anyone . . ." I was about to
conclude.

When an imperceptible noise made me question
whether the inhabitant of the shore was haunting my
leisure, or, unexpectedly, the pond.

The footsteps stopped: why?

Subtle secret of feet that come and go, leading the
spirit whither she wills, dear shadow buried in
cambric and in the lace of a skirt flowing on the

humidement impénétrable ne pouvant être que
conforme à mon goût. Sûr, elle avait fait de ce cristal
son miroir intérieur à l'abri de l'indiscrétion éclatante
des après-midi; elle y venait et la buée d'argent
glaçant des saules ne fut bientôt que la limpidité de
son regard habitué à chaque feuille.

Toute je l'évoquais lustrale.

Courbé dans la sportive attitude où me maintenait
de la curiosité, comme sous le silence spacieux de ce
que s'annonçait l'étrangère, je souris au commence-
ment d'esclavage dégagé par une possibilité féminine:
que ne signifiaient pas mal les courroies attachant le
soulier du rameur au bois de l'embarcation, comme
on ne fait qu'un avec l'instrument de ses sortilèges.

« —Aussi bien une quelconque… » allais-je ter-
miner.

Quand un imperceptible bruit me fit douter si
l'habitante du bord hantait mon loisir, ou inespéré-
ment le bassin.

Le pas cessa, pourquoi?

Subtil secret des pieds qui vont, viennent,
conduisent l'esprit où le veut la chère ombre enfouie
en de la batiste et les dentelles d'une jupe affluant sur
le sol comme pour circonvenir du talon à l'orteil,
dans une flottaison, cette initiative par quoi la marche
s'ouvre, tout au bas et les plis rejetés en traîne, une
échappée, de sa double flèche savante.

Connaît-elle un motif à sa station, elle-même la
promeneuse: et n'est-ce, moi, tendre trop haut la tête,

ground, as if to surround from heel to toe, floatingly, this initiative by which walking opens up as a fugitive space, very low and with the folds thrown back in a train, its knowing double arrow.

Has she a motive, then, for standing still, she herself, the stroller: and I, am I not holding up my head too high if, to interrogate the mystery, I raise it up beyond those reeds and all the mental somnolence in which lucidity is veiled.

"—To whatever pattern your features correspond, I sense their precision, Madame, interrupting something established here by the rustling of an arrival, yes! this instinctive charm of something underneath, which the most authentically fastened sash, with a buckle of diamonds, does not defend against the explorer. So vague a concept suffices and will not transgress against the delight imprinted by a generality that permits and ordains the exclusion of all faces, to the point at which the revelation of one (oh, do not incline it, confirmed, on the secret threshold where I reign) would drive away my turmoil, with which it has nothing to do.

I can try to present myself in this pirate's outfit, with the excuse that I came here by chance.

Separated, we are together: I inveigle myself in her obscure intimacy, in this moment suspended over the water in which my dream delays the undecided one, better than any visit, followed by others, will enable me to do. How many trifling conversations there would have to be, in comparison with this one which I held in order not to be heard, before we could recover as intuitive an understanding as we now have,

pour ces joncs à ne dépasser et toute la mentale somnolence où se voile ma lucidité, que d'interroger jusque-là le mystère.

« —A quel type s'ajustent vos traits, je sens leur précision, Madame, interrompre chose installée ici par le bruissement d'une venue, oui! ce charme instinctif d'en dessous que ne défend pas contre l'explorateur la plus authentiquement nouée, avec une boucle en diamant, des ceintures. Si vague concept se suffit: et ne transgressera le délice empreint de généralité qui permet et ordonne d'exclure tous visages, au point que la révélation d'un (n'allez point le pencher, avéré, sur le furtif seuil où je règne) chasserait mon trouble, avec lequel il n'a que faire. »

Ma présentation, en cette tenue de maraudeur aquatique, je la peux tenter, avec l'excuse du hasard.

Séparés, on est ensemble: je m'immisce à de sa confuse intimité, dans ce suspens sur l'eau où mon songe attarde l'indécise, mieux que visite, suivie d'autres, l'autorisera. Que de discours oiseux en comparaison de celui que je tins pour n'être pas entendu, faudra-t-il, avant de retrouver aussi intuitif accord que maintenant, l'ouïe au ras de l'acajou vers le sable entier qui s'est tu!

La pause se mesure au temps de ma détermination.

Conseille, ô mon rêve, que faire?

Résumer d'un regard la vierge absence éparse en cette solitude et, comme on cueille, en mémoire d'un site, l'un de ces magiques nénuphars clos qui y surgissent tout à coup, enveloppant de leur creuse blanc-

my ear flat against the mahogany toward the sand which has now fallen entirely silent!

The pause measures itself by the time of my decision.

Counsel me, O my dream: what shall I do?

Sum up with a glance the virginal absence dispersed in this solitude and, as one gathers, in memory of a site, one of those magical, closed water lilies which spring up suddenly, enveloping nothingness with their hollow whiteness, formed from untouched dreams, from a happiness that will never take place, and from the breath that I am now holding in fear of an apparition, depart with it: steal silently away, rowing little by little, so as not to break the illusion with a shock and so that the rippling of the visible bubble of foam unwinding from my flight does not throw at the feet of the lady who has arrived a transparent resemblance to my ravished ideal flower.

If, drawn by an unprecedented feeling, she happened to appear—she, the Meditative or Haughty, the Cruel or Gay—so much the worse for that ineffable face which I shall never know! for I accomplished the maneuver according to the rules: disentangled myself, put about, and was already skirting a river wave, bearing away, like a noble swan's egg, such as will never burst into flight, my imaginary trophy, which swells with nothing but the exquisite vacancy of self that many a lady loves to pursue in summer, along the paths of her park, as she stops sometimes and lingers, perhaps on the edge of a spring that must be crossed, or of some other body of water.

heur un rien, fait de songes intacts, du bonheur qui n'aura pas lieu et de mon souffle ici retenu dans la peur d'une apparition, partir avec: tacitement en déramant peu à peu sans du heurt briser l'illusion ni que le clapotis de la bulle visible d'écume enroulée à ma fuite ne jette aux pieds survenus de personne la ressemblance transparente du rapt de mon idéale fleur.

Si, attirée par un sentiment d'insolite, elle a paru, la Méditative ou la Hautaine, la Farouche, la Gaie, tant pis pour cette indicible mine que j'ignore à jamais! car j'accomplis selon les règles la manœuvre: me dégageai, virai et je contournais déjà une ondulation du ruisseau, emportant comme un noble œuf de cygne, tel que n'en jaillira le vol, mon imaginaire trophée, qui ne se gonfle d'autre chose sinon de la vacance exquise de soi qu'aime, l'été, à poursuivre, dans les allées de son parc, toute dame, arrêtée parfois et longtemps, comme au bord d'une source à franchir ou de quelque pièce d'eau.

Spring impels the organism to acts which, in another season, are unknown to it, and many a treatise in natural history abounds in descriptions of this phenomenon among animals. Of how much more plausible interest it would be to record certain of the changes that the climacteric moment brings about in the behavior of individuals fashioned for a spiritual destiny! As for myself, the irony of winter barely having left me, I hold on to something of its state of ambivalence, lest it be replaced by a naive or absolute naturalism capable of pursuing enjoyment in the differentiation of various blades of grass. Since nothing in the case at hand could bring profit to the crowd, I escape, in order to meditate upon it, beneath several shade trees formerly surrounding the town: so it is from within their almost banal mystery that I shall exhibit a palpable and striking example of springtime urges.

Keen was my surprise just now when—low somber commotion—in a rarely frequented corner of the Bois de Boulogne, I saw, through the interstices of thousands of bushes good for hiding nothing, completely, and from the high throbbings of his tricorn hat down to his silver-buckled shoes, an ecclesiastic, who, removed from all witnesses, was responding to the solicitations of the lawn. Far be it from me (and nothing of the sort serves the designs of providence) that, guilty as a scandalized hypocrite seizing a stone from the road, I should bring by a smile even of understanding a blush to the face hidden with two hands of this poor man, other than that which was doubtlessly discovered in his solitary exercise! Being

Les printemps poussent l'organisme à des actes qui dans une autre saison, lui sont inconnus et maint traité d'histoire naturelle abonde en descriptions de ce phénomène, chez les animaux. Qu'il serait d'un intérêt plus plausible de recueillir certaines des altérations qu'apporte l'instant climatérique dans les allures d'individus faits pour la spiritualité! Mal quitté par l'ironie de l'hiver, j'en retiens, quant à moi, un état équivoque tant que ne s'y substitue pas un naturalisme absolu ou naïf, capable de poursuivre une jouissance dans la différentiation de plusieurs brins d'herbes. Rien dans le cas actuel n'apportant de profit à la foule, j'échappe, pour le méditer, sous quelques ombrages environnant d'hier la ville: or c'est de leur mystère presque banal que j'exhiberai un exemple saisissable et frappant des inspirations printanières.

Vive fut tout à l'heure, dans un endroit peu fréquenté du bois de Boulogne, ma surprise quand, sombre agitation basse, je vis, par les mille interstices d'arbustes bons à ne rien cacher, total et des battements supérieurs du tricorne s'animant jusqu'à des souliers affermis par des boucles en argent, un ecclésiastique, qui à l'écart de témoins, répondait aux sollicitations du gazon. A moi ne plût (et rien de pareil ne sert les desseins providentiels) que, coupable à l'égal d'un faux scandalisé se saisissant d'un caillou du chemin, j'amenasse par mon sourire même d'intelligence, une rougeur sur le visage à deux mains voilé de ce pauvre homme, autre que celle sans doute trouvée dans son solitaire exercice! Le pied vif, il me fallut, pour ne produire par ma présence de distrac-

fast of foot, I had to use my dexterity in order not to produce a distraction by my presence; and steeled against the temptation of a backward glance, to picture to myself the quasi-diabolic apparition who continued to rumple the springtime renewal with his sides, from right to left and with his stomach, obtaining a chaste frenzy thereby. Everything, rubbing himself or tossing about his limbs, rolling or sliding, resulted in satisfaction: even pausing, abashed by some tall flower stem tickling his black calves, amid that special robe worn with the appearance that one is everything for oneself, even one's own wife. Solitude, cold silence dispersed in the verdure, perceived by senses less subtle than troubled, you have been acquainted with the furious flappings of a cloth; as if the night hidden in its folds came shaken out of it at last! and the dull thuds against the earth of the rejuvenated skeleton; but the possessed one did not have to contemplate you at all. It was enough to seek within himself mirthfully the cause of a pleasure or a duty which, confronted by a lawn, could hardly be explained by a return to the gambols of the seminary. The influence of a vernal breeze gently dilating the immutable texts inscribed in his flesh, he too, emboldened by this confusion agreeable to his sterile thought, had come to acknowledge the general well-being through a contact with Nature that was clean, violent, positive, denuded of all intellectual curiosity; and candidly, far from the obediences and constraints of his occupation, from the canons, prohibitions, and censures, he was rolling, in the beatitude of his native simplicity, happier than a donkey. Having attained the goal of his outing, that the hero of my vision at once got straight up, not without shaking off the pistils and wiping off the sap clinging to his person, in order to return, unperceived, to the crowd

tion, user d'adresse; et fort contre la tentation d'un regard porté en arrière, me figurer en esprit l'apparition quasi diabolique qui continuait à froisser le renouveau de ses côtes, à droite, à gauche et du ventre, en obtenant une chaste frénésie. Tout, se frictionner ou jeter les membres, se rouler, glisser, aboutissait à une satisfaction: et s'arrêter, interdit du chatouillement de quelque haute tige de fleur à de noirs mollets, parmi cette robe spéciale portée avec l'apparence qu'on est pour soi tout même sa femme. Solitude, froid silence épars dans la verdure, perçus par des sens moins subtils qu'inquiets, vous connûtes les claquements furibonds d'une étoffe; comme si la nuit absconse en ses plis en sortait enfin secouée! et les heurts sourds contre la terre du squelette rajeuni; mais l'énergumène n'avait point à vous contempler. Hilare, c'était assez de chercher en soi la cause d'un plaisir ou d'un devoir, qu'expliquait mal un retour, devant une pelouse, aux gambades du séminaire. L'influence du souffle vernal doucement dilatant les immuables textes inscrits en sa chair, lui aussi, enhardi de ce trouble agréable à sa stérile pensée, était venu reconnaître par un contact avec la Nature, immédiat, net, violent, positif, dénué de toute curiosité intellectuelle, le bien-être général; et candidement, loin des obédiences et de la contrainte de son occupation, des canons, des interdits, des censures, il se roulait, dans la béatitude de sa simplicité native, plus heureux qu'un âne. Que le but de sa promenade atteint se soit, droit et d'un jet, relevé non sans secouer les pistils et essuyer les sucs attachés à sa personne, le héros de ma vision, pour rentrer, inaperçu, dans la foule, et les habitudes de son ministère, je ne songe à rien nier; mais j'ai le droit de ne point considérer cela. Ma discrétion vis-à-vis d'ébats d'abord apparus n'a-t-elle pas pour récompense d'en

and to the habits of his ministry, I would not dream of denying; but I have the right to be unconcerned with all that. Has not my discretion vis-à-vis the incipient appearance of those frolics been rewarded by being fixed forever as the reverie of a passerby pleased to complete it, as an image marked by the mysterious seal of modernity, at once baroque and beautiful?

fixer à jamais comme une rêverie de passant se plut à la compléter, l'image marquée d'unsceau mystérieux de modernité, à la fois baroque et belle?

GLORY

Glory! Until yesterday I didn't know it in its indisputable essence, and from now on nothing else so-called will ever be of interest to me.

A hundred posters absorbing the uncomprehended gold of the days (treason of letters) flew by, as if to all the outposts of the city, my eyes being drawn to the horizon's edge by a departure on the rails before being gathered into the abstruse loftiness that an approach to a forest in the time of its apotheosis bestows.

But such discord amid the exaltation of that hour: the name of Fontainebleau—this name known for the unfolding of a continuous line of lately vanished summits—was howled with such violent distortion that I thought I would break the glass of the compartment and throttle the interrupter: Keep quiet! Do not, by means of your insensible barking, divulge the shadow which has here been instilled in my spirit to the carriage doors banging beneath an inspired and egalitarian wind, now that the ubiquitous tourists have been vomited out. A deceptive calm emanating from rich woods holds in suspension around it some extraordinary state of illusion. And what do you reply? That these travelers have today left the capital for your station? Good employee that you are, vociferating is your duty; far from monopolizing an ecstasy bestowed upon all by the conjoined liberalities of nature and the State, I ask only that silence be prolonged for the time it takes me to isolate myself from the urban delegation and reach the ecstatic torpor of yonder leaves that sit too motionless not to be soon scattered into the air by

LA GLOIRE

La Gloire! je ne la sus qu'hier, irréfragable, et rien ne m'intéressera d'appelé par quelqu'un ainsi.

Cent affiches s'assimilant l'or incompris des jours, trahison de la lettre, ont fui, comme à tous confins de la ville, mes yeux au ras de l'horizon par un départ sur le rail traînés avant de se recueillir dans l'abstruse fierté que donne une approche de forêt en son temps d'apothéose.

Si discord parmi l'exaltation de l'heure, un cri faussa ce nom connu pour déployer la continuité de cimes tard évanouies, Fontainebleau, que je pensai, la glace du compartiment violentée, du poing aussi étreindre à la gorge l'interrupteur: Tais-toi! Ne divulgue pas du fait d'un aboi indifférent l'ombre ici insinuée dans mon esprit, aux portières de wagons battant sous un vent inspiré et égalitaire, les touristes omniprésents vomis. Une quiétude menteuse de riches bois suspend alentour quelque extraordinaire état d'illusion, que me réponds-tu? qu'ils ont, ces voyageurs, pour ta gare aujourd'hui quitté la capitale, bon employé vociférateur par devoir et dont je n'attends, loin d'accaparer une ivresse à tous départie par les libéralités conjointes de la nature et de l'État, rien qu'un silence prolongé le temps de m'isoler de la délégation urbaine vers l'extatique torpeur de ces feuillages là-bas trop immobilisés pour qu'une crise ne les éparpille bientôt dans l'air; voici, sans attenter à ton intégrité, tiens, une monnaie.

Un uniforme inattentif m'invitant vers quelque barrière, je remets sans dire mot, au lieu du suborneur métal, mon billet.

a storm; here, now (I make no attempt on your integrity), take this coin.

An unresponsive uniform conducts me to a gate, and, without a word, in lieu of the suborning metal, I hand over my ticket.

I must have been obeyed, however, yes, to judge from the asphalt stretching out untrodden before me; for in this exceptionally magnificent October, I cannot imagine that of the millions of existences stacking their vacuity in the enormous monotony of the capital (whose spell is soon going to be effaced when the whistle blows through the mist), there is no one beside myself who has not stolen furtively away or sensed that there are bitter and luminous sobbings in the air this year, many an indeterminate drifting idea forsaking the fortuitous like a branch, such a quivering that one thinks of autumn beneath the heavens.

But there was no one, and enveloped in the wings of doubt, like one who carries off a prize in secret splendor, a trophy too inestimable in its worth to be visible! but without immediately rushing into that diurnal vigil of immortal tree-trunks sloping down with superhuman pride (the truth of which must be experienced) or crossing the threshold where torches, maintaining a lofty trust, consume all dreams before their brilliance can burst forth purple in the clouds with the universal consecration of the royal intruder who will only have had to come—I waited, in order that I might be that being, until slowly and gathered up in its regular motion, the train was reduced in its proportions to a childish monster carrying people somewhere, the train which had left me there alone.

Obéi pourtant, oui, à ne voir que l'asphalte s'étaler net de pas, car je ne peux encore imaginer qu'en ce pompeux octobre exceptionnel du million d'existences étageant leur vacuité en tant qu'une monotonie énorme de capitale dont va s'effacer ici la hantise avec le coup de sifflet sous la brume, aucun furtivement évadé que moi n'ait senti qu'il est, cet an, d'amers et lumineux sanglots, mainte indécise flottaison d'idée désertant les hasards comme des branches, tel frisson et ce qui fait penser à un automne sous les cieux.

Personne et, les bras de doute envolés comme qui porte aussi un lot d'une splendeur secrète, trop inappréciable trophée pour paraître! mais sans du coup m'élancer dans cette diurne veillée d'immortels troncs au déversement sur un d'orgueils surhumains (or ne faut-il pas qu'on en constate l'authenticité?) ni passer le seuil où des torches consument, dans une haute garde, tous rêves antérieurs à leur éclat répercutant en pourpre dans la nue l'universel sacre de l'intrus royal qui n'aura eu qu'à venir: j'attendis, pour l'être, que lent et repris du mouvement ordinaire, se réduisît à ses proportions d'une chimère puérile emportant du monde quelque part, le train qui m'avait là déposé seul.

UN COUP DE DÉS

PREFACE

I would rather that this note not be read, or, if glanced at, that it be forgotten; to the skillful Reader, it imparts little that is situated beyond his penetration: but it may prove a hindrance to the inexperienced one, who must apply his gaze to the first words of the Poem, so that those that follow, disposed as they are on the Page, lead to the final ones, the whole without novelty except for the way the reading process is spaced out. The "blanks," in effect, assume importance and are what is immediately most striking; versification always demanded them as a surrounding silence, so that a lyric poem, or one with a few feet, generally occupies about a third of the leaf on which it is centered: I don't transgress against this order of things, I merely disperse its elements. The paper intervenes each time an image, of its own accord, ceases or withdraws, accepting the succession of others; and, as it is not a question, as it usually is, of regular sound patterns or verses but rather of prismatic subdivisions of the Idea, at the instant they appear and for the duration of their concurrence in some exact mental setting, the text imposes itself, variably, near or far from the latent guiding thread, for the sake of verisimilitude. This copied distance, which mentally separates words or groups of words from one another, has the literary advantage, if I may say so, of seeming to speed up and slow down the movement, of scanning it, and even of intimating it through a simultaneous vision of the Page: the latter is taken as the basic unit, in the way that elsewhere the

PRÉFACE

J'aimerais qu'on ne lût pas cette Note ou que parcourue, même on l'oubliât; elle apprend, au Lecteur habile, peu de chose situé outre sa pénétration: mais, peut troubler l'ingénu devant appliquer un regard aux premiers mots du Poëme pour que de suivants, disposés comme ils sont, l'amènent aux derniers, le tout sans nouveauté qu'un espacement de la lecture. Les «blancs» en effet, assument l'importance, frappent d'abord; la versification en exigea, comme silence alentour, ordinairement, au point qu'un morceau, lyrique ou de peu de pieds, occupe, au milieu, le tiers environ du feuillet: je ne transgresse cette mesure, seulement la disperse. Le papier intervient chaque fois qu'une image, d'elle-même, cesse ou rentre, acceptant la succession d'autres et, comme il ne s'agit pas, ainsi que toujours, de traits sonores réguliers ou vers—plutôt, de subdivisions prismatiques de l'Idée, l'instant de paraître et que dure leur concours, dans quelque mise en scène spirituelle exacte, c'est à des places variables, près ou loin du fil conducteur latent, en raison de la vraisemblance, que s'impose le texte. L'avantage, si j'ai droit à le dire, littéraire, de cette distance copiée qui mentalement sépare des groupes de mots ou les mots entre eux, semble d'accélérer tantôt et de ralentir le mouvement, le scandant, l'intimant même selon une vision simultanée de la Page: celle-ci prise pour unité comme l'est autre part le Vers ou ligne parfaite. La fiction affleurera et se dissipera, vite, d'après la mobilité de l'écrit, autour des arrêts fragmentaires

Verse or the perfect line is. The fiction rises to the surface and quickly dissipates, following the variable motion of the writing, around the fragmentary interruptions of a central phrase, a phrase introduced from the title and continuing onward. Everything that occurs is foreshortened and, as it were, hypothetical; narrative is avoided. Add that from this stripped-down mode of thought, with its retreats, prolongations, flights, or from its very design, there results, for whoever would read it aloud, a musical score. The difference in the type faces, between the dominant motif, a secondary, and adjacent ones, dictates their importance for oral expression, and the range or disposition of the characters, in the middle, at the top, or at the bottom of the page, marks the rising and falling of the intonation. In a work lacking in precedents, only a certain number of very bold directions, infringements, and so forth, forming the counterpoint to the prosody, remain in an elementary state: not that I judge it expedient to be timid in one's first attempts; but it isn't appropriate, outside of one's own special pages or volume, to go too much against custom in a Periodical, however courageous, generous, and open to freedom it may be. In any event, I shall have indicated a "state" rather than a sketch of this Poem, a "state" that does not break with tradition at all; I shall have extended its presentation in many directions, but not so far as to offend anyone: just enough to open some eyes. Today, or at least without presuming upon the future that will emerge from this—nothing or perhaps what merely verges on art—let us openly acknowledge that the attempt participates, in a way that could not be foreseen, in a number of pursuits that are dear to our

d'une phrase capitale dès le titre introduite et continuée. Tout se passe, par raccourci, en hypothèse; on évite le récit. Ajouter que de cet emploi à nu de la pensée avec retraits, prolongements, fuites, ou son dessin même, résulte, pour qui veut lire à haute voix, une partition. La différence des caractères d'imprimerie entre le motif prépondérant, un secondaire et d'adjacents, dicte son importance à l'émission orale et la portée, moyenne, en haut, en bas de page, notera que monte ou descend l'intonation. Seules certaines directions très hardies, des empiétements, etc., formant le contre-point de cette prosodie, demeurant dans une œuvre, qui manque de précédents, à l'état élémentaire: non que j'estime l'opportunité d'essais timides; mais il ne m'appartient pas, hormis une pagination spéciale ou de volume à moi, dans un Périodique, même valeureux, gracieux et invitant qu'il se montre aux belles libertés, d'agir par trop contrairement à l'usage. J'aurai, toutefois, indiqué du Poëme ci-joint, mieux que l'esquisse, un «état» qui ne rompe pas de tout point avec la tradition; poussé sa présentation en maint sens aussi avant qu'elle n'offusque personne: suffisamment, pour ouvrir des yeux. Aujourd'hui ou sans présumer de l'avenir qui sortira d'ici, rien ou presque un art, reconnaissons aisément que la tentative participe, avec imprévu, de poursuites particulières et chères à notre temps, le vers libre et le poëme en prose. Leur réunion s'accomplit sous une influence, je sais, étrangère, celle de la Musique entendue au concert; on en retrouve plusieurs moyens m'ayant semblé appartenir aux Lettres, je les reprends. Le genre, que c'en devienne un comme la symphonie, peu à peu, à côté du chant personnel, laisse intact l'antique vers,

time: free verse and the prose-poem. They are joined under a strange influence, that of Music, as it is heard at a concert; several of its methods, which seemed to me to apply to Literature, are to be found here. Its genre, if little by little it should become one like the symphony, alongside personal song, leaves the ancient technique of verse—for which I retain a religious veneration and to which I attribute the empire of passion and of dreams—intact, while this would be the preferred place for treating, as may follow, subjects of pure and complex imagination or intellect, which there is no reason to exclude from Poetry—unique source.

auquel je garde un culte et attribue l'empire de la passion et des rêveries; tandis que ce serait le cas de traiter, de préférence (ainsi qu'il suit) tels sujets d'imagination pure et complexe ou intellect: que ne reste aucune raison d'exclure de la Poésie—unique source.

A THROW OF THE DICE

UN COUP DE DÉS

WILL NEVER

EVEN WHEN LAUNCHED IN ETERNAL

CIRCUMSTANCES

FROM THE DEPTHS OF A SHIPWRECK

JAMAIS

QUAND BIEN MÊME LANCÉ DANS DES CIRCONSTANCES

ÉTERNELLES

DU FOND D'UN NAUFRAGE

THOUGH IT BE
　　　that

　　　　　　the Abyss

blanched
　　　　spread
　　　　　　furious
　　　　　　　　beneath an incline
　　　　　　　　　　desperately plane

　　　　　　　　　　　　on a wing

　　　　　　　　　　its own
　　　　　　　　　　　　fallen　　　　　　back in advance from being unable to dress its flight
　　　　　　　　　　　　　　　　　　　　　and covering the spurtings
　　　　　　　　　　　　　　　　　　　　　　　cutting off the surges

　　　　　　　　　　　　　　　　　　most inwardly sums up

　　　　　　　　　　　　　　　　the shadow buried in the deeps by this alternate sail

　　　　　　　　　　　　　　　　　　　　to the point of adapting
　　　　　　　　　　　　　　　　　　　　　　to the wingspan

　　　　　　　　　　　　　　　　　　　its gaping maw like the shell

　　　　　　　　　　　　　　　　　　of a ship

　　　　　　　　　　　　　　　　　listing to starboard or larboard

SOIT
    que

        l'Abîme

blanchi
    étale
      furieux
          sous une inclinaison
             plane désespérément

                 d'aile

               la sienne
                  par   avance retombée d'un mal à dresser le vol
                                          et couvrant les jaillissements
                                            coupant au ras les bonds

                           très à l'intérieur résume

                   l'ombre enfouie dans la profondeur par cette voile alternative

                           jusqu'adapter
                                à l'envergure

                     sa béante profondeur en tant que la coque

                            d'un bâtiment

                      penché de l'un ou l'autre bord

THE MASTER

beyond ancient reckonings
the maneuver forgotten with the age

arisen
    inferring

formerly he would grasp the helm

from this conflagration   at his feet
    from the unanimous horizon

that there   is readied
    tossed about and mixed
    in the hand that would clasp it
as one shakes one's fist at   a destiny and the winds

the unique Number which cannot   be another

Spirit
    to cast it
    into the storm
    to fold back division and pass proudly on

hesitates
corpse by the arm   separated from the secret it withholds

rather
    than play
    as a hoary maniac
    the game
    in the name of the waves

one   invades the head
flows in the submissive beard

shipwreck this   pertaining to man

without vessel
    no matter
    where vain

LE MAÎTRE

                                              hors d'anciens calculs
                                           où la manœuvre avec l'âge oubliée

surgi
      inférant
                                                      jadis il empoignait la barre

                    de cette conflagration   à ses pieds
                                                     de l'horizon unanime

                              que se   prépare
                                               s'agite et mêle
                                                    au poing qui l'étreindrait
                  comme on menace   un destin et les vents

            l'unique Nombre qui ne peut pas   être un autre

                                                  Esprit
                                                      pour le jeter
                                                           dans la tempête
                                                    en reployer la division et passer fier

                              hésite
                  cadavre par le bras   écarté du secret qu'il détient

plutôt
      que de jouer
            en maniaque chenu
                  la partie
            au nom des flots
                              un   envahit le chef
                                          coule en barbe soumise

                  naufrage cela   direct de l'homme

                              sans nef
                                    n'importe
                                          où vaine

from ancient time not to open up the hand
                              clenched
                    beyond the useless head

          legacy amid disappearance

                    to someone
                              ambiguous

               the ulterior immemorial demon

having
          from nullified regions
                    induced
the old man toward this supreme conjunction with probability

                    this one
                              his puerile shade
caressed and polished and rendered and washed
                    made supple by the waves and removed
               from the hard bones lost among the timbers

                    born
                              of a frolic
the sea through the ancestor or the ancestor against the sea
               tempting an idle chance

                                        Nuptials
from which
          the veil of illusion sprung up against their haunting
          like the ghost of a gesture

                    will falter
                    will fall

                         madness   ABOLISH

ancestralement à n'ouvrir pas la main
                              crispée
                    par delà l'inutile tête

          legs en la disparition

                    à quelqu'un
                              ambigu

               l'ultérieur démon immémorial

ayant
          de contrées nulles
                    induit
le vieillard vers cette conjonction suprême avec la probabilité

                         celui
                              son ombre puérile
caressée et polie et rendue et lavée
                    assouplie par la vague et soustraite
               aux durs os perdus entre les ais

                    né
                         d'un ébat
la mer par l'aïeul tentant ou l'aïeul contre la mer
               une chance oiseuse

                                        Fiançailles
dont
          le voile d'illusion rejailli leur hantise
          ainsi que le fantome d'un geste

                    chancellera
                    s'affalera

               folie

                    N'ABOLIRA

AS IF

           An insinuation   *simple*

             in the silence   *enrolled with irony*

                                  or

                                      the mystery

                                          hurled

                                              howled

             in some nearby   *whirlpool of hilarity and horror*

               flutters   *about the abyss*

                                      without strewing it

                                          or fleeing

                              and out of it cradles the virgin sign

                                                                  AS IF

COMME SI

Une insinuation   simple

au silence   enroulée avec ironie

ou

le mystère

précipité

hurlé

dans quelque proche   tourbillon d'hilarité et d'horreur

voltige   autour du gouffre

sans le joncher

ni fuir

et en berce le vierge indice

COMME SI

135

solitary distraught feather

        unless   *a midnight toque encounters or grazes it*
                        and immobilizes
                  on the crumpled velvet by a somber guffaw

           this rigid whiteness

      ridiculous
                   in opposition to the sky
         too much so
             not to mark
                in the slightest detail
                   whoever

        bitter prince of the reef

        wears it as an heroic headdress
         irresistible but contained
        by his small virile reason
                  in a lightning flash

plume solitaire éperdue

sauf   *que la rencontre ou l'effleure une toque de minuit*
                                      et immobilise
                          au velours chiffonné par un esclaffement sombre

                                   cette blancheur rigide

dérisoire
                                   en opposition au ciel
           trop
                          pour ne pas marquer
                                      exigüment
                                              quiconque

                                   prince amer de l'écueil

                          s'en coiffe comme de l'héroïque
                          irrésistible mais contenu
                          par sa petite raison virile
                                              en foudre

anxious

    expiatory and pubescent

        mute   *laughter*

                                             that

IF

        The lucid and lordly crest   *of vertigo*
         invisible on the brow
        scintillates
          then shadows
         a delicate dark form   *standing upright*
      in its Siren twist

                     long enough
                      to slap
     with impatient terminal scales   *forked*

                     a rock

                  false manor
                      immediately
                           evaporated in mist

                    which imposed
                      a limit on infinity

soucieux

expiatoire et pubère

muet

rire

que

SI

La lucide et seigneuriale aigrette
au front invisible
scintille
puis ombrage
une stature mignonne ténébreuse
en sa torsion de sirène

par d'impatientes squames ultimes

de vertige

debout

le temps
de souffleter
bifurquées

un roc

faux manoir
tout de suite
évaporé en brumes

qui imposa
une borne à l'infini

IT WAS
born of the stars

THE NUMBER

WERE IT TO EXIST
other than as a scattered dying hallucination

WERE IT TO BEGIN AND WERE IT TO CEASE
springing up as denied and closed off when made manifest
at last
through some thinly diffused emanation
WERE IT TO BE NUMBERED

evidence of a totality however meager
WERE IT TO ILLUMINE

IT WOULD BE

worse
no
more nor less
but as much indifferently

CHANCE

Falls
the feather
rhythmic suspension of disaster
to be buried
in the original spray
whence formerly its delirium sprang up to a peak
withered
by the identical neutrality of the abyss

C'ÉTAIT

issu stellaire

LE NOMBRE

EXISTÂT-IL

autrement qu'hallucination éparse d'agonie

COMMENÇÂT-IL ET CESSÂT-IL

sourdant que nié et clos quand apparu

enfin

par quelque profusion répandue en rareté

SE CHIFFRÂT-IL

évidence de la somme pour peu qu'une

ILLUMINÂT-IL

CE SERAIT

pire

non

davantage ni moins

indifféremment mais autant

LE HASARD

Choit

la plume

rythmique suspens du sinistre

s'ensevelir

aux écumes originelles

naguères d'où sursauta son délire jusqu'à une cime

flétrie

par la neutralité identique du gouffre

141

NOTHING

of the memorable crisis
or might
the event   have been accomplished in view of all results   null

human

WILL HAVE TAKEN PLACE
an ordinary elevation pours out absence

BUT THE PLACE
some splashing below of water as if to disperse the empty act
abruptly which otherwise
by its falsehood
would have founded
perdition

in these latitudes
of indeterminate
waves
in which all reality dissolves

RIEN

de la mémorable crise
ou se fût
l'évènement   accompli en vue de tout résultat nul
humain

N'AURA EU LIEU
une élévation ordinaire verse l'absence

QUE LE LIEU
inférieur clapotis quelconque comme pour disperser l'acte vide
abruptement qui sinon
par son mensonge
eût fondé
la perdition

dans ces parages
du vague
en quoi toute réalité se dissout

EXCEPT

    on high

           PERHAPS

                as far as place   can fuse with the beyond

                          aside from the interest
                      marked out to it
                            in general
           by a certain obliquity through a certain declivity
                          of fires

            toward
              what must be
                the Septentrion as well as North

                      A CONSTELLATION

              cold from forgetfulness and desuetude
                  not so much
                  that it doesn't number
            on some vacant and superior surface
                  the successive shock
                      in the way of stars
            of a total account in the making

        keeping vigil
           doubting
             rolling
                shining and meditating

                  before coming to a halt
                at some terminus that sanctifies it

              All Thought emits a Throw of the Dice

EXCEPTÉ

    à l'altitude
          PEUT-ÊTRE

              aussi loin qu'un endroit   fusionne avec au delà

                       hors l'intérêt
                     quant à lui signalé
                           en général
             selon telle obliquité par telle déclivité
                          de feux

               vers
                  ce doit être
                    le Septentrion aussi Nord

                         UNE CONSTELLATION

                   froide d'oubli et de désuétude
                       pas tant
                     qu'elle n'énumère
               sur quelque surface vacante et supérieure
                     le heurt successif
                         sidéralement
                  d'un compte total en formation

  veillant

        doutant

            roulant

               brillant et méditant

                      avant de s'arrêter
                 à quelque point dernier qui le sacre

                  Toute Pensée émet un Coup de Dés

COMMENTARY

POÉSIES

The first publication of the *Poésies* in book form was issued in Belgium by the firm of Edmond Deman in 1899, the year after Mallarmé's death. Prior to the Deman edition, the poems had been published in reviews and, in 1887, many of them had appeared in successive issues of *La Revue Indépendante.* In 1913 Mallarmé's son-in-law, Dr. Edmond Bonniot, and his daughter, Geneviève, published a new edition of the *Poésies* through the *Nouvelle Revue Française,* which contained a number of previously unpublished poems. In general, the present volume follows the standard Pléiade edition of the *Œuvres Complètes* of 1951, edited by Henri Mondor and G. Jean-Aubry (hereafter referred to as *OC).* I have also consulted the critical edition of the *Poésies* prepared by Carl Paul Barbier and Charles Gordon Millan and published by Flammarion in 1983. Specific information concerning the publishing history of individual poems is noted in the following Commentary.

SALUT / SALUTATION

Although it was not composed until 1893, Mallarmé chose "Salut" to appear at the head of the *Poésies.* The title condenses at least three different meanings, and is one of those symbolically freighted terms that play so crucial a role in the *Poésies.* The poem offers a *salutation,* or greeting, to the poet's audience, and taking the form of a drinking song, it raises a *toast,* or a wish for good health, to the reader. Indeed, the sonnet was originally entitled "Toast" and was read by Mallarmé at a banquet for the journal *La Plume* prior to its publication in the February 1893 edition of that journal. In addition, "salut" can mean *salvation*, and on this level it points to the sacred character of poetry, as Mallarmé's poems frequently do. In "Cantique de Saint Jean" from *Hérodiade*, for example, the saint's severed head extends a salutation that carries with it salvation ("penche un salut").

A stamnos in the British Museum by the so-called Siren painter will take us some distance in understanding the poem's internal symbols and hidden narrative (a stamnos is an ancient Greek wine jug with a wide mouth and handles on either side). This particular stamnos shows two Sirens perched on boulders on either side of Odysseus's ship, while a third Siren falls headfirst into the water. The painting follows a Hellenistic (rather than a Homeric) tradition, according to which the Sirens commit suicide by drowning themselves if they are unable to seduce the hero from his quest (see Odette Touchefeu-Meynier, *Thèmes Odysséens* [Paris: Editions E. de Boccard, 1968], 175). The Siren symbol recurs, along with the shipwreck motif, in "A la nue accablante tu," a sonnet of 1895, and in *Un Coup de Dés*; it is connected to a central notion in Mallarmé: that the authentic poet, having been granted an experience of ecstasy, must be able to withstand or sublimate that experience through the discipline of form. "Toast Funèbre" and "Prose (pour des Esseintes)" are two major poems in the *Poésies* that take up this theme.

The poet holding up his cup in toast, a cup on which he imagines the figures of Odysseus and the Sirens to be depicted, thus, symbolically, becomes a kind of latter-day Odysseus. The cup, moreover, like Keats's Grecian Urn (and the connection between Mallarmé and Keats, as we shall see, is a very deep one), becomes a container for the ineffable. The foam of the champagne in line 1 ("écume") is connected metaphorically to the foam on the surface of the sea, and the "virgin verse" in apposition to "foam" indicates (like Keats's "still unravished bride of quietness") that although the mysteries of this sea are contained by the cup, they cannot easily be penetrated. What is contained, as it were, is not only "Salut" in particular, but because it is placed as a symbolic beginning, the entire contents of the *Poésies*; thus, the cup as a symbol is also connected to the symbol of the book, which Mallarmé will refer to as a "spiritual instrument" (see "Le Livre, Instrument Spirituel," *OC*, 378).

The ship, as another vessel or container, is itself connected to the book—or rather to the page or to poetry itself—by the "sheet's white care" (or "concern": "souci"—line 14). The poet, "already on the poop," signals thereby that his time is running out and that it will be left to his fellow shipmates "to cut / Through winter wave and lightning burst," or, in other words, to take up the struggles of the avantgarde. In the meantime, since the poet is drunk in his imagination (or imaginatively drunk), the ship listing from side to side is in danger of shipwreck, as the word "récif" ("reef") in the sestet indicates. That danger is underplayed in "Salut" because of the particular poetic occasion, but it is a central motif in the work as a whole. Having disciplined himself to the exigencies of form, the poet manages to preserve his work from the devastation wrought by the Sirens,

by desire, but that work could never be produced unless he were drawn by their songs of a transcendence that must end in death. Like Odysseus strapped to the mast who manages thereby to contain himself, the Mallarméan conception of the poet is of one who, hearing the songs, will strive to contain them, even though what they contain is precisely that which is uncontainable.

The analogy of the poet to Odysseus, Homer's "master seaman," is solidified by the final word of the sonnet, "toile" (literally "cloth"), which has the meaning of "sail" and the extended figurative meaning here of the poet's white page. (Fortunately, "sheet" in English can embrace both meanings.) Several times the poet is referred to as the "Master" in the *Poésies*. The analogy will culminate in *Un Coup de Dés*, where the Master of the shipwrecked vessel is also the poet.

PREMIERS POËMES / FIRST POEMS

LE GUIGNON / THE JINX

It is significant that Mallarmé placed "Le Guignon," the first version of which seems to have been written before he was twenty, in early 1862 if not before, as the initial poem in "Premiers Poëmes," immediately following "Salut," which provides a thematic greeting to the *Poésies* but was written much later. Mallarmé indicates thereby that "Le Guignon" is to be adjudged his first poem of maturity, the first in which he comes into his own as a poet and is no longer at the stage of the juvenilia. This is especially important given Mallarmé's emphasis on the book as a "spiritual instrument" and the rigorous manner in which he strove throughout his career to fit every individual poem into the larger totality that was his life's work.

As Harold Bloom has argued, a great poet comes into his strength by taking on that of his precursors; so it is not surprising that standing in the background to "Le Guignon," the poem in which Mallarmé receives the mantle of "poetic election," are Charles Baudelaire and Théophile Gautier, his two most important precursors, along with Théodore de Banville, in the French tradition. Interestingly, Baudelaire and Gautier seem to have merged as a composite influence on the Mallarmé of "Le Guignon." For example, line 16 of "Le Guignon," "Ils tètent la douleur comme ils tétaient le rêve," echoes Baudelaire's "Ils tètent la douleur comme une bonne louve" from "Le Cygne" and Gautier's "Ils tettent librement la féconde mamelle" from "Ténèbres" (see *OC*, 1408–1409). There are many echoes from the *Fleurs du Mal* in "Le Guignon," but the influence of Baudelaire is primarily drawn through a sonnet that Baudelaire alternately entitled "Le Guignon" and "L'Artiste Inconnu." This sonnet deals with the theme of the *poeta ignotus*, a theme that Baudelaire has obviously taken from Thomas Gray's "Elegy Written in a Country Churchyard"; indeed, the sestet is a paraphrase of the "Full many a gem" stanza of the "Elegy," and this is interesting because whether or not Mallarmé knew Gray at this stage, he will later directly echo the same passage from the "Elegy" in the "Scène" from *Hérodiade*.

Gautier's influence on "Le Guignon" is even more central. "Ténèbres," Gautier's magnificent poem in terza rima of 411 lines—a poem that dwells on the misfortune of all misfits, of those who are marginal to society, including the artist himself, and that culmi-

nates in an apocalyptic vision—supplies Mallarmé with Dante's measure and with a good deal of his own rhetorical power. The influence of Baudelaire has been more closely studied than that of Gautier, but Mallarmé regarded Gautier as his Virgil, as demonstrated in the concluding lines to "Toast Funèbre," Mallarmé's great elegy on Gautier.

Mallarmé wrote two poems in terza rima, "Le Guignon" and "Aumône"; both were begun in 1862 and both center on figures who are marginal to society: "beggars of azure" ("mendieurs d'azur"— line 3) in "Le Guignon" and an ordinary beggar in "Aumône." The style/content dialectic of these poems is, as we have noted, drawn from Gautier, but the relationship between Dante's measure (and hence his vision) and the thematics of marginality and misfortune is an interesting one. The Dante whom Mallarmé receives from Gautier is the Dante of the *Inferno*; and the Jinx who drives the "beggars of azure" unremittingly through the world (I follow Anthony Hartley's lead in rendering the title so as to capture the personification [see *Mallarmé*, 8]) is not unlike one of the devils of Hell: he stands for a cruelly deterministic Nature that is ruled by chance and from which God has absconded. Gautier's vision—and this is true of Baudelaire's as well—is essentially tragic; the feeling and tone of Mallarmé's poetry will take on a different coloring as the mature poet reaches for an affirmation in the realm of art itself. But that will occur later on.

Mallarmé was always concerned to bring his poetry before the public in a context that was thematically relevant to the work at hand, and so it is interesting that "Le Guignon" was initially published (in an early and truncated form) in the March 1862 issue of *L'Artiste* and that it was later included in Paul Verlaine's anthology *Les Poëtes Maudits* (1884).

Mallarmé's "beggars of azure," however, are not explicitly identified as poets—indeed, in the poem's conclusion they are reviled by what we might call the "official" poets of the society—perhaps because the "bitter ideal" ("l'idéal amer"—line 9; "bitter wish" in the translation) leading them on and torturing them at the same time (an ideal symbolized in many of the *Poésies* as the *azure* sky) can never be realized and will not even allow for a definite social identity. This transcendental striving is what distinguishes the "beggars of azure" from the "herd" ("bétail"—line 1), a word that Mallarmé will use in "L'Azur" and elsewhere (and that for present-day readers will have Nietzschean implications). The schism between the ideal and the real in the poem, between potentiality and actuality, can be gauged by the fact that the beggars of azure are referred to as "dieux effacés" ("effaced gods"—line 53; "vanquished" in the translation), and that in early versions of the poem the "héros excédés" ("surpassed heroes") of the penultimate line were "Hamlet abreuvés" ("Hamlets steeped in grief"). The suicidal implications attached to Hamlet are particularly interesting because of the concluding image of the lamppost. The poet Gérard de Nerval committed suicide by hanging himself in the Rue de la Vieille Lanterne—the Street of the Old Lantern (or Lamppost).

APPARITION

Though not published until 1883 when it was included in the *Poëtes Maudits* edited by Verlaine, "Apparition" belongs to Mallarmé's first period and was probably composed in 1862 or 1863. The poem is clearly indebted to an eighteen-line poem by Victor Hugo, also entitled "Apparition," which involves a dialogue with an angel and in which the final image is also of stars. There is a Proustian quality to Mallarmé's "Apparition" that I have tried to bring out in the translation—so that the white bouquets of perfumed stars, snowing from the hands of the fairy long ago, are scattered in drifts to us, as it were "through the years" and across the linguistic divide.

The deep lyricism of "Apparition" has made it one of Mallarmé's most popular poems. It may be, as Charles Mauron has argued, that the feeling-tone of the poem is connected in some way to Mallarmé's ruminations over his sister Maria, who died at the age of thirteen when the poet was only fifteen (see *Introduction to the Psychoanalysis of Mallarmé,* 87–88); but the various attempts of criticism to situate the poem concretely in terms of Mallarmé's feelings for Maria, for his wife, Marie Gerhard, before their marriage, or for Ettie Yapp, the fiancée of his friend Henri Cazalis, add nothing to our appreciation of it as a poem. Whether or not it was written in response to a request by Cazalis for verses to celebrate his "mystical union" with Ettie, however, Mallarmé's response to Cazalis in a letter of July 1862 is interesting for the light it sheds on his somewhat paradoxical relationship to *lyricism.* Explaining that Cazalis must allow him the necessary time to produce the exquisite verses he has in mind, Mallarmé remarks: "I do not want to compose them out of inspiration: the turbulence of lyricism would be unworthy of that chaste apparition which you love. One must meditate a long time: only art, limpid and impeccable, is sufficiently chaste to sculpt her religiously" (see *OC,* 1412–1413). Or, to shift the metaphor: the process of gathering the sweetness of life and distilling poetry from it, a process that is adumbrated in the poem itself, can only be accomplished (as Keats also knew) through "silence and slow time."

PLACET FUTILE / FUTILE PETITION

"Placet Futile" shows Mallarmé mining a rococo vein to which he was to turn from time to time throughout his career, as if for relief from his struggles with the Absolute. Although it was begun in 1862 and initially published in that year (it did not arrive at its final form, however, until 1887), "Placet Futile" bears a marked resemblance to a poem written almost thirty years later, entitled "Feuillet d'Album." The titles of both poems indicate that Mallarmé is consciously taking on the persona of a minor scribbler of occasional verse, as if he were satisfied with a conception of poetry as an ornamental adjunct to polite society. The poet of "Placet Futile" is represented, as Guy Michaud astutely notes, "as if painted by Boucher on a pink fan, 'a flute in his hands,' that is, in the eventual attitude of the faun" (*Mallarmé*, 12). Indeed, in a letter of 1862 to his friend Emmanuel des Essarts in which he mentioned that he had written "Placet Futile" in response to the request for verses of a young lady, Mallarmé refers to it as "ce sonnet Louis XV," and in an early manuscript he inscribes it with the date of 1762. We might suspect that there is a kind of trompe l'œil at work here, however, and the connection that Michaud draws between "Placet Futile" and "L'Après-midi d'un Faune" suggests that Mallarmé's "occasional" verse is not quite so circumscribed from his major work as might initially appear.

Both "Placet Futile" and "Feuillet d'Album" adopt pastoral conventions and attitudes that we associate with the Rococo decadence. In "Placet" the poet represents himself in relation to the "princess" he addresses as barely possessing the rank of a sober abbé; he is nothing to her and will remain nothing unless she bestows a name upon him, a name that, in the elaborately ornamented metaphor of the sestet, will invoke Amor, who, painting him as a shepherd with a flute—on the fan that is his own wings—will enable him to be present to her at least in that form. Similarly, in "Feuillet d'Album" the poet is represented as a faun or satyr whose crippled fingers lack the means to *imitate* the charming laughter of the young girl who had condescended to listen to his flute-playing. The implied aesthetic attitude of the poem, as of "Placet Futile," is that art has a merely mimetic function—to get as close to life as possible—which in the final analysis it is unable to perform. Thus, the breath that the faun of "Feuillet" blows out of his pipes, even if he plays to the very limits of artistic capability ("Jusqu'à la dernière limite"), is ultimately "vain."

The apparent modesty of such "occasional" poems as "Placet Futile" and "Feuillet d'Album" takes on a quite different coloration, however, if they are set in contrast to *Hérodiade*, a poem that is clearly one of Mallarmé's major accomplishments. In *Hérodiade*, as our discussion of that poem will elucidate, Mallarmé develops a metaphysics of poetry that, on the surface at least, is antithetical to the mimetic orientation of the sonnets we have been discussing. In the final analysis, however, it may be that the antithesis is more apparent than real; for to the extent that the princess Hérodiade becomes a symbol of *la poésie pure* by turning away from life and disappearing into the poem, the attempt to reach her is ultimately as *futile* as the attempt to reach the princess of "Placet Futile." Whether the princess is conceived as symbolic of Poetry or of Life, the distance between them becomes an unbridgeable chasm in Mallarmé's poetry, and thus the mimetic relationship breaks down.

LE PITRE CHÂTIÉ / THE CLOWN CHASTISED

"Le Pitre Châtié" was begun in 1864 but was not published until 1887; in the interim it was much revised, and the final version, displaying all the difficulties of Mallarmé's late style, remains radically ambiguous. The clown clearly stands in some sort of symbolic relationship to poetry; but there are questions that simply cannot be resolved on the basis of the text at hand: Why is he punished? Is the flight he describes toward another or toward himself? And therefore, to what is poetry being opposed in the implicit antithesis that seems to be formulated by the sonnet?

In 1929 Edmond Bonniot, Mallarmé's son-in-law, published an early version of "Le Pitre Châtié," which he had discovered among the poet's papers. The first quatrain of that early version reads as follows:

> Pour ses yeux,— pour nager dans ces lacs, dont les quais
> Sont plantés de beaux cils qu'un matin bleu pénètre,
> J'ai, Muse,— moi, ton pitre,— enjambé la fenêtre
> Et fui notre baraque où fument tes quinquets.

"For her eyes—to swim in those lakes, whose banks are planted with beautiful lashes that a blue morning penetrates, I, Muse, your clown, have skipped out of the window and fled our hovel where the stage lamps smoke."

It is fairly clear that the clown of the early draft has fled the circus tent—or, in other words, fled from the Muse—in order to immerse himself (the metaphor of swimming is carried through both versions) in a woman—which means that in the early draft the antithesis concerns love and poetry. Some critics would argue that the existence of the early draft clarifies the final version, where the eyes and lakes of the first line are left floating. As R.-J. Berg notes in a very fine study of the poem ("Le Pitre Châtié," 376–384), however, this raises the problem of intentionality and assumes that the final version merely involves a condensation of the early draft, such that the poetic conception remains unchanged. But suppose that the "eyes" of the final version are the clown's own (as Berg suggests, and as Joy Newton and Ann Prescott also argue in "Mallarmé's Clown: A Study of 'Le Pitre Châtié'"); suppose further that they are glimpsed as in a mirror, and that in wanting to disappear inside them the poet wants to divest himself of his own personality and/or of the trivial accoutrements of his art (those deployed by a "mauvais Hamlet," which is to say, by a false rhetorical tradition) and thereby enter into *la poésie pure*. From this point of view, the real opposition delineated in the poem is not between love (or life) and poetry (we remember Auguste de Villiers de L'Isle-Adam's famous phrase: "As for living, our servants will do that for us!") but rather between two kinds of poetry, or, to revert to a philosophical dilemma at least as ancient as Plato, between rhetoric and truth; moreover, from this point of view, the clown is being punished, not for giving up the muse in favor of a woman but for failing to recognize that the "sanctity" of poetry is inextricably bound up with the very rhetorical tradition that, on the most banal level, can be likened to the grease paint of the clown. Again, the radical ambiguity of "Le Pitre Châtié" seems to demand of criticism not that it adjudicate among these interpretive possibilities but that it bring them into play.

DU PARNASSE SATYRIQUE / FROM THE SATIRICAL PARNASSUS

UNE NÉGRESSE / A NEGRESS

Mallarmé's "Négresse" may appear as something of an embarrassment to a contemporary sensibility, not so much because of her overt *eroticism*, which would have been much more disturbing to a fin de siècle audience (indeed, the poem was not included in the 1899 edition of the *Poésies*, probably for this reason), but because the *exoticism* of the image is tainted by what we would now call racism, although I personally would resist such an interpretation. There is no question, however, but that the feeling and tone of Mallarmé's poem are strongly marked by the influence of Baudelaire and that the figure of the Negress has a familial resemblance to Baudelaire's amazons and giantesses. The poem dates from 1864 or early 1865 and was originally published in *Le Nouveau Parnasse Satyrique* under the title "Les Lèvres Roses." I translate the section heading, "Du Parnasse Satyrique," which includes only this one poem, as "From the Satirical Parnassus"; but note that Mallarmé's adjective is spelled with a *y*, not an *i*; he invokes the sense in which *satire* derives from the *satyrs* of mythology. This would connect "Une négresse" to the faun of "L'Après-midi."

Allen Mandelbaum has alerted me to the difficulty of deciphering precisely who is doing what to whom in the poem, a difficulty exacerbated by the fact that the child is also female ("une enfant"). Is the instruction she is receiving of a purely theoretical character or does it involve some sort of practical application?

Where criticism has had anything at all to say about "Une Négresse," it has tended to relegate the poem to the domain of the comic or the grotesque.

But this seems to me superficial. I would argue that the poem should be understood in the context of the religious crisis that Mallarmé underwent during this period—and perhaps also in the context of a larger historical crisis resulting from colonialism. In any event, the child saddened by the "fruits nouveaux / Et criminels" of the first quatrain—that is, simultaneously by the longings of her own pubescent body and by the woman's nakedness—is constrained by a religious morality that in the West reaches back through many centuries, a morality that the negress (at least in the poet's conception) simply does not feel. (Significantly the verb "darder" in line 7 can refer to the rapidly thrusting tongue of a serpent; hence the "forbidden fruits" of this translation.) The European image of uninhibited African sexuality is, of course, a myth, and from that point of view, one might almost say that it is the negress herself—rather than the child between her legs—who is the "victim." But that image allows for a juxtaposition, a joining or collision, of two bodies that are simultaneously two cultures, and this in turn releases certain metaphysical possibilities that may not have been otherwise attained. Granted that the negress is reified by the exotic sense of otherness she embodies; but what we are ultimately left with in the final quatrain is an image that is neither comic nor grotesque but deeply mysterious.

DU PARNASSE CONTEMPORAIN / FROM THE CONTEMPORARY PARNASSUS

LES FENÊTRES / THE WINDOWS

Published for the first time in 1866 in *Le Parnasse Contemporain*, "Les Fenêtres" was composed in 1863 when Mallarmé was living in London. To the extent that the dichotomization of the Real and the Ideal is at the root of the Mallarméan sense of tragedy, we can regard "Les Fenêtres" as opening a window on the work as a whole. Indeed, the window/mirror constellation is one of the most important symbolic constructs in Mallarmé, and the reason for this is that although the Real and the Ideal inhabit different metaphysical realms, they give out onto one another, as it were, and mirror one another, so that our awareness of an essential pathos at the heart of experience consists in our being able to see the one in the other. In a frequently quoted letter of June 1863—one that incidentally marks his growing distance from Baudelaire—Mallarmé writes to Cazalis:

> A modern poet has gone so far as to lament that "Action was not the sister of Dream" [Baudelaire, in "Le Reniement de Saint Pierre"] . . . Dear Lord, if it were otherwise, if the Dream were thus debased and deflowered, where would we retreat to, we unlucky ones whom the earth repels and for whom the Dream alone offers refuge? Henri, my friend, seek your sustenance from the Ideal. Earthly happiness is ignoble—you have to have hands full of calluses if you're to pick it up. Saying "I'm happy!" amounts to saying "I'm a coward"—and more often "I'm a fool." For you have to avoid seeing above that ceiling of happiness the sky of the Ideal, or else you have to close your eyes deliberately. I've written a little poem on this subject which I've called "Les Fenêtres" and I'm sending it to you. (*Selected Letters*, 22)

The metaphor of the world as a hospital, upon which "Les Fenêtres" is structured, is a venerable one. Mallarmé was probably influenced by Sainte-Beuve's "Sonnet, Imitated from Bowles," in which the poet, experiencing a resurgence of hope with the coming of spring, compares himself to a hospital inmate who drags himself out of bed to see the sky. The editors of the Pléiade edition produce an excerpt from the Sainte-Beuve sonnet as well as from the sonnet by William Lisle Bowles that inspired it (see *OC,* 1422). It is interesting that whereas in the poems by Sainte-Beuve and Bowles the comparison is immediately explicit—both begin with an adverb of comparison: *comme* or *as*—in the case of "Les Fenêtres" we are unaware that a comparison is being made until the sixth and seventh stanzas. This is a small detail, perhaps, but one that is illustrative of Mallarmé's often dazzling technique. Thus, the poem divides in two: the first five quatrains immerse us in the experience of a hospital inmate who is seen as representative of the human condition, while the last five quatrains focus on the desire for transcendence of the poet or lyric-I.

The third line of the poem, "Vers le grand crucifix ennuyé du mur vide," presents us with an interesting ambiguity. I have translated it, "Toward the large crucifix bored of the empty wall," but it could also be rendered "bored crucifix on the empty wall." The boredom of the crucifix could be something akin to a pathetic fallacy, underlining a sense of stultification that would apply more properly to humanity, and this would fit with the "horror of the holy oils" of the fourth quatrain. But the crucifix could also be a metonymy for Jesus, or God, who would then be represented as bored with the human race. In other words, the pronominal ambiguity reveals a religious one that can be explored in various ways.

We also see this in the climax, or turning point, of "Les Fenêtres," which is one of the most impassioned moments in all of Mallarmé's poetry, and which occurs in the eighth stanza:

Je me mire et me vois ange! et je meurs, et j'aime
— Que la vitre soit l'art, soit la mysticité —
A renaître, portant mon rêve en diadème,
Au ciel antérieur où fleurit la Beauté!

The first and fourth lines of the stanza are deeply ambiguous, and the ambiguities open up an *aporia* in Mallarmé's thought. With regard to the exclamation in the first half of line 29, the question is whether what is envisioned is an illusion or a truth that cannot normally be seen. Similarly, in line 32, the tense of "fleurit" can be either the *passé simple* or the present (or both); thus, the line can mean either "In the former sky where Beauty *flourished*" or "where Beauty *flourishes*." In both lines the two interpretations are held in balance, and perhaps the ambiguities themselves are what is finally the point, as most critics of Mallarmé would now argue, since everything depends, in any event, on what we mean by the Ideal.

LES FLEURS / THE FLOWERS

Composed at Tournon in 1864, "Les Fleurs" was first published in *Le Parnasse Contemporain* two years later. It was apparently not until after 1894, however, that Mallarmé substituted the phrase "Notre Dame" in line 18 for "Notre Père," a change that alters the meaning of the poem considerably (though critics have not commented on it), since it turns God the Father into God the Mother. The poem appeared with this important revision for the first time in *La Plume* in 1896 (Barbier and Millan, *Œuvres Complètes*, 165).

"Les Fleurs" owes something to Hugo's *La Légende des Siècles* (see *OC*, 1424), but it may be that Mallarmé was also influenced by an English poem, Percy Bysshe Shelley's "Sensitive Plant," which also contains a catalog of flowers. That Mallarmé was deeply influenced by Shelley is unquestionable. In July of 1865, Mallarmé wrote the following to Eugène Lefébure: "I've had a copy of Shelley since my days at College, and consider him one of the greatest poets I know" (*Selected Letters*, 54). In addition to Shelley, Mallarmé would have had the examples of Spenser's "Garden of Adonis" passage in *The Faerie Queene* and of Ovid's catalogs of flowers. Shelley's tendency in "The Sensitive Plant" is Platonic, but Mallarmé adopts a form of Catholic pantheism in which God appears to be consubstantial with the beauty of Nature, and for this reason the substitution of "Notre Dame" for "Notre Père" appears to me to have been always implicit in the poem. Shelley's garden is presided over by a lady who exerts a mystical influence upon the flowers she tends; her sudden death turns the garden into a wasteland, although this transformation is negated by the poem's strange and magnificent conclusion. His Sensitive Plant, which "desires what it has not, the Beautiful" (line 77)—Shelley is paraphrasing the *Symposium* here—is implicitly an avatar of the poet, whereas, at the conclusion of "Les Fleurs," the weary poet whom life enervates, or in Mallarmé's metaphor, *etiolates* ("le poëte las que la vie étiole"), has literally become a Sensitive Plant.

There is a strange ambiguity in the final lines of "Les Fleurs" that hearkens back to Baudelaire and that, as a matter of fact, is once again exploited by Mallarmé in the "Tombeau de Baudelaire" of 1893. The weary poet, "withering on the husk" (in my translation), is presumably nurtured by the Mother he invokes and by the flowers she offers; yet these are fatal flowers that contain a "deadly balsam" ("la balsamique Mort"). The Beauty that nurtures the poet is also what enervates him from the task of participating in ordinary life and what maintains him as an "âme exilée."

RENOUVEAU / RENEWAL

In June 1862 Mallarmé writes to Cazalis: "Emmanuel [Des Essarts] may have told you of a curious sterility that the Spring had installed in me. After three months of impotence, I've at last shaken it off, and my first sonnet is devoted to describing it, by which I mean cursing it" (*Selected Letters,* 11). The sonnet in question, originally entitled "Vere Novo," was first published in 1866 in *Le Parnasse Contemporain.*

According to Mallarmé in "Renouveau," the sap that rises in us at spring saps us of creative energy, engulfing us in yearnings that drive out lucidity. The poem hovers around a constellation of themes that will be with Mallarmé throughout his career. For one thing, the struggle for Beauty produces a relationship to Nature (a word that is rarely to be found in the *Poésies*) that is deeply ambivalent in Mallarmé. Note, for example, that *rêve* appears twice in the sonnet. The poet wanders after a vague and beautiful dream in line 7; but, a mere two lines later, hollows a grave for his dream with his face. Are the two dreams the same or does he face the danger that his own individual dream will be engulfed by the generic dream of springtime? To the extent that Nature, in Mallarmé's thought, stands opposed to the individual or—in a still more advanced formulation of a problem that is at the heart of the Romantic sublime—to the very possibility of meaning itself, it will often be figured as *l'Azur,* the "dividing and indifferent blue" that Wallace Stevens abjures in "Sunday Morning." That

figuration, of course, as well as the concomitant emphasis on *ennui,* is taken over from Baudelaire; but already in this early sonnet there is an *askesis,* a turning away from the merely natural, that is much more radical than anything in Baudelaire and that is at the root of Mallarmé's mature poetic thought.

ANGOISSE / ANGUISH

An irregular sonnet composed at Tournon in 1864, "Angoisse" has a form and rhyme scheme that is partly Shakespearean and partly Petrarchan: two Shakespearean quatrains are followed by two tercets in which the Petrarchan spacing is obviated by a concluding couplet.

The French title word encompasses *anguish, agony, distress,* and *anxiety.* I follow other translators in hewing to the nearest etymological line, but a Freudian reading of "Anxiety" would not be untoward in this case. Interestingly, the poem was initially entitled "A une Putain" ("To a Whore"); it was subsequently retitled "A Celle Qui Est Tranquille" ("To One Who Is Tranquil") when it appeared in *Le Parnasse Contemporain* in 1866, and was given the title "Angoisse" for the edition of the *Poésies* that was published in the *Revue Indépendante* in 1887. The editors of the Pléiade edition suggest that Mallarmé gave the sonnet its final title in an attempt to "de-Baudelairize" it ("débaudelairiser"; *OC,* 1426). For an English-speaking audience, to *de-Baudelairize* in this case could be construed as to *bowdlerize.*

The two earlier titles are interesting above all in terms of the problem of interpretation posed by the sonnet and, connected to this, the problem of relating Mallarmé to Baudelaire. If the prostitute of the initial title is understood literally and concretely as the interlocutor of the poem, the interpretive difficulties might seem to be minimized; and if the interlocutor is a "tranquil one," as with the second title, then this is antithetical to the anguish or anxiety of the final title. The Baudelairean resonances in "Angoisse" have been adumbrated by a number of commentators; Austin Gill, for example, relates the sonnet to no less than four separate poems in the *Fleurs du Mal* (*The Early Mallarmé* 2, 315–321); and Wallace Fowlie, emphasizing the original title, connects it to the lines on prostitution in the "Tombeau de Baudelaire" (*Mallarmé,* 65). The connection between the two poets as presented in a poem such as "Angoisse," however, is by no means easy to parse.

A number of critics have argued that Mallarmé had a Baudelairean obsession with prostitutes as a young man (see *The Early Mallarmé* 2, 320); but whether or not such was the case, the question remains, even with the original title, whether the prostitute addressed is to be taken literally or metaphorically, and with the final title, whether the "beast" of line 1 has some larger allegorical significance. A variety of answers could be supplied. For example, in asking what this beast is, one could say (ironically, with Baudelaire in "Au Lecteur"), "C'est l'Ennui!" But in any event, the beast would be as much a metaphysical quality or propensity within the self as an external object; and hence the anguish or anxiety of the title. My own sense is that the allegorical impulse is always strong in Mallarmé and that it deepens over the years as his aesthetic philosophy solidifies. This would suggest that whatever "de-Baudelairization" might have occurred would have been more a matter of developing an allegorical impulse that is already present in Baudelaire (as in "Au Lecteur," for example) than of playing down the influence of a precursor.

LAS DE L'AMER REPOS / WEARY OF BITTER SLEEP

Composed in 1864 and first published in 1866 in *Le Parnasse Contemporain*, "Las de l'amer repos," though only twenty-eight lines long, is written in alexandrine couplets, the vehicle for all of Mallarmé's longer poems. Its two stanzas of ten and eighteen lines contain several of the long periods for which Mallarmé is noted: the first stanza is one long sentence and the second begins with a ten-line sentence. I have translated the poem into poulter's measure (hexameters on fourteeners), a verse form that was regularly employed during the sixteenth century and has been used only sporadically since then.

The theme of artistic impotence (or what our own vulgar age refers to as "writer's block") is taken up in "Las de l'amer repos," as it is in several of the poems of this period. At the same time, however, the poem seems to contain *in nuce* a theory of poetic creation or originality and a theoretical contrast between occidental and oriental art. The poem begins with a rehearsal of the familiar Romantic notion that poetry is an attempt to recapture a glory that was once experienced innocently and without self-consciousness in childhood. There are three stages to this: the first is childhood innocence, in which glory is experienced as a radiance but is not yet equated with *fame*, since the latter already implies a kind of bad faith. Here we should note that Mallarmé's *gloire* is often deliberately ambiguous and ambivalent: it can mean both *glory* and *glorying* (or boasting); in "Toast Funèbre," for example (line 12), it has both of these meanings, but the second is more dominant. In "Las de l'amer repos" the primary meaning is *glory*, but the implications of *glorying* are also present. The second stage would be when the young poet of genius takes on the mantle of poetry by consciously identifying himself as a poet. There is not yet an "offense" against glory, the glory that was experienced innocently in childhood, and there is even a kind of "artlessness" to the quality of poetic perception at this stage. But the self-consciousness of art and the artistic struggle, at least where the occidental spirit is concerned, eventually breeds in the lyric poet a kind of impotent indolence (or indolent impotence), both because inspiration, though continuing to be a necessary, is no longer a sufficient condition of poetry, and because the self-consciousness necessitated by the insufficiency of inspiration now acts as a barrier against inspiration itself. This third stage can thus produce a consummate artist of the lyric type—a Mallarmé, for instance—but it can also lead to artistic narcissism such as that excoriated by Mallarmé in "Toast Funèbre."

The poet of "Las de l'amer repos" has become a master, a consummate lyric artist; but, as Freud knew so well, there is no human attainment or development of the spirit that does not ultimately take its toll on the spirit, and for the moment he finds himself deeply weary of the "harsh necessity" imposed upon him by his genius. He compares his nightly struggle to prepare a way for inspiration to the hollowing of a pit out of frozen soil by a grave digger. Moreover, in analyzing this necessary struggle against impotence, Mallarmé presents us with a brief allegory of the divided mind of the poet: the analytic self-consciousness that has emerged in order to fill in the lacunae left by an imperfect inspiration then becomes the enemy of inspiration, so that the "enormous burial ground," "frightened" of the roses of inspiration that "visit" it from time to time, works of its own accord to fill in the empty holes that have been hollowed by the grave digger in which the roses might take root.

This rather lugubrious process is comprehended in the second stanza as a consequence of the occidental spirit: the "ravenous Art of cruel lands." Thus, the poet expresses a desire to "bid goodbye" to the occidental past, to his own genius—that is, to the struggle for originality and perfection that are at once the glory and the pathology of our tradition—in short, to his "agony." He pictures to himself his own artistic antitype: a Chinese sage whose relationship to art is entirely serene and whose serenity results from the cultivation of a technique that is free not only of self-aggrandizement but of any tinge of selfhood, an artist whose technique seems an objective manifestation of the oriental acceptance of death. In the magnificent concluding lines to the poem, Mallarmé—by a grammatical shift from the subjunctive to the present—*becomes* that artist/sage, disappearing into the landscape of his own description.

LE SONNEUR / THE BELL-RINGER

"Le Sonneur," an irregular sonnet in that its octave employs alternating rhymes like the Shakespearean form but only two rhymes like the Petrarchan, was published in an early form in *L'Artiste* in 1862, and subsequently, in a thoroughly revised version, in *Le Parnasse Contemporain* in 1866. The fact that "Le Sonneur" was originally submitted to *L'Artiste* only confirms what seems clear from the sonnet itself: that it is an allegory of the poet's transcendental strivings.

The task of the poet is to "sound the Ideal" ("sonner l'Idéal"), but the poet inhabits the world below (the *Ici-bas* of "Les Fenêtres"), and the only passageway between that world and the realm of the Ideal is desire. Hence the deep-seated frustration of the poet, a frustration that has been misunderstood and hence misinterpreted from a psychoanalytic perspective—by Mauron, Sartre, and others—as peculiar to Mallarmé the man. It is not specific to Mallarmé *the man*; it is an ontological predicate of human existence that Mallarmé experienced with extraordinary depth and lucidity because of the kind of artist he was. Plato in the *Symposium*—as rendered by Shelley in "The Sensitive Plant" in a passage that we have already quoted in conjunction with "Les Fleurs"—understood that the lover "desires what [he] has not, the Beautiful." Artistic impotence can be neurotic, of course, but the more uncompromising the artistic quest for the absolute, the greater the technical difficulties of composition. Mallarmé's frustration with poetic impotence is tied to his astonishing poetic technique.

Mallarmé deliberately renders the dichotomy between the Real and the Ideal as starkly as possible, not only in "Le Sonneur" but in several of the other early poems. Thus, in "Le Sonneur," the poet is likened to a kind of Quasimodo, a pathetically grotesque figure who, if not entirely deaf, is able to hear the bells he rings only as the "tinkling of a far-off chime" ("un tintement lointain"), just as in "Les Fenêtres" he is likened to a man dying in a hospital. Austin Gill notes that the rhetorical shape of both poems is that of the extended simile, and that this is also the case in Baudelaire's "L'Albatros" (*The Early Mallarmé* 2, 331–332). But whereas Baudelaire's simile in "L'Albatros" suggests that the poet's "wings" make him unfit for any earthly activity, Mallarmé writes from the perspective of one who is earthbound. In "Les Fenêtres" the man who sees himself as an angel knows that he would have to break the crystal and fall through eternity in order to grasp hold of that image; in "Le Sonneur" the impossibility of "sounding the Ideal" has a similar suicidal denouement. The paradox of language, however, of the poetic art, is that somehow the Ideal *is* sounded, albeit by negation, through a statement of its impossibility. Years later, in the *tombeaux* for Baudelaire, Théophile Gautier, and Edgar Allan Poe, Mallarmé will register the same tragic dualism. It is only after death, when the poet becomes one with his poetry, that the split between life and art, the Real and the Ideal, is finally healed.

TRISTESSE D'ÉTÉ / SUMMER SADNESS

The earliest version of "Tristesse d'Été" was composed in 1862, not 1864 as was formerly believed. This would make it contemporaneous with "Renouveau," its companion piece as an expression of seasonal *spleen*. The woman in the sonnet may possibly be Marie Gerhard, whom Mallarmé was courting at this time and who later became his wife. Marie's hair was blonde, however, and in the 1862 version of the sonnet, as well as a version published four years later in *Le Parnasse Contemporain*, the second line reads: "A chauffé comme un bain tes cheveux ténébreux" ("has warmed your dark [or possibly "mysterious"] hair like a bath").

But whether Mallarmé depersonalized the image in his final revision of the poem, or whether the lapse of time enabled him to allow a personal association (one that he had previously obscured) to stand, the golden hair rising like a cloud is one of the central erotic symbols of the *Poésies*. Another, albeit less prominent, symbol is the *fard* (or paint) wept from the lady's eyelids in the final tercet; we have already encountered it in "Le Pitre Châtié" (where its removal did not release the clown from his mask but instead divested him of his sanctity), and we shall soon encounter it again in "L'Azur." The two symbols taken together indicate that sexuality stands in relation to the problem of identity in the sonnet, and that both of these themes are in turn implicated in the religious crisis that is condensed in two other central Mallarméan conceptions: "le Néant" ("Nothingness" or "the Void") and "l'Azur" ("the Azure"—Mallarmé's standard metonymy for the indifference of the heavens).

The sexual ambivalence of both the poet and the woman in "Tristesse d'Été" (a *lutteuse*, she has been wrestling both with and against him) is fraught with the saddened awareness that, because of the individual soul, the merging of bodies is always only partial and temporary. But what is the soul? On the one hand, from the standpoint of "le Néant," it, too, is a nothingness, a mere obsession that stands in the way of the instinctual life. But on the other hand, to what could the drowning of the soul—that is, the shedding of human identity—lead? Perhaps to nothing more than "the indifference of the azure and of stone."

L'AZUR / THE AZURE

"L'Azur," composed in 1864 and first published in *Le Parnasse Contemporain* in 1866, is the only poem in the *Poésies* for which Mallarmé himself provided a written commentary. In a letter to Cazalis that was probably composed in March 1864, he writes as follows:

> I send you at last this poem of *The Azure*, which you seemed so desirous of possessing. I have worked on it for the last several days, and I won't hide from you that it has given me an infinite amount of pain ["infiniment de mal": "mal" can mean both "pain" and "trouble" here, and probably has both meanings at once]—over

and above the fact that before taking up my pen it was necessary, in order to achieve a moment of perfect lucidity, to overcome my harrowing sense of impotence. It has given me a great deal of trouble ["mal"]because, banishing a thousand lyric graces and fine verses that incessantly haunted my brain, I wanted to remain implacably within my subject. I assure you that it doesn't contain a single word that has not cost me several hours of searching, and that the first word, which adorns the first idea, besides conveying the general *effect* of the poem, serves to prepare for the last word.

> That the effect should be produced, without any distracting dissonances or flourishes, even adorable ones—that's what I'm looking for. And I'm certain, having read these verses to myself perhaps two hundred times, that it has been achieved. It now remains to consider the effect from the other side, that of aesthetics. Is it beautiful? Does it contain a reflection of Beauty? . . . In any case, as I progress, I shall continue to be faithful to those austere ideas that my great teacher Edgar Poe has left me as a legacy. (*Correspondance de Stéphane Mallarmé* 1,103–104; translation mine)

As Mondor and Richard note, in this passage Mallarmé has in mind Poe's *Philosophy of Composition*, translated by Baudelaire in 1853, in which Poe had described, disingenuously as it turns out, the originating circumstances behind "The Raven" (see *Correspondance de Stéphane Mallarmé* 1, 104n). In the remainder of the letter Mallarmé discusses several stanzas of the poem, and it is clear from his discussion that he conceives of it as an allegory, or in the phrase of Adile Ayda, an interior drama (see *Le Drame Intérieur de Mallarmé*) in which the lyric-I has both a personal and a universal significance. He concludes his discussion with several fascinating sentences that suggest that the drama unfolded in the poem is mirrored by a compositional drama through which it was conceived:

> I want to flee once more, but sense my error and acknowledge that *I am haunted*. This entire poignant revelation was necessary in order to motivate the sincere and bizarre cry of the conclusion: "l'Azur"... You can see that for those who ... seek in a poem something more than the music of verses, there is a real drama. And it has been a terrible difficulty for me to combine, in an authentic harmony ["dans une juste harmonie"] the dramatic element hostile to the idea of a pure and subjective poetry with the serene and calm lines necessary to Beauty. (*Correspondance de Stéphane Mallarmé* 1, 105; translation mine)

The Azure is, of course, one of the most important symbols in Mallarmé's poetry; we have already encountered it in "Le Guignon," in "Renouveau," and elsewhere. But there is a sense in which the very word itself contains an allegory of the spiritual crisis it symbolizes (should one capitalize "azure" or not? Mallarmé is himself inconsistent in his practice). This is to say that the word, *Azure*, is a metonymy that swerves away from *Ciel*, which in French means both sky and heaven. The inability of the French language to say sky without simultaneously saying heaven is precisely what motivates—indeed, necessitates—the use of the term *Azure*, first in earlier poets such as Hugo and Baudelaire, and then, more self-consciously, in Mallarmé himself. Thus, the Azure as a symbol is, for Mallarmé, a way of avoiding religious assumptions that can no longer be assumed and, simultaneously, of concretizing the void that has interpolated itself in the space formerly occupied by those assumptions. The Azure, then, represents an absolute that is simultaneously perfection and noth-ingness—a perfection for which the poet strives in vain, a nothingness against which he beats his fists in impotent frustration.

The doubleness of the symbol leads eventually to the turning point of the poem, "Le Ciel est mort," a turning point that occurs in the sixth stanza and that coincides with the utterance of the very term from which the poet had initially swerved in producing the symbol of the *Azure*. We can read the sudden violence of this utterance in two ways: as the outcome of the symbolic attempts, delineated in the previous stanzas, to block or smother the Azure, or, alternately, as a consequence of the intuition that initiated those symbolic attempts. In one sense the poet wants to obliterate the *Ciel* (the Sky/Heaven), but, in another, it is the fact that the *Ciel* is already dead that makes him want to obliterate it. In either case the attempt is in vain because the *Azure* is felt to be present even when it is not seen. By the same token, in the following stanza, even though the poet feels himself to be as empty of poetry as a rouge pot at the base of a wall (or dressing stand in my substitute image—and we have previously encountered "fard" as a symbol for art or artifice in "Le Pitre Châtié" and "Tristesse d'Été"), he continues to be haunted by poetry. "Such is that haunting obsession with the Azure," writes Jean-Pierre Richard,

> that causes Mallarmé to cry out at the end of his famous poem: the forbidden transcendence has at this point come to haunt, that is, to occupy negatively, our soul, to paralyze our slightest attempts at autonomy. The forbidden plenitude now takes the form of a palpable void that ends by destroying, through the very impossibility of its name, every human gesture, every earthly solution. (*L'Univers Imaginaire de Mallarmé*, 56; translation mine)

BRISE MARINE / SEA BREEZE

In "Brise Marine," which was composed in 1865 and first published in *Le Parnasse Contemporain* in 1866, the poet manages to contain many of the characteristic symbols and motifs that are disseminated throughout his poetry. On the one hand, in expressing the theme of flight to a distant, exotic landscape, "Brise Marine" recapitulates the Baudelairean tendency of many of the earlier poems in the *Poésies*; but on the other hand, it looks forward to a more rigorous application of symbolism that will shortly coalesce in *Hérodiade*. Michaud says of "Brise Marine" that it is "a last echo of Baudelairean escape. . . . It was a farewell to [Mallarmé's] childhood dreams. . . . He scarcely heard the call of the sea again until the end of his life, when, in a tragic decor of storms and shipwreck, he wrote 'Un Coup de Dés'" (*Mallarmé*, 37). Indeed, the poem has often been linked to Baudelaire's sonnet "Parfum Exotique," which ends with the phrase "chant des mariniers," just as "Brise Marine" ends with the "chant des matelots." However, overt resemblances often camouflage subtle but important differences where the influence of Baudelaire on Mallarmé is concerned, and in this particular case the relationship of the two poets to the nature of *fantasy* is very different: in the Baudelaire sonnet, what is evoked is a landscape that is the concretization of desire; in "Brise Marine," that landscape is immediately comprehended as nonexistent ("Perdus, san mâts, sans mâts, ni fertiles îlots" / "No fertile isle, no spar on which to cling"), or rather, as existing only in poetry, in relation to the Ideal. Hence, in "Brise Marine," as earlier in "Les Fenêtres," the shipwreck of the Ideal on the shoals of actuality has what would otherwise appear to be suicidal implications, were it not for the space that is thereby opened up for poetry.

The ennui of the famous opening line, an ennui that can only be experienced by the literary man who is drowning in ink and suffocating from the dust of books (my translation gives a rather postmodern or poststructuralist slant to this predicament), will be echoed more than twenty years later by the sonnet with which Mallarmé chose to conclude the *Poésies*, "Mes bouquins refermés sur le nom de Paphos," where there is a less tormented, but equally romantic, conjunction of literature and the exotic. Mallarmé wrote "Brise Marine" shortly after the birth of his daughter, Geneviève, and it may be, as Robert Cohn suggests, that the old frustration with literature is amplified by a "desire to flee from bourgeois domesticity" (*Toward the Poems of Mallarmé*, 288). Cohn adds that "unlike his friend Gauguin, of whom he would say later, 'On n'a pas le droit d'abandonner ses enfants même pour fonder une religion,'" Mallarmé confined himself to dreaming (288). Indeed, Mallarmé's refusal to confuse the dream with reality is rigorously maintained throughout his work, as in "Toast Funèbre," where the poet is entrusted, paradoxically, with the task of standing guard against the dream itself.

The symbolic constellation associated with *whiteness*, which will figure so prominently in the later work, seems to emerge spontaneously and of its own accord in "Brise Marine," as if the symbol entered Mallarmé's work before its precise location in the symbolic lexicon of that work had become clear. This becomes apparent in a comparison of "Brise Marine" to "Don du Poëme," the sonnet written only a few months later that is the gateway to *Hérodiade*. Frank Lestringant has traced the phrase "que la blancheur défend" in "Brise Marine" (literally, "which defends itself by its own whiteness") first to Victor Hugo's poem "Les Contemplations," where it is associated with the image of the Virgin and Child, and then to "Don du Poëme" (see "Rémanence du Blanc," 64–74). The young mother suckling her child is figured in both poems against an exotic landscape, and in both poems the symbol of the lamp appears. In "Brise Marine," however, whiteness—together with its affines: purity, the void, and so forth—is unconnected to the mother-and-child motif; it is evoked primarily in relation to the empty paper that the poet wishes to flee and secondarily in relation to the fluttering handkerchief ("l'adieu suprême des mouchoirs"), where it echoes the conclusion to "La Pipe," a prose-poem that was also written in 1865. In "Don du Poëme" whiteness is self-consciously grasped as a symbol that reverberates in many directions at once: the "sibylline whiteness" of the mother's milk is proleptic of the figure of Hérodiade and of the poem that bears her name. What this comparison suggests is that "Brise Marine" is a transitional poem in Mallarmé's œuvre, in which images that have emerged unconsciously and, as it were, accidentally (through the birth of his daughter, Geneviève, for example) contain the seeds of a more rigorously ordained Symbolist method that will seek to ban all mere contingencies.

SOUPIR / SIGH

In the simile framing the ten exquisite lines of "Soupir," which was written in 1864 and first published in *Le Parnasse Contemporain* in 1866, just as the poet's soul ascends toward the "angelic eye's wandering heaven" of the woman being addressed, so a fountain rises toward the tender skies ("l'Azur attendri"—"compassionate" in this translation) of October. The religious analogy, by which a human relation is brought into alignment with Nature, is possible because the sky of "Soupir"—unlike that of "L'Azur," to take the most extreme counterexample—is humanized by a feminine presence who softens the poet's struggle with the Absolute. The "sœur" of "Soupir," however we ultimately come to understand her, is thus cognate with the saints, angels, and fairies that figure in such other poems as "Apparition," "Les Fleurs," and "Sainte."

In Charles Mauron's reading of the poem "sœur" is as much literal as metaphorical, in that it ultimately derives from the poet's loss of his sister, Maria (*Introduction to the Psychoanalysis of Mallarmé*, 100–109 passim). One advantage of this interpretation, however reductionary it may seem in other respects, is that it enables the critic to connect "Soupir" with "Plainte d'Automne," a prose poem written in 1864 or earlier, in which Maria is mentioned directly. "Since Maria left me," writes Mallarmé in "Plainte," "I have loved, strangely and especially, all that can be summed up in the word *fall* ['chute']. Thus, during the year my favorite season is the last, languid stretch of summer immediately before autumn." In "Soupir" the rising arc of the opening lines gives way to a drawn-out fall; the poem is itself a sigh, its syntax balanced in the shifts and modulations of a single sentence. Not surprisingly, "Soupir" was set to music by both Claude Debussy and Maurice Ravel; it is included in Debussy's *Trois Poëmes de Stéphane Mallarmé* of 1913 and in Ravel's *Trois Poëmes*, also of that year.

The "sœur" of "Soupir" is a chaste (and chastening) figure, but she is also an erotic presence, and even if Mallarmé's use of the term derives in part from the loss of his sister, he is obviously availing himself of an old metaphor (often used by Baudelaire), the implications of which are akin to the Jungian anima. "Sœur" will again figure in "Prose (pour des Esseintes)" and, in an especially erotic context, in a late sonnet addressed to Méry Laurent: "O si chère de loin et proche et blanche." In the latter poem the poet "rejoices in [no word] but the whisper of *sister*," which thus takes on the overtones of the drawn-out sigh of "Soupir." It is interesting, nevertheless—to give Mauron's biographical reading its due—that three of the most prominent women in Mallarmé's life had the same name: his sister Maria, his wife Marie Gerhard, and his friend Méry Laurent—not to mention the Mater Creatrix of "Les Fleurs."

AUMÔNE / ALMS

"Aumône," which like "Le Guignon" is in terza rima, was probably begun in 1862, around the same time as "Le Guignon," if the two poems did not originally stem from the same compositional source. In any event, "Aumône" was heavily reworked before receiving its final form and its final title in 1887. Earlier versions, of 1864 and 1866, were entitled "A un Mendiant" and "A un Pauvre," respectively. A manuscript dated 1862 and ambiguously titled "Haine du Pauvre" ("Hatred of the Poor Man") has often been taken to be the first version of "Aumône," since its discovery by Mallarmé's son-in-law, Dr. Edmond Bonniot (see *OC,* 1434); as Austin Gill has argued, however, the text of "Haine du Pauvre" is different enough from "Aumône" to make this assumption questionable (*The Early Mallarmé* 2, 216–226).

The first tercet of the poem exemplifies Mallarmé's distinctive wordplay and use of metaphor—and also, incidentally, the problematics of translation. First, the phrase "en égoutter" can refer either to "sac" or

to "tétine"; "égoutter" means "to drain" or "to drip," but the verb is sufficiently close to "goûter," "to taste," to carry the associations of that verb as well; "égoutter" is a metaphor of the first order in relation to "tétine" but of the second order in relation to "sac." Secondly, although "glas" means "death knell" or "passing bell," to Mallarmé, the author of *Les Mots Anglais,* it may have carried an undertone (or overtone) of "glass," and hence of "hourglass"; in any event, it does so for the present reader. I have translated "égoutter" as "strain" because the presence of "death knell" in the line allows the verb to take on a double meaning. But it seems to me that the line might just as well be translated "In order to drain your hourglass coin by coin," in which case, the English aural association would be foregrounded and the idea of death would be implicit.

The connection between "Aumône" and "Le Guignon" is heightened by phrases and rhymes that the two poems share in common. The "bizarre"/ "fanfare" rhyme in the second tercet of "Aumône" appears also in the twelfth tercet of "Le Guignon"; similarly, the "old god" ("vieux dieu") of the sixth tercet of "Aumône" echoes the "outworn heroes" ("héros excédés") of the twenty-first tercet of "Le Guignon."

DON DU POËME / GIFT OF THE POEM

As Michael Riffaterre observes, "Don du Poëme," which has already been briefly discussed in relation to "Brise Marine," functions as a kind of dedicatory epistle to *Hérodiade,* the major poetic project on which Mallarmé labored from his early twenties until his death (*The Semiotics of Poetry*, 150–163). Written in 1865 but not published until 1883 when Verlaine included it in *Les Poëtes Maudits,* the sonnet commemorates two births: that of Hérodiade ("l'enfant d'Idumée" of line 1 refers both to the character herself and to the poem composed about her) and that of his daughter, Geneviève (in November 1864). It employs a pattern of imagery (wing, palm, stringed instrument) that can also be found in "Sainte" and in "Le Démon de l'Analogie," a prose-poem that seems to have been composed around the same time (see Mauron, *Introduction to the Psychoanalysis of Mallarmé*, 49; Michaud, *Mallarmé*, 41). At the same time, the sonnet echoes a line from Virgil's *Georgics*: "Primus Idumaeas referam tibi, o Mantua, palmas" / "I shall be the first, O Mantua, to bring thee back Idumaean palms" (8.12).

Mary Ellen Wolf, in her study of *Hérodiade*, refers to the legend involving the kings of Edom, according to which Edom was "a mythical country that preceded Adam and the creation of women. The kings of Edom were sexless individuals who gave birth to monsters" (*Eros under Glass*, 2). The root meaning of "monster" is "something unnatural," and if the poet gives birth, it can only be, in the manner of the kings of Edom, by a process of parthenogenesis and thus to something that goes beyond Nature and that is even potentially *horrible* ("horrible naissance"; I have substituted "monster" in this translation). In some sense, then, Hérodiade herself will be a symbol of the Absolute, of the desire to penetrate beyond Nature to the Absolute; at the same time she expresses that desire and is a concrete expression of it.

Mallarmé's ambivalent relationship to *Hérodiade*, his creation of the night, manifests itself as a desire to bring that which has been separated from Nature back into alignment with Nature, so as to succor it and give it life. Thus, in "Don du Poëme" images of sterility are juxtaposed against images of fertility. The child of an Idumaean night, who is herself the poem, having been conceived through a struggle with impotence and sterility (the sexual overtones are certainly relevant, but they should be taken thematically rather than biographically, in my view), is therefore consonant also with nothingness: thus, paradoxically, not to give birth to her is to give birth to nothing, but also to give birth to her is to give birth to nothing. Since nothing will come of nothing, she is given a further metaphorical elaboration as a bird with bloodless and featherless wing. (In the final stanza of "Les Fenêtres," the poet spoke of taking flight "with my two featherless wings" in order to "burst the crystal that the monster has profaned": the terms of the equation remain constant, but their metaphysical alignment has been shifted.)

Against this backdrop of ambivalence and even antipathy, however, there is a sudden and inexplicable intervention of inspiration through the mediation of the Dawn, an intervention that has the symbolic effect of transforming the Idumaean desert to an oasis of palms. The transformation that occurs in the sonnet recalls similar transformations in English Romantic poems, such as Keats's "Ode to a Nightingale"; indeed, Mallarmé's interrogation of the relationship of Poetry to Nature, his ambivalence about the "unnaturalness" of Poetry, and his subsequent attempt to bring Poetry back into harmony with Nature, are all deeply Keatsian, I would argue, in their orientation if not origin. In the clear light of day, the natural image of mother and child takes on a quality of innocence and even sacredness that the poet seems literally to want to imbibe, as if to ensure, or justify, the existence of his own creation and his own creativity; the woman's voice, "recalling viol and harpsichord," reminds us also of Mallarmé's "Sainte," and in that angelic image the orders of Poetry and Nature are harmonized with each other in terms of the sacred. Thus, in the epiphanic moment that occurs with the sudden intervention of Dawn, the poet's lamp itself becomes "angelic," much as, in the moment of crisis in "Les Fenêtres," he suddenly sees himself as an angel ("Je me mire et me vois ange!").

The "faded finger" ("doigt fané") of line 12 and the adjective "sibylline" of line 13 will seem not only obscure but strangely out of context until we realize that the young mother nursing her infant daughter is simultaneously, through a Mallarméan transformation, the old nurse of the "Ouverture Ancienne" and of the "Scène," the first two sections of *Hérodiade*. This becomes clear when we connect these ideas in "Don du Poëme" to a complementary passage in the "Ouverture Ancienne," in which "prophetesses" ("sibylles") are described as "offering Magi withered fingers" ("offrant leur ongle vieil aux Mages"—line 25). In "Don du Poëme," as we have seen, there is a desire to link the prophetic moment that gives birth to or nurses the poem to the natural world itself; this linkage is much more tenuous in the "Ouverture Ancienne" and in the "Scène," but it is not entirely erased. The problem, however, is that despite his attempt to harmonize the orders of Poetry and Nature in terms of each other, the poet must perforce remain a "beggar of azure" ("Le Guignon"— line 3), hungering for an Absolute that is grounded in nothing. That the azure is described as "virginal" connects it to the princess Hérodiade herself, who, as we noted earlier, both expresses the desire for the Absolute and is an expression of that desire. Hence the ambiguity of the sonnet's final line, in which the lips are starved simultaneously *for* and *from* the air of the virginal azure.

AUTRES POËMES / OTHER POEMS

HÉRODIADE

Mallarmé began *Hérodiade* in 1864 at the age of twenty-two and continued working on it throughout his life. That the poem remained unfinished at his death is a testament to the struggle for purity and perfection that is one of its themes, and also to Valéry's melancholy dictum that a poem is never completed but only abandoned. Of the three sections of *Hérodiade* that have traditionally been included in editions of Mallarmé's *Poésies* since 1898, only the second, the "Scène," was published during the poet's lifetime. The "Ouverture Ancienne" and the "Cantique de Saint Jean," the two other sections, present themselves as finished pieces and contain poetry of the highest quality, but it is unclear what their ultimate disposition in the completed work would have been, or whether indeed they would have been included at all. In a letter of April 1866, Mallarmé writes to Cazalis: "I've written the musical overture, which is still almost completely in draft stage, but I can say in all modesty that it will create an unparalleled effect and that in comparison with these lines, the dramatic scene you know is like a mere vulgar scrawl compared with a canvas by Leonardo da Vinci" (*Correspondance de Stéphane Mallarmé* 1, 207; *Selected Letters*, 59–60). Later, however, he may have decided to substitute a "Prélude" for the "Ouverture Ancienne." Fragmentary drafts of this "Prélude," as well as a "Scène Intermédiaire" and a "Finale," exist in manuscript and have been analyzed by Gardner Davies in *Les Noces d'Hérodiade, Mystère* (1959), which is the title that Mallarmé seems to have been working with at the end. The three sections of *Hérodiade* that are included in the standard Pléiade edition constitute a kind of triptych and can be read (and translated) as a completed work; they are included in the present translation for that reason. The "Ouverture Ancienne" is spoken by the Nurse, the "Scène" is a Racinian dialogue between the Nurse and Hérodiade, and the concluding "Cantique de Saint Jean" is spoken by the saint himself.

The germination and early composition of *Hérodiade* coincides with the religious crisis (to which we have referred in the Introduction) that the poem itself dramatizes and with the development of aesthetic principles that we now associate with Mallarmé and with the Symbolist Movement in general. Mallarmé's letters during this period resemble no one's so much as Keats's, and make for equally exciting reading; for like Keats at the time the great odes were written, Mallarmé was distilling a philosophy of poetic composition directly from his work on *Hérodiade* in the middle 1860s. Thus, in the famous letter to Cazalis of October 1864, in which he refers to the poem for the first time, he writes:

> I have finally begun my *Hérodiade*. With terror, for I am inventing a language which must necessarily spring from a very new poetics, which I could define in these few words: *To paint, not the thing itself, but the effect it produces.* On this principle, verse should be composed not out of words but out of intentions, and every utterance should be effaced before its corresponding sensation. I don't know if you can divine my meaning, but I hope that you will approve it when I have succeeded. For I *want*—for the first time in my life—to succeed. I would never put pen to paper again if I failed. (*Correspondance de Stéphane Mallarmé* 1, 137; translation mine)

Because words have meanings, poetry must always have a content; but on the principles enunciated above, poetic content becomes a pretext for its own transcendence. This is made clear in a letter to Villiers de L'Isle-Adam of December 1865. "In a word," writes Mallarmé, "the subject of my work [he is referring both to *Hérodiade* and to his poetry in general] is Beauty and its ostensible subject is merely a pretext for approaching Beauty [Elle]" (*Selected Letters*, 58). The capitalized pronoun, "Elle," in this passage, emphasizes the identification of Mallarmé's heroine not only with the poem she names but also with Poetry itself, and indeed with Beauty.

The "ostensible subject" of the poem—the biblical story of Herodias, Salomé, and John the Baptist (Mallarmé seems to have collapsed Herodias and her daughter Salomé into one figure: he gives Hérodiade a father but no mother)—is merely a pretext for the real subject of the poem, Beauty. We can go further than this. The ostensible subject of the poem and its real subject are, in the case of *Hérodiade*, incommensurate with each other and even in contradiction with each other. Indeed, this contradiction was precisely what Mallarmé was aiming for in the poem, and this means that the ostensible subject of the poem was arrived at not in spite of the contradiction with its real subject but because of that contradiction. F. C. St. Aubyn reminds us of the many representations of the story in the art and literature of the period (see *Stéphane Mallarmé*, 38–41), and certainly, the Romantic-decadent overtones of the Salomé story made it a subject ready-to-hand. But for Mallarmé, in contrast to many of his contemporaries who revelled in the sadistic overtones of the story, what the "ostensible subject" provided was a vehicle for its own transcendence, and this means that the poem is ultimately an allegory of the poetic process itself.

The paradox of *Hérodiade* is that Mallarmé has chosen a subject deeply embedded in history precisely in order to overcome history, and hence to overcome language and "the subject" itself. This is made clear in his letter to Eugène Lefébure of February 1865:

> The most beautiful page of my work will be that which contains only this divine name *Hérodiade*. The little inspiration I have had, I owe to this name, and I believe that if my heroine had been called Salomé, I would have invented this word that is as dark and red as an open pomegranate: *Hérodiade*. For the rest, my intent is to create a being purely dreamt and absolutely independent of history. You understand me. I am not even invoking the paintings of the students of da Vinci and of all those Florentines who have had the same mistress and have named her as I do. (*Correspondance de Stéphane Mallarmé* 1,154; translation mine)

As Robert Cohn notes, the tonal associations of "Hérodiade" include *héros*, *Éros*, and *rose* (*Toward the Poems of Mallarmé*, 53), and this is perhaps why the name can serve Mallarmé as a metonym for Beauty. It originally appears in "Les Fleurs" as a species of rose ("And, like the flesh of woman, the cruel rose, / Hérodiade blooming in the garden light, / She that from wild and radiant blood arose!"—literally: "She that a wild and radiant blood waters" ["Et, pareille à la chair de la femme, la rose / Cruelle, Hérodiade en fleur du jardin clair, / Celle qu'un sang farouche et radieux arrose!"]). Perhaps we can say, therefore, that *Hérodiade*, Mallarmé's strange allegorical creation, on which he was to labor for more than thirty years, constitutes his "Romance of the Rose." It is interesting that Mallarmé associates the name "Hérodiade" with a pomegranate because of the famous passage in "L'Après-midi d'un Faune" in which the pomegranate appears as a figure of desire: "You know, my passion, that, crimson with ripe seeds, / Pomegranates burst in a murmur of bees; /

And that our blood, seized by each passing form, / Flows toward desire's everlasting swarm" ("Tu sais, ma passion, que, pourpre et déjà mûre, / Chaque grenade éclate et d'abeilles murmure; / Et notre sang, épris de qui le va saisir, / Coule pour tout l'essaim éternel du désir"). "Underneath all this related imagery," Cohn observes, "is the secret connection between sexual consummation and blood sacrifice" (53), and on the representational level there is certainly a sense in which this is so. But Hérodiade's desire for purity, her rejection of life—which, as Michaud maintains, makes her the perfect symbol of Mallarmé's poetry (*Mallarmé*, 33)—is tantamount to the poem's attempt to transcend the representational level through a process of distillation that aims at essentializing the rose itself, until all that is left is a name.

At the same time, however, *Hérodiade* is a poem that remains deeply enmeshed in history. This is true on a number of levels. First of all, it could be argued that the attempt on the part of a poet such as Mallarmé to transcend history is itself constitutive of a particular historical milieu, and this is essentially the argument that Sartre puts forward in his revealing though ultimately reductionary study of Mallarmé, *The Poet of Nothingness*. But more importantly, at the same time that it aims at the transcendence of history, *Hérodiade* contains within itself a historical vision that verges on the apocalyptic and that points ambiguously to the transformation of one historical epoch into another. This is where the salience of the biblical story line comes into play. At the end of the "Scène," for example, Hérodiade is left waiting for "une chose inconnue," and clearly this has something to do with her fatal meeting with John the Baptist. But, as always, the poet's meaning remains shrouded in mystery. Although the text evokes the coming of Christianity on the level of drama or plot, could it be that it points to something else entirely—indeed, to something entirely opposite? Or, to frame the question more explicitly: "And what rough beast, its hour come round at last, / Slouches toward Bethlehem to be born?"

I. OVERTURE ANCIENNE D'HÉRODIADE / ANCIENT OVERTURE OF HÉRODIADE

As Jean-Pierre Richard emphasizes (see *L'Univers Imaginaire de Mallarmé*, 70–72), the radical leap that Mallarmé took in the "Ouverture" coincides with and should be seen in terms of the spiritual crisis of 1866. Indeed, Mallarmé's most succinct account of that crisis is contained in the same letter to Cazalis in which he tells of having written the "musical overture" to *Hérodiade*:

> Unfortunately, in the course of quarrying out the lines to this extent, I've come across two abysses, which fill me with despair. One is the Void ["le Néant"], which I've reached without any knowledge of Buddhism, and I'm still too distraught to be able to believe even in my poetry and get back to work, which this crushing awareness ["pensée"] has made me abandon.
>
> Yes, I *know*, we are merely empty forms of matter, but we are indeed sublime in having invented God and our soul. So sublime, my friend, that I want to gaze upon matter, fully conscious that it exists, and yet launching itself madly into Dream, despite its knowledge that Dream has no existence, extolling the Soul and all the divine impressions of that kind which have collected within us from the beginning of time and proclaiming, in the face of the Void which is truth, these glorious lies! ["mensonges"]. (*Selected Letters*, 60)

The syntactical complexity of the last sentence is akin to what we begin to find in the "Ouverture Ancienne." In that sentence, empty matter, hurling itself into the Dream, sings praises of a nonexistent soul, which in turn proclaims the "glorious lies" it has woven around itself. The Real and the Ideal comprehend each other as in a mirror.

Mallarmé composed the "Ouverture Ancienne" mainly during the period from 1865 to 1866, but the poem never appeared in print during his lifetime and he may have continued to work on it in later years. The manuscript, which is housed in the Collection Mme. Edmond Bonniot in the Bibliothèque Littéraire Jacques Doucet in Paris, contains many variants, and since Mallarmé never authorized its publication, we are not in possession of anything even approaching a definitive text. The poem appeared for the first time in 1926, in the *Nouvelle Revue Française*, as edited by Edmond Bonniot. It has been included in all subsequent editions of the *Poésies*, including the standard Pléiade editions of 1945 and 1951. There are discrepancies between the Bonniot and Pléiade versions, however, and, as Gardner Davie's editing of the *Hérodiade* manuscripts has shown (see *Les Noces d'Hérodiade, Mystère* [1959]), the Pléiade text of the "Ouverture" contains a number of inaccuracies. A definitive text of the poem will probably continue to elude scholars because, as the manuscript shows, in certain lines of the poem Mallarmé was hesitating between variants (see *Les Noces d'Hérodiade,* 143–164); moreover, even if this were not the case, the poet may very well have returned to older solutions or may have arrived at entirely new ones if he had actually prepared the work for publication. The version of the "Ouverture" that is included by Mallarmé's most recent editors, Carl Paul Barbier and Charles Gordon Millan, in their critical edition of the

Poésies (*Œuvres Complètes,* 1983), was prepared on the basis of what seem to have been Mallarmé's latest emendations, but, in several cases at least, this version strikes me as poetically inferior to the Pléiade text. In preparing the French text of the "Ouverture," I have consulted all of the sources mentioned above and have made extensive use of Professor Davies's work to correct the Pléiade edition.

An incantation is the chanting of a magical spell or formula for the purpose of evoking something, and in the nurse's incantation it is Hérodiade herself who is being evoked. On the dramatic level, she has fled from her bed, but the opening word of the poem, "abolie," which is repeated in the second line, suggests that what she represents has been abolished or nullified and therefore requires to be evoked by the incantation of poetry. The metaphorical connection between poetry and magic occurs several times in the *Poésies,* most notably, in "Prose," where the "grimoire" (grammary of magic spells) appears in line 3, just as it does in line 61 of the "Ouverture." "Abolie" occurs in the same sentence as "tour," and this conjunction reminds us of one of the most famous lines in French poetry, "Le Prince d'Aquitaine à la tour abolie," from Gérard de Nerval's sonnet, "El Desdichado."

What is being both evoked and invoked in the opening lines of the "Ouverture" is a lost beauty that, on one level, existed in the past but, on another, never existed and could never exist, corresponding as it does to the Ideal. This conception of beauty is evoked metaphorically—but ambiguously and ambivalently—as a Dawn whose winglike rays are mirrored in a pool of water. The capitalized Dawn (Aurora) with heraldic wings of line 4 may or may not be the lowercased dawn "au vain plumage noir" of line 7, into which the "bel oiseau" of line 6 flees, but the orthography of the manuscript seems clear on this point, and, although the transformation from capitalized to lowercase "aurore" is difficult to parse, perhaps we can see in it an allegory of beauty struggling to materialize itself and being thrust back into the night of oblivion and nonexistence. In any event, the bird/dawn motif (which is carried over from "Don du Poëme") is then connected to the "plume" and the swan of lines 10 and 11; and like the swan of Mallarmé's famous sonnet, "Le vierge, le vivace et le bel aujourd'hui," the swan of the "Ouverture" is in turn connected to the stars. The "plume" is simultaneously the feather in which the swan buries its head in death and the poet's pen (hence my "quill" in line 10). The mournful water of the pool is no longer visited either by the swan or by the pen, and thus whatever beauty it contains is lost or held in abeyance. That beauty, we may say, has fled from the tower, the tomb, and the pyre, in connection with which beauty is habitually sacrificed. It is difficult to say, however, whether the bird that has fled from the sacrificial tower/tomb exists on the same symbolic plane as the swan, not only because the latter, like the swan in the sonnet, finds a tomb within its own feathers, but because in death it is unwillingly frozen in the eternity of its own constellation, Cygnus. If the bird is a univocal symbol, it seeks to escape simultaneously from a death-in-life and a life-in-death.

Beauty, in the opening stanza of the "Ouverture," is either in danger of being lost amid terror and inquisition (to paraphrase Eliot in "Gerontion") or, to adopt a still more sinister possibility, is actually predicated on terror and inquisition. In like manner, whatever sense of the sacred is projected by the poem is bound up with the horror of sacrifice. Thus, in lines 17–19 (which, following the Flammarion text, we give as a separate stanza [Barbier and Millan, *Œuvres*

Complètes, 208]), a stained-glass window ("vitrail"), anachronistically evoking the imminence of Christianity, gives out on a scene of imagined horror. Both Nature and Art are implicated in this horror, as the colors of the Dawn, evoking ritual sacrifice, are mirrored in the pool and blended with the colors in the stained glass itself.

We then move to an interior framed by the window, as in a still life. There is a lovely ambiguity in line 22, on which the temporal existence of the ambiance being evoked is hinged: either the room has always had an ancient snow-white tint or its former colors have faded ("ancienne" can mean both ancient and former). The tapestry has folds or creases ("plis") that will be echoed by the "yellow folds of thought" (line 41), which in turn will be likened to the folds of a cloth covering holy relics and to the folds of a shroud, and further echoed in the final stanza by the folds of the sheets on which Hérodiade had lain, the folds of the grammary, or ancient book of magic spells, and the folds of the imagination or reverie. The folds of the tapestry are uselessly closed to the viewer ("inutile"), much as the book with vellum pages (lines 59–60) is uselessly closed to the reader, "cloistered" from sight ("claustral"): whatever meaning or beauty they contain is lost or at least hidden away. But the folds of the tapestry contain the buried, or downcast, eyes of sibyls, who extend withered fingernails to Mages. St. Aubyn insightfully suggests that the sibyls, belonging to the pre-Christian or pagan world, are not only pointing to the Christian era but passing along their prophetic function to the Magi of the gospel story; he also notes that the word "ongle" ("fingernail") derives from the Greek *onyx* (*Stéphane Mallarmé*, 43–44)—and this reminds us of the first line of the famous "Sonnet-en-*yx*" ("Ses purs ongles très haut dédiant leur onyx" ["Her pure nails

on high displaying their onyx"]), which in turn suggests that the nails of the sibyls, raised in prophecy to the stars, are like the stars. At the end of the poem, the sky will be reflected in the fingernail, as in a mirror (lines 82–84).

The milk of the mother nursing her child in "Don du Poëme" had been described as "sibylline," and in that context the mother/nurse had been linked to the poet, as engenderer of the poem—a poem entitled *Hérodiade*, the name of a princess, and hence evocative, by the magic of naming, of her being. The connection in the "Ouverture" between the sibyls on the tapestry and the incantatory Nurse, who thus stands for the poet, is solidified through a very strange gesture. One of the sibyls, "avec un passé de ramages"—with a *past*, or embroidery, of flowering vines—seems literally to fly out of the tapestry (and out of the *past*) to become the Nurse: her past is embroidered on the Nurse's dress. Davies's collation of the manuscripts indicates that, at one point, Mallarmé was working with the possibility of "Une, qui s'en détache, avec un passé de ramages" ("One, who detaches herself . . ."—that is, from the tapestry [*Les Noces d'Hérodiade, Mystère*, 146]), and Barbier and Millan have interpreted the manuscript as reading "Je m'en détache" at this point (*Œuvres Complètes,* 208), although this makes the syntax that follows ungrammatical. In any event, the Nurse's gown is embroidered with birds, and the sibyl, having risen as a birdlike phantom from the tapestry, now enters into the ordinary objects of the room, endowing them with a sibylline quality of mystery: the roses, the snuffed-out candle (which shrouds the empty bed from which Hérodiade, birdlike herself, has flown), and the vase, in which the flowers drench their stems—which returns us to the poem's opening image.

Hence the apostrophe that opens the ensuing stanza: "Ombre magicienne aux symboliques charmes!" (line 38). The opening phrase (both words are feminine nouns, to match the "sibylle") can be translated either as "Magical shadow" or as "Shadowy magician." The Nurse hears a voice that is a distant evocation of the past, or of a past that never was, and it turns out to be her own, "prepared for incantation." The whole poem, however, is the Nurse's incantation, and thus, in a profoundly Keatsian moment, the magical shadow takes on substance in a moment of time that blots out time.

In the fourth stanza of Keats's "Nightingale" ode, the poet realizes that he is "already with" the Nightingale, that is, already in the presence of Poetry, because, although he had been lamenting his estrangement, he is already in the ode, already composing it. A similar moment occurs at this point in the "Ouverture," just as other moments of this kind will occur in the "Scène" and in "L'Après-midi d'un Faune." The sibyl, the voice of prophecy, rises from the past, from the aged—hence yellow—folds of thought itself, woven as in a tapestry. The participle "traînant" (line 42) is extremely interesting at this point because it connects the "ombre magicienne" (and hence the sibyl) to the Aurora dragging her wings in the basin's tears. But the larger issue at hand is whether there will be a *resurrection* of the ancient powers of poetry and prophecy that have now been evoked but that are still lingering and unexhumed. (Mallarmé's "Ouverture," it turns out, is an ode, in the manner of Blake, to the ancient power of prophetic poetry: "How have you left the antient love / That bards of old enjoy'd in you! / The languid strings do scarcely move! / The sound is forc'd, the notes are few!" ["To the Muses"].) The prophetic voice has been smothered but is not entirely extinguished; the metaphor the poet gives is of a shroud,

or sacramental cloth covering holy relics, which nevertheless allows "the old veiled brightness" ("le vieil éclat voilé"—line 46) to break free. The question that is then asked of that prophetic—indeed, apocalyptic—voice is whether it will be able to achieve a final, ultimate splendor ("dernière" has the force of both meanings), an idea that is expressed through one of Mallarmé's favorite metaphors, the golden shower ("Jettera-t-il son or par dernières splendeurs" [line 51]), returning us to the opening images of the poem and hence to the possibility of a new dawn taking shape against the blackness of the night. Will that voice, the poet seems to ask—even in its death agony, even insofar as it expresses the "swan song" of European, Christian civilization, and even as it turns into the past from which it arose—be able to serve as a new psalm of petition ("l'antienne aux versets demandeurs"—literally: "the antiphon to petitionary verses")? A great deal is at stake in these lines; indeed, not less than everything is at stake: "For all are alike in being brought to perdition / By the power of old silence and deepening gloom" (lines 54–55). Recall the sentence from the letter quoted at the beginning of the discussion of the "Ouverture": "Yes, *I know*, we are merely empty forms of matter, but we are indeed sublime in having invented God and our soul."

The prophetic voice of poetry that has been evoked from the past by the incantatory Nurse is, of course, Hérodiade herself, whose dawn flight from her bed can be taken to symbolize the loss or absence of beauty, of poetry, now considered as the object rather than from the standpoint of the subject. In the opening lines of the concluding stanza, as the word "grimoire" in line 61 indicates, Mallarmé begins to develop a conception that he will take up again more rigorously in "Prose (pour des Esseintes)," and this has to do with the very nature of the poetic process. To Mallarmé, as to the Greeks before him and to poets such as Yeats after him, poetry comes from the outside. The problem, however, is that in the moment of inspiration the poet is bombarded, as it were, by sense impressions that do not order themselves in a logically extended fashion but are instead contained in a moment of time. Thus, if Hérodiade's song is "incoherent" (line 58), this is not because poetry is meaningless but rather, as Paul de Man has written with reference to Mallarmé, because it contains so much meaning. Or, as Mallarmé will express the matter in "Prose," the vision of Beauty simply transcends the power of Reason to encapsulate it.

"Everything in the world," wrote Mallarmé in a passage quoted earlier, "exists in order to culminate in a book" (see above, p. xiv). The wordplay in lines 59 and 60 on "vélin" and "le lin" (the vellum sheets of a book and the linen sheets of a bed) connects Hérodiade's absence from her bed with her absence from the book, and therefore underlines the sense in which she corresponds to a beauty that has been lost to the ravages of time. And from here the poem modulates to lines on time that are among the most lovely that Mallarmé ever wrote. The crescent moon, visible at "wicked evening" (line 68), is Time's scythe slicing apart the pomegranates. The pomegranate, as we noted earlier, is a figure of desire in Mallarmé, and in the present context, as St. Aubyn observes, "is the red of the sun and the day that night effectively eliminates" (*Stéphane Mallarmé*, 46); but we should also recall the letter to Lefébure quoted earlier in which Mallarmé speaks of Hérodiade's name as being "dark and red as an open pomegranate" (see p. 170). As the moon traverses the heavens, it is also a pendulum on the iron clock face of night, anchored on Lucifer, the morning star. Time is the evil, and, as

the scythe wounds the hours, each one wanders, a shade of its former self, unaccompanied by any angel and wept over only by the clepsydra, the water clock. In lines 71–72, because of the repetition of "pas" as the end-rhyme, and also because of the sparse punctuation, we are presented with an angel who is then negated when the syntax becomes clear. The anguish in these lines is Pascalian: it is in relation to a dark, impersonal, meaningless nature against which man posits his conceptions.

There is no stanza break in the manuscript after line 74, but this point marks the denouement of the poem. The ensuing lines on Hérodiade's father, with his arms of steel, are perhaps motivated by the wounding scythe of the crescent moon. Whatever this bellicose father/king ultimately represents, the Nurse tells us that she is under his jurisdiction and that the breasts with which she formerly nursed the princess are now dry. On an allegorical level, the aging of the Nurse and the absence of the princess are one and the same fact. The Nurse asks, rhetorically, whether the father will ever return from the Cisalpines—that is, from the side of the Alps nearest Rome—and her prophetic answer is that this will occur soon enough. If the king represents a pagan past, then the Nurse's prophecy amounts to something like Nietzsche's cyclical conception of history, the idea of the Eternal Return. Again, if, on the most immediate level, the poem represents the coming of Christianity, at the same time, through a kind of Hegelian play of opposites, and with specific reference to Mallarmé's own historical situation, it also represents the demise of Christianity.

Thus, the fingernail, which had previously been connected to the sibyls in the tapestry, is raised prophetically amid the stained glass, where it mirrors the apocalyptic burning of the old sky. By a typically

Mallarméan association, the finger turns into a Christian candle, which, however, is melted by the sinking sun. The "Ouverture" had opened with the redness of a frightful dawn, and the apocalyptic meaning of that dawn is now fully grasped for the first time, almost in the manner of Revelations. The tears of the Nurse's prophecy fall on the child, who, insofar as she represents Beauty, is once again a Beauty unattainable. Exiled to her own proud heart, to the poem named after her, she is again compared to the swan that at death turns into its own constellation.

II. SCÈNE / SCENE

Mallarmé originally conceived of *Hérodiade* as a drama, partly along Racinian lines, and the first section of the poem to be composed, the "Scène" between Hérodiade and the Nurse, is reminiscent in many ways of dialogues in *Phèdre*. The poem has a classical polish and brilliance that critics have often associated with Byzantine art. To Albert Thibaudet, for example, it "takes on the aspect of a Byzantine mosaic, recalling the *Theodora* of Ravenna. The brightness of its colors is blended with the coldness of precious stones. The words ... are juxtaposed like jewels lit up by their own fires" (*La Poésie de Stéphane Mallarmé*, 389). The conception of art that Yeats develops in his "Byzantium" poems may well have been influenced by *Hérodiade*.

The "Scène" was begun in October 1864, shortly before the birth of Mallarmé's daughter, Geneviève, in November. In his letters of that period, the poet playfully refers to Hérodiade and Geneviève as his "two daughters," and sometimes complains that the cries of the latter make it impossible for him to attend to the former. He worked on *Hérodiade* throughout the winter of 1865 and then put it aside in the spring of that year in order to concentrate on a new poem, "L'Après-midi d'un Faune." He had originally hoped to have *Hérodiade* produced by the Théâtre Français and had been encouraged in this hope by Théodore de Banville, whose own *Diane au Bois* (which may have influenced both *Hérodiade* and "L'Après-midi") had been performed at the Odéon in October 1863 (*OC*, 1441). In a letter of 31 March 1865, Banville urges Mallarmé to "try to bring out the dramatic interest, along with the poetry, for you will do more for our cause by composing your work in a manner that will make it well received and acted than by making it more poetic and less actable" (*OC*, 1441; translation mine). Predictably, when Mallarmé resumed working on *Hérodiade* in the fall it was no longer as a drama. Indeed, one might observe that the transformation of dramatic action into pure lyricism is not only an aspect of the texture of Mallarmé's style but, in *Hérodiade* and particularly in the "Scène," has assumed thematic proportions. "The failure of 'Hérodiade' to be an *histoire*," writes Richard Goodkin, "is based on a double rejection of normative temporality: its heroine's refusal to instigate a love story by accepting a lover or husband, and Mallarmé's refusal to make his tragic poem into a 'story'" (*Around Proust*, 50).

Nevertheless, the "Scène" does hover around a series of dramatic actions, albeit in a manner that is at once operatic and lyrical. Mallarmé was deeply influenced by Wagner (although he never actually witnessed a performance of one of the composer's operas), and the slow pacing of the "Scène" may have been influenced as much by Wagnerian opera as by Racinian drama. (Debussy's great opera, *Pelléas et Mélisande* [1902], may, in turn, have been influenced not only by Wagner but by Mallarmé as well.) In operatic fashion, the "Ouverture" is interrupted by the Nurse's expression of astonishment at Hérodiade's return, and with that the "Scène" begins. As St. Aubyn notes, the dramatic movement of the "Scène" is punctuated by three actions on the part of the Nurse and three reactions on the part of Hérodiade: when the Nurse offers to kiss the princess's hand, when she offers perfume, and when she attempts to replace a fallen lock of hair, Hérodiade recoils violently (*Stéphane Mallarmé*, 49). Hérodiade's desire to remain "inviolate to the touch" (line 106), her desire to maintain a self-enclosed purity, clearly has a broad chain of symbolic implications, concretizing as it does the poet's meditation on the religious nature of art. There is a deep ambiguity here, however, which emerges at the outset of the "Scène," and this concerns the relationship between Beauty and Death. In one sense, Beauty achieves immortality by cordoning itself off from Life, which is to say, from Death; but in another sense, by doing so, Beauty *is* Death. Thus, "A kiss would kill me, woman, / If beauty were not death" (lines 7–8).

Art, for Mallarmé, and for the Symbolist imagination in general, is a mirror not of the external world but of the Ideal. In lines 45–51 of the "Scène," when Hérodiade asks the Nurse to hold up a looking glass, there is an echo of I Corinthians 13.12: "For now we see through a glass, darkly; but then face to face: now I know in part; but then shall I know even as also I am known." Mallarmé reverses the Pauline metaphor, such that the mirror of art can focus the otherwise scattered Dream and allow for a glimpse into the Ideal. Thus, Hérodiade says: "I've glimpsed the Ideal in all its nakedness!" ("J'ai de mon rêve épars connu la nudité!" [line 51], or more literally: "I've understood the scattered fragments of my dream in its nakedness").

As the Nurse intuits, however, the religion of art carries very definite risks, and the "Scène" as a whole is permeated by ambivalence and terror. In gazing at herself in the mirror, Hérodiade is an avatar of Narcissus, and to see the Dream in its nakedness is also to gaze into nothingness. According to the Nurse, Hérodiade feels no more than the shadow she contemplates in a state of anomie ("atonie" in the French—line 77); and she herself refers to the country she inhabits as single-toned or monotonous ("monotone"—line 113). Clearly, Mallarmé has thought through the negative as well as the positive implications of a religion of art in which the figures on the urn "pipe to the spirit ditties of no tone." In describing herself as an object of worship, Hérodiade does not hesitate to use the word "idolatry" (line 114).

There is tremendous pathos, however, in Hérodiade's long aria, "Oui, c'est pour moi, pour moi, que je fleuris, déserte!" (line 86), a pathos stemming from our sense that Beauty must always flourish in isolation. The word "déserte," in the context of line 86, can mean both "deserted" or "in this desert," and the whole passage, with its flower and gem imagery, descends from a famous stanza in Gray's *Elegy*:

> Full many a gem of purest ray serene,
> The dark unfathom'd caves of ocean bear:
> Full many a flower is born to blush unseen,
> And waste its sweetness on the desert air.

Hérodiade invoking the precious stones that lie buried is, herself, a buried precious stone, and thus the aria rises to a moment of Keatsian transcendence in which desire and fulfillment are made one in the poetic utterance itself. This occurs at the point at which Hérodiade invokes the Moon: "And your solitary sister, O mine forever now, / My dream shall rise toward you: already such" ("Et ta sœur solitaire, ô ma sœur éternelle / Mon rêve montera vers toi: telle déjà"—lines 110–111). Just as, in the "Ouverture Ancienne," the Nurse discovers that the prophetic voice she has been hearing is her own, so now the phrase "telle déjà" indicates that the princess is already at one with her desire. But as the ensuing lines indicate, this "final enchantment" (line 117) is purchased at very great cost.

Indeed, as Hérodiade's "marriage" to John the Baptist indicates, the cost is something akin to Pauline dualism. The evening star, Venus, whom Hérodiade hates, is the morning star, to which Christianity will give the name of Lucifer—and thus, the lines on Venus in the "Scène" resonate with those on Lucifer in the "Ouverture." The next logical step in this progression—before the pendulum shifts in the opposite direction, to the pagan revitalization of "L'Après-midi d'un Faune"—is the little canticle spoken by the saint himself.

III. CANTIQUE DE SAINT JEAN / CANTICLE OF SAINT JOHN

The "Cantique de Saint Jean" was not published until the 1913 edition of the *Poésies*. The editors of the Pléiade edition believe that it was composed around the same time as the "Scène" (*OC*, 1446), but this is not certain and internal evidence would seem to connect the "Cantique" even more strongly to the "Ouverture Ancienne." The poem is written in a four-line stanza that is unusual for Mallarmé and that he may have borrowed from Banville; the first three lines of each stanza contain six syllables, and the last line four. The very short lines, together with the rhymed couplets, produce an effect of condensation and immediacy, especially after the drawn-out alexandrines of the "Ouverture" and the "Scène."

The speaker of the "Cantique" is Saint John himself—at the very moment of his beheading. The feast of Saint John occurs on June 24, around the time of the summer solstice, and the moment at which the severed head is at its highest point before falling to earth coincides with the moment at which the sun is at its highest point in the sky at the solstice. In metaphysical terms, this *point* is outside of time, or marks the cessation of time, and thus the natural is raised (or "exalted") to the supernatural. The decapitating scythe ("faux") that exalts the saint and the metaphysical notion of time standing still have both been prepared by the "Ouverture": by the image of the crescent moon wounding the hours and by the apocalyptic conclusion.

There has been a tendency among critics to interpret the "Cantique" reductively. Thus, Mauron has argued that the poem should be understood in terms of castration anxiety (*Introduction to the Psychoanalysis of Mallarmé*, 123–128), and Michaud, that the death and transfiguration of the saint should be understood as the death and transfiguration of the poet (*Mallarmé*, 151). Michaud's argument at least has the virtue of allowing us to see the "Cantique" in connection with such poems as the sonnet on the death of Poe, but there is no need to see the saint as symbolizing the poet, or vice versa: instead, the saint and the poet should be seen as existing on the same symbolic plane, since in both cases a similar set of dualisms is being played out. The line concluding the "Cantique," "Penche un salut," means both "extends a salutation" (the saint doffs his head rather than a cap) and "offers salvation." "Salut," as we have already seen in connection with the poem that opens the *Poésies*, has both a secular and a sacred meaning, and whatever Mallarmé's ultimate intentions in regard to *Hérodiade* may have been, it is fitting that the poem should end on this ambiguity. Richard Goodkin suggests that by ending the "Cantique" on this note, Mallarmé offers a subtle intertextual "salute" to Racine, whose first name was "Jean-Baptiste" (see *Around Proust*, 51–56).

L'APRÈS-MIDI D'UN FAUNE / THE AFTERNOON OF A FAUN

The first mention of this, Mallarmé's most famous poem, which Valéry considered the greatest in French literature, occurs in a letter to Cazalis of June 1865: "I have left *Hérodiade* for the cruel winters," writes Mallarmé; "this solitary work had made me sterile, and, in the interval, I am rhyming a heroic intermezzo, of which the hero is a Faun" (*Correspondance de Stéphane Mallarmé* 1,166; translation mine). The poet's original intention was to send the "Faune" to the Théâtre Français, but he soon came to realize that it was no more suited to the theater than *Hérodiade* had been. Whether he realized this from the outset, or not until he had lived with the poem for some time, is unclear. In the same letter to Cazalis, he writes: "This poem contains a very lofty and very beautiful idea, but the verses are terribly difficult to compose, for I am making it absolutely scenic" —to which he then adds: "non *possible au théâtre*, mais *exigeant le théâtre*," a phrase that in context can mean either "not just capable of being staged but demanding the stage," as Rosemary Lloyd translates it (*Selected Letters*, 51), or "not . . . playable on the stage, but . . . need[ing] the stage," as Bradford Cook renders it (*Selected Prose Poems, Essays, and Letters*, 86). The ambiguous syntax may suggest that Mallarmé was overemphasizing the theatricality of his poem because on some level he was already aware, even at this early date, that its theatricality was undercut by its lyricism.

Mallarmé's "Faune" evolved between the years 1865 and 1876, when it was first published by Alphonse Derenne in an edition of less than 200 copies and with an illustration by Manet. Two earlier versions of the poem (both of which are given in the Pléiade and Flammarion editions) were entitled "Monologue d'un Faune" and "Improvisation d'un Faune." It is unclear when Mallarmé completed the poem and when he gave it the current title, but the final version contained in the *Poésies* is changed only slightly from the Derenne edition of 1876.

One aspect of the richness of "The Afternoon of a Faun" is the way in which it embraces the sister arts of painting and music. On the one hand, Mallarmé may have been inspired by François Boucher's *Pan et Syrinx* (1759) in the National Gallery of London, in which a satyr is depicted surprising two nymphs. Boucher's painting was acquired by the National Gallery only in 1880, but Mallarmé may have known it from an engraving or from a miniature done after the painting (see Souffrin-le-Breton, "The Young Mallarmé and the Boucher Revival," 305–308). On the other hand, nobody would argue with Thibaudet's assertion that the form of the poem is symphonic (see *La Poésie de Stéphane Mallarmé*, 398). Although "The Afternoon of a Faun" certainly does not require musical accompaniment, Debussy's "Prélude à l'Après-Midi d'un Faune," which was completed and first performed in 1894, bears a relationship to it that one feels is almost inevitable. Even in the title he gave to the music, which echoes a line from the poem itself ("au prélude lent où naissent les pipeaux"—line 30), Debussy is attentive to the spirit of Mallarmé's poetry. In a letter to the composer that probably commemorates the first performance of the piece, Mallarmé writes as follows: "Your version of *l'Après-midi d'un Faune* . . . would present no dissonance with my text if not for actually going further, in nostalgia and in light, with finesse, with malaise, with richness" (*OC*, 1465; translation mine). Poem and music were brought together in 1912 by Nijinsky in a ballet that was presented that year in Paris by his "Ballet Russes."

Like *Hérodiade*, which it mirrors in many ways, albeit antithetically, "The Afternoon of a Faun" is a poem that abounds in dualisms. The narrator/protagonist of the poem, the Faun, is himself the embodiment of a dualism. Part goat and part man, he figures forth the paradox of our existence as *animals*, that is, as beings that possess both a body and a soul (*anima* means "soul" in Latin). The faun, in Roman mythology, is related to the Greek god Pan, who, representing a primitive stage of Greek religion, was superseded by the Olympian god Apollo. In Book I of Ovid's *Metamorphoses*, parallel stories are told of Apollo pursuing the nymph Daphne, who turns into a laurel tree, and of Pan pursuing Syrinx, who turns into a reed. The laurel is worn on Apollo's brow and thus becomes a symbol of poetry, Apollo being the god of poetry. Similarly, Pan fashions his musical pipes out of the reed to which Syrinx has been transformed. Thus, both stories are myths of artistic sublimation, of desire metamorphosing into art. However, while the Pan-Syrinx story provides Mallarmé with the mythological germ of "L'Aprèsmidi," the erotic dualism of physical desire versus music is countered and joined in the poem by an equally important theme, the noetic dualism of illusion versus reality.

In its structure, "The Afternoon of a Faun" is a soliloquy, but the poem is subtitled an eclogue, and the eclogue, a pastoral form dating from Theocritus's *Idylls*, usually involves a dialogue of some kind. In this case the dialogue is an internal one; it centers around the Faun's attempt to make sense of the experience with two nymphs that he actually had or that he only imagined. The Faun's meditation is presented in roman type and the narrative of the events themselves is presented in italics. As Bernard Weinberg notes, Mallarmé's use of typography in "L'Après-midi d'un Faune" as a structural device foreshadows the much more complex use of typography in *Un Coup de Dés* (*The Limits of Symbolism*, 427). Reversing our expectations, the meditative section is in roman type and the narrative in italics, so that the meditation is given priority over the narrative, and, rather than being a commentary on experience, is, as it were, productive of experience.

"The Afternoon of a Faun" is a poem in which Mallarmé is able to bring together the primitive language of desire and the most sophisticated philosophical concepts, and this is certainly one aspect of its greatness. Mallarmé develops a poetic language that is delicately subtle and impressionistic in the manner of Debussy's music but at the same time is extremely precise. In the opening lines, for example, the verb "perpetuate" brings together both of the large-scale thematic centers of the poem, the erotic and the noetic. To perpetuate is to keep alive, and thus the subthemes of the imagination, the memory, and poetry itself are all delicately linked through the verb. Moreover, as Wallace Fowlie notes, to perpetuate in this context is also to copulate with: the Faun desires to copulate with the nymphs and thus to perpetuate them through the offspring he would engender upon them (*Mallarmé*, 152).

But the question immediately arises as to who and what these nymphs are, whether they are "real" or merely a product of the Faun's imagination, and, therefore, what reality is as opposed to illusion. Consider the noun "incarnat" in line 2, for example, a word that occurs also in the "Ouverture Ancienne" of *Hérodiade* (line 19). Here, the word refers to the rosy flesh tones of the nymphs, their "carnation" in the rather stilted English equivalent. But because the flesh tones of the nymphs are so clear or translucent that they float in the air, the concreteness of the nymphs themselves is put into question, and this is further established by the etymological connection between "incarnat" and "incarnation"—*embodiment* or *incarnation* in the English (I have acceded to "carnation" in the translation, awkward though it may be, because of this connection). In part, the nymphs are the embodiment or incarnation of the Faun's own desires, as he says a few lines further into the poem, and this is already suggested by the word "incarnat." Moreover, the rosy flesh tones of the nymphs, their "incarnat," connects them symbolically to "la faute idéale de roses" of line 7, and, through that symbol, to the larger issue of idealism that the poem raises. Thus, in the first two lines, and essentially through two words, both of the large-scale thematic centers of the poem, the erotic and the noetic, are broached and brought into alignment with each other.

A phrase such as "la faute idéale de roses" is at once so vague and so precise that it seems to harbor every possible interpretation that can be made of the poem. My own *gloss* (note the Faun's use of this scholarly term in line 8) would run as follows. The rose, besides being a sexual symbol, retains its classical status in the poem as a symbol of the Ideal, in both senses of the word: in the ordinary sense of an ultimate wish and in the philosophical sense of the mind cut off or liberated from the material world. Ironically, however, while the poetic symbol betokens a realm of timeless purity, it is itself drawn from Nature, and ultimately the two realms cannot be kept apart, even (or especially) in poetry. The ideal *fault* of roses, then, would be that, on the one hand, insofar as they pertain to an ideal dream world, they don't exist, and on the other, insofar as they exist, they are not ideal but are bound to a world of time and death. The Faun, who himself *embodies* or *animates* both principles, would like to separate them out in order to unify them, much as he would like to disentwine the two sleeping nymphs he encounters, since otherwise he will not be able to seize one and join himself to her. But that is not possible—the attempt, indeed, is deemed a "crime"—because the two principles have been inextricably mixed or raveled together ("mêlée") by the gods (lines 83–85). The Faun, in short, is a dualist who would like to be a monist but finds no way either of unifying the two principles or of disencumbering himself of one of them. The Faun is in the position of romancing a rose that is linked symbolically to the nymphs, to the "hymen" and "primal *A*" of lines 33–34, and even (by extension) to the mystery of his own nature, and his efforts to get back to the source are naturally in vain. Yet the Faun (in contrast to Hérodiade) has the good sense to see his failure as a comedy rather than a tragedy.

As far as the issue of truth is concerned, we are certainly in the realm of Cartesian doubt, as the Faun acknowledges in line 4. But to the High Romantic mode that connects Keats to Mallarmé, the problem of knowledge is swept away by the concreteness of the work of art, of Beauty, which is often specified in terms of music, the art toward which all the others aspire, as Walter Pater said. At the same time, however, there is a deep ambivalence toward music and toward art in general, which is expressed in the poem because of the Faun's desire for direct experience. (The same ambivalence can be felt in "Feuillet d'Album," a sonnet of 1890 that also makes use of pastoral trappings.) Words such as "artificiel" in line 21 and "monotone" in line 51 carry a heavy semantic weight of ambivalence: "artificiel," because it emphasizes the sense in which art is a construction of reality and hence unnatural; and "monotone," because the syntax makes it applicable both to the ordinary lines of the body and to the lines of a piece of music—in other words, to an ennui resulting from sexual satiety or to the fact that no matter how sweet heard melodies may be, one tires of them after a while. Music, in lines 48 to 51, tempers love in such a way that it makes the ordinary dream of the body vanish; therefore (as the translation indicates), my own sense is that "monotone" applies mainly to the lines of the body; but the syntax is dual and thus insists that we apply the word also to the musical line itself; and with Mallarmé—who liked to refer to himself as "un syntaxier"—we must always respect syntax.

Lines 45 to 51 (52 in the translation; I have added a line to this section) are among the densest and most difficult to parse in the entire poem, partly because they seem to question the relationship of Music to Nature and the nature of Beauty itself. At the beginning of the stanza, the Faun wonders how, if the nymphs are no more than a dream, he has come to have bite marks on his chest, and he concludes that there are certain mysteries that can be grasped by music but not by the intellectual mind. This is as much to say that "Beauty is truth, truth beauty,—that is all / Ye know on earth . . . ," except that Mallarmé seems to depart from Keats at this point by distinguishing the "artificial" beauty of Art from the beauty of Nature. Lines 45 to 47 suggest that we are *credulous* to assume a mimetic correspondence between Music (or Art in general) and Nature, and in the context of the earlier lines they suggest that all reality is constructed rather than reconstructed. But all of this remains ambiguous because, through a typically Mallarméan complication, the syntax indicates that the negation of the mimetic equation is dreamed by the music itself!

This dichotomization of Art and Nature does not prevent the Faun from invoking the secret connection between the two (and hence a higher level dualism) at the beginning of the next stanza, in the lines in which he begs Syrinx (that is, his pipe) to bloom once more. We thus have a double metamorphosis, leading from the animal to the vegetable to the purely spiritual: the nymph changes to a reed (which the verb "refleurir" connects to the rose symbol), and the reed changes in its turn to music. Though the Faun fondly hopes that the process can be reversed in such a way that his music will ultimately lead him back to the nymphs, the problem he faces—as Richard Goodkin astutely observes in his seminal reading of the poem (see "Zeno's Paradox: Mallarmé, Valéry, and the Symbolist 'Movement'")—is that he belongs to the class of *fauna*: in other words, that he is an *animal*, a being divided between a body and a soul. The nymphs, whom the Faun now refers to as goddesses (line 56), are associated with both the vegetable and the spiritual worlds, neither of which is divided, and thus they are unattainable to the Faun. The Faun hopes that by representing them—through the work of art, presumably ("par d'idolâtres peintures"—line 55; literally: "by idolatrous depictions")—he will be able, paradoxically, to strip them of the barriers—the veils or belts ("ceintures"—line 56)—which keep him from reaching the source; but this, of course, is a vain hope, for even if the Faun were to reach the source, by whatever means, he would still experience the postcoital sadness of the divided animal. Nevertheless, taking refuge in the pleasures of the grape, the Faun inflates his memories (though we can hardly be certain that they really are memories), experiencing thereby an ecstasy, albeit one that is inevitably secondhand.

What saves the Faun from undue bitterness at the loss he has experienced—and what turns the poem in the direction of life and away from the morbid austerities of *Hérodiade*—is the sense that although individual desires can never be attained, precisely because of the dividedness of the individual, there is a unifying force that transcends individuality and, as Wordsworth would say, flows through all things. Freud called it libido; the Faun, in lines that are among the most vividly sensual in European poetry (96–99), apostrophizes it as passion and personifies it as Venus. It is in this sense that he can be said to "hold the queen" (105).

In the end, the Faun accedes to his destiny as an animal, whose "soul, / Weighed down by the body, wordless, struck dumb, / To noon's proud silence must at last succumb" (lines 105–107). But in the weight of this failure, and as the poem draws a circle around itself, the Faun *has* succeeded in perpetuating the nymphs—or at least, their shades (but perhaps everything in the world is a shade). "The Imagination," wrote Keats in a famous letter, "may be compared to Adam's dream—he awoke and found it truth." As the afternoon draws to a close, the Faun's experience and his meditation have finally been fused and enclosed in the poem.

LA CHEVELURE VOL / THE FLIGHT OF FLAMING HAIR

"La chevelure vol," a sonnet in Shakespearean form, originally appeared in the body of the prose-poem "La Déclaration Foraine," in the 12 August 1887 edition of *L'Art et la Mode*. Exactly when it was composed is unknown, but the sonnet bears stylistic and thematic resemblances to other poems of the mid-eighties, such as "Victorieusement fui le suicide beau" from *Plusieurs Sonnets*, and it is likely that it was written around that time. It was first published on its own, apart from "La Déclaration Foraine," in the premier issue of the journal *Le Faune* in 1889, which is perhaps why Mallarmé chose to place it immediately after "L'Après-midi d'un Faune" in the *Poésies*.

In "La chevelure vol," as in other late poems, Mallarmé dispenses with punctuation (except for the final period, which does not appear in the version published in *Le Faune*). The elimination of punctuation enables the poet to draw together as many different meanings, and as many different levels of meaning, in as small a compass as possible, and is clearly in function of the heightened lexical and syntactical ambiguity of the later poetry. It should be noted, however, that in a poem such as "La chevelure vol," the mechanisms of rhyme, meter, and stanza remain in effect to mediate our response and to preserve the lyric integrity and the structure of the poetry.

The degree of ambiguity contained—or deployed—in the sonnet can be gauged by the fact that the word "vol" in line 1 can be taken to mean either "flight" or "theft" or both. The word has generally been translated as "flight," and this seems to me also to be the primary meaning, but Austin Gill has argued very plausibly for "theft" (see *Mallarmé's*

Poem "*La chevelure vol d'une flamme*). In Gill's interpretation of the sonnet, there is an opposition between natural beauty, as embodied in woman, and ideal beauty, as conveyed by poetry. "The opposition," notes D. J. Mossop in his review of Gill's study, "begins when the flame of ideal beauty, 'stolen' by woman, is said to return to the brow of the *poet* (who alone can confer it)" ("Review of *Mallarmé's Poem 'La chevelure vol d'une flamme,'*" 468). But the *flight/ theft* ambiguity is only one example of the extent to which "La chevelure vol" is an exercise in plurisignification. Barbara Johnson provides a useful schematization of many of the lexical possibilities in her study of the poem (*The Critical Difference*, 52–66).

In addition to the lexical ambiguities, moreover, we also have to deal with the syntactical problems posed by the sonnet. In the opening phrase we come upon a syntactical distortion that is of a different order from anything we have previously encountered in the *Poésies*. If we recall Mallarmé's famous apothegm of 1864, "To paint not the thing itself but the effect it produces" *(Correspondance de Stéphane Mallarmé* 1, 137), we can express this difference by noting that the impressionistic technique he had previously employed in poems such as the "Ouverture Ancienne" is now being applied not only to imagery but to syntax as well. However, while the syntactical distortion of line 1 can be analyzed in perceptual terms, as a way of producing a certain kind of effect or impression, it is the vehicle of a distinctly Mallarméan type of continuous metaphor (or allegory) in which different orders of experience are fused. A recurring pattern in a number of the late sonnets is of an earthbound, hence temporal, symbol being linked to an astral, hence eternal, phenomenon. In "La chevelure vol," the woman's golden-red hair being combed out at dusk—and hair, of course,

is one of the most prominent symbols in Mallarmé's poetry—takes on cosmic proportions by being seen as a comet (the Greek root of which, *komé*, means "hair"), or as the setting sun. Thus, in the opening line, all three of the nouns—"chevelure," "vol," and "flamme"—have both a literal and a metaphorical sense, depending on whether they are taken to refer to the woman or to the comet or sun, and this is in addition to the two senses of "vol" we have already noted. The peculiarity here is that the metaphor (if metaphor it is) is completely reversible; there is no tenor and no vehicle; the woman's hair does not "stand for" the astral body any more than the astral body stands for the woman's hair, but each is mirrored in the other.

The woman's hair is not only an erotic symbol but represents a kind of ultimate in erotic experience: it stands at the extreme verge of desire ("à l'extrême / . . . de désirs"), beyond which there is only darkness or nothingness, much as the sun disappears into the western sky. (The use of the word "Occident" for "West" is fascinating because it seems to suggest that a transcendental erotic vision of this kind is embedded in the Occidental, or Western, imagination.) With the setting of the sun, the horizon is encircled by a "diadem" of fading light, which, because the process is a cyclic one, finally disappears into the hearth from which it arose; analogously, the woman's hair, now perhaps braided, either crowns the brow or (with the pun on "couronne") settles on the crown of the head.

The fifth line of the poem is intractably ambiguous because "or" can mean both "gold" and "then," and "nue" can mean both "cloud" and "nude." The general meaning, however, seems to be that since the hair possesses a kind of erotic ultimacy, one should desire no other "gold" than the "nakedness" of this "cloud" of hair hovering above the head; in other words, one should not demand any other form of sexual gratification. The two senses of "nue" come together, and "gold" has both a literal reference as color and a metaphorical meaning (in the sense of an ore that must be mined) as the ultimate fruition of desire. (I follow Robert Cohn's hint in regard to "soupirer" that the infinitive contains an implicit imperative [*Toward the Poems of Mallarmé*, 147].) Moreover, line 6 is doubly ambiguous because the cloud or the nude both kindles and is kindled by the "interior flame," which seems to be some sort of transcendental life energy or even Freudian libido *avant la lettre*.

The sestet fills in the blanks as to why woman, seen in these exalted—not to say cosmic—terms, requires nothing that the poet could give her and would even be "defamed" by any overt erotic advances. "Héros" in line 9, as every commentator has noted, is a pun on "Éros," and "tendre" can have a verbal meaning as "to tender" or "to extend" as well as an adjectival one. The woman requires no rings (the astral metaphor in line 10 connects us back to the first stanza) to accomplish the "exploit" alluded to in the third quatrain; she is "simplified with glory" by her "dazzling head," by the hair that encircles her like a nimbus.

That exploit is to sow with rubies, or ruby, the darkness, or doubt, that her hair touches ("rubis" can be singular or plural). We are again in the realm of Cartesian doubt (as in the opening of "L'Après-midi"), where the blackness of the night sky—that is, of the physical universe—takes on the characteristic of nothingness, of a complete loss of meaning. The woman's flaming hair, which sows either rubies (as jewels) or ruby (the red of the sunset), has the effect of "scorching" the doubt with which it comes into

contact: "écorche" has the literal meaning of "grazes," "touches," or "flays," but Mallarmé may have chosen the word because of its aural connection to the English "scorch." The hair thus becomes a torch that is held aloft against the void, in the same way that the rays of the sun, even as it is about to disappear, are posed against the consuming blackness of night. On a cosmic level, the beauty of the hair, like that of the setting sun, interposes the hope of meaning against a background of meaninglessness.

SAINTE / SAINT

"Sainte" was composed in December of 1865, but was not published until 1884, when Verlaine included it in *Les Poëtes Maudits*. It was set to music by Ravel in 1896. The original version, which differs slightly from the one published in the *Poésies*, was entitled "Sainte Cécile Jouant sur l'Aile d'un Chérubin" ("Saint Cecilia Playing on the Wing of an Angel"). The plangent rhythms of the poem's four octosyllabic quatrains are slightly reminiscent of Poe, especially in the first two strophes where four of the rhyme words are present participles that end on the same phoneme. To convey them in English, it has been necessary to alternate feminine and masculine rhymes.

The religious function of art, as we have often noted, is one of Mallarmé's most important themes, perhaps *the* most important theme of his poetry. Thus, in the figure of Saint Cecilia, the patron saint of music, we have the perfect Mallarméan symbol of the transumptive power of art, in which music and holiness are intertwined. There is something deeply Baroque about the poem, in spite of its quiet simplicity. Bernini's angels and Corelli's music hover in the background.

Charles Mauron notes that the poem is constructed like a diptych (cited by Michaud, *Mallarmé*, 42); and Guy Michaud adds that "the two panels . . . are superimposed in a sort of double exposure" (42). The poem is divided at the colon and each half begins by focusing on a window or glass. The window symbol is, of course, central to Mallarmé's poetry, and the collocation of the saint and then the angel with the window is reminiscent of the climactic stanza of "Les Fenêtres":

Je me mire et me vois ange! et je meurs, et j'aime
— Que la vitre soit l'art, soit la mysticité —
A renaître, portant mon rêve en diadème,
Au ciel antérieur où fleurit la Beauté!

Mallarmé's "Sainte" transcribes a kind of mystical process that is metaphorically akin to transubstantiation, and for which transubstantiation serves as a metaphor. There are windows within windows within windows, and each seems to take us closer to the ontological essence at which the poem is aimed. We enter into the poem as into a painting or stained-glass window. Within that initial frame, we immediately encounter a second window. This window both conceals and reveals: it conceals the old instruments associated with the saint, whose music was once heard, and it reveals the Saint herself with the old missal or manuscript in which the music the instruments played is contained (notice the repetition of "vieux" and "jadis" in the first two quatrains). The movement is from music to silence, from present to past, and from presence to absence; but we should note that what is spatially concealed on the representational level is revealed by being poetically imagined or named.

The Saint's music was once heard during the Mass, at vespers and compline, and this leads us to another window, the glass monstrance that holds the consecrated host. There is something puzzling about the demonstrative pronoun ("ce") in line 9: does it refer to something already mentioned or do we simply encounter it as another object in the room? If it is connected to the window of line 1, as suggested by the symmetrical syntax, then it would seem metaphorically to contain the Saint herself, or at least that aspect of her that has been mystically translated. In any event, the glass monstrance serves as the poetic container, so to speak, for the ineffable; it is the last window, and when we arrive upon it we have reached the middle point of the poem. It contains what ordinary language cannot articulate, and what the *via negativa* of the poem articulates by negation. From this mystical center, the poem radiates out to the phenomenological world of space and time, and back to the supernatural, by a series of gradual mediations. Barely touching the monstrance (as indicated by the verb "frôler") is an ethereal harp that has been formed from the flight of an Angel at evening; and much as the harp barely touches the monstrance, the fingertip of the Saint barely touches the harp, an effect that is beautifully conveyed by the enjambment between the third and fourth quatrains. The definite article in line 10 creates an ambiguity similar to the one created by the demonstrative pronoun in line 9: it either allows us to connect the Angel and the Saint or it points to a kind of latent presence for the Angel. Whether the harp is visible or invisible, seen or only imagined, depends on the representational standpoint from which we are approaching it; but by forming the harp not from the Angel's wing but from its flight, Mallarmé is hinting at precisely this dialectic. The Angel is a messenger between the supernatural and the natural realms (*angelos* in Greek means

186

"messenger"), and the Saint represents a further mediation between humanity and divinity.

In the concluding quatrain, not only the viol but the book as well is absent, and the adjective "vieux" is again repeated, as if to emphasize the fading away not only of old things but of time itself. There is now only the fingertip on the "plumage instrumental." Do we have a new tableau in the fourth quatrain or has the scene remained unchanged? It is perhaps impossible to say. The movement seems to be from the sensible to the super-sensible, but the duality of the paradox is never completely left behind.

TOAST FUNÈBRE / FUNEREAL TOAST

Written in 1873 in response to the death of Théophile Gautier in October of the previous year, "Toast Funèbre" was a contribution to an anthology of poetic tributes, a *Tombeau de Théophile Gautier*, which had been organized by the *Parnasse Contemporain* grouping. Although it was composed for a specific occasion, it is Mallarmé's most straightforward and, in some ways, most complete statement in verse on the fundamental problems that concerned him as a poet. It is a deeply serious poem—in my own view, one of the most profound and beautiful philosophical poems of a middle length in European literature. The high solemnity of its alexandrines has seemed to call for hexameters as an English response.

From his earliest phase as a poet, Mallarmé was deeply influenced by Gautier, as we see already in "Le Guignon," one of the earliest poems in the *Poésies*, where he borrows not only the subject matter but also the terza rima of Gautier's poem "Ténèbres" (see above, p. 151). What Gautier meant to him is summed up in an illuminating letter to François Coppée, in which he refers to the poem he was planning to contribute to the *Tombeau*. "I want to praise," writes Mallarmé, "one of the most glorious qualities of Gautier: the mysterious gift of seeing with the eyes (delete mysterious). I shall praise the *seer*, who, set down in this world, has looked at it, which is something that most people do not do" ("ce que l'on ne fait pas"; *Correspondance de Stéphane Mallarmé* 2, 37; translation mine). Mallarmé's parenthesis "delete[s] 'mysterious,'" but without actually erasing or obliterating it, for reasons that will have everything to do with the visionary conception (or conception of the visionary) that is developed in "Toast Funèbre." In one sense, to "see with the eyes" (as opposed to without them) is to be capable of distinguishing what can be seen from what cannot be seen, and hence of demystifying a relationship to religion that is merely self-consoling. (Most people do not look at the world, as both Sophocles and Freud saw; in particular, they do not see what they cannot see because to do so is simply too painful.) But this capacity of "seeing with the eyes" is still a "mysterious gift," because the process of demystification—as performed by the poem in general, and as "Toast Funèbre" will itself delineate—allows at the same time for an affirmation of mystery that is fully consonant with the demands of modernity. Indeed, it is precisely in this sense that "Toast Funèbre," however agnostic its initial assumptions might be, establishes itself as one of the great religious poems of our time.

As far as its relationship to genre is concerned, we should note that "Toast Funèbre" is a funeral elegy that begins by refusing the elegiac occasion. "Funèbre" can mean both "funeral" and "funereal," and there is a sense in which Mallarmé disdains the funereal (or lugubrious) platitudes of funeral elegies. The basic cliché that stands behind the funeral elegy as a genre, insofar as it is directed toward the death of the poet, is that the poet is not dead but will "live forever." Mallarmé, as one might expect, has utter contempt for posturing of this kind, although that has not stopped the critics from attributing to him precisely the argument against which he is polemicizing in the poem. Bernard Weinberg, for example, asserts that the theme of "Toast Funèbre" is that "other men may be considered as passing and the poet as eternal" (*The Limits of Symbolism*, 190). To Mallarmé, on the contrary, a distinction of this sort, founded on pride, on *amour propre*, remains implicated in the same tissue of illusions that allows for the perpetuation—in veiled form, of course—of sacrificial rituals; it is merely another version of the spiritual blindness against which the figure of Gautier is posed as a corrective in the poem.

Thus, in the opening line, although "notre bonheur" has been read as referring specifically to the tribe of poets (in the manner of Wordsworth's lines from "Resolution and Independence": "We Poets in our youth begin in gladness; / But thereof come in the end despondency and madness"), the reference is simply to the human condition. The poet is a representative man (in Emerson's phrase), and Gautier is a representative poet, but that is all. Our happiness (*bonheur*—"good hours" says the French) is shadowed by death, and, as if to emphasize the Pascalian finality of that thought, the line is separated from the body of the poem. The dead poet is apostrophized in the familiar ("toi")—partly, perhaps, because it is really an aspect of the self that is being addressed—but this is ironic because what follows is not the toast itself but rather an explanation for why it is being refused: the pale champagne ("libation blême") is associated with the liquid offerings of a grisly sacrificial rite, and hence with the

dementia of magical thinking. Insofar as the rite has any real significance, Mallarmé seems to be saying, it is not to invoke the ghost of the dead poet but simply to grieve for his absence. The dead poet does not "live on"; his spirit having been extinguished, or having returned to its source (in the classical metaphor of the flame), he is now entirely enclosed in his tomb.

The opening movement of the poem is thus deeply Lucretian in the austerity of its negations, but those negations are mainly directed against pride, and specifically the pride of poets. "Gloire" in line 12 has generally been translated as "glory," but I take it that in this context it means "glorying" or "boasting," the boasting of the *trade* ("métier" has to be pejorative here). In other words, if all of this is nothing more than the braggadocio of poets, who would raise themselves above ordinary mortals, even in the common hour of death (line 13), then the true glory of the spirit consists in remaining true to the modesty of nature, and hence in returning "toward the fires of the pure *mortal* sun" (line 15). In the Lucretian creed of the opening movement, the spirit returns to its invisible source while the body goes the way of all flesh.

There has been much discussion of line 4, "J'offre ma coupe vide où souffre un monstre d'or." If the symbols remain somewhat enigmatic, this is not because they are impregnable to interpretation but rather because they are attached to such a rich web of associations that interpretation seems endless. Both the cup and the monster are recurring motifs in Mallarmé, and both are associated with the poetic process. The poet José-Maria de Heredia tells of having been asked the meaning of the line by Mallarmé himself. "To justify his confidence in my powers of divination," remarks Heredia, "I gave him the following explanation: 'It's very clear; it has to do with an ancient cup in which an artist, Benvenuto Cellini, if you will, engraved in solid gold a golden monster writhing with an expression of suffering.'" Heredia adds that Mallarmé was immensely pleased with his suggestion (cited in Mondor, *Vie de Mallarmé*, 347). In itself, this story does not elucidate the line, of course, but in connecting the cup to the artistic tradition, and hence to a series of paradoxes that emanate from Keats's Grecian Urn, it allows us to see the cup as a symbol of poetry. Thus, after mentioning Heredia's anecdote, James Lawler asks: "[I]s it not true that the magnificent glass the poet is offering in a gesture of libation is nothing but the tributary poem we are reading?" (*The Language of French Symbolism*, 7). We have already encountered the cup in "Salut," the sonnet of 1893 that Mallarmé placed at the head of the *Poésies*; in that poem, the cup "contains" a depiction of Odysseus and the Sirens, those figures of desire who would destroy the serenity of art. As for the suffering monster of gold, one of its avatars is to be found in "Quelle soie aux baumes de temps," a sonnet of 1885, in which a chimera, imaged in a watermark, struggles to free itself from the paper in which it is entrapped (see p. 236). As Robert Cohn points out, the figure occurs in a similar guise in two passages from Mallarmé's prose—both of which, interestingly, are concerned with music, and both of which make it clear that the figure is associated with an ideal that is embodied in music, in art generally, but that can never be fully realized in the materiality of the work (*Toward the Poems of Mallarmé*, 98). In "Richard Wagner: Rêverie d'un Poëte Français" (1885), the figure occurs as "le Monstre-Qui-ne-peut-Etre" (*OC*, 541), and, in a particularly convoluted passage from "La Musique et les Lettres," the lecture that Mallarmé delivered at Oxford and Cam-

bridge in 1894, it occurs as "la Chimère versant par ses blessures d'or l'évidence de tout l'être pareil" ("the Chimera pouring out through its golden wounds the proof that it is always entire"; *OC*, 648; translation mine).

We are further indebted to Cohn for tracing the symbol to a poem by Gautier himself, "La Chimère," which, as the critic notes, is about "the poet's eternal hopeless dream" (*Toward the Poems of Mallarmé*, 98), and which begins with the line, "Une jeune Chimère, aux lèvres de ma coupe." As it occurs in "Toast Funèbre," the golden monster is thus a subtle intertextual salute to the dead poet. From this point of view, the monster/Chimera symbolizes the Ideal struggling against the material circumstances in which it is embodied, and this, of course, is a central Mallarméan theme; but we can also see it more simply as a figure of human suffering. Weinberg reminds us that on ancient sarcophagi "the suffering and struggling monster was an 'emblem' of the pains of this life on earth" (*The Limits of Symbolism*, 194). A monster, commonly, is something unnatural, something paradoxical, something that, in possessing a dual nature (like humanity itself), surpasses nature. But if we trace the word "monster" back to its roots (recalling that Mallarmé was always concerned with etymology), we find that it derives from the Latin *monere*, "to warn," and that it originally has the meaning of an omen or divine portent, which is consonant with the prophetic quality of the poem.

We return, then, as the second movement of the poem begins, to "the pure mortal sun" of line 15, which (in the translation) "stands as an *admonition* [also from *monere*] to the foolish pride of men." (These lines have often been mistranslated—as in Hartley's otherwise admirable prose version, where the three adjectives of line 16 are absurdly made to refer to "the false pride of men.") The syntax is particularly difficult here because the three adjectives are in apposition to "tel" ("such"), and refer back to "soleil," but "tel" acquires something of an adverbial force. The condensed meaning is something like the following: "So magnificent, total and solitary is the sun that the false pride of men trembles to exhale itself; that is, is ashamed to display itself." The prophetic attack on pride involves a kind of stripping away of our disguises, of the way in which we insulate ourselves from death—to the extent that what we are turns out to be nothing more than "the sad opaqueness of the future ghosts we bear" (line 19). The poet disdains all the accoutrements of mourning, including the formal conventions of verse, because (as Pascal was aware) these things merely enable us to avoid reality; they enable us to avoid "seeing with the eyes." At this point, the thought of Gautier interposes itself. But who is (or was) Gautier? In one sense, being human, he is a man like every other man; the poetic fiction that the poet occupies a special destiny is explicitly rejected. Gautier—*qua* Gautier—is merely "[o]ne of these blind men passing, mute, puffed-up with pride, / The inmate of his winding-sheet" (lines 23–24). Yet, at the same time, it turns out that Gautier had transformed himself ("se transmuait") "[i]nto the virgin hero of posthumous unveiling" (24–25). This occurred because of his heroic ability, at least in his poetry, to "see with the eyes"—that is, to confront the void. Lines 26–31 are among the most difficult—as well as the most powerful—that Mallarmé ever wrote; but it is my interpretation that a kind of absence/presence dialectic is in operation here, such that the words of the authentic poet, representing as they do a confrontation with truth, evoke a larger reality beyond themselves; metaphorically (and in circular fashion), the "words that

he did not say" (line 27), invoking the abyss, are breathed out not by the poet himself but by an "irascible wind" that is both nothing and, perhaps, everything. Authentic poetry, the poetry of Gautier, Mallarmé seems to be saying, puts Man ("Homme"; here defined only in terms of his "memories of horizons" [lines 28–29]) and his shifting relationship to the Earth into question. To pose this another way, it is as if the authentic poet evoked the "corridor" between life and death, not as a "magic hope" (line 3), but as a confrontation with reality. That which "speaks," in this regard, is not the individual himself but something that can only be defined in terms of its absence—metaphorically, the wind in line 27, or space in line 31. And the question that all poetry implicitly asks can only be answered: "I do not know!" There is a strangely Dantean quality to these lines, reminiscent especially of Canto III (the Limbo canto) of the *Inferno*, which brings home to us the sense in which Gautier is Mallarmé's Virgil, the "Master" who (as the ensuing lines will suggest), having come before, has shown him the way. And this says something more about why the early "Le Guignon," influenced by Gautier's "Ténèbres," is in terza rima.

In any event, from the seemingly all-encompassing negations of the second stanza, we arrive, in the third, at a series of astonishing affirmations. If man is defined by his confrontation with the Void, and in terms of his "memories of horizons," then the question arises as to whether nothing remains of his destiny (line 36). What remains, of course, is Poetry itself. Developing a conception of the realized poet that he will later return to in the conclusion of "Prose (pour des Esseintes)," Mallarmé defines the "Master" as one who, having disciplined his own ecstasy, is able to awaken in the Rose and the Lily the mystery of a name—that is, as one who is able to articulate, and memorialize, the Ideal. Poetry is not only the vehicle by which experience is memorialized but is itself that which is memorialized. From this standpoint, all of us who are gathered in witness are enjoined to "forget that gloomy creed" (line 37), which, ironically, is not so much that nothing remains after death as that the soul, or shade, passes to another existence. The "O vous tous" of line 37 includes Mallarmé's readers as well as his immediate audience of fellow poets; it resonates against the "O vos omnes qui transitis per viam" of Lamentations 1.12, and, for English readers, perhaps, against the "All you who passe by, behold and see" of George Herbert's poem "The Sacrifice." "The splendid, the eternal genius has no shade," proclaims the poet (line 38). There is no contradiction with the negations of the opening stanza, although such might seem to be the case. As an individual, Gautier has now "vanished," but as one who partook of the "eternal genius," he has vanished "into the ideal / Duty we are given by the gardens of that star" (lines 40–41)—that star being simultaneously the "pure mortal sun" of line 15, the source of all earthly energy, to which all individual flames return, and something better approaching a Platonic ideal. The "disaster" of the poet's death (the word literally means "fall from a star," although in this case Gautier's death seems more a return to a star) can be accepted with tranquility because the flowers to which the poet has given the mystery of a name do not fade and are like no other ones.

The hope of the elegiac poet is that by following in the Master's footsteps, he will not only commemorate the disaster of his death but will himself produce a work that will "survive" (line 42). To do this, however, the poet's motivation must be absolutely pure;

the poet must be free of the "anxiety of influence" and devoid of any desire to survive in his own person, which, as we have seen, is an illusion. Gautier, a man with "the mysterious gift of seeing with the eyes," has led the way, and "Toast Funèbre" itself—even as it is being written—is *already* the proof that the gardens he has cultivated are the true groves in which we sojourn (line 48). There, the dead poet resumes his paradoxical task—but now for the benefit of others, including poets to come—of standing guard, "with large and humble gesture," against the dream, which is to say, against that which would render us mute in the face of experience (an idea that is also adumbrated at the end of "Prose"), and perhaps also against the false hopes of personal immortality. In the magnificent concluding lines to the poem—and particularly in line 52, with its very strange syntax (the standard Pléiade edition has destroyed the line for generations of readers by incoherently substituting an "et" for an "est")—Gautier has taken on the dignity of "ancient death." The task imposed upon Gautier by ancient death is not to open his "sacred eyes" (again the emphasis on this poet's gift of vision) and to keep his secrets ("de se taire" in line 53 can also mean keep his silence, and perhaps this is the more immediate meaning, but the word "silence" occurs in a very different key in the last line of the poem); in Mallarmé's syntax, however, it is as if ancient death and Gautier had somehow merged, as if Gautier had now taken on the dignity of ancient death. The "solid sepulcher," which has come into existence as a result of Gautier's poetic accomplishment, now guards his physical remains, forming a metaphysical boundary between "all things harmful" and the "eternal genius" of which he is now an avatar.

PROSE (POUR DES ESSEINTES) / PROSE (FOR DES ESSEINTES)

"Prose," which was first published in *La Revue Indépendante* in January 1885, is one of Mallarmé's most extraordinarily difficult poems and one that has elicited perhaps a greater amount of commentary than any other in the *Poésies*. The poem is dedicated to des Esseintes, the hero of J.-K. Huysmans's novel of 1884 entitled *A Rebours* (usually translated as *Against the Grain*), and the dedication has often been read as part of the title—with the correlative assumption that "Prose" was conceived directly in response to the novel. However, recently discovered manuscripts, including a partial autograph version of the poem that Henri Mondor published in 1954, indicate that "Prose" probably originated during the 1870s and, as Marshall C. Olds observes, that only its dedication is occasional (*Desire Seeking Expression*, 16–17). This possibility is interesting because, as we shall have occasion to note, "Prose" resonates in important ways with "Toast Funèbre," the elegy to Gautier of 1873 that it immediately follows in the *Poésies*. "Prose" is written in octosyllabic quatrains of alternating rhymes, rather than in the alexandrines of "Toast Funèbre," but both poems contain fifty-six lines.

In Chapter 14 of *A Rebours*, des Esseintes meditates for some eight pages on the poetry of Mallarmé: "[H]e loved the works of this poet who, in an age of democracy devoted to lucre, lived his solitary and literary life sheltered by his disdain from the encompassing stupidity, delighting, far from society, in the surprises of the intellect, in cerebral visions, refining on subtle ideas, grafting Byzantine delicacies upon them, perpetuating them in suggestions lightly connected by an imperceptible thread" (*Against the Grain*, trans. John Howard [New York: Boni, 1924], 294–295). Huysmans's novel became notorious as a touchstone of decadence, and, ironically, it was largely responsible—along with Verlaine's *Poëtes Maudits*—for lifting (or rather, dragging) Mallarmé out of the obscurity in which he had long labored (*OC*, 1472).

To the extent that Mallarmé epitomizes the modern lyric poet, the poet in whose work theory and practice, the intellectual and the sensual, are ultimately one and the same, "Prose" stands not only as Mallarmé's *ars poetica*, not only as the poem in which his theory of poetry is most fully elaborated, but, at the same time, as the quintessential modern lyric. The poem is its own allegory of the poetic process, and its own explanation for why it—and lyric poetry in general—is so difficult to interpret.

We begin with the ambiguous title, an example of Empson's seventh and final type, in which meanings that are antithetical to one another come together. In the first place—but this will not be obvious to most readers—the word "prose" refers to a hymn that is sung during the Mass. A *prosa* is a Latin hymn, such as the *Dies Irae*, that is sung between the gradual and the reading from the Gospels (*Desire Seeking Expression*, 18); but Mallarmé's use of the term may also refer to the *hymnes chrétiens* of the Byzantine Church, and the significance of Byzantium to the poem will emerge later. This sense of the title word serves, incidentally, to set the poem's dedication to des Esseintes in relief, since the latter is a connoisseur of late Latin literature and of the early Christian theologians, including those associated with the Byzantine Church. But more importantly, as Georges Poulet notes, the title word indicates that Mallarmé's purpose in the poem, at least in part, will be "to create something equivalent to the ancient religious hymn . . . tantamount to what Mallarmé calls elsewhere 'liturgical remembrances' [in his essay "Catholicisme," *OC*, 394]. Like the medieval prose, Mallarmé's poem will be an incantation directed toward a transcendence" (*The Metamorphoses of the Circle*, 290).

But if "Prose" is a hymn (to Beauty? to Poetry itself?), it is simultaneously an inquiry into the nature of lyric poetry. Thus, in addition to the associations listed above, Mallarmé's title has all of the connotations that we ordinarily associate with the word in English or French: prose as the opposite of verse, as the opposite of poetry, as the vehicle of the analytic rather than the rhapsodic, and so forth. These ordinary connotations of "prose" are further complicated by the fact that they have both an ironic sense and a nonironic sense in the poem. They are ironic in the sense that the poem contains a polemic against the "prosaic world," but they also convey a straightforward, nonironic sense (although this itself is ironic in the context of a poem) of the importance, for modern poetry, of incorporating intellectual analysis, or that which has traditionally been construed as foreign to poetry, within the confines of the poem itself.

The poem begins with an apostrophe, which, by calling attention to the outlandishness of apostrophe, is simultaneously an analysis of apostrophe. The trope of apostrophe is central to Romantic poetics, as recent criticism has informed us, because it poses the very question of our *embarrassment* in the face of poetry, an embarrassment mandated by the prosaic world. Apostrophe, as Paul de Man observes, is related to prosopopoeia, or personification, the root meaning of which is "to give a face to" ("Lyrical Voice in Contemporary Theory," 57). In the modern world, personification, and hence Poetry itself, is embarrassing; to give a face to the dehumanized, faceless world of our prosaic science is to "lose face."

And the poem immediately insists upon its modernity: the placement of "aujourd'hui" in line 3 allows it to mean both that memory should arise *today* and that the "grammary" ("grimoire"; Mallarmé had previously employed this metaphor in the "Ouverture Ancienne") should be a modern one. The Greek word from which "hyperbole" is derived means "to throw beyond the mark"; and thus, the act of invoking Hyperbole is a profoundly ambivalent, not to say paradoxical, one; for at the same time that it calls up what from the standpoint of the prosaic world, the world that does not believe in poetry, is an unbridgeable gulf between Prose and Poetry, by the very act of calling, it manages to bridge that gulf. The metaphysical boundary separating the prosaic world from the realm of Poetry will be allegorized in "Prose" as a symbolic journey to a magical island—the island, of course, representing Poetry, and the mainland, Prose.

Apostrophe is central above all to the ode, and with the apostrophe to Hyperbole we have a situation that is once again reminiscent of Keats's "Ode to a Nightingale." In the latter poem, as so often in the ode tradition, the poet begins in a state of depression and unbelief, a state in which poetry seems very remote. The act of calling, however, even in the face of what the prosaic world regards as inadmissible hyperbole, lifts him out of his spiritual torpor. Thus, in the fourth stanza of the Nightingale ode, at the point at which the poet determines to join the Nightingale, "Not charioted by Bacchus and his pards, / But on the viewless wings of Poesy," he suddenly realizes that he is already there, that, as far as Poetry is concerned, imagination and reality are one, and that the act of invoking brings what is invoked into existence. The "Already with thee!" of Keats's ode is a moment that we have seen matched in a number of poems from the *Poésies*, in the "Ouverture

Ancienne," "L'Après-midi d'un Faune," and "Toast Funèbre." Similarly, but perhaps more ambivalently, in "Prose," the act of calling upon an other—even though both the act itself and what is called upon are seen, from the standpoint of the prosaic world, as hyperbole—immediately (magically) bridges the gulf between the mainland and the island on which the poet and his "sister" will sojourn. The trope of apostrophe, though comprehended as hyperbolic, thus functions for modernity like the magic spell of an epoch that had not yet experienced the crisis of modernity: the magic is all the more powerful in that its effect is not dependent upon belief; like Proust's madeleine, the act of calling sets memory into action, as if of its own accord.

The question of whether "Prose" is a hymn, as its title ambivalently asserts, or whether it should not rather be regarded as an ode, is one that is worth considering because, in a sense, it is raised by the poem itself. Comparing the two genres, Paul Fry notes that "like the hymn, the ode . . . longs for participation in the divine, but . . . never participates communally, never willingly supplies the congregation with common prayer because it is bent on recovering a priestly role that is not pastoral but hermetic" (*The Poet's Calling*, 7). While there could hardly be a more hermetic poem in any language than "Prose," it may be that in this poem the hymn/ode dialectic has evolved yet another turn, and that the ode, having come into existence as a result of the disappearance of the possibility of establishing poetic communion in a congregational or public setting, had become a hymn once again—as if the self, driven into the exile of its own solitude, had now disappeared into the otherness, not of God but of the Poem itself.

As noted in the Introduction, the religious crisis of the nineteenth century had deep-seated effects on poetry, not only on poetic content or poetic form but on the very existence of poetry as a form. If Poetry becomes more hermetic, if it becomes more resistant to popular appropriation, this, paradoxically, is because, having stepped into the breach of the sacred, it has now become more important. Poetry is no longer merely the vehicle of spiritual experience (as it is in the hymn) but the container and even the locus of the spiritual; consequently, the question of poetic *technique*—which in "Prose" encompasses both "magic" and "science"—takes on increasing complexity. The mystical burden of Poetry, for Mallarmé, is that of containing the uncontainable, of expressing not only the ineffable but the inexpressibility of the ineffable. We see this even in Mallarmé's astonishingly radical use of rhyme in "Prose," where, as noted in the Introduction, polysyllabic homonym chains extending beyond word boundaries—such as "désir Idées" and "des iridées," in lines 29 and 31, or "par chemins" and "parchemins," in lines 50 and 52 (far beyond the capacities of the translator, of course)—make it seem as if sound is not an echo to the sense but sense to the sound, or as if, in the hands of the Master, words had taken on the magical properties attributed to the Irises that are glimpsed on the island. "The pure work of poetry," wrote Mallarmé in one of his most famous pronouncements, "involves the elocutionary disappearance of the poet, who cedes the initiative to words" (*OC*, 366; translation mine); and the very title of the essay from which this statement is drawn, "Crise de Vers," suggests that for Mallarmé the problem of poetic technique assumes a larger existential or religious dimension. Indeed, the problem of poetic technique that is raised in and by "Prose" is by no means merely formal: it is associated with the paradoxes of experience and duration that Proust was later to analyze in his own way in *A la*

Recherche du Temps Perdu, and, as such, is figurally inscribed in Mallarmé's allegory.

When "Prose" was first published in *La Revue Indépendante*, the first two stanzas were separated from the rest of the poem as a kind of prologue; for it is after these stanzas that we reach the heart of the epiphanic experience the poem develops. The problem that is posed by the poem is as follows. Suppose that somehow we manage to arrive at the Island of Poetry, whether prompted by "magic," by "inspiration," by the "Muse," or by any other agency that the modern mind feels compelled to set in inverted commas. We have contrived to evade the pseudo-authoritative judgments of the prosaic scoffers—those still living in an "era of authority" (line 13; "age of certainty" in the translation), which has clearly broken down—and we have been vouchsafed a vision of the magic Irises (lines 17–32). I say "we" because the self, having "fallen" (as in Blake's cosmogony), is now divided, in Mallarmé's traditional metaphor, into a percipient "feminine" component and a rational "masculine" component. On that island, *vision* (in the mystical or transcendental sense) is simply *sight*, that which "ordinarily" occurs. (We recall that Mallarmé's conception of Gautier, which he was concerned to develop in "Toast Funèbre," was as a man "with the mysterious gift of seeing with the eyes.") The problem, however, is that your "sister" has no intention of informing you of what she has experienced; her wisdom remains inscrutable. You are thus left with the problem of *translating* (here a raft of paradoxes associated with the translation process are raised) her experience into a form that will not be evanescent but will somehow be lasting, and that therefore will provide you with a bridge to get back to the Island of Poetry when you are again stranded on the prosaic mainland, as you know you will surely be. (Here, the connection to the English Romantic tradition would be to "Tintern Abbey" and the "Ode to the West Wind," where memory and poetry itself are consciously viewed as vehicles of the creative transformation of consciousness.) In order to comprehend her, you have to cultivate your ancient skill (lines 35–36).

If the problem of poetic technique can be essentialized, it is that the epiphanic vision (of God, of Beauty—however one wants to label it) simply transcends the power of Reason to encompass or encapsulate it. Those living on the "shore" (line 41)—which includes everyone, at least most of the time—do not believe that "this country" ever existed (line 48; the syntax of lines 41–48 is particularly difficult, but the passage opens up if we set invisible parentheses from the beginning of line 42 to the end of line 47). Nevertheless, they have the illusion that the poet can simply spill out the plenitude he has experienced in "profuse strains of unpremeditated art"—and, as it happens, the poets themselves help to foster this illusion, perhaps because they want to become like the Skylark or Nightingale, or like Mallarmé's "sister" in "Prose" or Wordsworth's sister in "Tintern Abbey"; but the paradox, as Shelley enunciates it in the West Wind ode, and Keats in the Nightingale ode, is that if poets could simply do that, Poetry would not exist. Thus, the discipline imposed on the poet is to *sublimate* his ecstasy and, through the patient labor of prosody, to *translate*—that is, to carry across or bring back—that ecstasy in the form of poetry. In Mallarmé's allegorical representation of this process, the sister and the brother, the child and the adult, are one and the same: "L'enfant abdique son extase." The child abdicates from her ecstasy in order to become a master of the ways (lines 49–50), for the lucid vision of the Irises, of the Ideal, has imposed this duty ("devoir") upon her (lines 25–32). By the same token, in "Toast Funèbre," the Master calms "the unquiet marvels of Eden's wild delights" (line 33) before vanishing "into the ideal / Duty we are given by the gardens" (lines 40–41). Poetry thus represents a species of *resurrection*—and "Anastasius," the name that the child utters in the penultimate quatrain (line 51), is the Byzantine Greek word for "resurrection." The "ancestor" ("aïeul") of Beauty ("Pulchérie"—*pulcheria* in the Latin) in the final quatrain is, of course, Death. As Wallace Stevens tells us in "Sunday Morning," it is Death that is the mother of Beauty, the awareness of Death that spurs the poet to create Beauty. ("Avant" in line 53 has consistently been mistranslated as "before," thus rendering the final stanza unintelligible, but if it is translated as "lest" the meaning becomes clear.) For if the poet refused to defer his ecstasy through the sublimation of form, Beauty would be swallowed up by Death—Death would bear the sacred name of Beauty; the poem as an articulation of the noumenal would be swallowed up by the phenomenal realm— "Hidden by the too large lily flower."

ÉVENTAIL (DE MADAME MALLARMÉ) / A FAN (OF MADAME MALLARMÉ)

Of the eighteen *éventail* poems that Mallarmé wrote, often on the spur of the moment, three were included in the *Poésies*: poems addressed to his wife, to his daughter, Geneviève, and to his friend Méry Laurent. In each of these, a fan is likened to a wing, the traditional symbol for poetic inspiration, and thus by analogy the fan comes to stand for poetry. The underlying conception, then, which is borne out in many of Mallarmé's later poems beside the three "Éventails," is that poetry elevates the ordinary commonplaces and appurtenances of the domestic world to the condition of mystery. As we see from the fact that Mallarmé wrote several of his *éventail* poems on actual fans, the object *becomes* the poem; the conception thus involves the mysterious transformation of the animate to the inanimate, the concrete to the abstract, the material to the spiritual. "The *aile* [wing] springs poetically," as Robert Cohn observes, "from the final letters of *éventail*" (*Toward the Poems of Mallarmé*, 113).

The "Éventail de Madame Mallarmé" was first published in June of 1891 in the review *La Conque*, with a text that differs slightly from the one that appears in the *Poésies* (it does not include the parenthesis in the third quatrain). The original, contained in the "Collection Henri Mondor," is written in red ink on a fan of silver paper ornamented with white daisies.

In the elaborate compliment that the poet addresses to his wife, the same hand that holds the fan (and also, incidentally, the duster that cleans up the ashes from his ever-present cigarettes and cigars: see the magnificent portrait of the poet by Édouard Manet) is the "lodging-place" ("logis"—line 4) out of which his poetry shall arise. Thus, once again, in the paradox that Mallarmé loves so well, the poem itself becomes the objective correlative of what it attests. In the first quatrain, Cohn notes, "The lady's fan seems to 'beat out,' or scan, in the air the poetry it inspires"; and he adds that this is similar to what happens in the *Tombeau d'Anatole* (the collection of poetic fragments that Mallarmé wrote on the death of his son), "where the mother's cradle-rocking was the source of the poet's rhythm" (111).

The fan thus gives rise to the wing symbol in the second quatrain. But beside the wing symbol, the poem contains two other important Mallarméan symbols: the mirror and the ash. As glimpsed in the mirror (often associated with mystery in Mallarmé), the ash from the poet's cigarette or cigar is about to fall; and this makes him nervous, for he has often, no doubt, been reproached by his long-suffering wife for scattering ashes on the furniture. The ash symbol thus connects the poem to another Shakespearean sonnet of the 1890s, "Toute l'âme résumée," in which the image of a smoke ring, mysteriously summing up the nature of the soul for the poet, also signifies to him that the poetic process must burn up and "shed" the material circumstances from which it has arisen, lest the poem be prevented from arising phoenix-like from its ashes (see below, p. 231). Madame Mallarmé's fan takes wing for the poet, and even her ordinary occupation of dusting the furniture has the propaedeutic function of reminding him that, in order for poetic elevation to occur, there must first be a spiritual clearing away of the debris of reality.

AUTRE ÉVENTAIL (DE MADEMOISELLE MALLARMÉ) / ANOTHER FAN (OF MADEMOISELLE MALLARMÉ)

"Autre Éventail," which Mallarmé dedicated to his daughter, Geneviève, was first published in 1884. Written in octosyllabic quatrains (which I have rendered in lines that contain 3, 3, 4, and 4 stresses), the poem takes on the voice of the fan and addresses the young lady.

Robert Cohn helpfully connects "Autre Éventail" to the sonnet entitled "Placet Futile." The latter was begun much earlier than the three fan poems, but Mallarmé returned to it in the 1880s, and, interestingly, both "Autre Éventail" and "Placet Futile" were set to music by Debussy and included in his

Trois Poëmes de Stéphane Mallarmé. In any event, the desire of the poet to become the fan, so as to come as close as possible to the "dreamer" who is being addressed, is parallel to his desire, in "Placet Futile," to be depicted, on the fan that is the love-god's wings, as the shepherd of the princess's smiles. Moreover, in "Autre Éventail" the fan's transformation into a "scepter," in the concluding stanza, has the effect of transforming Mademoiselle Mallarmé into a princess herself. The laughter of the princess in "Placet Futile" is transformed into the bleating lambs in the pastoral scene on the fan: life in all its transience is held and contained in the work of art. Similarly, the Edenic freshness of life that the poet associates with his daughter's laughter flows to the depths of the fan's inner folds. Both poems—but perhaps "Autre Éventail" more maturely—express a deep sense of nostalgia for the mysterious pulse of life, which art captures as that which always eludes us.

ÉVENTAIL (DE MÉRY LAURENT) / A FAN (OF MÉRY LAURENT)

Written in white ink on the gilt paper of a fan decorated with roses, this sonnet was presented in 1890 by the poet to Méry Laurent, Mallarmé's close friend and perhaps mistress in later years, whom he had met through Manet. The sonnet was not published during the poet's lifetime, and appeared for the first time in the 1945 Pléiade edition of the *Œuvres Complètes.* Barbier and Millan, the editors of the Flammarion text of the *Poésies,* note that Paul Valéry copied it out by hand (*Œuvres Complètes,* 375).

The roses, in the first stanza of the sonnet, are frigid, both because they are white and (implicitly) because of the onset of winter. The syntax of lines

1–2 is ambiguous: "pour vivre" can stand alone or can take "Toutes la même" as a predicate complement, and the latter phrase can also be an adverbial modifier of "interromprent." Thus, in order for the roses to survive, they must join together as a single rose—an image evoked by the white fan when it is closed in the winter time. The closed, white fan, which now looks like a rose, will interrupt or break in upon the breath of Méry; that is to say, it will remind her of the joys of summer.

But if the beatings of the reopened fan, in the second stanza, can deliver a deep enough shock, the tuft of flowers will be freed and the cold will be melted up in the rapture of a new blooming. Richard points out that "la touffe" can have a sexual connotation in the stanza (*L'Univers Imaginaire de Mallarmé*, 122); but if it is plausible to read the "battement" of line 5 as phallic, one can also read it as the metrical pulsing of the poem—in which case, as in the other "Éventail" poems, the fan is a symbol for the poem.

In the sestet the relationship of the fan to Méry is transferred by analogy ("Voilà") to the relationship of Méry to the poet. "Comme" in line 10, as often in Mallarmé, can mean both "like" and "as"—so that Méry is like a fan in her impact on the poet, or has the effect of a fan; in any event, she, or the natural scent she emits (a scent perhaps of roses), is better suited than a perfume vial "at focusing fragments of the sky" ("A jeter le ciel en détail" —line 9); that is, at powerfully stimulating the senses and thereby making reality ("ciel"—the sky or heaven) especially vivid.

FEUILLETS D'ALBUM / ALBUM LEAVES

FEUILLET D'ALBUM / ALBUM LEAF

Mallarmé noted in the bibliography he prepared for the 1899 edition of the *Poésies* published by Deman that "Feuillet d'Album" was recopied from verses he had written in the album of the daughter of his friend, the Provençal poet Joseph Roumanille (*OC*, 1475). The poem was first published in the 1892 edition of the review *La Wallonie*.

Like "Placet Futile"—in the context of which it has already been discussed (see above p. 153)— "Feuillet d'Album" corresponds to a rococo or pastoral vein in Mallarmé's work that makes of poetry (and the poet) something deliberately minor and self-effacing. (In "L'Après-midi d'un Faune," however, this minor vein is retransformed into something major.) Mallarmé's ambitions for poetry being what they were, it is not surprising that he would have taken a kind of antithetical pleasure in depicting the artist as a crude satyr whose flute-playing "lacks the means to imitate" the laughter of a young girl. The "paysage" in line 6 indicates that we are in the territory of the artificial picturesque—or would be, if it were not for the irony with which the entire sonnet is framed. In one sense, the poet expends his breath in order to come as close as possible to the breath of life, concretized in this case, as in "Placet Futile" and "Autre Éventail," as a young girl verging on womanhood. Poetry, from this standpoint, has a merely mimetic function—which it cannot even fulfill—and exists solely to adorn the album of one who possesses the "natural and clear" existence that the poet himself can never possess. Of course, this "picturesque" conception of poetry (which comes with its own sorrows) is only a resting place for Mallarmé in the movement toward the sublime.

Formally, the sonnet poses few difficulties. What the narrator/satyr says about breaking off his performance in the second quatrain is mimed by the breaking off of the syntax in the first. The tense-construction of the verbs in the second quatrain is deliberately skewed, so that whether the performance seemed good to the narrator *when* he ended it, or seems good to him *in that* he ended it, is ambiguous.

REMÉMORATION D'AMIS BELGES / REMEMBRANCE OF BELGIAN FRIENDS

During February of 1890 Mallarmé delivered a lecture on Villiers de L'Isle-Adam, who had died the previous year, at a number of cities in Belgium. At Bruges, he was entertained by the poets of the Excelsior Circle, and "Remémoration d'Amis Belges" derives from this experience. The poem was privately printed by the Circle, and subsequently appeared in the Brussels journal *L'Art Littéraire* in 1893. In the bibliography that he prepared for the 1899 edition of the *Poésies*, Mallarmé writes: "J'éprouve un plaisir à envoyer ce sonnet au livre d'or du Cercle Excelsior où j'avais fait une conférence et connu des amis" ("I experience pleasure at sending this sonnet to the gold book of the Excelsior Circle, where I delivered a lecture and made a number of friendships"; *OC*, 1477). Thinking of this passage, Robert Cohn suggests that the *or* of the title is connected to the circumstances of the poem's origins (*Toward the Poems of Mallarmé*, 298, n. 1). The suggestion may seem farfetched until one realizes that the stripping away of the stone in the opening quatrain is reminiscent of the faded goldwork of the chamber in the "Ouverture

Ancienne," and, more generally, of Mallarmé's meditation on time.

Indeed, in the sensorial/spiritual paradoxes of the sonnet, the poet's vision of time, of *ruin*, is connected to a vision of transcendence. What Spenser after du Bellay called "The Ruines of Time" is concretized in the weather-stripped stone of the first quatrain ("la vétusté"), which, through the fog of an incense-colored dawn, is experienced not in a melancholy light but as a liberation from the banality of the ordinary. The experience of time is thus *poured out*, as it were, as "ancient balm" on those "immemorial ones"—the poets—who experience time as a reaching beyond time (lines 6–7).

The absence of punctuation in the sonnet is once again a function of the poet's deployment of syntactical ambiguity, but in "Remémoration" it confirms the sense of floating weightlessness that is central to the experience of the poem. Thibaudet notes that the difficulty of the opening lines will be lessened if we insert imaginary parentheses between lines 3 and 4 (*La Poésie de Stéphane Mallarmé*, 146), but the increase in intelligibility that is gained thereby runs counter to Mallarmé's poetic intentions. In line 6, around the phrase "le temps," we have what is appropriately, considering the nature of the poet's meditation on time, the most interesting example of syntactical ambiguity in the poem and an extraordinarily beautiful effect: "le temps" is both the object of "d'épandre" and connected as part of an ablative absolute to the "immémoriaux quelques-uns" of the next line. In other words, time is the ancient balm that is poured out *on the time* and *at the time* of the sudden beginning of the friendship of the immemorial ones.

This, in turn, makes us aware that the immediacy of the poet's experience of time in the opening quatrain is distanced in time and comprehended by memory—and also that the two experiences are ultimately one and the same. The time that is poured out as ancient balm on the immemorial ones, on those who reach through memory beyond time, is simultaneously the time of the experience and the time of its recollection, so that time is comprehended under the aspect of eternity. Beauty, experienced as and through the interpenetration of the temporal and the eternal, and here symbolized as the Mallarméan swan, irradiates the flight of the wingèd spirit, or in my translation, "lights the wingèd spirit to its home."

DAME SANS TROP D'ARDEUR / LADY WHO BURNS

An earlier version of this sonnet was addressed directly to Méry Laurent and presented to her on 31 December 1887 as a New Year's present. Mallarmé eventually depersonalized the poem, however, substituting "Dame" in the opening line and "disons" in line 9 for the name "Méry"; he also substituted "d'ardeur" for "d'aurore" in line 1. This revised version of the sonnet was published in the *Gazette Anecdotique* in 1896 and subsequently in the *Figaro* in the same year. An intermediate version of the sonnet, dated 1888, in which the name "Méry" was changed to "Chéry," was published by Robert de Montesquiou in the *Diptyque de Flandre, Triptyque de France* (1921).

In "Dame / sans trop d'ardeur," as also in "O si chère de loin" (which immediately follows it in the *Poésies*), the rose exists both inside and outside of time, divesting itself of itself and yet remaining itself. The two sonnets are gentle, erotic compliments, and

yet there is a spiritual dimension to the symbol that enters into the texture of the poetry. Syntactically—and hence the absence of terminal punctuation in the sonnet—the rose in line 2 of "Dame / sans trop d'ardeur" is both burned by the lady being addressed and the lady herself, depending on whether or not we insert a mental comma after "enflammant." The white rose that blooms eternally, engendering passionate devotion in others while remaining unaffected by that passion, forever enflamed and yet unconsumed by the flames, stems ultimately from Dante's *Paradiso*. The continual recurrence of the rose symbol in the *Poésies*, in poems such as "Les Fleurs" and *Hérodiade* (where it is also associated with cruelty) and "Toast Funèbre" (where it also occurs in conjunction with the diamond image), suggests that Dante had a greater impact on Mallarmé than has generally been recognized. But Mallarmé's more immediate debt in "Dame / sans trop d'ardeur" is to two poems by Pierre de Ronsard: the "Ode à Cassandre" and the "Sonnet sur la Mort de Marie," the former a love poem, the latter an elegy, and both centering on the image of the rose. The opening lines of the ode are familiar to every French school child: "Mignonne, allon voir si la rose / Qui ce matin avoit declose / Sa robe de pourpre au soleil." Ronsard's rose discloses its crimson gown to the sunlight, whereas Mallarmé's flaming rose divests itself of its gown (unlacing it with crimson) in order to disclose what is beneath the gown and what is shrouded by it. The carpe diem topos underlying the Ronsard ode enters into the tone and the texture of the Mallarmé sonnet, but is undercut in the latter by a suggestion of eternity, which in turn recalls Dante. The phrasing of the opening quatrain of Ronsard's sonnet ("Comme on voit sur la branche, au moi de mai, la rose / En sa belle jeunesse, en sa première fleur, / Rendre le ciel jaloux de sa vive couleur, /Quand l'aube de ses pleurs au point du jour l'arrose") is echoed in the poem by Mallarmé—and the title of the Ronsard would have resonated for Mallarmé because of his own dead sister, Maria, and because of the other Marias in his life. (Ronsard's homonymic rhyme of "la rose"/ "l'arrose" is echoed in Mallarmé's "Les Fleurs.")

The immediate image presented by the opening quatrain is of a white rose whose petals are delicately "laced" with crimson at the tips, such that when the rose opens (is unlaced) the crimson lacing becomes more prominent. Insofar as the rose and the lady are one, there is also the possibility that the opening of the rose, by which it divests itself of its white gown, denotes a sexual yielding, with the diamond at the center or essence. Thus, the lady enflames the rose and is the rose that is flaming, but without too much *ardor* ("sans trop d'ardeur")—the root meaning of which is "burning." There is clearly a deep ambivalence in these lines and a concomitant sense that passion can only continue to burn if it is controlled and held in check. On the one hand, the diamond weeping inside the open rose is a dew drop ("rosée"), and in the second quatrain Mallarmé plays on the "rose"/"rosée" conjunction. By holding passion in check, the lady protects the rose from the climatic disturbances of rain and wind, tears and gusts of emotion that would mar the atmosphere of love being celebrated. On the other hand, there is the recognition that if there were no storms, the storms would never pass, and therefore that even the storms have a role in furnishing a "spacious haven / For the simple day, the veritable day of feeling" (lines 7–8).

In the compliment of the sestet the poet observes that whereas the roses can only be renewed through the cycle of death and rebirth, the lady's grace is always spontaneously renewed and always sufficient, although the appearance it takes changes. "Monotone," in the final line of the sonnet, is charged with an ambivalence that is somewhat similar to the feeling and weight of the word in line 51 of "L'Après-midi d'un Faune"; in my view, however, it does not have the pejorative connotation of the English "monotonous" in this context (in spite of the many translations in which it is so rendered), and should instead be taken to signal the constancy and unwavering quality of the relationship. Newness and constancy are balanced against each other in the concluding lines, with the fan awakening intimacy in the way that spring breezes awaken the earth. The sonnet passes through three of the four elements, from fire to water to air.

O SI CHÈRE DE LOIN / SO DEAR FROM FAR

This sonnet, with the subtitle "pour elle," first appeared in *La Phalange* in 1908, ten years after Mallarmé's death. The editors made use of a manuscript that had been presented to Méry Laurent, probably in 1886. However, the text of the sonnet that was printed in the 1913 edition of the *Poésies* (and subsequent editions), a text that was copied out by Geneviève Bonniot, Mallarmé's daughter, differs in a number of respects from the one printed in *La Phalange*. The *Poésies* text eliminated the subtitle, changed "Méry" to "Mary" in line 2, made "sœur" in line 11 lowercase, and eliminated the punctuation after lines 4, 10, and 11. In a version of the poem published by Robert de Montesquiou in *Diptyque de*

Flandre, Triptyque de France, the name "Méry" is changed to "Chéry," as it also appears in "Dame / sans trop d'ardeur." The text presented here follows the Barbier and Millan edition (*Œuvres Complètes,* 318–319) in returning "Mary" to "Méry"—among other reasons, because "Mary" does not scan in either French or English. It should, however, be noted that although "sœur" is certainly a metaphor, and a traditional one at that, it may have acquired its force for Mallarmé from the death of his own sister, Maria, at the age of thirteen, when he was fifteen. Also, since Mallarmé's wife was named Marie, most of the significant women in the poet's life had variations of the same name.

The *trouvaille,* or discovery, of line 1, with its repetition of "si" and the lovely enjambment emphasizing that repetition, underlies the structure of the entire poem. "Si" is the adverb *so,* but the musical note *si* (or *so,* fortuitously, in the translation) seems also to be struck in so deliciously musical a poem: it is the syllable on which four of the rhyme words in the octave conclude. The prolongation of the note *si* seems to correspond to the prolongation of the rose, even as it "plunges with its fair sea- / son into the past and the future also." Mallarmé's language of the heart attains to the condition of music in this sonnet, so that the sibilants of line 11 culminate in a word that is a kiss, a word that seems capable of summing up the entire sonnet, or even passing beyond language. (That "sister" matches "whisper" so closely on the tonal level is another fortuitous circumstance, one for which the beleaguered translator of Mallarmé is grateful.)

Yet the reality principle would insist that we confront the "songe/mensonge" connection in the opening quatrain, where the dream in which the poet is embalmed is grasped as being in some sense a lie or falsehood—though one that is perhaps mitigated by the truth of the beauty it reveals. In opting for "fantasy" as a translation, a word that prolongs the musical *si,* I have accepted the terms of that mitigation.

RONDEL I

The first of two rondels that Mallarmé chose to include in the *Poésies*—he wrote five in all, as well as two rondeaux—was initially published in the June 1896 edition of the review *La Coupe.* The date of composition is unknown, but an earlier version of the poem, addressed to Méry Laurent, is contained in a manuscript of 1885 (compare *OC,* 1479; Barbier and Millan, *Œuvres Complètes,* 305).

Mallarmé's interest in the rondel and the rondeau may have been sparked by Théodore de Banville, who wrote a number of poems in these forms. The circular motion of the rondel form is mimed in "Rondel I" by the constant iteration of the long *a* sound, which not only occurs as the end rhyme and, hence, in the last syllable of seven of the poem's thirteen lines, but is doubled in the penultimate of all of those rhymes, and sounded internally another seven times during the course of the poem. Furthermore, on the level of content, the sad circularity of life and the futility of our dreams is mimed by the tonal clustering of the *a* sound and by the form itself. As often in Mallarmé, the wing symbol expresses the potentiality of a human essence that is always negated by the actuality of existence. The astonished dreams startled into being by Beauty leave nothing behind to waking life—or at least nothing that, from the standpoint of waking life, can be looked upon without bitterness.

RONDEL II

First published in *La Plume* in 1896, the second of the two rondels was composed in 1889. An earlier version of the poem was entitled "Chanson, sur un vers composé par Méry," and it is likely that Méry Laurent contributed the first line.

The underlying theme of the poem is once again the superiority of life to art and the incapacity of language to express the ethereal beauty of our highest moments. Just as the flowers and diamonds of the first Rondel vanish with the dream, so, in the second poem, the rose and the "radiance of a sudden smile" cannot be made to last either through language or song; indeed, the attempt to articulate the experience of love leads only to a worse silence. The wing symbol functions in the second rondel in much the same way as in the first. The figure of the sylph recurs in another poem in the *Poésies*, "Surgi de la croupe et du bond," which was actually written earlier than the second rondel but is positioned toward the end of the volume. A sylph can mean simply a slender or graceful young woman, but the term was apparently coined by Paracelsus to refer to a class of mortal, but soulless, beings inhabiting the air. It is unlikely that Mallarmé would have used this term loosely, and the soullessness of the sylph suggests an opposite meaning: that we, as human beings, are weighed down by our souls, which separate us from the immediacy of life—a theme that connects the poem, however tangentially, to "L'Après-midi d'un Faune."

CHANSONS BAS / STREET SONGS

The little poems included in the "Chansons Bas" were written in 1889 to accompany the designs of Jean-François Raffaëlli for the seventh issue of his illustrations, *Les Types de Paris*, which appeared in the *Figaro*. "Le Vitrier" was not included in Raffaëlli's album but was added to the 1913 edition of the *Poésies*. For the 1899 edition of the *Poésies* published by Deman, Mallarmé had retained only the two sonnets in the series, "Le Savetier" (originally entitled "Le Carreleur de Souliers") and "La Marchande d'Herbes Aromatiques" (originally entitled "La Petite Marchande de Lavande"). In the sequencing of the "Chansons Bas" presented by Barbier and Millan (which is based on a manuscript copied out by Geneviève Mallarmé), the two sonnets appear as the fourth and fifth rather than as the first and second pieces in the group (see Barbier and Millan, *Œuvres Complètes,* 366–367). We retain the sequencing of the Pléiade edition. The "Chansons Bas" were set to music in 1917 by Darius Milhaud.

Mallarmé, the very antithesis of a demotic poet, must have seen the "Chansons Bas" as a relief from the increasingly rarefied complexities of his style, or at least as a way of counterbalancing those complexities. The poems present him with an opportunity of working in a comparatively "low" style and of drawing sketches of working people—and hence of drawing out complexities from the deceptive simplicity of the surface representation. The adjective "bas" in the title has sometimes been taken to refer to the tone of the voice, but, as my translation, "Street Songs," indicates, I have interpreted the term to refer primarily both to the subject matter and to the stylistic treatment it occasions.

I. LE SAVETIER / THE SHOEMAKER

In "Le Savetier" the Nature/Culture dialectic is

allegorized through the symbol of the shoes. The poem seems to be saying that it is only through culture that anything can be accomplished: "Without the wax, what can one do? / The lily's white from birth." The lily is itself from the beginning; it does not become anything. "Consider the lilies of the field . . . they toil not, neither do they spin." The feet would not be aware of themselves as naked, were it not for the existence of shoes, and without shoes they would perhaps be content to "stay put." But as soon as shoes come into existence, we are filled with an infinite longing to be elsewhere than where we are; that longing becomes our nature—to the point at which it becomes impossible to distinguish the sole of the foot from the sole of the shoe ("semelle" can refer to both, in the same manner as our English "sole"). Paradoxically, as several critics have noted, it is not bare feet but rather shoes that are a sign of the human condition for Mallarmé; bare feet are associated with the gods, as for example in the lines on Venus at the conclusion of "L'Après-midi d'un Faune" (see Noulet, *Vingt Poèmes de Stéphane Mallarmé*, 204). The enigmatic verb "recréerait" in the couplet may point to the realm of Art or to a level beyond the antinomies of Nature and Culture, or it may suggest that because of our infinite longings we are always in the position of having to re-create ourselves.

II. LA MARCHANDE D'HERBS AROMATIQUES / THE WOMAN SELLING AROMATIC HERBS

The scatalogical atmosphere of this sonnet is coupled, as Jean-Paul Richard suggests, with oblique references to the Azure, Mallarmé's sign for the Absolute. The azure-colored, lavender-scented straw, which is hung by hypocrites on the walls of lavatories (that is, as the attempt on the part of Culture to deny Nature), "is the lowest [plus basse], most intestinal reality, which here mocks the ancient dream of the Azure" (*L'Univers Imaginaire de Mallarmé*, 332; translation mine). The conjunction of that lowest reality and the dream of the Azure had occurred much earlier, but in quite another key, in "Les Fenêtres": "And the foul vomit of Stupidity / Forces me to hold my nose before the azure" (lines 35–36). "Ventre," in line 7 of the sonnet, certainly has the primary meaning of "stomach" or "belly," but it can also mean "womb" (an ambiguity that Mallarmé will play upon in the late sonnet "Une dentelle s'abolit"), and the doubleness inherent in the word is given free rein by the unpleasant merging of scatological and sexual associations in the poem itself. Whether the stench is derived from Reality or only from Culture, the aromatic herbs that the lady is selling will have a lot to cover.

III. LE CANTONNIER / THE ROADMENDER

The analogy between the roadmender breaking stone and the poet violently opening up his brains had been prepared twenty-five years earlier by "Las de l'amer repos." In that poem Mallarmé had lamented a weariness stemming from "the harsh necessity / Of hollowing a pit each evening once again / Out of the cold and avaricious soil of [his] own brain" (lines 4–6). Although "Le Cantonnier" is punctuated, the ambiguous syntax allows us to refer "comme troubadour" either to the "tu" of line 1 or to the "me" of line

4; this in turn allows us to think of the roadmender either as an actual figure who is being compared to the poet or as an externalized metaphor of the poet.

IV. LE MARCHAND D'AIL ET D'OIGNONS / THE SELLER OF GARLIC AND ONIONS

The metaphysical question that this subtle little poem seems to be raising has to do with the relationship between emotional and physiological states, or between spirit and matter. Normally, we think of the physiological state—tears, for instance—as following from the emotion, but one prominent twentieth-century theory of emotion reverses this ordering, and if the order is reversed, then that has an effect on the way in which we conceive of poetry. In the materialist reduction of "Le Marchand d'Ail et d'Oignons," the grandiose elegy originates in something as simple, or "low," as an onion.

V. LA FEMME DE L'OUVRIER / THE WORKMAN'S WIFE

The quarryman who cuts into the rock, just as he "cuts out" a life for himself by marrying and fathering children, provides Mallarmé with a metaphor for the poet who, "married" to his art, must make a "cut" in reality through the delineations of his verse. The artist is confronted with the whiteness of the page, with the azure, with the amorphous rock—in short, with an irreducible totality that he must make meaningful. To make a cut in the rock, to create a work of some kind, is to impose limits on the world, and

hence, sadly, to delimit oneself, to give oneself over to contingency; but to refuse is finally to remain as amorphous as the rock. Even in so slight a poem as "La Femme de L'Ouvrier," we see a movement of thought that will eventually lead the poet to *Un Coup de Dés.*

VI. LE VITRIER / THE GLAZIER

As Richard notes (*L'Univers Imaginaire de Mallarmé*, 495), the phrase "pur soleil" also occurs in lines 14–15 of "Toast Funèbre": "Through the windowpane illumined by the evening's proud descent / Return toward the fires of the pure mortal sun!" Thus, even in the deceptively simple terms of "Le Vitrier," the window is not merely translucent but reflects and concentrates the rays of the sun in such a manner that the human being glimpsed through it is seen, as it were, in his "glory," under the aspect of eternity.

VII. LE CRIEUR D'IMPRIMÉS / THE NEWSPAPER VENDOR

The picture of the newspaper vendor can be taken as a simple image (after the manner of what will later be called Imagism), one that is without symbolic intrusion of any kind, or it can be regarded as a symbol of the poverty, either of the human condition in general or of social existence. The newspaper vendor is oblivious not only to what is contained in the papers he sells but to the weather, to the seasons. He has carved out a niche for himself in the division of labor, in the social (or perhaps we should say, cosmic) economy, and he is unperturbed by what seems to us the narrowness and weightlessness of his existence. He can be taken as a symbol, in other words, of our narrowness, of our weightlessness.

VIII. LA MARCHANDE D'HABITS / THE OLD-CLOTHES WOMAN

In "La Marchande d'Habits," Émilie Noulet observes, clothes are the sign of the human condition while nakedness is the privilege of the gods, just as in "Le Savetier" the same was true for shoes (*Vingt Poèmes de Stéphane Mallarmé*, 204). I have translated "hardes" (literally "clothes" or "old clothes") as "rags" in order to emphasize this irony, and also to bring out a certain ambiguity that is attached to beggars in Mallarmé's poetry as early as "Le Guignon" and "Aumône." In both of those poems, there are references to beggars as "gods." "Unaccommodated man is a poor forked animal," writes Shakespeare in *King Lear*; but the civilization that clothes us also deprives us of our nature and perhaps of our divinity as well. This is an unexpectedly Rousseauian moment in Mallarmé's thought. The old-clothes woman is a figure who is on a par with the prophetic Nurse or the Sibyl of the "Ouverture Ancienne."

BILLET A WHISTLER / NOTE TO WHISTLER

In 1890 Mallarmé was asked by James Abbott McNeill Whistler (his close friend in later years) to contribute to *The Whirlwind,* an English journal with which Whistler was then involved and to which he had contributed a number of lithographs. In the correspondence that ensued Mallarmé agreed to compose a sonnet especially for the journal, and promised that it would include Whistler's name as one of the rhymes. The result was "Billet à Whistler," which appeared in *The Whirlwind* in November 1890. Mallarmé was inspired by the title of the journal; by the symbol that appeared at the head of each issue, a dancer in a "whirlwind of muslin" (Barbier and Millan, *Œuvres Complètes,* 385); by Whistler's art; and also perhaps by Whistler's irascible personality.

In the "Billet à Whistler," the purity of art and of the artistic moment, as symbolized by the ballerina, is situated polemically against the journalistic clichés of public discourse. The "gusts of wind that hold the streets . . . Subject to dark flights of hats," in the opening quatrain, are the received opinions enthralling the masses, the "hot air" spoken by the politician or by "the man in the street" (to borrow two of our own expressions), which tormented Gustave Flaubert and so many other nineteenth-century artists. Against this whirlwind—the whirlwind of bourgeois society that threatens to sweep away everything that is beautiful in life—Mallarmé poses the furious whirlwind of art, specifically of Whistler's art, which, though it confines itself to representations of the beautiful, disdaining all conventional gestures, all attempts to "speak to the people," is nevertheless, by its very existence, a "blast" against the prosaic world. The premises that motivate the "Billet à Whistler" are by and large the same premises that motivate the "Prose (pour des Esseintes)" and later the "Tombeau d'Edgar Poe"; if understood correctly, they indicate that Mallarmé, far from being a mere aesthete, is actually a deeply committed, even a *political*, poet—though one whose conception of the polis is so rigorous that it would be difficult to translate into any terms that are not purely artistic.

The syntactical dislocations of the "Billet à Whistler," as in so many of Mallarmé's later poems, stand in function of a poetic purity that refuses to be translated into any conventional gestures; but here they function specifically to allow what is said about the dancing girl to be said also about the two artists, Whistler and Mallarmé, the "we" of line 8. By lifting her knee, the dancing girl, by whom, or for whom, "we lived" (both meanings of "dont" are intended), "blasts with a tutu" everything that pertains to the realm of cliché, which includes everything but the artist himself, who in fact will be inspired (or fanned—as in the *eventail* poems) by the air from her skirt. The syntax, however, allows for the simultaneous possibility that the dancer, as represented in the work of art, is the instrument by which the artist thunders against all platitudes—in other words, that the artist is the one who "blasts with a tutu" (the infinitive construction and the article in line 11 make this reading possible). I take it that the rage of the artist in line 12 refers partly to the dancer herself and partly to the "we" of line 8; in any event, that rage is not expressed directly (or rhetorically) but only through the mediation of the beautiful; it is sublimated in beauty, but in that form it expresses itself also as an implicit polemic against the prosaic world.

The dancer is herself an artist, but, as represented in Whistler's art (and, further, in Mallarmé's poetry), she is also a symbol of spiritual horizons that we associate with art. Paradoxically, although she arises as a "muslin whirlwind," she is described in line 10 as "spirituelle, ivre, immobile" ("Rapt motionless in her own dream" in the translation). Within herself, she contains "the still point of the turning world," to borrow T. S. Eliot's phrase. That motionlessness, that perfect unity of being, represents what for Mallarmé, as for many of the poets after him, is the

only possible transcendence; it is an image that will evoke Yeats's famous question: "How can we know the dancer from the dance?"

PETIT AIR I / LITTLE AIR I

The first of the three "Petit Airs," composed in 1894 and originally entitled "Bain," was initially published with its present title in November of that year in the journal *L'Épreuve*. As St. Aubyn notes, this sonnet makes use of several of Mallarmé's most frequent symbols: the swan, the setting sun, whiteness, and water (*Stéphane Mallarmé*, 85). For both this poem and the second "Petit Air," I have employed a stanza of 3, 3, 4, and 4 stresses (in the quatrains) to render Mallarmé's seven-syllable lines.

As Robert Cohn suggests (*Toward the Poems of Mallarmé*, 117), the presence of the verb "abdiquer" in line 4 and the noun "gloriole" in line 5 connects "Petit Air I" to "Victorieusement fui le suicide beau" (from *Plusieurs Sonnets*), where a glorious sunset is personified as a dying king (see below, p. 216). We have noted on a number of occasions that Mallarmé likes to play on the antithetical meanings of *gloire* as "glory" or "glorying"; and in the word "gloriole" (literally "vainglory") we can see a condensation of these antithetical meanings, such that to attempt to hold on to the glory that is here being resigned would be vainglory. The feeling of ambivalence is heightened by the sense that the glory in question pertains to the realm of the human precisely by transcending the realm of the human—which is why it must be given up. By contrast, a king abdicates from a realm that belongs to him. Perhaps the conflict can be resolved, or at least put into perspective, if we remember that in "Prose (pour des Esseintes)" the child "abdicates" from her ecstasy ("L'enfant abdique son extase"—line 49), in order to "resurrect" it in poetry. Cohn observes that the poet of "Petit Air I" "'abdicates' from his highest dream of glory, in favor of human love" (*Toward the Poems of Mallarmé*, 117), but if the standpoint of "Prose" is continuous with that of "Petit Air I," then it would be more correct to say that the "abdication" that occurs is not a real abdication because the glorious realm that is resigned is only resigned in order to be taken up again in the form of poetry. That glory is both given and not given; it is given but it must also be earned.

Insofar as the poet must "abdicate"—at least temporarily—from a glory that has not yet been earned, the descent to reality will be experienced, in the first instance, as pure negation: "Some sort of solitude / With neither swan nor dock." On one level, the closing couplet allows us to infer that the poet (or, in New Critical parlance, the speaker) happened to find himself with his mistress in a desolate spot of some kind; but since the desolation of the scene in the opening quatrain is marked by the absence of the swan, that quintessential Mallarméan symbol, an allegorical reading would seem more likely—and of course, Mallarmé's language is never directed toward an immediate or empirical level of referentiality. As in Kant's "Analytic of the Sublime," such a reading would describe a trajectory in which an initial disjunction between the Imagination and external Reality was the necessary prelude to a higher movement of the Imagination.

Indeed, the way in which negation is mirrored in the blankness of the poet's gaze is typical of the "Romantic Sublime," especially as manifested in English poetry. One is reminded, for example, of Coleridge's expostulation in "Dejection: An Ode": "And still I gaze—and with how blank an eye!" With

respect to Mallarmé's œuvre, the first quatrain of "Petit Air I" is reminiscent of the gloomy opening of the "Ouverture Ancienne," with its absent swan and mirroring pool. In the sonnet, however, the chasm between the desolate landscape and the glory that unfolds in the sunset but is nevertheless beyond the poet's grasp would seem to be bridged harmoniously in the sestet. There is clearly an attempt in the sestet to bring heaven and earth into alignment with each other, to turn the swan into the woman and the woman into the swan. In the couplet the attempted reconciliation between Imagination and external Reality is effected via the figure of the woman who, plunging into the waves, becomes her own "naked jubilation."

The reconciliation is not complete, however, and the tone of the poem remains wistful despite the "jubilation" of the final line. It is significant that Mallarmé does not designate the languorously gliding bird of the sestet as a swan: it is simply "tel fugace oiseau" ("some passing bird"). Furthermore, the association that allows the bird to hover over the sestet is oddly asymmetrical: the bird is likened both to the white linen thrown off by the bather and to the bather herself. Perhaps it is only the ghost of a bird that hovers in the poem. "Comme" in line 10 can mean both "like" and "as"; with the former possibility, the bird is likened to the linen; with the latter, the linen floating down to the ground merely seems to take the shape of a bird.

PETIT AIR II / LITTLE AIR II

The second of the three "Petit Airs" was not published in Mallarmé's lifetime, but appeared for the first time in the 1899 edition of the *Poésies* published by Deman. In the bibliography he prepared for that edition Mallarmé's note on the poem reads: "belonging to the album of M. [Alphonse] Daudet." An 1893 manuscript of the poem has the variant "*Tomber* sur quelque sentier" in the last line (*OC*, 1484; Barbier and Millan, *Œuvres Complètes,* 407).

On the most immediate level, the image of the bird functions in terms of fairly traditional Romantic expectations in "Petit Air II," as a symbol of the poet or of his aspirations. The bird gives itself over entirely to its flight and to its song, without thought of being seen or heard, so that in the moment of its death it rises, in both flight and song, to an apex. (The verb "éclater" in line 3 gives the sense of both a bursting apart and a brilliance.) In the second quatrain, however, the symbol appears to leave the realm of nature and to take on the connotation of pure spirit; for this is a voice that is "foreign to the wood." That it is followed by no echo suggests perhaps that the song is heard at the moment of death, but also that this is an unheard melody. An English reader will be reminded of Keats, and of the opening lines of Shelley's ode "To a Skylark": "Hail to thee, blithe Spirit! / Bird thou never wert."

The third quatrain is extremely enigmatic (apparently to the poet as well as to the reader), but a number of points can be made to set the various enigmas in perspective. First, "cela" in line 10 is ambiguous; syntactically, it can refer to the music that dies (away) or is breathed out ("expire" has a dual meaning), and to the question being asked in lines 11 and 12. Secondly, "doute," also in line 10, is a word that frequently—and prominently—occurs in the *Poésies,* in the context of the poet's interrogation of the relationship between music (or poetry) and nature or reality, as in the opening of "L'Après-midi d'un Faune" ("My doubt, night's ancient hoard"—

line 4). Actually, a number of questions remain in doubt ("dans le doute expire"): among them, whether the bird dies ("expire") in midflight; and whether the music that is breathed out and that dies away ("expire") is an extension of nature or a construction (or reconstruction) of reality (as in "L'Après-midi"). In comparing himself in Romantic fashion to the bird, Mallarmé seems to be asking, moreover, whether the pathos of Nature is equivalent to, or more or less powerful than, the pathos of Art. The play on "sein / sien" in line 11 would appear to be in function of that question. One is reminded again of Shelley, who, envying the skylark for its spontaneity and its embeddedness in Nature, nevertheless comes to the realization that "If we were things born / Not to shed a tear, / I know not how thy joy we ever should come near." But Mallarmé is much more ambiguous than Shelley, and the question asked in lines 11 and 12 also has to do with the problem of illusion versus reality.

The couplet glides over an idea that will later be articulated more definitely by Yeats in the concluding lines of "Crazy Jane and the Bishop": "For nothing can be sole or whole / That has not been rent." As is so often the case, however, Mallarmé's ambiguous syntax allows us to read the couplet as a question, as a statement, or (if "va" is subjunctive) as a kind of prayer. The underlying conception, if applied to the lyric poet, would seem to represent the poetic process in sacrificial terms as a kenosis, or emptying out of the self, so that the poet becomes analogous to the martyr (see Peter Hambly, "Cinq Sonnets de Mallarmé," 42–43). Mallarmé's technique of indirection enables him to suggest a connection of this kind—without breaching decorum—via the symbol. The conception of poetic sublimation that he develops (a conception that is diametrically opposed to the "egotistical sublime" of a Wordsworth or Whitman) is a general undercurrent in all of those poems in the *Poésies* that reflect on the poetic process, and is more or less implicit in "Prose" and "Toast Funèbre."

PETIT AIR (Guerrier) / LITTLE AIR (Martial)

This witty sonnet originally appeared as the epigraph to "L'Action" (subsequently retitled "L'Action Restreinte" and grouped with several other short pieces under the rubric "Quant au Livre"), an essay included in the *Variations sur un Sujet* that Mallarmé published in the *Revue Blanche* during 1895. The poem was first published on its own in the *Poésies* in 1913.

The opening line contains one of Mallarmé's more fantastic puns, since "hormis l'y taire" resonates against its homonym "hors militaire." In other words, it suits the poet ("Ce me va"), except for keeping quiet about it ("hormis l'y taire"), to remain outside of the military ("hors militaire"). (In the phrases "It suits me" and "not to hold my peace," the translation attempts to capture something of Mallarmé's untranslatable pun.)

Shadows flickering from the fireplace, together perhaps with the reflection of the late afternoon sun, form the image of a military costume reddening on the poet's leg. With regard to the poem's background, we should recall that it was written in the aftermath of the Franco-Prussian War (1870–1871), at a time in which patriotic fervor directed against things German (as the mention of "Teuton" in line 10 subtly underlines) was again on the rise. The Dreyfus Affair, as a case in point, began in the middle 1890s. The military metaphor that emerges in the sonnet is exceedingly complex, however, for it functions both with reference to the poetic process and with reference to the emotional frenzy that regimes try to whip up in the public in order to further their military adventures. The military metaphor is the vehicle for a chastening and disciplining of raw emotion, which, as so many of the *Poésies* delineate, Mallarmé regards as a necessary propaedeutic to the poetic process; but at the same time, the raw emotion that the poet wishes to "weed out" (in the couplet) is itself subtly associated with the military fervor of his day. Thus, if we read between the lines, it suits the poet to remain outside the military ("hors militaire") and, by speaking out ("hormis l'y taire"), to adopt a military posture against the military frenzy being whipped up in the masses, which is the same sort of frenzy that results in the rhetoric of bad poetry.

PLUSIEURS SONNETS / SEVERAL SONNETS

The four *Plusieurs Sonnets* are among Mallarmé's greatest and most characteristic achievements. From a philosophical point of view, they are aimed very high—at the cosmos and our relation to it; hence, at the human condition and the meaning of poetry; and through Mallarmé's technical virtuosity in the handling of the sonnet form, they achieve a power of condensation and a beauty of phrasing that are often astonishing. All four of the sonnets make use of cosmic imagery, the central image, or trope, being a constellation in three of them. The first three are Petrarchan sonnets, while the last is a sonnet on two rhymes. Taken together, they constitute one of the "limits of art."

I. QUAND L'OMBRE MENAÇA DE LA FATALE LOI / WHEN THE SHADOW MENACED WITH ITS FATAL LAW

"Quand l'ombre menaça," the first of the group, has often been compared to "Toast Funèbre" for the directness with which it articulates Mallarmé's fundamental vision. It has been argued that the sonnet originated around 1870, during the period in which "Toast Funèbre" was composed and not long after the religious crisis of the 1860s (see Austin Gill, "From 'Quand l'ombre menaça,'" 415). There is no direct evidence for this, however, and the sonnet did not actually appear in print until 1883 when it was included, under the title of "Cette Nuit," in the *Poëtes Maudits* edited by Verlaine. The title was retained in subsequent publications of the sonnet, until finally being suppressed in the 1887 edition of the *Poésies*.

In the opening quatrain the "religious crisis" is adumbrated with extraordinary succinctness, not only in itself but as it bears upon the poetic process. Whether we ascribe that crisis to Mallarmé personally, or see it more generally as impinging upon the European spirit of his time, ultimately does not matter, since, in any event, the "moi" of line 4 is a "concrete universal." The abstractness of the lines allows us to read a great deal into them, but my own tendency would be to interpret "That old dream" ("Tel vieux rêve") as the religious dream (of a God or of plural gods) that, having been shared by men over the centuries (the "hideous centuries," Mallarmé writes in line 11), is now "menaced" by the "shadow." The "shadow," from this point of view, is at once Doubt and a figure for the universe rendered meaningless by the "Death of God"—which is to say, by

Doubt taken to its extreme. If we were to historicize this perception, which the adjective "indubitable" in line 4 seems to allow us to do, we might point not only to the Scientific Revolution, which, from its beginnings in the seventeenth century, had arrived at another focal point in Mallarmé's own day as a result of Darwin, but, more specifically, to Cartesian Doubt. For Mallarmé, however (as perhaps for Keats before him), the Dream is not annihilated by doubt, by the shadow, precisely because it is able, so to speak, to fold itself within the individual as experience—in other words, to emerge as Poetry. The metaphorical wing that is folded within the poet is *indubitable*; it cannot be denied, much as Descartes' "pure and distinct ideas" cannot be denied, because it is an aspect of the individual's sensuously felt experience, which is what allows him to refer to a "moi" in the first place (line 4). In short, if we pose this in Hegelian terms, the "Death of God" leads to the full emancipation of Poetry.

We are clearly in the realm of infinite Pascalian spaces in the opening quatrain—which is why it seemed reasonable to transform the "plafonds funèbres" ("funereal ceilings") of line 3 to "night's black maw." But Mallarmé's metaphor conveys a peculiar sense of boundedness that will carry over to the second quatrain. There we encounter the universe as a theater in which the lone spectator is a sadistic king who is entertained by "celebrated garlands [being] twisted in death"—that is, by the constellations. Mallarmé's conception, I take it, is that in order to avoid the problem of infinity and meaninglessness, the mythological imagination develops a closed system, as it were, by way of positing some sort of explanation or rationalization for what it is unable to grasp; in short, it invents a theater of some kind.

Such a "closed system" may have a consolatory function, but even if it begins in a consolatory vein it inevitably comes upon certain *aporiae*—occasioned by the existence of evil, death, and suffering—which the human condition must inevitably confront. The "king" in "Quand l'ombre menaça" is depicted as cruel or sadistic—as one who is "seduced" or "beguiled" by suffering and death, because, if there is a king—that is, if the system is "closed"—there is no other way of explaining the existence of those evils. Even a monotheistic frame of reference cannot, for Mallarmé, wholly escape the taint of religious sadism.

All of this, however, is merely a proud lie that has been constructed in order to avoid the nothingness that the shadows standing as figures of nothingness ("ténèbres" in line 7, "l'ombre" in line 1) expose as a lie. (Mallarmé's syntax in line 7 is extremely complex; however, I take it that "orgueil" carries the sense of "proud lie" and that "menti" means both "belied" and "lied" in this context: "belied" in the sense that the shadows expose the lie and "lied" in the sense that they, or the attempt to avoid them, are the ultimate source of the lie.) If it were not for that "indubitable wing" enfolded within the self, we would be on the horns of a hideous dilemma: a dilemma between an antiquated mythological system imbued with sadism, on the one hand, and sheer nothingness, on the other. Indeed, because of that wing, faith has not only not been lost but is grounded on something "indubitable." Each word in line 8 strikes the reader with tremendous precision and finality. Mallarmé writes "solitary" rather than "poet" (although clearly "poet" is implied) in order to convey the inwardness of an ecstatic but also deeply painful spiritual struggle; he refers to the solitary as being "dazzled" by his faith ("ébloui" is singular and must therefore modify "solitaire" rather than "yeux"), at the same time that the

solitary sees behind the deception exposed by the shadows; and he concludes the octave with the most daring of all monosyllables. Like the Gautier whom he lionizes in "Toast Funèbre," Mallarmé's solitary is endowed with "the mysterious gift of seeing with the eyes" (see above, p. 189); paradoxically, the more clearly he sees into the emptiness, the more he is dazzled by the inner light of faith. Radical skepticism is combined with, and issues forth in, the affirmation of a hymn—as in "Prose," the title of which merges both of these vectors.

There could, however, be a darker reading of these lines, one that would construe human limitations in a much more pessimistic light. Such a reading would take a different perspective on the participle "ébloui" and the prepositional phrase "aux yeux" in line 8. The "dazzling" that the solitary experiences is profoundly ambiguous because it is an experience that the sense organs are unable to sustain—and this is part of the definition of the verb "éblouir." To be dazzled is, in a way, to be blinded, and so there is a sense in which the participle cuts both ways. From this point of view, the solitary, dazzled by his faith and also by the brilliant display of the constellations in the night sky, remains "benighted," as it were, even though his affirmation is built on a poetic rather than a theological "lie." In this connection we should recall the passage from a letter that Mallarmé wrote in 1866 to Cazalis in regard to the composition of *Hérodiade*:

Yes, I *know*, we are merely empty forms of matter, but we are indeed sublime in having invented God and our soul. So sublime, my friend, that I want to gaze upon matter, fully conscious that it exists, and yet launching itself madly into Dream, despite its knowledge that Dream has no existence, extolling the Soul and all the divine impressions of that kind which have collected within us from the beginning of time and proclaiming, in the face of the Void which is truth, these glorious lies! (*Selected Letters*, 60)

From this point of view, "aux yeux" suggests not that the solitary sees through the lie but that it is reflected in his eyes. The question is whether Man can live without his fictions and whether the path of aestheticism does not merely reinscribe those fictions in a new key.

The affirmation of human genius in the sestet would seem to relegate the latter, more pessimistic interpretation to the background, however; for Mallarmé's conception is that far off in space and time from "this night"—far off, that is, from the moment of creativity—the Earth throws off the light of an unprecedented mystery ("l'insolite mystère") beneath the hideous centuries. In a version of the sonnet published in 1886 Mallarmé substituted "pour" for "sous," before returning to "sous" in subsequent printings. Both prepositions are applicable to the conception he is developing, but "sous" makes the line more abstract and ambiguous: it enables the line to suggest either that the "hideous centuries" nevertheless rest upon the unprecedented mystery of the creative moment or, more tragically, that they loom over the creative moment without actually being touched by it. At any rate, something *radiant* has been achieved—even if the eyes, being dazzled, are also blinded—which can be set as an affirmation against the implacable darkness and emptiness of material processes, on the one hand, and of human history, on the other. It is notable that "siècles hideux" has the effect of linking history to the cosmos, since, as A. R. Chisholm suggests, in a certain sense both are "inhuman." "This radiance," remarks Chisholm, "has been achieved by the efforts of many creative minds, making their way up from the obscure beginnings of thought and the barbarity of past ages—'les siècles hideux.' The ancient savagery of man can no longer hide this splendor, or at any rate it now obscures it less" ("Mallarmé: 'Quand l'ombre menaça,'" 148). Mallarmé probably would not have agreed with Shelley, that "poets are the unacknowledged legislators of the world"; yet, "Quand l'ombre menaça," like Shelley's "Ode to the West Wind," concludes with the suggestion of genius kindling genius through the ages, in an unbroken chain of human solidarity. Shelley asks that the wind "Scatter, as from an unextinguished hearth / Ashes and sparks, my words among mankind." To Mallarmé, at the conclusion of this great sonnet, the "vile fires" that are given off by the meaningless process of the stars, and that roll in the "boredom" of a space that is always the same, nevertheless stand as external witness to an interior light that, once kindled into genius, reaches across the centuries.

II. LE VIERGE, LE VIVACE ET LE BEL AUJOURD'HUI / THE VIRGINAL, VIBRANT, AND BEAUTIFUL DAWN

Mallarmé's best known and, according to Madame Noulet, least understood sonnet (see *Vingt Poèmes de Stéphane Mallarmé*, 131) was first printed in the *Revue Indépendante* in March 1885 and subsequently in the 1887 edition of the *Poésies*. As Thibaudet notes, the fourteen rhymes of the sonnet all have the *i* sound: "They develop on that contracted and piercing vowel the monotony of a vast space, solitary and silent, as white and hard as ice" (*La Poésie de Stéphane Mallarmé*, 250; translation mine). In order to replicate in some measure the intricacies of Mallarmé's sound patterning, I have constructed the translation on two basic rhyme endings. "Aujourd'hui" in line 1 is rendered here as "dawn" to rhyme with "swan" and to capture the metaphorical transformation of the day to the swan, the poem's central symbol.

Exactly when the sonnet was composed remains unknown, but one senses that the symbolism it employs has been refined in the alembic of Mallarmé's earlier work as well as in that of the poetic tradition in general. Two great poems by Baudelaire, "Le Cygne" and "L'Albatros," stand behind the sonnet, and critics have also pointed to images from Gautier's *Émaux et Camées*, to Ronsard's sonnet, "Ma plume vol au Ciel pour estre quelque signe," and to a number of other poems. Three primary Mallarméan symbols are brought together in the sonnet and interwoven with one another, and this accounts, in part, for the poem's extraordinary richness. First and foremost, of course, is the swan symbol, which, as we have seen, figures importantly in the "Ouverture Ancienne" as well as in several other early poems. Christine Crow, in calling our attention to Ronsard's "Ma plume vol au Ciel," emphasizes the significance to Mallarmé of the "cygne"/"signe" homophone and of the double meaning of "plume" as feather and pen ("Le Silence au Vol de Cygne," 18, n. 24). While these elements play a role in the sonnet, however, the whiteness of the swan and the beauty it symbolizes must be understood against the background of the two other primary symbols in the sonnet: the ice and the snow. The ice that entraps the bird is also the mirror in which its antitype, or negative, can be glimpsed as the "transparent glacier of flights never flown" (line 4)—in the way that Hérodiade glimpses herself as a "far-off shadow" in the passage beginning "Mirror,

cold water frozen in your frame" from the "Scène." The manner in which the desire to shatter the ice is expressed as a question in the opening quatrain is reminiscent of the concluding stanza of "Les Fenêtres": "Is there a way, O Self, thou who hast known bitterness, / To burst the crystal that the monster has profaned, / And take flight, with my two featherless / Wings—at the risk of falling through eternity?" Finally, the vast expanse of the snow, which, in its whiteness, will eventually swallow up the whiteness of the swan, is related as a symbolic construct to the vast expanse of the azure in "L'Azur" and other early poems. Both stand in function of an absolute, toward which and against which humanity heroically strives.

Can the privileged moment of inspiration triumph over the vast expanse of undifferentiated time into which it must ultimately be swallowed up and reabsorbed? The poem begins by asking this metaphysical question, and, in its opening quatrain (as also in "Don du Poëme"), inspiration "dawns" as a double metaphor: on the wings of a bird and in the vibrancy of a new day. But the metaphysical problem from which the bird flies, and against which it takes flight, assumes the form of a double exile. The actual, lowercase swan is in exile on earth, in the here-and-now or here-below (the *ici-bas* of "Les Fenêtres"); it yearns for an absolute realm "in which to exist / When the boredom of the sterile winter has shone," and its "pure brightness" (or perfect whiteness, "pur éclat") is a sign, on the metaphorical level, of the absolute it contains and seeks to actualize. Paradoxically, however, that absolute realm can never be realized—even when it is realized. On the one hand, insofar as it is an individual, the swan will eventually be swallowed up in the ice and snow, its whiteness lost in the greater whiteness. But on the other hand—and here Mallarmé's greatness, and the divergence of his tragic vision from all (Romantic) systems of consolation, makes itself felt—even insofar as the swan, the moment of inspiration, can be constellated as pure form, as the uppercase Swan, it can only assume what is essentially a new exile, one in which its nostalgia turns back upon the living swan of memory, "haunted," as it were, either "beneath the ice" or beneath the mirror of the stars—for ultimately it amounts to the same thing—"by the transparent glacier of flights never flown." The Swan is trapped in the stars in the same way that the swan is trapped in the ice; what is congealed in the achieved form of the poem is the same desire for transcendence—that is, for life—that led to the poem in the first place.

There are a number of ambiguities in the poem that are extremely interesting in light of these themes. In line 6 the swan "frees itself without hope" ("sans espoir se délivre"), which is to say, struggles hopelessly (and unsuccessfully) to free itself; similarly, in line 9, its neck both shakes *from* and shakes *off* "this white agony" ("secouera" being both transitive and intransitive). That these verbs express their own opposites says something about the metaphysical double bind into which the poem is locked—and this relates also to the two questions that are implicitly being raised in lines 7 and 8: (1) why the swan failed to sing of a land in which it might live "when the boredom of the sterile winter ha[d] shone"; and (2), even more subtly, why it failed to praise a land in which one might live "when the boredom of the sterile winter has shone" (the verb in line 7 can also be both transitive and intransitive). Those critics who are in the habit of reducing everything to Mallarmé's biography point to the problem of artistic impotence, as if the poet were simply lamenting the paucity of his output in these lines. Certainly the problem of "death-in-life" (to borrow Coleridge's

phrase) is one that is inescapable, no matter how "full" the life that is lived; and certainly the glacier metaphor of line 4 will remind us of Freud. But the swan, it seems fair to say, did not sing (of) the land in which one might live for the simple reason that, in Mallarmé's vision, such a land does not exist. Our transcendental hopes and dreams are ungrounded, and though art presents itself as a kind of ground—that is, though we can think of the swan as finding a home in the sonnet itself—what is really grounded in the work of art is our ungroundedness. The swan stiffens into form, into the Swan, when the individual becomes one with the species, but the species takes on life only in its concrete embodiment as an actual individual existing in time. In contrast to Keats's Nightingale, Mallarmé's swan *is* born for death, and to the extent that it becomes an "immortal Bird," it nevertheless refuses—to its credit—to regard that dispensation with anything other than "disdain" and as anything other than a "useless exile."

III. VICTORIEUSEMENT FUI LE SUICIDE BEAU / THE BEAUTIFUL SUICIDE VICTORIOUSLY FLED

An early version of "Victorieusement fui le suicide beau," preceded by an essay on Mallarmé by Verlaine, was published in 1885 in the *Hommes d'Aujourd'hui* series edited by Léon Vanier. The sonnet was substantially revised for the 1887 edition of the *Poésies*.

Like "La chevelure vol d'une flamme à l'extrême," to which it has often been compared, "Victorieusement" is an articulation of the "solar myth" that Mallarmé, in *Les Dieux Antiques*, his study of Occidental mythology, referred to as the "Tragedy of Nature" (*OC*, 1216). (*Les Dieux Antiques*, an adaptation of several works on mythology by the Englishman George Cox, appeared in 1880 [see Gardner Davies, *Mallarmé et le Drame Solaire*, 32–39].) In Mallarmé's solar myth the descent of the sun is tantamount, on the cosmic plane, to the death of a god (or the death of God), and, on the human plane, to a fall into the material world of sexuality, a fall that has been occasioned by the loss of a previous source of plenitude and power. Hence the rapid (indeed radical) movement from the third to the first person in the opening quatrain. As in certain gnostic versions of the Creation story, in which the Creation and Fall are simultaneous events, the poet/hero of Mallarmé's solar myth accedes to sexuality only after forfeiting an anterior *glory* and, even more ironically, takes on the lineaments of a specifically human creativity only after losing his divine powers.

The deep ambivalence registered by the sonnet strikes an immediate chord in the first word of the poem, the adverb "Victorieusement." According to Robert Cohn, it signifies "both the glorious sunset and the literal 'victory' of the poet who did not perish in that conflagration" (*Toward the Poems of Mallarmé*, 134). But this interpretation, in separating the sunset from the poet, strikes me as too flat; for as the words "fui" and "suicide" indicate, that which has survived and that which has fled has done so only at the expense of having perished in another, perhaps more *glorious* form. The glory of the sunset occurs only in the context of the sun's descent and, hence, the victorious apotheosis of the god occurs in the context of his death. The laughter of line 3 is thus doubly ironic (hence my translation "What irony"), and not, as some critics would have it, a simple laugh of victory (St. Aubyn, *Stéphane Mallarmé*, 89), because survival has also meant the forfeiture of the royalty signified by the color purple.

The section on Heracles in *Les Dieux Antiques* offers fascinating insight into the poem at hand, Heracles being, in Mallarmé's conception, a prime avatar of the solar deity. In the sophist Prodicos's discussion of Heracles, Mallarmé notes, the hero is affianced to Iole but is soon separated from her "because all the heroes that represent the sun are separated from their first loves, just as the sun leaves the beautiful dawn behind it when it rises in the heavens" (*OC*, 1214; translation mine). The name Iole, Mallarmé then observes, signifies the color violet; thus, Heracles (the sun) must leave Iole, whose color of violet or purple is the royal color, to descend into the world (*OC*, 1214).

In the scenario of the second quatrain, which has the woman combing out her golden hair, we are given (as in "La chevelure vol") what amounts to a microcosm of the solar drama that has been played out on the cosmic level. (One of the salient features of allegory, as Angus Fletcher points out in his study of the mode, is the play between microcosm and macrocosm [see *Allegory*, esp. 70–146].) But the "trésor . . . de tête" referred to in line 7 is appropriately deemed "presumptuous" because the human situation represents a "fall" from a former glory. Nevertheless, as Wordsworth says in the "Immortality" ode—a poem that is curiously akin to "Victorieusement fui" in its emphasis on lost glory—"Earth fills her lap with pleasures of her own" (line 77); in other words, the woman's hair brings with it delight because it retains a "puerile" vestige of triumph—"puerile," like "presumptuous," signalling the essential incommensurability of the two realms being measured. The sonnet concludes with a typically Mallarméan tribute, gracefully modest and self-effacing, to the lady in question; but this gesture is played off against the "ciel évanoui," the vanished sky that at the same time is a vanished heaven.

IV. SES PURS ONGLES TRÈS HAUT / HER PURE NAILS ON HIGH

One of Mallarmé's most widely discussed poems, the "Sonnet en-*yx*," originally entitled "Sonnet allégorique de lui-même," dates from the spring of 1868, when the poet was living and teaching in Avignon, but was not published until 1887, when it appeared in the *Poésies* in a thoroughly revised version. From a technical point of view, as St. Aubyn notes, "Mallarmé set himself the complicated task of inverting the gender of the rhymes between the quatrains and the tercets: the masculine *-yx* of the quatrains becomes the feminine *-ixe* in the tercets while the feminine *-ore* of the quatrains becomes the masculine *-or* of the tercets" (*Stéphane Mallarmé*, 90). Thus, in the very rhyme scheme of the sonnet, we have a chiasmus, or cross, which is echoed in the *ix* rhyme itself, as well as being mirrored, both imagistically and linguistically, in the "croisée" of line 9. Robert Cohn has pointed to the epistemological importance in Mallarmé's work of the cross or "double polarity" (see *Toward the Poems of Mallarmé*, 276–278); but one should not underestimate the possibility that the cross has a more traditional iconographic significance.

In any event, one aspect of the fascination that this poem has always engendered has to do with the fact that the technical problem of finding rhymes ending in *ix* (which in French are extremely few) cannot be separated from the *content* or *meaning* of the poem—and it is for this reason, perhaps, that Mallarmé considered it a sonnet "allegorical of itself." The mirroring of form and content, technique and meaning, is of course focused upon the *ptyx* of the second quatrain. In May of 1868 Mallarmé writes to Eugène Lefébure: "I may write a sonnet and as I have only three rhymes in -ix, do your best to send me the true meaning of the word ptyx, for I'm told it doesn't exist in any language, something I'd much prefer, for that would give me the joy of creating it through the magic of rhyme" (*Selected Letters*, 85). There is "no ptyx" "on the credenzas in the empty room" (line 5), for the simple reason that the word does not exist in French— or at least, *did not* exist prior to the existence of the sonnet. Nevertheless, the word *does* occur in Greek, where it seems to designate a fold (a favorite Mallarméan concept) and, by implication, a seashell. (The *Thesaurus Linguae Graecae*, note the editors of the Pléiade, "gives the sense of the fold of an organ and cites an example in which 'ptyx' means oyster shell" [*OC*, 1490].) The word has been interpreted variously by the critics: as a seashell, a writing tablet, a fold, and a receptacle (see Ellen Burt, "Mallarmé's 'Sonnet en-*yx*,'" 56).

As is often the case in the *Poésies*, by the time the "Sonnet en-*yx*" had arrived at its definitive form certain symbolic connections that had been more evident in the original version had been obscured; and thus, the original version may shed light on the published poem:

La nuit approbatrice allume les onyx
De ses ongles au pur Crime lampadophore,
Du Soir aboli par le vespéral Phoenix
De qui la cendre n'a de cinéraire amphore.

Sur des consoles, en le noir Salon: nul ptyx,
Insolite vaisseau d'inanité sonore,
Car le Maitre est allé puiser l'eau du Styx
Avec tous ses objets dont le rêve s'honore.

Et selon la croisée au nord vacante, un or
Néfaste incite pour son beau cadre une rixe
Faite d'un dieu que croit emporter une nixe

En l'obscurcissement de la glace, Décor
De l'absence, sinon que sur la glace encor
De scintillation le septuor se fixe.

In the original version, the ptyx is clearly a vessel or container (line 6), and this implication remains in the published version; furthermore, in the original version, the ptyx serves the function of the Dream, whereas in the published version it is that by which Nothingness honors itself. We might say, then, that the ptyx, literally signifying nothing, serves the Master as a container of nothing, of nothingness, of that which cannot be contained, of those dreams which, "burnt by the Phoenix," no funeral amphora contains (lines 3–4).

The ptyx is thus, as A. R. Chisholm maintains, an alternative to the funeral amphora (see "Mallarmé: 'Ses purs ongles,'" 231)—but this does not require us to conclude, as Chisholm does, that the ptyx *is* an amphora, for that would be to deny its essential nothingness. Moreover, as Chisholm notes—and this is fascinating in light of the possible religious significance of the *ix* rhyme and the cross shape, and also in light of Mallarmé's involvement with English words—the word *pyx* in English is "a container in which the host is kept for communion—an idea that is by no means remote from that of *cinéraire amphore*" (232). I have rendered, not the (non) word "ptyx" itself, but the "aboli bibelot" (literally: "abolished trinket") that qualifies it in line 6, as "abolished shell": first, because of the Greek etymology that resonates against the significance of the seashell as a symbol of poetry (one thinks, for example, of Wordsworth's "Dream of the Arab" in Book V of *The Prelude*), and secondly, because of the possible sense of "shell" in English as the *husk* of that which has vanished in substance.

Language in the sonnet, writes Richard Goodkin, implicitly connecting the ptyx to the imagery of the opening quatrain, "is simultaneously an earthly tool pointing with admiration to something which it is not, *indicating*, as would a finger, phenomena which are outside of itself and distinguishable from it, and a celestial mirror, a reflexive locus of meaning *delineating* and sacralizing the site of the linguistic utterance" (*The Symbolist Home and the Tragic Home*, 159). The paradox of the opening quatrain would seem to be that Anguish, the lampbearer—whose fingernails are the stars of the constellation Ursa Major, although this does not become clear until the conclusion of the poem—sustains our dreams, precisely insofar as her existence testifies to the fact that those dreams cannot be *contained* otherwise than in the poem. The Phoenix rises from its own ashes, but this process is a merely cyclical one and, thus, the problem posed by the sonnet as a whole is how to contain, how to memorialize, that which is intangible and that which would otherwise be merely consumed. It is the same problem that is posed in "Prose," in "Toast Funèbre," in the *tombeau* sonnets, and, in general, in the *Poésies* as a whole.

The poem itself, of course, is the only container for expressing the ineffable—and from this point of view the ptyx of the second quatrain is nothing else than the poem. But what is the poem? In empirical terms it is nothing, and yet it has the magical property of containing the uncontainable, of expressing the inexpressible. It is by means of the poem that "the Master" (in what I regard as one of the greatest single lines in all poetry) goes down to the underworld to "draw tears from the Styx." Like the hero of epic, his task is to confront the reality of death; but at the same time (and here Mallarmé conflates the river Lethe with the Styx), by evoking the "tears of things" he manages to contain that which would otherwise be swept into oblivion.

A remarkable letter written in July 1868 to Henri Cazalis, testifying to the quasi-cabalistic function that poetry has by now assumed for Mallarmé (a sense of the poem that is overtly concretized in such poems as the "Ouverture Ancienne" and "Prose"), sheds light on the difficult imagery of the final six lines of the "Sonnet en-*yx*":

> I'm extracting this sonnet . . . from a projected study of The Word ["parole"]: it is inverted, by which I mean that its meaning, if there is one (but I'd draw consolation for its lack of meaning from the dose of poetry it contains, at least in my view) is evoked by an internal mirage created by the words themselves. If you murmur it to yourself a couple of times, you get a fairly cabbalistic sensation. . . . [T]here is a window open, at night, the two shutters fastened; a room with no one in it, despite the stable appearance provided by the fastened shutters, and in a night made of absence and questioning, without furniture apart from the vague outline of what appear to be tables, a warlike and dying frame of a mirror hung up at the back of the room, with its reflection, a stellar and incomprehensible reflection, of Ursa Major, which links to heaven alone this dwelling abandoned by the world. (*Selected Letters*, 86–87)

The "septuor," in the final line of the sonnet, refers to the seven stars of Ursa Major, also known in English as "the Big Dipper," and hence linked to the "ptyx" as a container of the "tears of things." (Chisholm argues that Mallarmé has chosen a musical term, "septuor," to substitute for the "septentrion," the seven stars of the northern sky, and that this substitution suggests the "music of the spheres" ["Mallarmé: 'Ses purs ongles,'" 231]; Noulet, for her part, adds

that the "septuor," doubled by being reflected in the mirror, makes up the fourteen lines of the sonnet: hence Mallarmé's description, "Sonnet allégorique de lui-même" [*Vingt Poèmes de Stéphane Mallarmé*, 191].) In any event, standing behind the sonnet is the myth of Callisto that Mallarmé adumbrates in *Les Dieux Antiques* (see *OC*, 1243–1244; Davies, *Mallarmé et le Drame Solaire*, 136n.). Callisto, incurring the wrath of Artemis, is changed into a bear before being transformed into a star in the constellation that will henceforth be called Ursa Major. In the definitive version of the sonnet, the traces of the myth are obscured because the "god" of the early version has been transmogrified into the unicorns. Nevertheless, the female figure of the second tercet ("Elle"), who is either dead or departed from (or into) the mirror—Mallarmé's syntax is particularly strange here—is connected to her constellation in much the same way as the swan is connected to the constellation Cygnus. Her death or absence is connected to the waning of the light ("un or / Agonise"—lines 9–10), and perhaps is what has given rise to the Anguish of the opening quatrain. The phrase "défunte nue" in line 12 is deeply ambiguous, first, because "défunte" can mean "dead" (or "defunct"—as in Ravel's "Pavanne pour une Infante Défunte") or, by extension, "absent" or "departed," and secondly, because "nue" (as in other sonnets, notably "La chevelure vol d'une flamme à l'extrême") can mean both "nude" and "cloud." With the latter possibility, as Chisholm suggests, "the nymph in the glass becomes an absent cloud of golden hair" ("Mallarmé: 'Ses purs ongles,'" 233), and this would connect the sonnet to "Victorieusement fui le suicide beau," the previous one in the sequence.

The symbolism of the unicorns and the nix, which are engraved on the frame of the mirror, remains enigmatic. A "nix" is a water sprite, and the opposition of fire and water (and perhaps of male and female) in the tercets seems to represent the reprise of a motif that has already been played out in the quatrain, with the Phoenix and the Master drawing tears from the Styx. (Why the Phoenix is capitalized in the quatrains and the unicorns are not in the tercets presents another enigma, unless capitalization serves the play of macrocosm against microcosm that seems to obtain in general in the *Plusieurs Sonnets*.) Mallarmé's letter to Cazalis, referring to "a warlike, dying frame of a mirror," is reminiscent of the mirror frame in the "Ouverture Ancienne" of *Hérodiade* ("La chambre singulière en un cadre, attirail / De siècle belliqueux . . ." / "The strange chamber, framed in all the baggage / Of a warlike age . . ."—lines 20–21), and perhaps the war being enacted is something like the eternal war of earth and cloud, or earth and heaven, that is posed in the "Tombeau d'Edgar Poe": "Du sol et de la nue hostiles, ô grief!" (line 9), in which case, the problem again would be to find a container for, or raise a monument to, that which would otherwise be burnt by the Phoenix or drowned in the waters of the Styx.

HOMMAGES ET TOMBEAUX / HOMAGES AND TOMBS

SUR LES BOIS OUBLIÉS / IN THE FORGOTTEN WOODS

The paradox of memory is a central theme in the *Hommages et Tombeaux* as a whole, as well as in the *Poésies* generally; but it is significant that the first poem in the sequence focuses not on a famous artist but on an anonymous lady, who addresses her husband from the tomb. Probably composed in 1877 but not published until the 1913 edition of the *Poésies*, this sonnet evinces qualities of simplicity and tenderness for which Mallarmé is not always noted but which, in my own view, undergird even his most hermetically intellectual compositions.

It is likely that the sonnet was composed to the memory of Ettie Maspero, née Yapp, who at one time had been the fiancée of Mallarmé's close friend Henri Cazalis, and for whom the poet always retained deep affection. Married to the Egyptologist Gaston Maspero, she had died suddenly of a puerperal fever in 1873, at the age of twenty-seven, after the birth of her second child. By addressing Maspero in the dedication to the sonnet, Mallarmé seems to have been aware that the latter had become an adept of the theosophy of Madame Blavatsky and that he was in the habit of attempting to enter into contact with his dead wife by means of spiritual exercises (see Barbier and Millan, *Œuvres Complètes,* 280–281). But the supernatural is, as it were, naturalized in the sonnet; for that the dead lady should actually speak to her living husband does not strike us as extravagant or arcane but rather as the natural extension of a human love that, in fact, remains unbroken. Thus, in a certain sense, the spirit of the dead lady *is* corporealized by the breath of the living husband whispering her name—and this is what is most extraordinary about the poem.

Because of the syntactical inversion that opens the sonnet, winter passes over the forgotten woods, but also the complaint is made over (or to) the forgotten woods. The lady speaks from within the forgotten woods, and the inversion also serves to underline that fact. "Seuil" in line 2 can mean both "sill" or "threshold," and thus can refer to a window, to a grave site, or to a hearth or fireplace; the word is balanced against "foyer" in line 12, which has the meaning of both "hearth" and "entranceway."

LE TOMBEAU D'EDGAR POE / THE TOMB OF EDGAR POE

Mallarmé not only translated Poe's poetry but, like Baudelaire before him, who had translated the prose, he felt that he had virtually been *created* by Poe, so palpable was the influence. Why Poe haunted the imaginations of Baudelaire, Mallarmé, and (to a lesser extent) Valéry, while exerting an essentially negligible impact on poetry in English, is a question that remains mysterious, although many attempts have been made to answer it. It is hard for modern ears to ignore what seems to us Poe's vulgarity, but perhaps we are now deaf to an original tone that the French poets heard in his work. In any event, there is no doubt that Poe had a formative influence on the Symbolist aesthetic, both through the daemonic quality of his personality, in Robert Cohn's phrase (*Toward the Poems of Mallarmé*, 153), and through the argument set forth in his important manifesto, "The Poetic Principle."

The sonnet to Poe appeared for the first time in 1877 in a volume entitled *Edgar Allan Poe: A Memorial Volume*, which was published in Baltimore to accompany the erection of a monument to the American poet. (Poe had died of *delirium tremens* in 1849, and for many years his grave was without a tombstone.) The sonnet was subsequently printed in one of Verlaine's articles in the *Poëtes Maudits* series and, in a revised form, was included in the 1887 edition of the *Poésies*.

In a letter of July 1877 to one of the editors of the Poe memorial volume, Mallarmé provided a translation and a gloss of the sonnet ("une traduction probablement barbare que j'ai fait mot à mot" [*Correspondance de Stéphane Mallarmé* 2, 154; cited by Barbier and Millan, *Œuvres Complètes,* 274]), which sheds wonderful light on his thinking:

Such as into himself at last Eternity changes him,
The poet arouses with a naked (1) hymn
His century overawed not to have known
That death extolled itself in this (2) strange voice:
But in a vile writhing of an hydra, (they) once
    hearing the Angel (3)
To give (4) too pure a meaning to the words of the
    tribe,
They (between themselves) thought (by him) the
    spell drunk
In the honourless flood of some dark mixture (5)

Of the soil and the ether (which are) enemies, O
    struggle!
If with it my idea does not carve a bas-relief
Of which Poe's dazzling (6) tomb be adorned,
(A) stern block here fallen from a mysterious
    disaster,
Let this granite at least show forever their bound
To the old flights of Blasphemy (still) spread in the
    future. (7)

(1) Naked hymn means when the words take in
    death their absolute value.
(2) This: his own.
(3) The Angel: the above said Poet.
(4) To give: giving.
(5) —: in plain prose—charged him with always
    being drunk.
(6) Dàzzling: with the idea of such a bas relief.
(7) Blasphemy: against Poets, such as the charge of
    Poe being drunk. (*Correspondance de Stéphane
    Mallarmé* 2, 155)

In the original version of the sonnet, which Mallarmé is here translating, line 6 contained the phrase "un sens trop pur"; it was later revised to "plus pur." That is a small—though not unimportant—point, but a larger issue concerns Mallarmé's translation of "glaive nu" in the second line (literally "naked sword") as "naked hymn." The word "hymn" is interesting, not only because of the relationship between death and the sacred in Mallarmé but because it connects us to one of the meanings of "Prose." In English it supplies a homonymic rhyme with "him," and partly because of Mallarmé's fondness for homonymic rhyme (in "Prose" and elsewhere) I have transposed this word to line 4.

Mallarmé's explicit identification in the gloss of the Poet (capital *p*) with the angel is fascinating in view of the conjunction in the sonnet of a number of symbolic constructs that had previously been brought together in two early poems, "Le Guignon" and "L'Azur." (The translation mutes this possibility by turning the singular angel into plural seraphim.) In "Le Guignon," the "beggars of azure," who stand apart from the "bewildered human herd" (lines 1–3), are destroyed (as "poètes maudits") by a powerful angel waving a naked sword (lines 13–15). In "L'Azur," where Mallarmé himself takes on the voice of a "poète impuissant," he yearns for refuge among "the happy herd of men" (line 24). Although the angel is absent from this poem, his role is taken over by the semipersonified Azure wielding a sword in the final quatrain. In the Poe sonnet, however—or at least, in Mallarmé's gloss upon it—the poet, having been victimized by the "tribu," becomes the sword-bearing angel after his death. I have turned the tribe into a "horde," largely because of the sound, but I might also have translated it as "herd" (with all of the Nietzschean implications accruing to that word), because of the homonymic rhyme with "heard" and

because "tribu" seems to function in much the same manner as "bétail" does in "Le Guignon" and "L'Azur." A few other notes on the translation: I have rendered "suscite" ("arouses" or "awakens") in line 2 as "reawakens"; Mallarmé's verb is transitive, but in my rendering it can refer intransitively to the poet himself or transitively to his "siècle épouvanté" in line 3; similarly, the adjective "triumphant," in my translation of line 4, can refer to "voice" or to "death." Richard Goodkin's analysis alerted me to the possibility that "jamais" in the penultimate line of the sonnet pays tribute to the resonating "Nevermore" of Poe's "Raven" (see *The Symbolist Home and the Tragic Home*, 63); hence my "evermore," which translates it back again. In the "Tombeau d'Edgar Poe"—as also in "Toast Funèbre," and perhaps for similar reasons—the alexandrine has fallen naturally into English hexameters.

The poet, in the oft-quoted first line of the sonnet, becomes himself in death; but there is nevertheless a chastened awareness (as also in the "Tombeau de Charles Baudelaire" of 1893) that the purity of the work and the muddiness of the life are inescapably entwined. In "Les Fenêtres" the poet had glimpsed himself as an angel, but only tragically, and, as it were, through a glass, darkly. Poe was a drunkard, as the gloss candidly, and the sonnet itself more obliquely, admits; and the "war between earth and heaven" (line 9), which is always unfolding on a cosmic plane, is being played out in microcosm within the poet himself. This conception of the poet as inevitably *maudit*, a conception that Mallarmé inherits from Poe himself, is partly predicated on the widening gulf between the public and the private realms. The many-headed hydra of the second quatrain is a traditional symbol for the "public" or "crowd." Being an impure "mélange" (that is, a monster), but speaking

222

in one voice, the voice of bourgeois conformity, the crowd is altogether incapable of distinguishing beauty from ugliness; it therefore attributes the "magic" of the poetry to the poet's alcoholism. But the poet is not the angel that he glimpses in the mirror of his poetry, unless we take a rarefied platonic view of the matter. Victimized by the attitudes of the crowd, he himself becomes a "mélange" of opposites, to the extent that his very creativity is mediated by the ugliness from which he seeks to escape. Yet, in both the Poe and the Baudelaire sonnets, beauty—pure form—somehow arises or escapes from the content of the poetry, a content in which the monstrous ugliness of the time is undisguisedly rendered. Thus, the paradox of the sonnet is that the poet is himself, necessarily, a microcosm of the very struggle between earth and cloud, beauty and ugliness, which distinguishes the angel from the hydra.

Noulet has pointed to the close resemblance between the Poe sonnet and "Toast Funèbre" (*Vingt Poèmes de Stéphane Mallarmé*, 53). Indeed, in both poems the sepulcher or tombstone functions to mark a necessary boundary and to maintain a crucial distinction. In "Toast Funèbre" the "solid sepulcher where all things harmful lie" serves to contain "avaricious silence and night's immensity" (lines 55–56); and in the "Tombeau d'Edgar Poe," the granite tombstone is meant to hold in check the "dark flights of Blasphemy hurled to the future." One need not go quite as far as Marian Zwerling Sugano, who argues that the *tombeau* sonnets demonstrate a "breakdown of the monumentalizing function of literature itself" (*The Poetics of the Occasion*, 109); but perhaps the very concreteness of the physical monument in the Poe sonnet indicates that it is inevitably tied to a debased public sphere, and hence to the monstrous hydra. Sugano cites the *Scolies* appended to Mal-larmé's translation of Poe's verse, in which Mallarmé refers to "a useless and belated tombstone, rolled there [as] a boulder, immense, heavy, misshapen, deprecatory, as if to fully stop up the place from which might give forth toward the sky, like a pestilence, the just demands of a Poet's existence censored by all" (*The Poetics of the Occasion*, 113–114; *OC*, 226). Mallarmé's comment in the *Scolies* intensifies the contrast drawn in the sonnet itself between the physicality of the tombstone and the "idea" of line 10—which, in the circular syntax of the tercet, must ornament a dazzling tomb that it already ornaments ("Dont la tombe de Poe éblouissante s'orne"; literally: "By which the dazzling tomb of Poe ornaments itself"). In other words, the true monument, ideal in both senses of the word, is not something that can be concretized or made public. And yet the granite block is necessary, if only as a marker. Having fallen from some "obscure disaster"—literally, from a star—like the angel or the poet himself in Mallarmé's "solar myth" (see above, p. 216), the granite block marks off a distinction that tragically breaks down—or, if it is maintained, is maintained only on a transcendental plane, with respect to the angel.

The "Tombeau d'Edgar Poe" thus confronts the problem of poetic mediation on two planes at once. On one level, as in the Pentecost story—in which, reversing the story of Babel, the Holy Spirit is comprehended by people of different languages who are then sneered at as drunkards (Acts 2.1–12; see Jacques Morel, "Le 'Sortilège Bu' et la Pentecôte")—the angel "bestow[s] a purer sense on the language of the horde," only to encounter "dark flights of Blasphemy." But on another level, the "disaster" has always already occurred; the angel is merely a form seen through a glass, darkly; and the poet is a "dark mélange" of antagonistic elements—in short, a "monster."

LE TOMBEAU DE CHARLES BAUDELAIRE / THE TOMB OF CHARLES BAUDELAIRE

In July of 1892 Mallarmé was asked by the editor of *La Plume* to assume the presidency of a committee charged with preparing a subscription to erect a monument to Baudelaire. Rodin had already agreed to execute the work, and a dedicatory volume, *Le Tombeau de Baudelaire*, composed of poems written by the members of the committee, was to be published in conjunction with the unveiling of the monument. Mallarmé did not immediately accept the presidency of the committee, deferring to Leconte de Lisle, a contemporary closer in age to Baudelaire, but he participated in its work, and upon de Lisle's death in 1894, became its president. Mallarmé's *tombeau*, composed in 1893, was included in the volume published by *La Plume* in January 1895, and subsequently in the 1899 edition of the *Poésies* (*OC*, 1494–1495; Barbier and Millan, *Œuvres Complètes,* 411).

Mallarmé's sonnet has sometimes been accused of being less a tribute to Baudelaire than a satire on him; but if the poem is dominated by its oxymorons, how could a more fitting tribute be paid to the poet who, in the *Fleurs du Mal*, made of himself an emblem of modernity and of the city that Walter Benjamin termed "the capital of the nineteenth century"? And in any event (as the poem's conclusion indicates), how is it possible to erect a monument or compose a tribute to one who, for better or worse, has become the very air we breathe?

The ambiguities and ambivalences attached to modernity, to Baudelaire, are evoked in the sonnet by the oxymoronic imagery, by the absence of punctuation, and by a variety of other means. In the opening quatrain the idol Anubis that has been disgorged from the buried temple (of Baudelaire's œuvre) is the dog-faced Egyptian god of death. I have rendered "bouche" as "bowels," because of the sewer image in line 2, but there is a parallel between the mouth of the temple and the muzzle of the disgorged idol. The "dog"/"god" anagram in English (and we should recall that Mallarmé is the author of *Les Mots Anglais*) mirrors the oxymoronic conjunction in the Egyptian deity of the bestial and the divine, the two sides of the human that are always conjoined in Baudelaire's poetry. The idol is an *abomination*—that is, both an object of revulsion and an ill omen—but the art of Baudelaire is not afraid to risk dredging up even the most loathsome images in pursuit of its prophecies.

The invention of the gas lamp, illuminating the cities with a garish, artificial light—and thereby putting an end to the crepuscular serenity and solemnity of evening—becomes an ambiguous symbol, in the second quatrain and in the poem as a whole, both of modernity and of Baudelaire's art. The gas lights up both the street lamps and the lamp by which the poet composes his visions of the street—and what is illuminated specifically is an "immortal pubis," a metonymy for the prostitution that so fascinated Baudelaire because, as an oxymoronic conjunction of the sacred and the profane, it presents itself as an emblem of the modern city. "Mèche" has the primary meaning of "wick," but also the secondary meaning of "lock of hair" (see Cohn, *Toward the Poems of Mallarmé*, 160), and thus is connected on a subterranean level to the pubis, much as the poet is connected to the prostitute. What the poet and the prostitute have in common is that they are both scapegoats and must thus bear the *opprobrium* ("opprobres" in line 6) of their time. "Essuyeuse" in line 6 means "assuager" or "wiper"; it is feminine because it modifies "mèche," but the adjective may have been chosen because the hair of the prostitute, however "louche," offers a consolation not entirely unrelated to the consolations of the poet's lamp. There would also, then, be a subtle allusion to Mary Magdalene, the reformed prostitute, wiping Christ's feet with her hair.

The absence of punctuation produces a particularly marvelous effect in the first tercet, where "Votif" can modify either "feuillage" or "soir," and can thus have either a literal or a metaphorical sense: in the first case, there would be a slight pause after line 9; in the second, a full enjambment. The full meaning, then, is something like the following: "What votive leaves (or wreaths) that have been dried out in the cities without (prayerful) evening." Evening, together with its metaphorical (and perhaps literal) prayers, has disappeared because of the gas lamps, and any votive wreath that might be placed at Baudelaire's tomb would tend to wither in their glare.

The uncanny atmosphere of the sestet is partly produced by the pronoun "elle" in line 10, which (alas for English), is deliberately ambiguous and can be rendered by either a personal or an impersonal pronoun. "Elle" can modify the grammatically feminine "Ombre" in line 13 (and from this point of view the pronominal reference would be impersonal; logically, it is Baudelaire's shade, after all); but there is something strange in the appearance of the pronoun three lines before its referent, and this has the effect of conjuring a *female* shade, who, in Jungian terms, would be the *anima* of the poet. If Baudelaire's shade is envisioned as female, she would be congruent with the metonymically evoked prostitute of the octave. But "elle" can also perhaps modify "mèche" in line 5, in which case the image conjured is of a third kind of gas lamp, this one placed at Baudelaire's tomb. (Such a reading is made possible by the fact that "se rasseoir," in line 10, can refer to the settling down of liquid, and "voile," in line 12, to the cover of a container.) From this perspective, the absence/ presence paradox of the final tercet is centered around the *gas* (etymologically derived in both French and English from the Indo-European root for *spirit*) illuminating the tomb but also poisoning the atmosphere; but if "mèche" is interpreted as "lock of hair" as well as "wick," the genie in the bottle becomes female once again. (I have dealt with the pronoun difficulty in the translation by giving both an impersonal and a personal rendering—"that which settles down" in line 10 and "her absence" in line 12.)

To add to the difficulty of the sestet, Baudelaire's Shade (or Wraith in the translation—and note the capitalization of "Ombre"), whether conceived as a person or a thing, *blesses* him but also settles down *vainly* against his tomb. The adverb "vainement" is particularly puzzling here, but if we recall that, in "Toast Funèbre," "The splendid, the eternal genius has no shade" (line 38), the meaning begins to come into focus—although in a situation such as this one we may be confronted by a kind of radical unintelligibility. In any event, if the sestet is read against the argument Mallarmé is framing in "Toast Funèbre" and in the "Tombeau d'Edgar Poe," we seem to be left with the notion that, having been turned into itself by eternity, Baudelaire's genius has now fled from all material constraints. He is absent: we can speak of his "Shade" as perhaps of a kind of earthly residue that frames his absence, much as it provides the content of his poetry (the *mal* to his *fleurs*); but whether we think of it as the immaterial gas emanating from the lamp illuminating his tomb, or as a kind of *lamia* figure, guarding his tomb from harm, that Shade can no longer touch him.

Finally, what we are given in the sonnet is a chastened, anti-utopian, ambivalent but nevertheless undiminished vision of poetry. If the air is poisoned, poetry, in order to come into existence, is going to have to breathe that poison in; but at the same time, poetry rises above its own atmosphere. Baudelaire must be distinguished from the Shade that, by virtue of its own harmful existence, guards him from harm.

TOMBEAU (DE VERLAINE) / TOMB (OF VERLAINE)

The *tombeau* on Paul Verlaine was published in the January 1897 issue of *La Revue Blanche*, before being included in the 1899 edition of the *Poésies*. Written to commemorate the first anniversary of Verlaine's death, and suffused with the deep personal affection Mallarmé felt for a poet with whom he had been in close contact for thirty years, it is the last of the three literary *tombeaux* contained in the *Poésies* and perhaps the very last poem that Mallarmé, who was himself to die in 1898, ever wrote. "La tombe aime tout de suite le silence" ("Suddenly the tomb loves its silence"), Mallarmé had said in the eulogy he delivered at Verlaine's grave (*OC*, 510); the omission of Verlaine's name from the title of this *tombeau* should perhaps be understood in that light.

The "noir roc" of line 1 is clearly in some sense Verlaine's tombstone, but it has also been seen as a cloud, as the fabled bird of the *Arabian Nights*, and (against the background of *Un Coup de Dés*) as a rolling die. If the meaning of the phrase cannot finally be pinned down, this attests to the protean quality of Verlaine, in death as in life, that Mallarmé wants to emphasize in the poem. Verlaine is everywhere and nowhere; neither he nor his meaning will be "stayed even for pious hands" (line 2—with the pun on "staid" intended).

The problem of representation that the sonnet poses, and perhaps even thematizes, has made it the focal point for a theoretical debate on the status of the object in modern lyric poetry. In his noted essay, "Lyric and Modernity," Paul de Man regarded the Verlaine sonnet as exemplifying, what must always be the case with poetry, "the ambivalence of a language that is representational and nonrepresentational at the same time" (*Blindness and Insight*, 185). Responding directly to de Man's argument, Michael Riffaterre suggested ("Prosopopeia," 107–123) that the sonnet is closed off to a strictly mimetic reading, but that its terms become meaningful when they are brought into alignment with the two textual "hypograms" from which they originate: one of them a proverb, "Pierre qui roule n'amasse pas mousse" ("A rolling stone gathers no moss"), and the other a stanza from Verlaine's own "Chanson d'Automne": "Et je m'en vais / Au vent mauvais / Qui m'emporte / Deçà, delà" ("And I go off into the cruel wind, which carries me here and there"). If we extend Riffaterre's insight, we might say that perhaps Verlaine gathers no moss because, as the first tercet indicates, he is now *in* the moss and has *become* the moss. At the same time, however, Verlaine has disappeared into his *name* and has become his name: *verte laine*, green wool, the green woolly grass in which the poet lies hidden.

The erotic imagery of the second quatrain seems to be motivated by the notion that Verlaine, the poet of eros and of the natural world, has now, in death, ripened to the point at which the future will be seeded by his songs. The "nubile folds" can refer to the clouds that inseminate nature, much as Verlaine's poems will inseminate the future ("des lendemains"), but also to the folds or pages of a book—and note that the French "nubile" is a play on the "nue" of "cloud" (which is why I have translated "immatériel deuil" as "cloudy grief"). The ringdove, bird of eros, is an emblem of Verlaine; but perhaps it also hints, ever so subtly, at the Paolo and Francesca canto of the *Inferno*, in which the doomed lovers, driven by the winds, are likened to doves.

Whether the infinitive that opens the final tercet refers to the one who seeks ("Qui cherche"—line 9) or to Verlaine himself cannot be determined from the syntax, and the ambiguity is a telling one. Perhaps the discovery that death is not, after all, entirely different from life, at least from a certain point of view, and that death has been calumniated by our shallow conceptions of it, pertains equally to Verlaine and to the one who seeks him out.

HOMMAGE (À WAGNER) / HOMAGE (TO WAGNER)

The relationship of the Symbolist Movement in France to Wagner is a large subject that has been taken up by a number of studies, the most important of which is still *The Symbolist Aesthetic in France* by A. G. Lehmann. Clearly, there is a certain "family resemblance" between the Mallarméan symbol and the Wagnerian leitmotif; yet Mallarmé came to know Wagner's music rather late and he remained somewhat ambivalent to what the German composer represented. Mallarmé was apparently introduced to the music of Wagner by Edouard Dujardin, who founded the *Revue Wagnérienne* in 1885, two years after the German composer's death. Many of the contributors to the *Revue Wagnérienne* were members of the Mallarmé circle, and for a time Dujardin wanted Mallarmé to serve as its spiritual director (Michaud, *Mallarmé*, 112). Mallarmé's essay, "Rich-

ard Wagner: Rêverie d'un Poëte Français" (actually, it is part essay, part prose-poem) was published in the *Revue Wagnérienne* in August 1885, and his "Hommage à Wagner" (subsequently retitled "Hommage") in the January 1886 edition of that journal.

One must beware of confounding the sonnet with the prose piece, but the ambivalence of Mallarmé's homage to Wagner—an ambivalence that makes itself felt by such gestures as the word "dieu" in line 13—is intensified by a reading of the "Rêverie." The sonnet, like the essay, pays tribute to Wagner for having transformed and revivified a moribund theatrical tradition, which was previously suitable only for popular farces and for the manipulation of the masses. (L. J. Austin has argued that in the sonnet Mallarmé had the French Romantic theater, and especially that of Victor Hugo, specifically in mind [see "'Le Principal Pilier'"; cited by Hartley, 94].) This is more or less the argument set forth in the octave. The physical theater in the opening quatrain thus becomes a metaphor for a pre-Wagnerian theatrical tradition that is literally crumbling. In line 1, either the old-fashioned silk cloth ("moire") draping the furniture is a figure for silence, or the silence, "already funereal" (and we should recall how negatively valenced that adjective is in "Toast Funèbre"), is a figure for the cloth. The two terms stand as both tenor and vehicle of one another in what amounts to a double metaphor, the meaning of which is perhaps more deliberately vague in the original than as rendered in the translation.

Something in the drama both attracted and repelled Mallarmé; he originally planned both *Hérodiade* and "L'Après-midi d'un Faune" for the theater (as we saw in connection with those poems), and had been forced to conclude that his poetry would be inaccessible to a theatrical audience. In any event, what repelled Mallarmé—not only in the popular theater but, I would argue, in the theater as a whole—is made manifest in the second quatrain of the "Hommage." The noun "grimoire" (which occurs in both the "Ouverture Ancienne" and in "Prose"), literally "grammary," is a key term in the poet's lexicon of symbols, representing as it does the sorcerer's book of magic spells, and hence the "magical" powers of poetry. But in a theatrical context, the power of poetry is used to manipulate a vulgar audience, to give it a sort of "cheap thrill" ("frisson familier"). If poetry is debased in this manner, if it is merely the bourgeois equivalent of a primitive religious rite in which the masses are essentially hypnotized into the violence of a catharsis (and here again we must refer to "Toast Funèbre" as the locus classicus for this problem in Mallarmé), then it would be better if it ceased to exist entirely; in short, let the "grimoire," the source of the poet's magic spells, be *buried* in a closet (the verb "enfouir" literally means "to bury").

The octave-sestet division of the sonnet would tend to mask Mallarmé's ambivalence to Wagner and to the theater in general because it underlines the contrast between the banalities of the popular theater and the "master clarities" (line 10) of Wagnerian music drama that somehow emerge from them. This contrast forms part of the meaning of the sonnet, but not the whole meaning, and to unearth the larger intellectual context for the ambivalence of Mallarmé's tone in the sonnet we must turn to a page in the prose "Rêverie."

Mallarmé pays tribute to Wagner in the "Rêverie" not just for revivifying a moribund theater but, more specifically, for restoring what was true of Greek drama, "the amazement and intimacy that the audience feels when it is face to face with the myths"

(translation by Cook, *Mallarmé: Selected Prose Poems, Essays, and Letters*, 76). This is no small praise, and it will be amplified in the passage that follows; and yet that passage will also clarify why Mallarmé, in the uncharacteristic emphasis of his title, was so concerned to differentiate himself from Wagner as a *French* poet:

> For the second time in history, the people (first Greek and now German) can borrow sacred feelings from the past and look upon the secret of their origins, even as that secret is being acted out. Some strange, new, primitive [*barbare*] happiness keeps them seated there before that mobile veil of orchestral delicacy, before that magnificence which adorns their genesis.
> Thus, all things are restrengthened in the primitive [*primitif*] stream. Yet not in its spring.
> It is not in this way that the strictly imaginative, abstract, and therefore poetic French mind shines forth. For that mind shrinks back from Legend; therein it resembles perfect Art, which is invention. From days gone by, the French preserve no looming, no half-misty memory; it is as if they knew in advance that to do so would be anachronistic in a theatrical performance, that is, in the Rite of one of Civilization's accomplishments. (76)

In the context of these remarks, the religious diction of the sestet seems to raise the "case against Wagner" slightly *avant la lettre*. (Nietzsche's *Case of Wagner*—his last book—was completed in 1888.) The "master clarities" in the sestet spring "Unto a parvis born for their simulacrum" (line 11). A "parvis" is literally a "paradise," and the word also signifies the courtyard in front of a church, specifically Saint Peter's in Rome; a "simulacrum" is an image but also a mere pretense or semblance, a counterfeit. The Wagnerian artist becomes a "god," a metaphor that cuts both ways; it can suggest a kind of magisterial artistic transcendence of what had previously seemed possible or a will to power that turns art into idol worship. There is something prophetic, or sibylline, in Wagner—but the content of that prophecy remains ambiguous—much as the content of the apocalyptic prophecy in the "Ouverture Ancienne" of *Hérodiade* remains ambiguous. We have the benefit of hindsight, of course, but from our perspective the brass section—even on the manuscript page—is too large and too loud.

HOMMAGE (À PUVIS DE CHAVANNES) / HOMAGE (TO PUVIS DE CHAVANNES)

The sonnet to Puvis de Chavannes was published for the first time in January 1895 in an issue of *La Plume* that was devoted entirely to the artist; in the same year it was also included in an album presented to Puvis at a banquet held in his honor, which Mallarmé did not attend. Unlike the other sonnets in the *Hommages et Tombeaux* sequence, it is in lines of seven syllables, perhaps, as St. Aubyn suggests, "to differentiate this tribute to a living artist from those for the dead which are in alexandrines" (*Stéphane Mallarmé*, 103), but perhaps also (as Aimée Brown Price has suggested to me) as an appreciation of the emphasis on rhythm in Puvis's own work. The *a* and *b* rhymes in the octave are more closely related than usual in Mallarmé, and the use of homonymic rhyme in a Petrarchan octave has led to both of the *a* rhymes ("gourde" and "sourde") being doubled; I have tried to reproduce the former but not the latter stylistic feature in the translation.

The sonnet replicates the static eeriness of Puvis's pastel landscapes, his attempt to infuse a distinctly modern anxiety into what may seem on the surface a mere return to the neoclassical spirit of pastoral allegory. A personified Dawn, seemingly too weak to emerge, nevertheless sounds the trumpet of a bright blue sky: the allegory here is of an artistic reawakening that, because it cannot be grasped by the present, imposes a kind of solitude upon those in the avant-garde. And the shepherd of the second quatrain, searching for water in the wilderness, is an emblem of that artistic solitude. Only the artist, Mallarmé seems to be saying, has a sense of the demands of the future; only the artist can discover the fountain at which his time can slake its thirst.

That Mallarmé should have attached an allegory of this kind to Puvis de Chavannes is interesting not only because it suggests that the critical tendency to view Puvis as a backward-leaning artist is shallow but because it implies that what is truly "radical" or "revolutionary" in an artist's work (one is obliged to resort to clichés of this kind) is rarely going to be seen as "radical" or "revolutionary," and essentially for the same reason that the artist must stand alone in the first place. Puvis de Chavannes, Mallarmé seems to be saying, is in the forefront of his time because he had the courage not to seem to be in the forefront of his time; therein lies his solitude and artistic Glory.

AU SEUL SOUCI DE VOYAGER / FOR THE SAKE OF VOYAGING— HEEDLESSLY

A Shakespearean sonnet in octosyllabics, "Au seul souci de voyager" is a tribute to Vasco da Gama, who, as an explorer of the unknown, is seen as a type of the artist. Although the poem was long thought to have been unpublished in Mallarmé's lifetime, it actually appeared in 1898 in a volume, under the patronage of the Queen of Portugal, commemorating the four-hundredth anniversary of Vasco's voyage round the Cape of Good Hope (see Léon Cellier, *Mallarmé et la Morte Qui Parle*, 208). The sonnet was subsequently included in the 1899 edition of the *Poésies*.

Although the sonnet was apparently written for the commemorative volume (see Barbier and Millan, *Œuvres Complètes*, 447–448), the sea voyage motif (with its corollary of shipwreck) is central to Mallarmé and can be found in such poems as "Brise Marine," "Salut," and *Un Coup de Dés*, poems that stretch over a period of more than thirty years. In "Au seul souci de voyager," which must cleave to the historical circumstances surrounding an actual explorer, the shipwreck motif is less explicitly foregrounded than it is in the three poems mentioned above, but it is present all the same in the final image of a pale Vasco fighting off despair. The shipwreck motif, interestingly, is connected to some of the meanings that coalesce in the word "salut," which functions as another symbolic motif in Mallarmé's poetics. "Salut" in line 3 of the sonnet is primarily a greeting, but as A. R. Chisholm suggests (in a fine analysis of the poem), Mallarmé implicitly lifts a glass to Vasco, much as the poet in "Salut" raises a glass to his followers ("Mallarmé's Vasco Sonnet," 139–140).

If the semantic densities of the sonnet's opening line are unravelled (and if we disregard, for the moment, the optative mood of the implied toast), the rough-and-ready literal meaning of the line, "To the sole concern [or care] for [or of] voyaging," yields something like the following: To be concerned only with the voyage, and with the voyage only for the sake of the voyage, and to have no other cares; (hence) *to be careless and without cares*. Mallarmé is praising the singlemindedness of the hero (whether artist or explorer) who can make his concern his only care and who can be unconcerned with all other cares, even if that carelessness leads him to death. Vasco da Gama, rounding the Cape of Good Hope, might have been falling off the edge of the world, for all he knew; and thus the cape his vessel rounds in line 4 becomes a metaphor for death. In 1898, four hundred years after his momentous voyage, Vasco had already rounded that cape, but Mallarmé, who was writing the sonnet and who would die later that year, had not; thus, the greeting that Mallarmé sends Vasco is a message from time to eternity, while the poem itself, as Chisholm movingly says, is the messenger of time.

The fact that one of the variants for line 8 is "Un oiseau d'ivresse nouvelle" (see Chisholm, "Mallarmé's Vasco Sonnet," 140–142) alerts us to the connection between "Au seul souci" and "Brise Marine," in which the poet had written, "Je sens que des oiseaux sont ivres" (line 2). "Brise Marine" was composed in 1865, near the beginning of Mallarmé's poetic career, and the "chant des matelots" that he hears in that poem is a kind of siren song that he will seek to master during the next thirty years, as we have seen especially in "Prose" and "Toast Funèbre." However, if the echoes between "Au seul souci" and "Salut" are even more numerous, this is because both poems come at the end ("Salut" was composed in 1893, five years earlier than "Au seul souci"), and because, in both, Mallarmé's greeting is to the past as well as to the future. The word "poupe," for example, appears in both poems, as Chisholm explains, because in "Salut" explicitly, and in "Au seul souci" implicitly, Mallarmé "sees himself standing at the stern of the poetic argosy, looking back, while his younger confrères are looking forward from the bows" (141). In seeking a passage to India, Vasco was searching for the land of precious jewels; but the syntactical echo between line 12 of the Vasco sonnet, "Nuit, désespoir et pierrerie" ("Night, despair and precious stones"), and the final tercet of "Salut"—

> Solitude, récif, étoile
> A n'importe ce qui valut
> Le blanc souci de notre toile
>
> *Solitude, rocky shoal, bright star*
> To whatsoever may be worth
> Our sheet's white care in setting forth

—in which the word "souci" is also contained, points us to "the divine unrest that can never be satisfied with the attainment of a material goal" ("Mallarmé's Vasco Sonnet," 140).

TOUTE L'ÂME RÉSUMÉE / THE ENTIRE SOUL EVOKED

In 1895 the critic Austin de Croze conducted a series of interviews with poets in *Le Figaro* on the subject of *vers libre*. In the interview with Mallarmé, which appeared in August, the poet contrasts *vers libre* with "official" verse written in alexandrines. Since "Toute l'âme résumée," a Shakespearean sonnet in lines of seven syllables, is appended to the interview, it may be that Mallarmé considered any poem not in alexandrines to constitute *vers libre,* or it may be that he was simply playing a joke on the interviewer, as de Croze seems to have thought ("And here are verses which, in sport [par jeu], the poet wrote directly for our investigation"). The sonnet was not collected until the 1913 edition of the *Poésies* (Barbier and Millan, *Œuvres Complètes,* 432–433).

Mallarmé's remarks in the interview are interest-ing both in themselves and in relation to the sonnet he produced for the occasion (especially as the latter seems to function as a minor *ars poetica*):

> To me, classical verse—I would call it *official verse*—is the grand nave in the basilica of French poetry; free verse, for its part, constructs the aisles and fills them with attractions, mysteries, rare sumptuosities. Official verse must continue to live [doit demeurer], for it is born from the soul of the people, it bursts from the soil of our ancestors, it has long known how to flower in the sublime. But free verse is a beautiful acquisi-tion: it has sprung up in revolt against the banality of received ideas [il a surgi en révolte de l'Idée contre la banalité du "convenu"]; only, that it might *exist*, let it not set itself up as a dissident, rival church, in a solitary chapel of its own! . . . Let us know how to listen to the grand organs of official verse, on which virtuoso fingers bring glorious cantatas to a state of exultation . . . moreover, let us not forget that Art is infinite.... Yes, Poetry is nothing but the intensely musical and emotional expression of the state of a soul; and that is what free verse is as well. In summary, small but good. (cited by Barbier and Millan, *Œuvres Complètes,* 433; translation mine)

Clearly, the distinction that Mallarmé wants to draw in these remarks is not the purely formal one that we would now tend to make between rhymed metrical and unrhymed unmetrical verse but rather between poetry that has the solidity of a public provenance and poetry that is private and of the moment. Yet the second kind of poetry, ethereal though it may be, must be able to sum up and evoke the entire state of a soul: "Toute l'âme résumée."

The sonnet may have been inspired by the marvel-ous portrait of Mallarmé painted by his close friend, Manet, in 1876. In the portrait, as Harry Rand ob-serves, the poet holds a cigar, rather than a pen, in his right hand, "as though Mallarmé wrote in smoke" (*Manet's Contemplation*, 150); and, as the smoke from the cigar, half regarded by the poet's right eye, curls lazily upward in spirals, his left eye, focused on nothing, seems to turn its gaze within. What is evoked by the painting, in short, is the mystery of a soul contemplating itself.

By the same token, in the sonnet, the cigar smoke being exhaled makes it possible to see or to envision the breathing out of the soul or spirit (spirit=breath), and thus evokes the paradoxical linkage of the immaterial to the material, the atemporal to the temporal. The soul that is breathed out is also, of course, the poem, which thus exists both in and out of time. The heroism required of the soul, as the metaphor of the second quatrain indicates, is to be true to the moment and to shed the ash of what it can no longer hold on to and what it no longer is.

An implied ethics as well as an implied aesthetics can be found in this little poem, which, in being true to its own moment, seems thereby to sum up a world. The stipulation posted against poetic ecstasy ("le chœur des romances" / "choirs of romance") in the sestet is that "the real in its vile shapes" must be excluded. Mallarmé's phrase "Le réel parce que vil" is ambiguous and problematic. I take it that the polemic here is not against reality as such but against a kind of Zola-esque naturalism that would identify reality with ugliness. The verb is absent, but my own predilection would be to interpret the line as meaning not that reality is vile and should, therefore, be excluded but that a definition of reality that stems from that which is vile should be excluded.

AUTRES POËMES ET SONNETS / OTHER POEMS AND SONNETS

I. TOUT ORGUEIL FUME-T-IL DU SOIR / DOES PRIDE AT EVENING ALWAYS FUME

The three sonnets, "Tout Orgueil fume-t-il du soir," "Surgi de la croupe et du bond," and "Une dentelle s'abolit," are often referred to as a triptych. When they originally appeared in the January 1887 issue of *La Revue Indépendante*, they were joined together by Roman numerals, which were retained for the 1887 and all subsequent editions of the *Poésies*. "Sumptuous allegories of the void," in St. Aubyn's phrase, they are connected by the capitalization of *Orgueil* in the first, *Chimère* in the second, and *Jeu* in the third, and also by a temporal progression from evening to the depths of night to early dawn (*Stéphane Mallarmé*, 106–107). "The parallelism of the three sonnets is striking," writes Michaud in his fine discussion of them. "All three take their point of departure from the sight of a familiar object chosen from the poet's room. . . . But all three objects are merely pretexts. Through the intervention of the 'demon of analogy,' each one *suggests* another image" (*Mallarmé*, 59).

Pride, in "Tout Orgueil fume-t-il du soir," is so called because it attempts to hold on to its objects, to its manifestations, but is obliged to "come upon the grave of its own life," as Hegel says of the Unhappy Consciousness. The immortality of the soul is perhaps juxtaposed against the perishing of objects, but—in an irony that corresponds to Hegelian negation—what is immortal in the opening quatrain of the sonnet is precisely the gust of wind ("l'immortelle bouffée") that blows out the torch by which Pride's objects are illuminated and to which Pride itself is likened. The syntax allows us to read that opening quatrain as either a statement or a question (nuanced between a real and a rhetorical question), and "du soir" can be rendered as either "at" or "of" evening. Evening, in Mallarmé's poetics, is the time just before "the abandonment about to come" but also the time at which Glory (to which Pride is here connected) is most fully manifested.

"Orgueil" is capitalized in the Pléiade text and this spelling has been retained; however, Barbier and Millan, the editors of the Flammarion edition, render it in lowercase and they do not indicate that the word was capitalized in any publication that appeared during the poet's lifetime. This is not merely an orthographical matter because, from an interpretive point of view, there are good grounds for both emphasizing and deemphasizing the personification of pride. The verb "fumer" can mean "smoke" (though I have rendered it as "fume"), and, insofar as pride is personified in the opening line, we can draw the picture of a man smoking in the evening—perhaps the poet himself, as in the famous portrait of him by Manet. In a number of poems in the *Poésies* cigarette smoke and the cigarette itself stand in a metaphoric relationship to poetry, to the pen, to mystery, and so forth. In line 2, however, the metaphor shifts away from the human to the image of a smoking torch. Mallarmé very often associates clusters of metaphors, and in this instance it is possible that he would have wanted "orgueil" to remain lowercase in order not to limit the range of meaning. The question of orthography is a vexed problem in the editing of Mallarmé, and, as the collations undertaken by Barbier and Millan indicate, we often find the poet changing his mind about the capitalization of particular nouns because of his awareness of the hermeneutic issues involved.

In the second quatrain the "chambre ancienne" recalls Hérodiade's room in the "Ouverture Ancienne." The "heir," whoever he may be (Michaud suggests that he is "the inheritor of the race, that is, the poet" [60]), is heir not so much to the room insofar as it is a *living room*, as to death—but perhaps the room itself is emblematic of death. "Ancienne," in an ambiguity that Mallarmé deploys so often, can mean both "ancient" and "former." The "couloir," or "passageway," is akin to the "corridor" of "Toast Funèbre."

We have to let go our grip on all of the objects to which Pride attaches itself; but, in the sestet, they seem to exert a grip on us of their own, perhaps because of the way in which they absorb the past within themselves. In a fine paradox, the marble console (recalling the credenzas of "Ses purs ongles très haut") is likened to "disavowal's sepulcher"; in other words, it is not only one of the objects that must be relinquished but a tomb that has been formed from renunciation itself.

II. SURGI DE LA CROUPE ET DU BOND / SPRUNG FROM THE CROUP AND THE FLIGHT

The second of the three sonnets in the triptych is one of the most enigmatic poems in the Mallarméan corpus, simply because of the difficulty of visualizing the images (or image) being delineated. The enigma has recently been penetrated, however—successfully, in my opinion—by Rae Beth Gordon, who, in a discussion of Mallarmé's trompe l'oeil effects, recognizes that the poem functions as a gestalt image in which figure and ground are reversible, such that we either see two lovers about to kiss or a vase rising in the empty space between them (see *Ornament,*

Fantasy, and Desire in Nineteenth-Century French Literature, 154–155). "In freezing [the] proximity [of the two lovers] in the timeless immobility Symbolism prizes," notes Gordon, "the resurgence of the vase obliterates their presence as well. This paradox elevates the physical desire of the lovers to a virtual, metaphysical desire. . . . [I]t is out of this absence . . . that the ideal vision springs" (155).

Mallarmé's sonnet consecrates the "marriage" of something with nothing. Although the two lovers are unable to kiss, they give birth to the "sylph" who, looking down from her cold ceiling ("ce froid plafond"—line 8), is not only speaking the poem but *is* the poem. (The figure of the sylph—a term coined by Paracelsus to refer to a class of mortal but soulless beings inhabiting the air—appears also in "Rondel II.") Similarly, although the neck of the vase is cut off by the top of the image, "[w]ithout flowering the long, bitter night," at the end of the sonnet a rose rises in the darkness, if only by negation.

The lovers—in a paradox that once again recalls Keats's "Ode on a Grecian Urn," as does the entire sonnet, for that matter—are unable to kiss, because they are phantoms who, with the emergence of the vase into the foreground, disappear into nothingness. Yet what they represent, in the second quatrain, is reality; for in asserting that two mouths never drank from the same Chimera, Mallarmé is pointing to the tragic fact that our dreams of the Ideal are solitary and cannot be shared. The "mother" of the sylph is thus widowed by the Ideal, in the same manner as the only liquor contained in the drinking goblet, to which the vase is transmogrified in the first tercet, is the "inexhaustible widowhood" of the poem. The sylph addresses us from her own "Cold Pastoral" (to borrow Keats's phrase), frozen on the boundary between being and nonbeing.

III. UNE DENTELLE S'ABOLIT / LACE SWEEPS ITSELF ASIDE

The tendency of Mallarmé's poetry to allegorize the creative process through a progressive purification and essentialization of language reaches a kind of limit in "Une dentelle s'abolit," the third sonnet in the triptych. Describing a quasi-Hegelian movement in which birth is necessarily predicated upon death and the creative moment upon negation and an encounter with the void, the sonnet resonates against several earlier poems in the *Poésies*, and is especially reminiscent of "Don du Poëme," which was written more than twenty years earlier when Mallarmé was engaged in the early stages of the composition of *Hérodiade*. The poet of "Don du Poëme," as we saw, had spent a sleepless night of impotent labor working on *Hérodiade*, his poem of purity and sterility; and the sonnet itself, conceived at dawn through the contemplation of that sterility, was thus the "child of an Idumaean night," to be set in contrast to his own recently born flesh-and-blood daughter. Now, in "Une dentelle s'abolit," the poet (although the lyric-I is no longer explicitly in evidence) has again apparently spent a sleepless night of labor—this time, I would suggest (despite only circumstantial evidence) on the great free-verse poem that occupied his later years, *Un Coup de Dés* (1897)—and the sonnet itself is again conceived at dawn and in the wake of a futile struggle. In both poems the simultaneous and contradictory desire of the lyric poet for purity, on the one hand, and fecundity, on the other, can only be resolved by a birth that is entirely self-generated and that the emerging poem allegorizes.

In the opening quatrain of "Une dentelle s'abolit" the image of the white lace curtains blowing against a window—an image that must be visualized in order for the poem to be at all intelligible—can only be inferred from the abstraction that is explicitly presented. What is clearly at issue is the self-cancellation or self-abolition of consciousness; but what we are presented with is not even an object, the lace curtain, but, simply, a piece of lace—that is, the effect or impression the object produces. (The translation, "Lace sweeps itself aside," attempts to convey both the abstraction and the concrete image of the curtains being blown in the wind.) The image of the curtains can be inferred from the context, but we are then immediately swept up into images and ideas that pertain to the realm of doubt. The "Jeu suprême" of line 2 (with "Jeu" significantly capitalized) brings us into the orbit of the central problematic of *Un Coup de Dés*: it can be interpreted in relation to the act of poetic conception or in relation to a cosmic process of some kind; both possibilities are latent and mutually reinforcing in a play of microcosm to macrocosm. The bed that is half-exposed by the play of the curtains against a window pane whitened by the first rays of dawn (in a ghostly concatenation of whiteness) is either empty or absent; both possibilities are again latent. It has sometimes been seen in relation to eros, but, given the octave, Émilie Noulet is certainly correct to observe that it is primarily a bed of childbirth (see *Vingt Poèmes de Stéphane Mallarmé*, 106), although here again the symbolism allows for a range of interpretations.

In his discussion of the sonnet Paul de Man points us to one of Mallarmé's most important aesthetic pronouncements, a passage from his Foreword to René Ghil's *Traité du Verbe*. In de Man's translation: "What use is the wonder of transposing a phenomenon of nature into its resonant near disappearance, according to the game of speech ['le jeu de la parole'], unless there emanates from it, without the hindrance of an immediate or concrete prompting, the pure idea?" ("Poetic Nothingness," 21; *OC*, 857). This was written in 1886, the year before the publication of the three sonnets in the triptych, and, as de Man suggests, it is an apt description of the process evoked by the opening of "Une dentelle s'abolit." "The 'supreme Game,'" remarks de Man, "is the act of (poetic) consciousness, and the 'lace' that 'does away with itself' is a sort of fringe of the evanescent object in its 'resonant near disappearance.' The action is 'doubt' by its suspension between being and nonbeing" ("Poetic Nothingness," 22).

In "Quand l'ombre menaça de la fatale loi" the constellations, writhing in their death throes before a sadistic king, were seen as "guirlandes célèbres," and similar cosmic overtones are apparent in the likening of the lace curtains to garlands in the second quatrain. The symbolism has become so over-determined at this point that it is perhaps impossible to fix on any clear meaning; but my own predilection would be to see the curtains and the constellations as joined in a kind of inverse relationship through the metaphor of the garlands; for as the curtains become increasingly visible with the dawn, the constellations become less visible; hence, as the curtains are blown against each other in their "conflict," they enact the death throes of the constellations.

The resolution of "Une dentelle s'abolit" occurs by way of music; and in the sestet, several of the symbols that had appeared in "Sainte" (the mandolin, the window) again make their presence known. The sestet contains a number of syntactical difficulties, but these are nothing compared to the problems posed by the octave. What seems to be articulated is the sad knowledge that even if the dream cannot be expressed, it nevertheless persists as a kind of unheard music. "Au creux néant musicien" (line 11) is susceptible of various readings: "In the hollow musical nothingness," "In the hollow nothingness [a] musician," "To the hollow nothingness [a] musician," and so on. Similarly, in the final tercet, "le sien" can be either "his own" (a reference to the one who gilds himself with dreams—line 9), or, as I have translated it, "its own," a reference to the dream that gives birth to itself. "Ventre," in line 13, can mean either womb or belly; the evoked image is of the bulge in the mandolin, a member of the lute family. In any event, the birth that occurs in the final line produces one of the most beautiful and sadly poignant cadences in the *Poésies*.

QUELLE SOIE AUX BAUMES DE TEMPS / WHAT SILK STEEPED IN THE BALMS OF TIME

Mallarmé's struggle against Glory, and the tendency he exhibits in some of his slighter poems of privileging Life against Art, are both in evidence in "Quelle soie aux baumes de temps," a sonnet that was published for the first time in *La Revue Indépendante* in 1885 (although an earlier version of the poem, "De l'Orient passé des Temps," was composed in 1868). As in "La chevelure vol d'une flamme à l'extrême," another sonnet of the mid-1880s, the initial image is of a woman combing out her hair. The association of the hair with a flag, which occurs between the first and second quatrains in "Quelle soie aux baumes de temps," can be found as early as "Le Château de l'Espérance," a poem of 1862 that was not published in Mallarmé's lifetime.

In the first quatrain, the hair of the mistress (probably Méry Laurent) is compared to costly silks, but the presence of the "Chimère" in line 2 indicates that the hidden reference is to a beautiful book of poetry and that the mistress's hair is thus being exalted above poetry. The writhing Chimera, a watermark in fine book paper, is a Mallarméan symbol of poetry; it appears in "Surgi de la croupe et du bond" and in *Igitur*, and its avatars include the suffering golden monster of "Toast Funèbre" and "le Monstre-Qui-ne-peut-Etre" of the essay on Richard Wagner (see *OC*, 541; see above, pp. 189–190).

The holes in the flags of the second quatrain are undoubtedly from bullets, as Robert Cohn observes (*Toward the Poems of Mallarmé*, 220), for what the flags denote is military triumph. In the two quatrains, we are thus given the two antithetical and traditional routes to Glory, both of which, along with the heroic conception of eternity they represent, are dismissed in favor of the woman's hair and the pleasures of the moment.

Beyond the sonnet's accession to the erotic, however, there is a deeper moral conception, which emerges in the sestet, and this is that in order to experience anything, in order to accomplish anything—including the work of poetry itself—one must be willing to give up the dream of Glory and live in the present without ulterior motives and without any hope of reward. Cohn has caught the pun on "morsure" in line 10 with "mort sûre," and the sense in which "expirer" in the penultimate line means both "breathe out" and "die" (220). These are fine insights, and they indicate the extent to which the truth of experience, for Mallarmé, is bound up with the death of vanity.

There is, however, at the same time, an ambivalence in regard to sexuality, which is manifested both in "Quelle soie aux baumes de temps" and in "M'introduire dans ton histoire," the following poem in the *Poésies*. The "tuft" of line 12 (or, as I have translated it, "brake") would seem to point to a type of hair that does not sit on the head (and, if so, this would suggest an ambivalence to pubic glory as well as to the public glory adumbrated in the octave). From this point of view, "expirer," like the Elizabethan sense of the verb "die," would betray a fear that ecstasy—often represented by the diamond symbol in Mallarmé—involves envelopment and dissolution; and this, in turn, would have a bearing on "the cry of Glories" that the princely lover snuffs out or stems.

M'INTRODUIRE DANS TON HISTOIRE / TO INSERT MYSELF INTO YOUR STORY

First published in *La Vogue* in June 1886, "M'introduire dans ton histoire" germinates from the same symbolic and mythical elements that are also at the root of "La chevelure vol d'une flamme à l'extrême" and "Victorieusement fui le suicide beau": namely, the "solar myth" and the identification of the woman's hair with the sun. As with "La chevelure vol" and "Victorieusement," the woman addressed in "M'introduire" is almost certainly Méry Laurent, and once again we have the same gently ambivalent attitude being expressed, an attitude quasi-erotic and quasi-platonic, melding the human realm with the cosmic order.

"Histoire," in the opening quatrain, can refer to the life of the woman being addressed, to a story that the poet is telling her or about her (Mallarmé's *Contes Indiens*, which make use of images that enter into "M'introduire," were written for Méry; see Cohn, *Toward the Poems of Mallarmé*, 223), or to the woman's sexual organ. "Héros" in line 2 joins the *hero* to *eros*, a conjunction that also occurs in "La chevelure vol" and in *Hérodiade*—although, as we saw in "Victorieusement," sexuality, in Mallarmé's solar myth,

represents a fall from an anterior order of plenitude—which explains the habitual ambivalence of his heroes. If we read the "grass plot of that territory" of line 4 as a euphemism or circumlocution (as it is difficult not to do), then it follows that the hero's naked heel is a metonymy—one that was perhaps chosen, as several commentators have suggested, because the heel was Achilles' only area of vulnerability. The heel frequently has erotic associations for Mallarmé; Venus, treading the lava of Mount Etna in "L'Après-midi d'un Faune," has "talons ingénus" (line 102), innocent heels that at the same time are naked, since "ingénus" contains "nus."

As a matter of fact, the hero of the second quatrain resembles the Faun in his apparently unsuccessful assault on the glacial attitude of the woman in question. There is an ambiguity here because a "naive sin" ("naïf péché"—"peccadillo" in the translation) might actually be more threatening ("attentatoire"—"minatory") to the glaciers jutting out of the ocean (hence the "glacial ridges" of the translation) than a more serious "sin"; evidently, one proceeds by degrees.

In any event, the poet, in the joyousness of the sestet (although the latter may be more interrogative than declarative), is apparently content to substitute the hair cascading over the woman's shoulders for another kind of "territory." I read the thunder of line 10 partly as a substitution for the metaphorical lightning of the hair, which flashes red and gold and pierces the air with fire. The hair is associated with the sun, and the poet contemplating it becomes the sun-god driving his chariot westward as evening draws on (toward the Occident, as in "La chevelure vol"), the wheels of the chariot flashing with thunder and rubies at their axles or hubs. The purpled clouds at sunset attest to a glory, to a kingdom, which in one sense has now passed away, but which also—to one who has studied the nostalgias as deeply as Mallarmé—can only come into existence by passing away.

A LA NUE ACCABLANTE TU / HUSHED TO THE CRUSHING CLOUD

As Madame Noulet observes, many commentators have seen in "A la nue accablante tu," which was first published in 1895 in the Berlin review *Pan*, the drama animating *Un Coup de Dés* played out in miniature (*Vingt Poèmes de Stéphane Mallarmé*, 247). The shipwreck motif is so central to Mallarmé that one is reminded of the epigraph to the volume in which Milton's *Lycidas* first appeared: *Si recte calculum ponas, ubique naufragium est* ("If you measure things correctly, there is shipwreck everywhere"); it occurs explicitly in "Brise Marine" and more subtly in "Salut" and "Au seul souci de voyager."

The cloud in the opening quatrain can be either literal or metaphorical; it can signify a storm cloud that has the form of basalt and lava—or that lowers ("basse") with basalt or lava—or it can signify the shoal ("basse") on which the ship has been wrecked. Mallarmé plays very frequently upon the double meaning of "nue" as "cloud" and "naked," as we have seen, and the choice of "nue" in the opening line must have been dictated partly by the way in which the possibility of "shipwreck" in human life renders us *naked*, so to speak, strips us bare to the universe, just as the mast in the second quatrain is stripped bare. Cloud and rock are interchangeable, just as they are in the opening of the Verlaine sonnet, where "The black rock raging that the wind has rolled / It" can be seen as a tombstone or as a storm cloud—and perhaps this interchange has to do with the theme of fate, with the inevitable shipwreck of the human

on the shoals of that which is indifferent to humanity. The foam, in the second quatrain, "slobber[s] on," despite the shipwreck buried in its midst; but the mast, stripped of its sheet, remains supreme, that is, continues to stand tall, a symbol—among the flotsam and jetsam—of the nobility of human aspirations.

The question posed by the poem as a whole, however, is whether the world ends with a bang or with a whimper—which is to say, whether our life is tragic, as the shipwreck motif of the octave would suggest, or simply meaningless and inconsequential. The fury of the sea in the first tercet "defaults" from some "high perdition." "Perdition," in French as in English, has the root meaning of loss and the connotation of hell or damnation, but if the cosmos is nothing more than a game of chance then there is nothing really to win or lose; there is only "the vain [or empty] abyss outspread" (line 11).

Is it, then, not a shipwreck that was drowned in the waves but merely a young Siren? Why Siren? In "Salut" (published in 1893, two years before "A la nue accablante tu"), the poet, as a kind of latter-day Odysseus, binds himself firmly to the mast of his vessel so as not to succumb to the Sirens, who, as a result, are drowned (see above, p. 149). The Sirens, as we saw, symbolize the seductions of the world and even of the Dream, seductions that the poet must guard against if he is to achieve his heroic quest. This motif is played out again and again in Mallarmé's poems, as we have seen. But what if the heroic quest is meaningless because the world has no meaning? What if the shipwreck, that symbol of human tragedy, will not have occurred or will have occurred in vain? In that case, what remains is only the pathos of a young Siren—drowning, because she symbolizes our unfulfilled, unrequited, or unacted-upon desires.

MES BOUQUINS REFERMÉS SUR LE NOM DE PAPHOS / MY OLD BOOKS CLOSED UPON PAPHOS'S NAME

"Mes bouquins refermés" initially appeared under the title "Autre Sonnet" in the January 1887 issue of *La Revue Indépendante* and, subsequently, in the edition of the *Poésies* published later that year. The sole variant in the poem is the adjective modifying "ébat" in line 7; originally "pur," it was changed to "vierge" and then finally to "blanc" in 1893 (Barbier and Millan, *Œuvres Complètes,* 329).

"Salut," with its allusion to the story of Odysseus and the Sirens, had greeted the reader of the *Poésies*; and in closing his book on the name of Paphos, with a sonnet that makes reference to the closing of old books, Mallarmé is again incorporating the realm of desire through the material of Greek mythology. Paphos was an ancient city of Cyprus, famous for its temple to Aphrodite. According to one story, it was founded by the Amazons (hence the final line of the sonnet), and according to another, by Cinyras, the son of Paphus, the son of Pygmalion and Galatea. Cinyras's name means "plaintive cry"; Paphus means "foam," and thus returns us to Aphrodite, who was born out of the foam (Robert Graves, *The Greek Myths* [New York: George Braziller, 1959], 386, 403).

In the opening quatrain, the ruin hallowed by the foam (one is reminded of a similar ruin in "Remémoration d'Amis Belges") could thus be a specific reference to the temple of Aphrodite or any imaginary ruin. The foam is a metonymy for the sea, but also a metaphor for the evanescence of the imagination, of "génie" (spirit or genius—line 2; *génie*, notes Fowlie, comes from the Latin *ingenium*, which means a game of the mind [*Mallarmé*, 55]), of life itself. The "hyacinth"—like the "azure" in so

many of Mallarmé's poems—is a figure for the sky, but Mallarmé has deliberately chosen an antique word, such as would be found in one of his "bouquins." "Hyacinthe" is the early form of the modern French "jacinthe"; it is also, as St. Aubyn notes, "the color blue-red, the color of the clear sunny skies of Greece" (*Stéphane Mallarmé*, 115). Noulet adds that the "hyacinthe . . . was a ceremonial cloth, blue-red in color, which would have been worn on days of triumph" (cited by St. Aubyn, *Stéphane Mallarmé*, 115); and thus, as in Mallarmé's solar myth generally, we have a correspondence between macrocosm and microcosm, between the sky and the human situation.

The fourth line contains one of those marvelous ambiguities in the *Poésies* that turn on a simple preposition—in this case, the fact that "de" can mean both "of" and "from." The ruin to which the poet delights to return is simultaneously beneath the distant hyacinth of the days *of* its fame and distant *from* the days of its fame. With the second reading, there is a double nostalgia, as if the horizon of longing stretched back to another horizon of longing, and so on, ad infinitum. Presence and absence, the presence of absence and the absence of presence, converge in the imagination. And always there is the same sky.

In the second quatrain of the sonnet, that marvelously idealized Greek landscape of the imagination is swept aside, as by a sickle (note the play of "faux" on "faux" in the rhyme), giving way to the chill winds of reality. Paphos is the realm of desire, but, as James Lawler reminds us ("Three Sonnets," 85), the pun on "pas faux" indicates that we are also—at least in the poem, if not in the place—in the realm of truth, although what the relationship between desire and truth may be remains undetermined. I noted above that Mallarmé hesitated for some time about which adjective, from the whiteness-virginity-purity symbolic constellation, to choose as a modifier for "ébat" (sport, frolic, gambol). In any event, the wind and the snow *frolic*, in the quatrain, out of a kind of spiteful glee at eviscerating human longings and strivings; they denude the ruin of its fictional honors, so to speak—and thus there is a double denuding or deconstruction: the temple becomes a ruin and the ruin is stripped of its glamour.

Nevertheless, none of this will make the poet "howl an empty moan" (line 6); in other words, he will not ululate ("hululerai") the *nénie[s]*—the latter being Greek funeral chants that, as Fowlie notes, are used here in the singular by poetic license (*Mallarmé*, 115). He will not utter a "plaintive cry"—in the manner, perhaps, of Cinyras, the founder of Paphos, whose name as we noted means "plaintive cry."

On a thematic plane, one is inclined to think in this connection of the transcendence of history via poetry; but Mallarmé's old books are closed and, alas, the sickle cuts both ways, as far as the resolution of the sestet is concerned, because the yearning of poetry is ultimately for *life*. Does the word "ici" in line 9 refer to the landscape of the opening quatrain or to the environment in which the poet is himself situated? In other words, is his frustration in relation to his existential situation or to the fact that the poetic imagination is disembodied?

Mallarmé's monsters, as we have seen, are generally *threshold* figures stretched between two modes of being, and the wyvern ("guivre") carved into the fireplace of line 12 represents a doubleness of that order. As Michaud observes, the same holds for the two breasts of one of the Amazons, whom the mention of Paphos had evoked for the poetic imagination: "One is bursting with flesh, symbolizing real life; the other, burned according to the ancient rite to permit the drawing of the bow, symbolizes absence. And it is on the latter that Mallarmé . . . would prolong his dream" (*Mallarmé*, 128).

POËMES EN PROSE

Published separately between 1864 and 1895, the twelve poems included in the *Poëmes en Prose* section of the *Œuvres Complètes* first appeared as a group in *Pages* (Brussels, 1891) and then subsequently in *Divagations* (Paris, 1896) under the heading "Anecdotes ou Poëmes."A thirteenth piece, "Conflit," added to the *Divagations*, was omitted from the *Poëmes en Prose* section of the Pléiade edition and included under *Variations sur un Sujet* (see *OC*, 355-360). The present edition follows the sequencing of the Pléiade text, which in turn (except for the omission of "Conflit") follows that of *Divagations*.

LE PHÉNOMÈNE FUTUR / A PHENOMENON OF THE FUTURE

"Le Phénomène Futur" was composed in 1864, along with a number of the other *Poëmes en Prose*, but was published only in 1875 when it appeared in *La République des Lettres*. Although it was not the first of the prose-poems to be composed, it may well have been placed at the head of the group because of its prophetic character, as Ursula Franklin suggests (*Anatomy of Poesis*, 18).

The conflict between the Real and the Ideal is a deep-seated theme in Mallarmé's poetry, particularly in the early work, but nowhere is that conflict more pessimistically staged than in "Le Phénomène Futur." One of the senses of "phénomène" is that of a

"curiosity" or "sideshow," and in the metaphorical setting of the poem, Beauty is seen as something outlandish, as a curiosity or sideshow, so far removed has it become from the immanent reality of human beings—indeed, of nature itself, which in the opening lines of the poem is in an advanced state of decrepitude and decline. The Beauty that is unveiled to the masses by the "Showman of things Past" is ironically reminiscent of Botticelli's Venus—but the age Mallarmé prophesies (which is clearly intended to reflect his own) is certainly not the Renaissance. In this future age, already glimpsed as a real possibility, the advancement of science seems to be in direct proportion to the decline not only of art but of natural happiness and vitality; this "sovereign science" is touted by the Showman in his "claptrap" or "sales pitch" to the audience ("boniment") for having preserved a "Woman of a former time" as a specimen of an outmoded beauty.

The poem, in short, is a deeply grieving, deeply political, vision of history and of the poet's own time (and, to that extent, should dispel any lingering conception of Mallarmé as an apolitical aesthete). The incongruity of the vision of Beauty and the debased context in which that vision is materialized is a frequent theme with apocalyptic consequences in Mallarmé's poetry—for example, in *Hérodiade*, which was begun in the same year "Le Phénomène Futur" was composed. But paradoxically, that incongruity or contradiction does not invalidate poetry, and may even be the proving ground in which poetry itself is materialized. One should note that in Mallarmé's parable, pessimistic as it is, the poets have not disappeared; at the end of the piece, they "make their way toward their lamps, their brains momentarily drunk with an obscure glory, haunted by a Rhythm and forgetting that they exist in an age that has outlived beauty."

The clown of "Le Pitre Châtié," another poem of 1864, bears an obvious symbolic relationship to the poet, and a number of critics have suggested that the same holds true for the "Showman of things Past" (see Franklin, *Anatomy of Poesis*, 24). I would argue, however, that to interpret "Le Phénomène Futur" in this manner is to disregard the texture of its metaphorical setting and to render the poem unintelligible. For one thing, it turns poetry into "claptrap"; for another—and this relates to a larger aesthetic question—it reduces Mallarmé's concern with Beauty to an attitude of nostalgia. Certainly "Le Phénomène Futur," like many of the early poems, is imbued with a quality of nostalgia that we associate with Baudelaire; but, already at this stage, Mallarmé's vision of Beauty is located in the past in order to concretize a transcendental horizon that the poet is as yet unable to locate in any other way. In "Les Fenêtres," a poem written in 1863, this produced the strange ambiguity we commented on in regard to line 32 ("Au ciel antérieur où fleurit la Beauté"), where the verb is past and present at the same time (see above, p. 157). The poets of "Le Phénomène Futur" forget that they live in an age that has outlived beauty; but, as I read Mallarmé, not only would the same hold for all poets in all ages, but the disjunction between the Real and the Ideal that produces the sense of loss is itself, ironically, the enabling condition for poetry. It is interesting in this regard that Baudelaire, commenting on

"Le Phénomène Futur," felt the need to distance himself from Mallarmé; and although what he had to say should not be pressed too far, it points to the possibility of an aesthetic divergence between the two poets:

> A young writer has recently had an ingenious conception, but one not absolutely justified ["juste"]. The world is coming to an end. Humanity is decrepit. A Barnum of the future shows the degraded men of his time a beautiful woman artificially preserved from a former age. "What!" they say. "Could humanity have been as beautiful as that?" I say this isn't true. *Degraded man would be astonished ["s'admirerait"] at the sight of beauty and would call it ugliness.* (*Correspondance de Stéphane Mallarmé* 1, 201; cited in *Anatomy of Poesis*, 25; translation mine)

PLAINTE D'AUTOMNE / AUTUMN LAMENT

Composed in 1864, "Plainte d'Automne" appeared for the first time in July of that year under the title "L'Orgue de Barbarie"; it was initially published in *La Semaine de Cusset et de Vichy*, together with another prose-poem, "La Tête" (subsequently "Pauvre Enfant Pâle"), and with a dedication to Baudelaire. It was reprinted several times as "L'Orgue de Barbarie," and then as "Plainte d'Automne" in a December 1875 issue of *La République des Lettres*.

As Charles Mauron notes, "Plainte d'Automne" is the only Mallarméan text in which the poet's sister, Maria, is explicitly mentioned (*Introduction to the Psychoanalysis of Mallarmé*, 27); as mentioned earlier, she had died in 1857 at the age of thirteen, when the poet was fifteen. In a letter of July 1862 to Henri Cazalis, in which Mallarmé ponders Cazalis's reference to his fiancée, Ettie Yapp, as Mallarmé's "sister," the poet refers to Maria as "this poor young phantom who was my sister for thirteen years and who was the only person whom I adored, before I knew all of you" (cited in *Introduction to the Psychoanalysis of Mallarmé*, 28). We have already discussed Mallarmé's metaphorical use of "sister" in the *Poésies* (for instance, in "Soupir," "O si chère de loin," and "Prose") and the strength that metaphor acquired for him because of his loss of Maria.

The dedication to Baudelaire is, of course, significant; and as Ursula Franklin notes, by changing the title Mallarmé may have been reflecting the influence of two poems from the *Fleurs du Mal*, "Chant d'Automne" and "Sonnet d'Automne" (*Anatomy of Poesis*, 29). Aside from their titles, however, there is very little connection between the Baudelaire poems and "Plainte d'Automne." My own speculation would be that Mallarmé retitled the piece because of his concern with the thematics of decline and fall, in the multiple senses of *fall*, and even with reference to the word that is given in English. The poem is a fall meditation; it alludes to the decline and fall of the Roman Empire; and, as Franklin suggests, it hints at a fall from an anterior paradise or state of plenitude associated with the figure of the sister (see *Anatomy of Poesis*, 38). It is significant that Mallarmé explicitly focuses on the word itself in the poem: "Depuis que Maria m'a quitté . . . depuis que la blanche créature n'est plus . . . j'ai aimé . . . tout ce qui se résumait en ce mot: chute" ("Since Maria left me . . . since that white creature has been no more . . . I have loved . . . all that can be summed up in the word *fall*"). English has the advantage here of summing up in one word what French needs two to express. Robert Cohn points out that the brother/sister motif in "Plainte d'Automne" may derive from Poe's "Fall

of the House of Usher," which in the French translation becomes "La Chute de la Maison Usher" (*Mallarmé's Prose Poems*, 34).

There is a historical meditation embedded in Mallarmé's lament for his sister, the poles of which are fall and spring, decadence and barbarism, "high" and "low" culture. In his solitude, Mallarmé's narrator expresses a preference "for the last authors of the Latin decadence . . . [for] the moribund poetry of the last days of Rome, so long, however, as it exudes nothing of the rejuvenating approach of the Barbarians and does not stammer the infantile Latin of the first Christian hymns ['proses chrétiennes']." An identical preference, by the way, is expressed by des Esseintes, the decadent protagonist of J.-K. Huysmans's novel, *A Rebours* (1884), a novel that was clearly influenced by "Plainte d'Automne," which it mentions, along with a number of the other prose-poems and along with several of the *Poésies*. Mallarmé's "Prose (pour des Esseintes)," as we have seen, takes up a different stance toward material that is touched on for the first time in "Plainte d'Automne."

The poem is divided into two paragraphs, and the break occurs at the moment the narrator/protagonist, reading his favorite decadent authors and thinking himself sealed off from the world in a kind of hermetic cocoon, happens to hear a hurdy-gurdy (or barrel organ) droning beneath his window. The French term for that instrument is *l'orgue de Barbarie*, the original title of the poem, and (alas for English!) translation must at this point throw up its hands; for implicated in the French phrase, in a manner that English cannot reach, is the dialectic on which the entire poem hangs; the phrase heralds, as the instruments sound, "the rejuvenating approach of the Barbarians," which the narrator, in his protective sadness, had disdained and rejected.

Mallarmé, of course, is the most hermetic of authors and the least given to popular gestures. Even in 1864, at the age of twenty-two, he must have sensed that this was his destiny, and furthermore—as writers such as Walter Benjamin have emphasized—that the age in which he lived was one in which great art was becoming less and less accessible to the masses. He must have sensed the psychological dangers of becoming "out of touch," of ceasing to feel, which even then were posed by the rigorous demands of his own artistry. In "Le Phénomène Futur," Mallarmé envisions a future in which decadence has become barbaric and has lost even the excuse of refinement: he must have known that this would be the inevitable outcome unless technical sophistication could be achieved without loss of *humanitas*. The polarity between the "moribund poetry of the last days of Rome" and the "old-fashioned, banal tune" of the hurdy-gurdy, "l'orgue de Barbarie," was the *enantiodromia*, the shuttling between opposites, that poetry compelled him to face.

FRISSON D'HIVER / WINTER SHIVER

"Frisson d'Hiver" was composed, like the two previous poems, in 1864, and was first published in October 1867 under the title "Causerie d'Hiver" in *La Revue des Arts et des Lettres*. It was reprinted several times as "Causerie," and was subsequently retitled for its appearance in the December 1875 issue of *La République des Lettres*.

Mallarmé is not exactly what one might call a "domestic" poet, and "Frisson d'Hiver" is the only text in the corpus that focuses openly on his household arrangements. Judging from this little piece—and notwithstanding its narrator's protesta-tions—they don't seem to have been altogether satisfactory. Indeed, I would go so far as to say that "Frisson d'Hiver" is one of the few relative failures in the work, and this because the feeling and tone it engenders is overwhelmed by ambivalence and by the poet's "good intentions." The reader feels smothered by the petit-bourgeois rococo atmosphere being described and senses that the same holds true for the narrator and the poet (intentional fallacy or no); yet the reader also feels expected not to recognize the unhappiness of the situation and to lend his approbation in some way. The title (in its definitive version) must be ironic (or at least must be taken in this way) because, with the exception of the spiderwebs on top of the high casements, nowhere can there be found even the slightest *frisson*; the atmosphere is entirely static. It may indeed be that the title was changed in order to provide an ironic echo against the famous opening of Alfred de Musset's first sonnet, "Que je l'aime le premier frisson d'hiver." In that sonnet, critics have seen "images of inconstancy, impermanence, and change" (Lloyd Bishop, "Musset's First Sonnet," 457).

One striking feature of the text, given its brevity, is the extraordinary number of different words the poet uses to express time and aging: *autrefois, usées, longtemps, vieux, amortis, dénués, anciennes, vieilleries, déteints, jadis, antique, fanées*. The windows and the mirror are, of course, among the constants in Mallarmé's lexicon of symbolic images. The woman bathing the sin of her beauty in the mirror is a pale reflection of Hérodiade.

Mauron (in his inimitable way) sees a "grafting" of Mallarmé's wife on his sister: "Marie is united with Maria by her look, and by the fact that one is dead and the other cherishes the past" (*Introduction to the Psychoanalysis of Mallarmé*, 92). Indeed, the narrator addresses his companion as "sister" (as well as "child"); but where in other poems the metaphor is richly erotic (for example in "Prose" or "O si chère de loin"), here it contributes to the desexualized atmosphere of sterility that is symbolized—as a framing device or refrain—by the recurring image of the spiderwebs. The syntax of the penultimate verse-paragraph, in the passage beginning "et, sur l'antique tapis couché," is deliberately ungrammatical, and, as a result, the male and female figures seem to merge in a sinister loss of boundaries. "There no longer are any fields and the streets are all empty," says the narrator, in an unanticipated moment that is surely the strangest in the poem.

LE DÉMON DE L'ANALOGIE / THE DEMON OF ANALOGY

Composed either in 1864 or 1865, "Le Démon de l'Analogie" was not published until March 1874 when it appeared in *La Revue du Monde Nouveau* under the title "La Pénultième." It was reprinted several times with that title and finally, in its definitive form, in *Pages* and again in *Divagations* in 1891. The piece must have achieved a certain notoriety early on. Gustave Kahn, in an amusing passage from *Symbolistes et Décadents* (1902) that is often quoted, comments as follows:

> When Mallarmé published these verses, the *Pénultième*, that famous *Pénultième*, was talked about for ten or twelve years everywhere on the Left Bank. The *Pénultième* was then the *nec plus ultra* of the incomprehensible, the Chimborazo of the insurmountable, and the Chinese head breaker. (*OC*, 1557; translation mine)

Though it originated around the same time as the three pieces that precede it in the "Poëmes en Prose," "Le Démon de l'Analogie" represents a dramatic advance in Mallarmé's handling of the prose-poem as a form. Those three pieces (and especially the first two), though suffused with poetic feeling, are essentially prose vignettes; but whatever that ineffable hybrid, the prose-poem, may ultimately be (should we hyphenate the phrase as I have done?), "Le Démon" certainly falls under the category. One reason for this, perhaps, is that "Le Démon" is at once a poem and a meditation on the poetic process that necessarily stands outside the poem. As Ursula Franklin observes, the poem is entitled "Le Démon de l'Analogie" and is simultaneously about the creation of "Le Démon de l'Analogie" (*Anatomy of Poesis*, 63–64). It hovers on the boundaries, and consequently the essential experience it conveys is what Freud referred to as the *uncanny*. That, indeed, may be the distinguishing feature of the prose-poem in general—along with the syntactical complexity that in Mallarmé's prose-poems begins to make itself felt in "Le Démon."

In its title, "Le Démon" recalls Poe's story, "The Imp of the Perverse," which Baudelaire had translated as "Le Démon de la Perversité." *Demon* is derived from the Greek *daimon*: one thinks of Socrates' *daimon*, which (or who) came to his aid when there was a problem he was unable to resolve on his own; and, in the realm of poetry, of the Muses who sang through their chosen vessels, the poets. Both Socrates' *daimon* and the Muses are figures of *otherness*; they pertain to a supernatural or supersensible realm to which we are sometimes given access, if we are open to it. One might say that the Greek *daimon* is *demonized* by the Christian terror of the irrational sources of our power. In the realm of poetry those irrational sources seem to operate according to the twin processes of condensation and association—*analogy*, which is what we are given here. There is a sense also in which the analogical process is experienced as demonic by Mallarmé because its lack of terminus gives it an obsessional quality: once mobilized it cannot easily be put to rest.

The Greeks regarded poetry as a gift, and Michaud points out (see *Mallarmé*, 41) that "Le Démon de l'Analogie" was written around the same time as "Don du Poëme,"the poem that introduces *Hérodiade*. (The editors of the Pléiade edition give the date of "Le Démon" as 1864 and that of "Don du Poëme" as 1865, but both are still within the same general time frame, and Michaud's observation points to an important convergence.) The wing, the palm branch, and the stringed instrument—all central symbols in Mallarmé's work—appear in both poems in combination. All three, moreover, function in terms of what Mallarmé referred to as the "Orphic explanation of the earth, which is the sole task of the poet" (*OC*, 663).

In her analysis of "Le Démon," Franklin brilliantly alerts us to the Orphic element in the poem, both to "the Orphic association of poetry and music" and to "the poet's Orphic function of resurrecting the past and bringing back the dead" (*Anatomy of Poesis*, 55, 57). She describes how the wing, the poem's initial image, a synecdoche for bird and a symbol for poetic inspiration, stands for and connects both of these processes, one associated with birth and the other with death. The wing, "gliding over the strings of an instrument" in the opening movement of the poem (p. 93), is replaced by a voice, and Franklin suggests that "the voice is born out of the wing's contact with the instrument," just as in "Une dentelle s'abolit" a birth occurs from the belly or womb of the instrument (55). In "Don du Poëme," the mother cradling

her child has a "voice like viol and harpsichord," and is connected to the sibylline nurse of the "Ouverture Ancienne." One is also reminded, of course, of "Sainte," where a harp is given its shape by the wing of an angel in flight.

The wing gliding over the instrument is immediately replaced by the voice pronouncing the death of the *Pénultième*. As an aspect of the Orphic equation of poetry and music, Franklin connects the wing with the *Pénultième*, suggesting that the former evokes a feminine presence—the *aile* an *elle*—and, by a process of association or analogy, an angel (as in "Sainte") and the poet's dead sister, Maria (54–56). The symbolism of "Le Démon de l'Analogie" is clearly so overdetermined—so relentlessly demonic in its refusal to arrive at any fixed meaning, by virtue, indeed, of an analogical process that is itself thematized in the poem—that it would be absurd to disagree with Franklin on this point; but certainly one could argue that it is unnecessary to resort to Mallarmé's biography in this way. Franklin's biographical reading differs from that of Mauron, who resolves the enigma (to his own satisfaction, at least) by arguing that everything leads back to the poet's *mother*: "Who is the next to last one dead? The last is Maria; the next to last, his mother" (*Introduction to the Psychoanalysis of Mallarmé*, 48).

Despite these attempts to fix meaning in a biographical terminus, part of the obsessive phrase, *Est morte*, "detache[s] itself from the fateful suspension, trailing uselessly off into the void of signification" (p. 93). In the passage that immediately follows, the poet recognizes "in the sound *nul* the taut string of the musical instrument which had been forgotten and which glorious Memory had just now surely visited with her wing or with a palm": *nul* means "void" and is the penultimate syllable of *Pénultième*.

Franklin notes that "Souvenir" and "Pénultième" are the only two words capitalized in the poem (*Anatomy of Poesis*, 57). Memory is traditionally linked to poetry, and the personification intensifies the sense of *otherness* associated with the poetic process. The palm is a symbol of poetic triumph, but in "Don du Poëme" it symbolizes a state of warmth and plenitude that banishes an earlier condition of emptiness and sterility, and perhaps that meaning applies here as well.

In any event, what is now emphasized is the way in which the phrase, "La Pénultième est morte," having detached itself from the visual and auditory sensations to which it was formerly connected, achieves an independence of its own—which is to say, forms the beginning of a poem. This is important because—as Mallarmé once emphasized to Edgar Degas when the latter complained that he had many poetic ideas but was unable to compose a poem—poetry is made out of words, not ideas. The poem has now begun to take shape and continues to obsess the poet, even though he tries to avoid it through rationalizations of various kinds. A passage in the middle of the long (penultimate) paragraph is syntactically difficult and worthy of special note: "le reste mal abjuré d'un labeur de linguistique par lequel quotidiennement sanglote de s'interrompre ma noble faculté poétique" (p. 94). "The imperfectly abandoned residue," here, is the result of a linguistic labor that is at the essence of the poetical faculty; but whether the poetical faculty "sobs" on account of the frustrating interruptions it must endure (this is probably the primary meaning), or whether the sobbing out of its interruptions *is* the poetical faculty, cannot be determined from the syntax. The second possibility is the darker of the two, but both are latent and both are very real to Mallarmé.

The emphasis that Mallarmé gives to the otherness of the poetic process makes poetry analogous to prayer, and it is not by accident that the words "oraison" and "psalmodie" (prayer and psalm) both occur in this context. A psalm is a hymn, and as we noted, one of the meanings of "prose," the title word of "Prose (pour des Esseintes)," is "hymn." Indeed, "Le Démon de l'Analogie" has the same status of *ars poetica* for Mallarmé's prose-poetry that "Prose" has for his verse.

As the poem draws to a conclusion, and just before the uncanny recognition in front of the lutemaker's shop, the poet senses that the voice in which he is chanting the phrase (which has now taken on the status of a psalm) is the same voice he originally heard chanting it and that seemed then to belong to another. (One is reminded of Rimbaud's famous assertion: "Je est un autre.") The phrase "l'unique," in "qui indubitablement avait été l'unique" (p. 94), can mean "the only one," "the original one" (as it is rendered here), or "the unique one"; the reference can be to the poet's own voice, or—if we give this an Orphic or a Platonic interpretation—to the voice of some *other*, to an original or unique voice that is the voice of Poetry and that the poet recognizes as his own only when it has finally spoken through him.

Whatever personal associations the "Penultimate" may have had for Mallarmé the man, it must remain "inexplicable" as far as the poet and poetry are concerned because it corresponds to an ideal that is always sought and never attained. The poetic process thus manifests a strange combination of mastery and triumph, on the one hand (as in the uncanny synthesis arrived at in front of the lutemaker's shop, where all of the symbols suddenly coalesce), and helplessness, frustration, even grief, on the other. The poet flees from the "Penultimate" as he fled from the Sky in "L'Azur" (also composed in 1864), but, because of the *daimon* (or *demon*) to which he has access, he is condemned to bear its grief.

PAUVRE ENFANT PÂLE / POOR PALE CHILD

Mallarmé wavered on the title of "Pauvre Enfant Pâle" for many years, as he did with several of the other prose-poems. The poem was first published in *La Semaine de Vichy* in July 1864 under the title "La Tête," reprinted in October 1867 in *La Revue des Arts et des Lettres* as "Pauvre Enfant Pâle," given the title "Le Fusain" ("The Sketch") for its appearance in the August 1886 issue of *Le Décadent Littéraire et Artistique*, and finally returned to "Pauvre Enfant Pâle" for the March 1887 issue of *La Revue Rose*. It was included in *Pages* and subsequently in *Divagations* under its definitive title in 1891.

The aura of fatalism pervading this visionary sketch of mid-nineteenth-century social conditions could not possibly be greater if its protagonist were the hero of a Greek tragedy. The young street singer on whom the poem focuses is destined by the bad luck of his birth (one is reminded of "Le Guignon") to come to no good, to "turn out badly," as we say. Inevitably, he will be drawn to a life of crime and just as inevitably he will be punished by the state. Mallarmé envisions the child's head, bobbing up and down as he strains to sing, severed by the guillotine from his shoulders.

Perhaps because its surface content is of such straightforward simplicity, criticism has tended to allegorize the poem. The little boy is a street singer, and thus it is possible to view him as a "beggar of azure" (again, like the *poètes-manqués* of "Le Guignon") and perhaps even as a self-reflexive image of the poet himself. The decapitation motif, moreover, allows us to draw a parallel between "Pauvre Enfant Pâle" and the "Cantique de Saint Jean" from *Hérodiade*. In the "Cantique" the saint's head is described as "drunk from fasting," and in "Pauvre Enfant Pâle" the little boy is ironically said to be "fasting"—that is, because he can't get enough to eat. Continuing the parallel, we might say that the boy is a "martyr" to society. Like any sacrificial victim, he will have to "pay" (note Mallarmé's use of this verb in the penultimate paragraph) for those members of society whose collective sin he expiates. "That's probably why you came into the world and you are fasting from now on," writes Mallarmé—as if the judicial systems of "advanced" societies, for all their apparent "rationality," were really nothing more than elaborate mechanisms of ritual sacrifice.

All of this is in the poem; nevertheless, there is a danger of sentimentalizing the image, by identifying the boy with the poet or martyr, and, simultaneously, of deflecting the meaning from the socio-political to the metaphysical realm. Mallarmé is not a poet of the "egotistical sublime," and he has too fine a sense of poetic decorum to open himself up to the kind of wholesale associations that some of his critics delight to engage in. The little boy is neither a poet nor a martyr; furthermore, he is going to end up badly: "on te rendra mauvais et un jour tu commettras un crime." "They will make you wicked": who is *they*? The other ragamuffins, the "criminal classes" . . . finally, society as a whole. "Mauvais" also has a range of meanings in this context: bad, wicked, evil, rotten, corrupt, and so on.

The extraordinary thing is that Mallarmé is able to suggest hidden depths—the stuff of Greek tragedy—without breaching the decorum imposed by the poetic image. The little boy is a symbol of nothing. And yet his lament is "so high, so high." The song he bawls out at the top of his lungs is perceived imaginatively as a plaint or lament and its loudness is turned into "height." The poem thus hints at the "high style" while remaining true to its own material.

LA PIPE / THE PIPE

Composed in 1864, "La Pipe" recalls the period between 1862 and 1863 when Mallarmé lived in London. The poem was first published in January 1868 in *La Revue des Arts et des Lettres*; it was reprinted in several other journals before being included in *Pages* and in *Divagations* in 1891.

Like "Plainte d'Automne," "La Pipe" is strongly marked by nostalgia and by the antithesis between high and low, or elite and popular, culture. In "Plainte," as we recall, the narrator, a connoisseur of the literature of the Latin decadence, is moved by a popular tune played by a hurdy-gurdy; similarly in "La Pipe," the narrator, while gravely pondering the serious books he is planning to write, is struck by an involuntary memory of a very simple, not to say sentimental, kind. The hurdy-gurdy and the pipe, like Proust's *madeleine*, become instruments for the evocation of memories, memories that, although sad in themselves, are also fructifying in that they substitute for a previous state of aridity. Note how the syntactical complexity of the second sentence, with its strange phrasing ("Jetées les cigarettes . . . " / "Thrown aside were my cigarettes . . . "), coincides with an emphasis on the way *things*, the ordinary things with which we are most familiar, *illuminate* (to borrow the metaphor that Mallarmé himself uses) what Wordsworth had earlier called "spots of time." The method that Proust was to develop may well

have been distilled through the alembic of the *Poëmes en Prose*.

The pipe is at first associated (ironically in retrospect) with the high seriousness of the man of letters; but with the tobacco smoke, the poet breathes in the air of the fogs of London, a London he had come to know during his sojourn there the previous winter. Smoke has the connotation of mystery, and hence of poetry, for Mallarmé, as in "Toute l'âme résumée," and fog offers protection against the "Azure"—which is to say, the Absolute (as in "L'Azur," also of 1864). One is reminded once again of Manet's magnificent portrait of the poet swathed in tobacco smoke.

The trajectory of associations charted by "La Pipe" culminates in the image of a woman—as is also true of "Plainte d'Automne." Insofar as we can relate the woman in the poem to Mallarmé's life—and of course, there is a sense in which the poem is directly autobiographical—she is Marie Gerhard, whom Mallarmé had married in August 1863. (They lived together for a time in London, and the correspondence of that period indicates that the relationship was rocky and almost broke up on several occasions.) The conclusion of the poem, with its image of the steamer and of the handkerchief "that one waves when saying goodbye forever," is reminiscent of "Brise Marine" (1865), where the Romantic ambivalence to human attachments as inevitably leading to ennui is more overtly expressed.

UN SPECTACLE INTERROMPU / AN INTERRUPTED PERFORMANCE

The date of composition of "Un Spectacle Interrompu" is unknown; however, it would not be unreasonable to assume that the poem was written around the time of its initial publication, which occurred in December 1875 in *La République des Lettres*. If that assumption is accurate, then "Un Spectacle" would occupy an intermediate position between the prose-poems that come before it in the sequence, all of which were composed in 1864, and those that come after it, which belong to the period of 1885–1888. Certainly "Un Spectacle" is much longer than the earlier poems, but I would be hesitant to argue, as Ursula Franklin does, that it occupies a middle ground from a stylistic point of view (see *Anatomy of Poesis*, 95). It has been suggested, as Franklin notes, that Mallarmé's style underwent a transformation in the 1870s, but "Le Démon de l'Analogie" dates from 1864, and so the argument strikes me as overly schematic. Mallarmé's development does not move in a straight line, and from almost the beginning the extraordinary stylistic capabilities he commanded could be deployed in various ways depending on the circumstances.

In any event, it is in a letter of 1864 (a letter we have previously quoted; see above, p. 169), that Mallarmé sums up his new poetics: "To paint, not the thing itself, but the effect it produces" (*Correspondance de Stéphane Mallarmé* 1, 137). That dictum seems particularly germane to "Un Spectacle Interrompu," with its skepticism about "objective reality." "*Reality*," says the poet at the outset, "is but an artifice, good only for stabilizing the average intellect amid the mirages of a fact." The anecdote or narrative that follows from this assertion—the performance that is interrupted—seems to have the dual purpose of concretizing a poetic conception that regards the immediate object as mere raw material and of distinguishing between an ordinary, conventional, *prosaic* conception of reality and a poetic one. Here again, as in "Le Démon de l'Analogie," we have the uncanny

hovering on the borders of prose and poetry that, for Mallarmé at least, seems to be intrinsic to the prose-poem as a genre.

Once again, as he will do so often in the *Poëmes en Prose*, beginning with "Un Phénomène Futur," Mallarmé presents us with a *spectacle* (a word that has deeply ironical resonances in both French and English). Etymologically, notes Franklin, the word "points to its Roman origin and the games which included confrontations of man and animal in the arena" (*Anatomy of Poesis*, 96). Here, the spectacle is a slightly more sophisticated version of the Elizabethan practice of bearbaiting; in short, it is a mere outlet for the cruelty of the mob. Yet ironically, the piece that is being performed at "the little theater of the Prodigalities" is a version of "The Beast and the Genius," and is intended to illustrate the superiority of man to the animals: "What was happening in front of me? Nothing, except: from the evasive pallor of muslins taking refuge on twenty pedestals constructed in the Baghdad manner, there came a smile and open arms to the sad heaviness of the bear: while the hero, the evoker and guardian of those sylphs, a clown, in his lofty nakedness, was taunting the animal with our superiority" (p. 99). The syntax of that last clause is particularly difficult, and deliberately so: "sortaient un sourire et des bras ouverts à la lourdeur triste de l'ours" could be (and has been) translated as though the smile and open arms were going out from the clown to the bear; but here, I believe, Mallarmé is purposely misleading the (prosaic) reader, setting him off on a wild goose (or rather bear) chase. Since the clown is taunting the bear, I follow Hartley in translating the passage so as to emphasize the sense in which the smile and open arms come as if from within the bear itself (see *Mallarmé*, 130–131).

What the "mirages of a fact" camouflage is what

ancient philosophy, modern physics, and Darwinian biology perceive—that is, that everything in the world is in continuous flux, that all of its beings are related to one another with respect to the larger process of which they form a part, and that the boundaries we erect between them are factitious. The crowd at the theater, reveling in "a myth enclosed in every banality," wants to applaud "Man's incontestable privilege" (p. 100); in a sense, they are the actors and the interrupting of the performance constitutes a rebuke to their hubris. What the poet sees, first of all, is that the myth includes the audience as well as the immediate performers; secondly, that the bear and the human being taunting him are locked into a reciprocal relationship, a kind of dance, that the bear is "on the way" to becoming a man and the man (by virtue of his very arrogance) still submerged in "bestiality"; and finally (as in Hegel's Master/Servant dialectic), that there is a sense in which the bear is superior to the man, precisely because the man thinks he is superior. It is difficult to visualize the scene because Mallarmé paints not the thing itself but the effect it produces; however, the sequence of impressions suggests the following reversal: at the beginning of the performance, the clown taunts the bear by pretending to catch a paper and gold fly suspended over his head, but once he has been "embraced" by the bear, his head, shaking with terror, comes to resemble that of the fly: "but as for him! he himself was raising, his mouth crazed with vagueness, a frightful head shaking by a thread visible in the horror the veritable denegations of a paper and gold fly" (p. 100).

The passage in which the bear asks the clown to explain the meaning of the theater is a marvelous parody of Hegelian dialectic and civilized politesse, but nevertheless serious for all that. The bear's paw is pressing down on the clown's shoulder, and so his request is a "pressing" one (Mallarmé is not above slapstick on occasion; earlier, incidentally, we had been told that the bear's paw was posed on the "ribbons" of the human shoulder, which made it unclear as to whether "ribbons" was literal or metaphorical, the ribbons of a clown costume or the torn flesh of a mauled shoulder). The bear's request is "launched into the regions of wisdom . . . toward myself"—in other words, toward the man, the "subtle elder," who is further along the path that the bear himself is traveling. The bear wants to "authenticate" a "reconciliation" between man and animal that would itself denote a higher stage of human existence than that which is implied by an arrogant anthropocentrism. The crowd is "effaced, magnifying the stage as the emblem of its spiritual situation," but the poet experiences the shock of recognition that "one of the dramas of astral history" has been played out before his eyes (p. 101).

In "Un Spectacle Interrompu," as in several of the other prose-poems (for example, "Le Phénomène Futur" and "La Déclaration Foraine"), the theatrical metaphor or mimetic frame by which the poet measures the banality of his own society and charts the difference between poetry and prose as in a kind of double mirror is continually expanding and contracting so that it is not always clear what is the object of focus and where the boundaries between inside and outside lie. Is the performance or spectacle that is interrupted the original farce and is it interrupted by the bear's unexpected "embrace" of the clown, or is what transpires the spectacle and is it interrupted by the piece of meat thrown out to distract the bear's attention? The incomprehensible "relief" that the audience experiences is "almost free of disappointment"; on some level the crowd would have preferred that a death had been "enacted." The bear, by contrast, eats only out of hunger and does not turn the human image into something *abject* in the way the clown had done with him.

None of the commentators have remarked on the very enigmatic last sentence of the poem. The poet's statement that his way of seeing "had been superior, and even the true one" will seem like uncharacteristic boasting—and hence the mimetic equivalent of the "steady din of glorying" that the performance was intended to celebrate—until we realize how deliberately ironic it is. Mallarmé (or his narrator, if one prefers the New Critical formulation) grasps the sad fact that like everyone else he desires to set himself above everyone else, and that precisely in this respect he is like everyone else. (This fundamental insight, which connects the weakness or fallibility of the poet to that of human beings in general, is also made in "Toast Funèbre," another poem written in the 1870s.) Once we have grasped the irony of the poem's last sentence, moreover, we can elucidate another enigma that has not been explained, one that occurs in the opening paragraph. We have already commented on the passage in which Reality is seen as mere "artifice, good only for stabilizing the average intellect amid the mirages of a fact." However, because Reality nevertheless "rests on some universal understanding," the challenge that is posed to the poet, and that the anecdote is intended to illustrate, is whether "there is not, ideally, some quality—necessary, evident, simple— that can serve as a type" (p. 99). By ending the poem as he does, Mallarmé seems to hint that the "type" defining the species (and reducing all of its members to the sameness of a theater crowd) is precisely the drive to maintain its superiority and dominance—or what Nietzsche called the "will to power." The poet discovers it in himself, in his own disgust for the mob—and the reader, even the attentive reader, is

forced to a similar discovery. (The critic who believes that he has elucidated an enigma posed by the text comes upon the same dynamic.) The desire of the poet at the conclusion of "Un Spectacle Interrompu," then, would seem to be to rid himself of the trammels of what René Girard, who has focused on precisely this problem, has called "mimetic desire"—in other words, to achieve on a higher level the condition still possessed by the "lower" animals.

RÉMINISCENCE / REMINISCENCE

"Réminiscence," probably begun in 1864, first appeared under the title "L'Orphelin" in *La Revue des Arts et des Lettres* in November 1867; it was reproduced in the Brussels journal *L'Art Libre* in February 1872. Before settling on "Réminiscence," Mallarmé apparently conjured two other titles in his mind, "Le Môme Sagace" and "Le Petit Saltimbanque" (*OC*, 1560). As it appeared in *Pages* in 1891, the poem was radically transformed from the version originally entitled "L'Orphelin"—so radically, in fact, that Ursula Franklin considers "Réminiscence," which she dates from 1888, to constitute a new and separate poem (*Anatomy of Poesis*, 109). Alison Finch, comparing "Réminiscence" to "L'Orphelin," points out that the former has 286 words to the latter's 473 ("'Réminiscence' and the Development of Mallarmé's Prose Poems," 212). The text of "L'Orphelin" is reproduced on pages 1559–1560 of the Pléiade edition.

The uncanny *wavering* between poetry and prose that is characteristic of Mallarmé's prose-poems generally is refigured in "Réminiscence" as a wavering between allegory and accident, between meaning as completion and meaning as emptying out. Mediating between the orphaned self that the narrator recalls and the older acrobat engaged "in feats of strength and banalities consistent with the day" is the little urchin in the nightcap "cut like Dante's hood" (p. 103). As Mallarmé's rejected titles, "Le Môme Sagace" and "Le Petit Saltimbanque," would suggest, it is this figure who is central to the poem. He is described as "trop vacillant pour figurer parmi sa race"—"too unsteady in his wavering" (I have deliberately doubled the meaning of "vacillant") "to figure [or appear] among his people" or "to stand as a figure for his people." The urchin, a mirror for the narrator's younger, orphaned self, is cut off from his people, and in being cut off, stands as a figure for the Poet, who, as in the sonnet on Poe, is removed from his time and who is changed into himself by eternity. Dante, reflecting his time under the aspect of eternity, stands as a type or figure of all poets from this point of view. At the same time, however, because we are dealing with a prose-poem that wavers between the fulfillment and the emptying of meaning, there is also the very real possibility that none of these details (the cap in the shape of Dante's hood, for instance) have any meaning beyond themselves.

The radically stripped-down syntax seems to serve as a vehicle for the wavering I have described. The starkness of "orphelin," the very first word of the poem, is intensified by the fact that the noun appears without the article, an effect that I have tried to preserve in the translation, though the result is somewhat awkward in English. (Mallarmé lost his mother at the age of five, and thereafter was committed to the care of his grandparents.) In the early version, entitled "L'Orphelin," the first sentence had read: "Orphelin, déjà, enfant avec tristesse pressentant le Poëte, j'errais vêtu de noir, les yeux baissés du ciel et cherchant ma famille sur la terre" ("Already an or- phan, a child embodying with sadness a presentiment of the Poet, I wandered dressed in black, my eyes low- ered from the sky, searching the earth for my fam- ily"). Here the connection between the orphan and the Poet he embodies as a presentiment was made explicit; there was an intimation of the Hamlet figure, central to *Igitur* and to the early poetry generally. In the revision, these implications are still present but are more subtle: "vêtu de noir," for example, has be- come "en noir," which, as Finch notes, can mean both "dressed in black" and "in a black mood" ("'Réminiscence' and the Development of Mallarmé's Prose Poems," 207). The clauses of the new first sen- tence are strung out paratactically, separated only by commas, as if grammar itself were wandering, cut off as an orphan from the experience it strives to repre- sent.

The circus metaphor—together with its avatars of sideshow, theater, fairground, stage, and so forth—is a profoundly ambivalent one in Mallarmé's lexicon of symbols, and this contributes to the parabolic wavering of meaning that "Réminiscence" describes. The tents of the fair, to which the orphan is attracted, become the site for the materialization of both the sacred and the profane. The child comes upon the "vagabonds" (the word literally means "wanderers" and thus replicates the orphan's own wandering) before the commencement of the performance they are about to give— and we should pay close attention to the opening phrases of the second sentence: "No cry of a chorus clamoring through the canvas rift, nor distant tirade, the drama requiring the holy hour of the footlights, I wanted to speak with an urchin." Is this the chorus of Greek tragedy or merely the noise made by the spectators of a banal sideshow? Is the sacred being enacted here or merely the profane? Grammatically, "the drama requiring the holy hour of the footlights" is wandering and orphaned: is it connected to the opening phrases or to the ensuing clause? Again, are we in the arena of allegory or mere accident, of meaning or emptiness? We then come upon the urchin in Dante's hood, and here again the language must be closely analyzed. He "was already returning to himself ['rentrait en soi'], in the guise of a slice of bread and soft cheese, the snow of mountain peaks, the lily, or some other whiteness constitutive of internal wings." "Rentrait en soi" is a very peculiar phrase: the verb takes "tartine" (the slice of bread on which there is a slice of cheese) as its object, but it also implies an *extasis*, a going out of the self and a return to the self, an association with the sacred that is consistent with the *whiteness* symbolization and with the internal wings. Who is this little boy? The orphan wants to be admitted to his "superior meal." The narrator had asked, in the opening sentence: "did I experience the future and that I would take this form?" Is the form to which the orphan is attracted embodied (perhaps as a presentiment) in the urchin? There seems to be a sense in which the orphan goes out of himself and returns to himself with the internal wings of the urchin.

But what do we make of the poem's conclusion? If a larger meaning is encoded, criticism has certainly failed to establish it. With the intervention of the older acrobat, "engaged in feats of strength and banalities consistent with the day," meaning becomes impoverished, the sacred gives way to the profane, allegory to mere anecdote. The older boy tells the orphan about his parents, and if poetry, the realm of the sacred, is somehow connected to the state of being orphaned, then the connection between the orphan and the older acrobat would take the form of a chiasmus that passes through the urchin. The wandering orphan sees his future in the vagabonds he encounters, but perhaps any future that can be embodied or materialized is inevitably a profane one. In "Le Pitre Châtié" (of 1864) the clown wished to be reborn "other than as an actor," other than as the "bad Hamlet" he was compelled to impersonate on the stage. Sartre would say that any fixed identity pertains to the factitious "in-itself"; as such, it is antithetical to the "whiteness constitutive of internal wings" that the urchin incorporates.

One of Mallarmé's rejected titles for "Réminiscence," "Le Petit Saltimbanque," suggests that the poem establishes an important intertextual relationship to Baudelaire's prose-poem, "Le Vieux Saltimbanque." (Michael Riffaterre has argued that the prose-poem always compensates for the lack of prosody by selecting an intertext as a formal model ["The Prose Poem's Formal Features," 131].) The conclusion of Baudelaire's prose-poem is as follows:

> And, turning around, obsessed by that vision [of the old acrobat], I tried to analyze my sudden sorrow, and I told myself: I have just seen the image of the old writer who has survived the generation whose brilliant entertainer he was; of the old poet without friends, without family, without children, debased by his wretchedness and the public's ingratitude, and whose booth the forgetful world no longer wants to enter! (*The Parisian Prowler [Le Spleen deParis: Petis Poèmes en prose]*, trans. Edward K. Kaplan [Athens: The University of Georgia Press, 1989], 30)

Just as the mature Baudelaire sees his fate in that of the *vieux saltimbanque*, so the young Mallarmé, the disciple of Baudelaire, envisions what he will become in the *petit saltimbanque*—although that phrase will eventually be written out of the poem. But Mallarmé establishes his distance from Baudelaire by envisioning a *double* destiny, one abstract and the other concrete, one allegorical and the other realistic and accidental, one associated with Dante and the "whiteness constitutive of internal wings" and the other connected to the "banalities consistent with the day." Henri Peyre remarks that Picasso came to Paris largely because of Mallarmé (cited by Cohn, *Mallarmé's Prose Poems*, 60).

LA DÉCLARATION FORAINE / THE DECLARATION AT A FAIR

"La Déclaration Foraine" was first published in *L'Art et la Mode* in August 1887 and subsequently in *La Jeune Belgique* in February 1890 before being included in *Pages* and in *Divagations*. When exactly the poem was composed is unknown, but this was probably around the time of its initial publication. The date of composition of "La chevelure vol d'une flamme à l'extrême," the poem in verse that is framed within "La Déclaration Foraine," is also unknown. Mallarmé later included it in the *Poésies*; it is discussed on pages 183 to 185 above.

"Foraine" can mean both "pertaining to a fair" and "foreign" or "strange"; and thus the word contains within itself both the *uncanniness* that permeates Mallarmé's prose-poems and that seems to mark them off generically and the dominant theater metaphor by which that uncanniness is projected in all of its ambivalence. The uncanny vacillation between sacred and profane elements, characteristic of all of the prose-poems, takes a new turn in "La Déclaration Foraine," the longest poem in the sequence; for here, with the actual framing of a poem in verse within a poem in prose, an illusion or trompe l'œil, is created by which the prose-poem seems to represent an actual world and the verse-poem an allegorical one.

Moreover, the verse-poem, "La chevelure vol," is one of Mallarmé's most hermetically private creations; and yet, within the frame of "La Déclaration Foraine" (difficult though *it* may be), it is given a *public* recitation, as if poetry of this kind, poetry so supremely removed from ordinary discourse, could be addressed to an immediate audience. Here, it is as if the artificial poems of the Latin decadence, mentioned in "Plainte d'Automne," could be sung to the accompaniment of the hurdy-gurdy.

The Mallarméan polarities of private to public, sacred to profane, silence to cacophony, and so on, are immediately invoked in the opening paragraph, where the narrator, driving through the countryside at sunset with a lady friend, is torn from his dream by the "ordinary strident laughter of things" (p. 104). As Ursula Franklin suggests, "idée," in the final sentence of the paragraph, has the connotation of "ideal" as well as "idea" (*Anatomy of Poesis*, 122), and the ambiguity is important because it mirrors the very tension between the Real and the Ideal that the poem as a whole manifests. Like the prose-poem itself, the narrator remains on the (uncanny) borderline between an ideal realm and "the obsessive hauntings of existence." Within the world of the prose-poem, however, the ideal must be redefined by an encounter with reality; thus, after the announcement made by the little girl has been "conveyed to [the narrator's] distraction," the narrator explains that the only "compensation for that shock [was] the need it occasioned to construct a figurative explanation plausible to the mind" (p. 104). In other words, poetry is created by its own need to reconstitute itself from the experience of its own destruction, a destruction administered by a reality to which it is antithetical. This dynamic seems to be fundamental to Mallarmé's relationship to the prose-poem as a genre.

In giving themselves over to the experience that ensues, the narrator and his lady enter into an abandoned fairground booth, which, despite its tawdriness, is described as if it were the temple of a sacred rite. The language is ironic, but only partly so, because the poetic challenge posed by the experience—indeed, by experience in general—is precisely the transformation of the real to the ideal, but in a way that does not lose touch with "things as they are." Mallarmé uses the phrase "très prosaïquement" (p. 105) as a marker for the way the plain prose of things is both negated and left intact by a baroque elaboration of syntax that strains almost to the breaking point. In plain prose, the booth has been abandoned by the Showman who was its possessor, and so it is impossible to ascertain the charade that had formerly been staged therein. An old man with a drum remains, however, and the narrator and his lady spontaneously decide to stage a show for his benefit. The narrator thus takes on a role analogous to that of the Showman of "Le Phénomène Futur," and, as in that poem, his lady is displayed as a figure of Beauty to the gathering crowd. There is a deep ambivalence in all this, which perhaps corresponds to the poet's ambivalence about externalizing, making public, his most intimate, mysterious, hermetic insights: the use of the word "pitre" (p. 106) indicates that he is caught in the role of the clown of "Le Pitre Châtié." Yet what distinguishes the Poet from the Showman, as Mallarmé acknowledges in one of the philosophical generalizations to which the narrative gives rise, is the "absolute power [of] Metaphor," without which there is "no earthly way of averting the defection of Beauty to mere curiosity" (p. 107).

"La chevelure vol d'une flamme à l'extrême," the sonnet recited by the narrator after the lady has mounted the platform and displayed herself to the crowd, has one meaning in the context of the *Poésies* and quite another in that of the anecdote that is unfolded in "La Déclaration Foraine." In the latter context it is the "claptrap" ("boniment" [p. 109]—the same word that is used in "Le Phénomène Futur") by which the narrator deludes the crowd into thinking that the performance being staged possesses "authenticity" and by which he convinces them that they have gotten something for their money. And of course if the crowd *believes* that it has gotten what it wanted, then it *has* gotten what it wanted—which means that even on the lowest, the most prosaic, level the performance possesses a kind of authenticity. It is not merely a question of "the emperor's new clothes" here because the relationship between reality and fiction, truth and illusion, is too complex to be stabilized; as the poet writes at the beginning of "Un Spectacle Interrompu," "*Reality* is but an artifice, good only for stabilizing the average intellect amid the mirages of a fact" (p. 99).

When the narrator has concluded his recitation, he "support[s] the waist of the living allegory, in order gracefully to cushion her descent to earth" (p. 108). The lady, mounted on her platform, has figured as an allegory of Beauty, as in "Le Phénomène Futur"; but the significance of allegory seems to burst its bounds here, almost as if it, too, had descended to earth, because, as at the conclusion of "Un Spectacle Interrompu," a prosaic spectacle has taken on the lineaments of "one of the dramas of astral history" (p. 101). Allegory is itself refigured—from the vantage point of the prose-poem—because it is precisely through the prosaic that the beauty and poetry of "La Déclaration Foraine" emerge. What arises, ambiguously, is the "lieu commun d'une esthétique"

(p. 108): from a poetic standpoint, the common place (that is, the place that can be shared in common) of a (new) aesthetic; and from a prosaic standpoint, the commonplace of an aesthetic—since (from the jaundiced perspective of prose) all aesthetic statements ultimately amount to commonplaces or clichés.

The concluding dialogue between the narrator and the lady is syntactically dense and, as befits a narrative that has refigured allegory, "open to the multiplicities of comprehension" (p. 109). The opening of the third-to-last paragraph, in which the lady speaks, can be parsed in several ways: (1) "An aesthetic that you would not perhaps have introduced … if it were not for the pretext of thus formulating it before me"; or possibly (2) "Would you not perhaps have introduced that aesthetic as the pretext of thus formulating (it) before me ?" The connection between aesthetics (the root meaning of which is *perception*) and eros is clear, in any event, and this reminds us that in the sonnet he had recited, the narrator consigned eros to aesthetic contemplation. He now agrees with the lady that the crowd is vulgar and brutal specifically because of a need to "hurl themselves naked . . . across the public" (p. 109)— that is, to insist on the public, concrete, material manifestation of things that might better be left hidden, mysterious, unactualized. However, he reminds her that she would not have been able to grasp the sonnet "if each term had not been echoed to you from various drums" (p. 109)—which is to say, if it were not for its prosodic structure. Prosody, without which poetry fades into incoherence or nothingness, is here subtly connected to the drum that the old man in the abandoned booth was asked to bang (although Mallarmé makes use of two words for drum: "caisse" and "tympan"). The significance of the analogy would seem to be that poetry, in order to exist, must descend into the depths of the cave, which (notwithstanding the lady's apparent prudishness) is the realm in which eros also abides.

LE NÉNUPHAR BLANC / THE WHITE WATER LILY

"Le Nénuphar Blanc" was first published in August 1885 in *L'Art et la Mode*, having probably been composed during the previous June or July. Mallarmé had a little villa at Valvins on the Seine, with a boat he called his "yole" which he was fond of sailing. The sense of timelessness he experienced on the water, and which he describes in his letters, is beautifully conveyed in this, the most Proustian of the prose-poems. The title, as well as the feeling and tone of the piece, is also reminiscent of Claude Monet's many paintings of water lilies, which were done considerably later. Mallarmé and Monet were very close, and (not to make too much of the affiliation) it is pleasant to imagine that the poet's water lily exerted some slight influence on those of the painter whom Proust was to fictionalize as Elstir.

Indeed, Mallarmé's painterly eye is very much in evidence in this piece; but what is depicted above all—in true Impressionist fashion (and here poetry may have some advantage over painting)—is surely the sense that all depiction is vain and that what the eye does not see the inner eye can conjure. "Toute je l'évoquais lustrale" ("Completely lustral did I conjure her"), writes the poet in a sentence that seems to sum up the entire poem and that is set off as its own paragraph (p. 111). "Paint not the thing itself but the effect it produces" (*Correspondance de Stéphane Mal-*

larmé 1. 137); "I say: a flower! and outside the oblivion to which my voice relegates any shape, insofar as it is something other than the calyx, there arises musically, as the very idea and delicate, the one absent from any bouquet" ("Crise de Vers," *Selected Poetry and Prose*, 76; *OC*, 368). Aesthetic dicta of this kind are often to be encountered in Mallarmé, and they coincide with an orientalizing tendency and a privileging of light over substance that are also found in the art of Monet and Debussy. In Mallarmé's work we already find this tendency in such early poems as "Las de l'amer repos" (1864), where the poet, turning toward an Oriental art of suggestion and of resignation to the transience of things, vows to "forsake the ravenous Art of cruel lands."

The final word of "Las de l'amer repos," significantly, is "roseaux"—"reeds"; and it is into a clump of reeds ("quelque touffe de roseaux") that the poet's boat runs aground in "Le Nénuphar Blanc," recalling him to his "worldly identity" (p. 110). That clump or tuft of reeds will remind us of the reeds in "L'Après-midi d'un Faune," through which the faun gazes on the bathing nymphs and out of which he fashions his musical instrument. A number of commentators have noticed the connection between "L'Après-midi" and "Le Nénuphar Blanc." Charles Mauron is the first to have suggested that the prose-poem "in many ways repeats the theme of the *Faune* . . . if the transposition into a modern tonality is taken into account" (*Introduction to the Psychoanalysis of Mallarmé*, 174–175); and he is followed by Franklin, who points to other important images that the two works share in common (for example, the *ceintures* that seem at once to focus eros and hold it in place; compare "Le Nénuphar," p. 112; "L'Après-midi," lines 54–56) and who emphasizes the sublimation of desire at which both poems are aimed (*Anatomy of Poesis*,

144–145). Mauron suggests further that in "Le Nénuphar" the woman and the flower become interchangeable, so that at the end of the piece the "ravished ideal flower" "rapt de mon idéale fleur"—p. 113) becomes a benign version of the rape that the faun attempts to accomplish (*Introduction to the Psychoanalysis of Mallarmé*, 175–176).

There is something, indeed, in the richness of the imagery of "Le Nénuphar Blanc" and in the fluidity of its syntax (a syntax that mimes the "meandering stream" [p. 110] on which the poet's boat also meanders), which allows us to connect the poem to the central vein of Mallarméan imagery and to many other poems in the corpus besides "L'Après-midi." The whiteness of the water lily and the water itself are caught up in a web of associated images that include the mirror, the diamond, the swan, and virginity, all of which have many resonances with the poetry at large. The poet's imagined lady, forming from the "crystal" of the water "an interior mirror to shelter her from the brilliant indiscretion of the afternoon" (p. 111), makes Franklin think of Hérodiade with her mirrors (see *Anatomy of Poesis*, 141). But the "silvery mist glazing the willows" (p. 111), the mirror, the boat meandering down the stream, the magic spells and the presence of a stranger on the shore, and the water lily itself—all of these remind the present reader, at least, of Tennyson's great poem, "The Lady of Shalott," which must have made a considerable impression on Mallarmé, who translated "Mariana" and wrote a memorial essay on Tennyson (see *OC*, 703; 527–531). In the Tennyson poem the lady has been cast under a spell that bars her from engaging with reality except through the mediation of a mirror: she is literally trapped in the world of art, in the work of art that bears her name. In her desire to break free, which comes upon her when she hears Sir Launcelot singing, she looks down from the tower in which she is imprisoned, and at that moment the mirror cracks and the curse comes upon her. Entering a boat that appears on the water, she floats down to Camelot; but "ere she reached upon the tide / The first house by the water-side, / Singing in her song she died." A similar melancholy pervades "Le Nénuphar Blanc," but here the poet floating down the river refuses to crack the mirror of art by actually making contact with his imagined lady. That would entail the death of the dream, but the choice that is made cannot but leave regret in its wake, a regret that bursts into flower in the exquisite final paragraph, and particularly in the final phrase, "or some other body of water," where a powerful poetic emotion is deflected, as it were, onto a prosaic utterance.

L' ECCLÉSIASTIQUE / THE ECCLESIASTIC

First published in Turin in the journal *Gazzetta Letteraria, Artistica e Scientifica* in December 1886, this poem was then reproduced under the title "Actualité" and with the subtitle "Printemps au Bois de Boulogne," in April 1888 in *La Revue Indépendante*. It was included in *Pages* and subsequently in *Divagations* under its definitive title.

The anecdote forming the basis of this meditation allows for a consideration (in deft but very broad strokes) of the relationship between nature and that aspect of the human spirit (comprising religion and art) that would set itself in opposition to nature. Moreover, the meditation takes up this relationship not only in itself but from the standpoint of a modernity that would cast our traditional outlook on the relationship into question.

When Mallarmé takes up metaphysical questions, they are often concretely posed in the context of lexical or syntactical ambiguities, and such is certainly the case in "L'Ecclésiastique." The poem begins by referring to the way in which natural organisms are impelled by spring, and to the fact that treatises in natural history abound in descriptions of this phenomenon. The word "poussent," incidentally, was also used in Mallarmé's sonnet of 1862 on the spring, "Renouveau," in which the poet, "Biting warm earth in which the lilacs push" ("Mordant la terre chaude où poussent les lilas"—line 11), takes up an attitude to the spring that is much more ambivalent and burdened than that of the ecclesiastic of the prose-poem. More will be said about this later; but for the moment, we should focus on the poem's difficult second sentence: "Of how much more plausible interest it would be to record certain of the changes that the climacteric moment brings about in the behavior of individuals fashioned for a spiritual destiny" ("Qu'il serait d'un intérêt plus plausible de recueillir certaines des altérations qu'apporte l'instant climatérique dans les allures d'individus faits pour la spiritualité!"—p. 114). "Plausible," in addition to its ordinary sense, retains its etymological meaning of "worthy of applause"; thus, the meaning of the opening portion of the sentence would be something like the following: "How much more laudable, because congruent to humanity, and hence to what is plausibly in the interests of humanity, would it be," and so forth. As in "Un Spectacle Interrompu," where the poet asks for an "association of dreamers [that would take] notice of events in the light peculiar to dreams" (p. 99), the poet of "L'Ecclésiastique" is asking for a scientific approach to a particular phenomenon, one that in this case goes beyond not only the ordinary but, strictly speaking, the "natural." But the phrase "l'instant climatérique" is especially ambiguous, and here is where the real questions emerge. "Climatérique" probably has the primary meaning of the "climacteric"—that is, of a physiological phase that emerges spontaneously from the mechanisms of biology, as it were. The French word can also have the meaning of "climatic"—although the Littré dictionary (to which Mallarmé continually referred, even as a way of generating material) makes it clear that the word should not be derived from "climat" or used instead of "climatologique." In addition to "climacteric" and "climatic," there may also be the included connotation of "climactic." How do we parse all of these lexical relations? In a sense, that question is another way of asking about the relationship between nature and the human. Does climate, or seasonality, play a role in human life in the way it does with the (other) animals? And, if so, what does this say about the way in which we attempt to distinguish ourselves from them? If one accepts the position of Littré, then "climactérique" would be a catachresis because "climatic" is more immediately relevant to the context at hand than "climacteric"; and yet, the very fact that from a lexical perspective "climatic" is not strictly speaking correct may be an indication of the problematic relationship that the poem itself is posing.

In any event, whether because of climate or an internal climacteric—or else, as seems reasonable to infer, because of a personal and/or cultural crisis that has arrived at its climax—the ecclesiastic is "responding to the solicitations of the lawn" (p. 114). What interests Mallarmé in this situation is nothing that "could bring profit to the crowd" (p. 114), that many-headed hydra (in the metaphor used in the sonnet on Poe) that alternates between hypocritical piety and gloating prurience, but rather the *uncanni-*

ness of an encounter that seems to serve as an emblem for modernity—that is, for the end of a long epoch in which the spiritual aspirations of humanity seemed to promise nothing less than the transcendence of nature. The tone of the poem is gently ironic, but not at all gloating; for, as a comparison with "Renouveau" would suggest, Mallarmé is aware that the spiritual aspirations of religion are on a continuum with those of poetry. "Lucid winter, season of art serene, / Is sadly driven out by sickly spring" ("Renouveau," lines 1–2); the discipline essential to a life that reaches beyond the senses is shattered by the inexorability of the instinctual realm.

The act of writing the prose-poem at hand thus becomes a way of holding on to "the irony of winter" and not succumbing to "a naive or absolute naturalism capable of pursuing enjoyment in the differentiation of various blades of grass" (p. 114). The ecclesiastic succumbs, "amid that special robe worn with the appearance that one is everything for oneself, even one's own wife" (p. 115), because of "the immutable texts inscribed in his flesh" (p. 115)—a truly astonishing figure, which transposes the realm of necessity in such a way as to subvert human strivings. Often in Mallarmé's prose-poems, boundaries are shattered and categories are opened up; and beneath the somewhat bland exterior of the anecdote of the ecclesiastic, there is a climactic sense of history, of an opening up to reality that mankind had wanted at all costs to keep at bay, and that he had been able to keep at bay. In the extraordinary sentence that opens with the apostrophe to Solitude, the black robe of the ecclesiastic is transformed to a darkness it had once served to hide—"as if the night hidden in its folds came shaken out of it at last!" (p. 115); the symbol of the folds ("plis"), as it so often appears in Mallarmé (the "Ouverture Ancienne," for instance) stands for a mystery that is finally intractable. The "canons, prohibitions, and censures" of religion are fixed (p. 115), but poetry, by contrast—and therein lies its significance to modernity—is able to accommodate itself to an intuition of this kind. The image presented by the ecclesiastic in spring, "an image marked by the mysterious seal of modernity, at once baroque and beautiful," is thus finally one in which religion is subsumed by poetry.

LA GLOIRE / GLORY

"La Gloire" first appeared in 1886, in the *Hommes d'Aujourd'hui* series edited by Verlaine, under the title "Notes de Mon Carnet" ("From My Notebook"); it was reprinted in April of the following year in *Écrits pour L'Art*, then subsequently in *Pages* and in *Divagations* under its definitive title.

Glory is central to the Mallarméan lexicon, as a number of scholars have stressed, and it seems fitting that the *Poëmes en Prose* should end on this note, although the sequence was ordered variously in the publications in which it appeared during Mallarmé's lifetime (see above, p. 241). The conception of glory—and not only the conception but the word "gloire" itself—encompasses a great deal for Mallarmé, as James R. Lawler has observed (see "Mallarmé's 'La Gloire'")—indeed, more than can perhaps be expressed. On the positive side, in the "solar drama" that Gardner Davies has analyzed (see *Mallarmé et le Drame Solaire*), it is that which connects the beauty of a sunset to the gold of a woman's hair to the exaltation of the poet; on the negative side (as in "Toast Funèbre"), it is vainglory or hubris, a human propensity that, in fact, separates us from the experience of glory itself.

The poem, accordingly, begins by distinguishing implicitly between a true glory, which has only now been discovered or grasped, and a false one, which, if given that name (for such is the nature of language), will no longer be of interest. Mallarmé has made use of a somewhat arcane philosophical term, "irréfragable," in order to express not only that the thing cannot be refuted but that it cannot even be opposed. ("Irréfragable" is reminiscent of another inkhorn term, "irrécusable," which occurs at the close of "Le Démon de l'Analogie" [p. 94].) The form or essence of glory has been experienced, and the positioning of the adjective allows it to refer both to glory and to the experience of *knowing* it. (The same syntactical maneuver would have been awkward in English, and I have chosen instead to draw out the syntax by interpolating the implicit sense of an essence.)

Having posed the possibility of an experience of this kind, the poet places us immediately in the phenomenological "train" of his observations, in medias res. This is the method of all of the later prose-poems, and often, as here, it coincides with the metaphor of a journey. Bradford Cook observes that the poet-traveler of the prose-poems "undertakes an inner voyage in search of solitude and ideality, but first must pass through the slough of reality" (*Mallarmé: Selected Prose Poems, Essays, and Letters*, 112–113). In "La Déclaration Foraine" the poet and his lady are in a carriage; in "Le Nénuphar Blanc" he is in a boat; here he is on a train traveling to the countryside. He is struck, as one often is when one's train is pulling out of a station, by the placards or posters ("affiches") flying by, with their advertisements and their commonplaces. The same observation occurs at the end of "Un Spectacle Interrompu," when the curtain comes down and we return from the sublime to the ridiculous. A central theme of Mallarmé's prose-poems, as we have seen time and again, is the tension between the sacred and the profane, the sublime and the ridiculous, poetry and prose; and in the long sentence that forms the second paragraph of "La Gloire," we move from the banalities of the billboards to the "abstruse loftiness . . . [of] a forest in the time of its apotheosis" (p. 117). The irony that mediates between these two conditions in the sentence is the way in which the posters absorb "the uncomprehended gold of the days" ("l'or incompris des jours"—p. 117). "Incompris" means both misunderstood and unappreciated; the primary suggestion, given the context, is probably that the uncomprehending *masses* fail to appreciate the gold of the days; but I have rendered "incompris" as "uncomprehended" in order also to convey the sense of some transcendental quality that eludes even the most enlightened and sensitive spirit. In any event, the posters absorbing the gold of the days represent the "treason of letters" ("trahison de la lettre"—p. 117), the treason of letters against letters, the betrayal of a human potential (specifically, the potential to grasp the "gold of the days") that is rooted in letters, in literature, but that humanity has managed to turn into something profane. There is a loftiness here that aspires to match the difficult (or abstruse) loftiness, or pride ("l'abstruse fierté") of the forest; for it is bestowed by the forest.

As in "La Déclaration Foraine," the poet's contemplation of the Ideal is interrupted by the banality of everyday life: in this case, the station of Fontainebleau being howled out discordantly by the conductor. "Discord amid the exaltation" (p. 117): that is only the first of a series of oxymorons contained in the paragraph; but I have suggested that the generic existence of the prose-poem is itself an oxy-moron. There is a marvelous moment—at once deeply serious and uproariously funny—in which the poet imagines himself breaking down the conductor's door and throttling him, or, at the very least, bribing him to keep quiet. In the imaginary dialogue that ensues, however, we have a beautiful figure for the onset of poetic composition that the exaltation of the hour has set in motion; the poet asks the conductor not to "divulge the shadow which has here been instilled in my spirit to the carriage doors banging beneath an inspired and egalitarian wind" (p. 117). The covering shadow is proleptic; it anticipates an opening out to language; but if it is "divulged" too soon, the process will be short-circuited. "The inspired and egalitarian wind" is another oxymoron, and a strange one at that. In Mallarmé's essentially Romantic conception, although the inspired poet is withdrawn into his own spirit, because the inspiration he experiences is enabled by Nature, by the wind, it is accessible to everyone and, hence, is "egalitarian." To the masses, however, the appreciation of Nature is a form of kitsch; and in the irony contained in "an ecstasy bestowed upon all by the conjoined liberalities of nature and the State" (p. 117), we have as full a critique of modernity and mass society as anyone could ever require. The violence of "vomis" in "les touristes omniprésents vomis" is reminiscent of "le vomissement impur de la Bêtise" ("the foul vomit of Stupidity") of the penultimate stanza of "Les Fenêtres," as Ursula Franklin reminds us (*Anatomy of Poesis*, 164n.).

The vision of Modernity and the vision of Glory seem, indeed, to run along parallel rails in this poem, and each is intensified in the context of the other. Thus, in the penultimate paragraph, the poet imagines "the millions of existences stacking their vacuity in the enormous monotony of the capital" (p. 118).

This occurs in the context of a strange (almost Thoreauvian) moment in which the poet, withdrawn into his own solitude, reaches out companionably, as it were, to another solitude; for only in such solitude can there be true companionship and true equality. That paragraph, like the one that follows it and completes the poem, contains only a single sentence; against the desperate image of "existences stacking their vacuity," it seeks to grasp hold of Nature (the "bitter and luminous sobbings in the air") in order to hold on to "an indeterminate drifting idea forsaking the fortuitous like a branch" (p. 118). The emphasis on "the fortuitous" ("les hasards") is reminiscent of *Un Coup de Dés*, and indeed of Mallarmé's life-struggle as a poet.

"But there was no one," begins the final paragraph, and the transition strikes me as being as moving as anything in the prose-poems. "Personne," the first word in that final paragraph, has an extraordinary quality, not only because standing alone it stands for what it represents, but because in the French "no one" is also "anyone." In its solitude, "personne" is matched by "seul," the last word in the poem and in the sequence as a whole. The transition is powerful even in English, which can do nothing but render the bare conception. The prose, "enveloped in the wings of doubt," rises in this final paragraph to a sense of distilled beauty that one also finds at the conclusion of "Le Nénuphar Blanc." Indeed, the invisible trophy that the poet carries off is like the one at the conclusion of that poem; it is not any one thing but the experience as a whole, the poem in its entirety. The "immortal tree trunks" with their "superhuman pride" ("d'orgueils surhumains"—p.118) connect us back to the "fierté" of the forest and to the "gloire" at which the poetic conception is aimed. And the concluding apotheosis resonates with so much in Mallarmé: with "Victorieusement fui le suicide beau," with the conclusion of "L'Après-midi," with the sense one derives of the work as a whole.

UN COUP DE DÉS

UN COUP DE DÉS JAMAIS N'ABOLIRA
LE HASARD / A THROW OF THE DICE
WILL NEVER ABOLISH CHANCE

Un Coup de Dés, a poem that occupies a singular position not only in Mallarmé's oeuvre but in European literature as a whole, appeared for the first time in the international journal *Cosmopolis* in May 1897. It was not published on its own until 1914, when it was issued by the *Nouvelle Revue Française* in an edition prepared by the poet's son-in-law, Dr. Edmond Bonniot. Before his death in 1898, Mallarmé had corrected the proofs to a deluxe edition of the poem, measuring approximately fifteen-and-one-half inches in height and eleven-and-one-half inches in width, which was to be published with illustrations by Odilon Redon by the firm of Lahure. This edition never appeared in print, and both the proofs and the Redon lithographs were eventually sold by the publisher (see Cohn, *Mallarmé's Masterwork*, 77). For the present University of California edition of the poem, we have made use of an edition of *Un Coup de Dés* prepared by Mitsou Ronat and published in 1980, which comes closer than other modern editions to the specifications that Mallarmé designated for the Lahure text. The Ronat text has been reduced to sixty-four percent of its original size in order to accommodate the nine-inch page height of the present edition, and to preserve the spatial and typographical proportions that Mallarmé seems to have desired.

For the *Cosmopolis* edition, because the poem was not printed in the double-page format that he had intended for it, Mallarmé reluctantly supplied a Preface, and this is perhaps the best place to begin a consideration of *Un Coup de Dés*, especially since the Preface is sufficiently difficult in itself and fraught with ambiguity. Although (or perhaps because) *Un Coup de Dés* was so radical a departure, Mallarmé's primary concern in the Preface was apparently to align the work with traditional lyric poetry and to demonstrate how the techniques and devices that went into its composition compensate for the absence of traditional versification; the poem, he tells us, "participates . . . in a number of pursuits that are dear to our time: free-verse and the prose-poem," but these are joined under the influence of Music (p. 123). The "blanks . . . assume importance," but previously they were there as a "surrounding silence," and Mallarmé insists that the poem does not "transgress against [the received] order of things" ("mesure") but merely "disperse[s] its elements." "Mesure" in French encompasses "order," "measure," and "meter," and thus gives a sense of how deep Mallarmé's anxiety about the "transgression" involved in his "attempt" ("tentative") must have been—not, one hastens to add, because of any undue fear that he would offend the bourgeois sensibilities of his readers (he had already done that time and again) but because he "retain[s] a religious veneration" for "the ancient technique of verse," which continues to be connected to "the empire of passion and of dreams"(pp. 122–123). One of the fascinating aspects of the Preface, in other words, is Mallarmé's awareness that the poem enacts the very crisis of modernity to which it responds. He acknowledges that the future that will emerge from *Un Coup de Dés* remains unclear: "rien ou presque un art"—perhaps nothing, perhaps some "half-art" or "almost-art," perhaps (as I have translated the phrase) "what merely verges on [fulfilling the function of] art"(p. 122). There are negative implications to Mallarmé's prophecy that critics have generally failed to take into account. Nevertheless, at the end of the Preface there is a sense that there is no turning back, that the "subjects of pure and complex imagination or intellect" issuing from modernity cannot be excluded, that, in any event, Poetry will remain, "unique source"(p. 123).

The formal properties of *Un Coup de Dés*, the physical layout of the poem—these things are immediately striking and were radical innovations for the time in which the poem was composed. The "blanks" assume importance, as Mallarmé remarks, and one critic has even gone so far as to assert that they take precedence over the printed words (see La Charité, *The Dynamics of Space*, 83–85 passim); however, the problem of emptiness, of the void, of white spaces, is everywhere to be found in the *Poésies*. There is a complete absence of punctuation and a corresponding ambiguity of syntax, but, again, this had already been prepared for by the late sonnets. The "basic unit" is no longer the line but the page, or rather the double-page, and each double-page has a character of its own. (The California edition has rendered each of the poem's two-page spreads on a single, very wide page—a procedure that has both advantages and disadvantages; it allows for the French text to remain *en face*, but it eliminates the physicality of the "gutter" separating the verso and recto elements of the two-page spread.) What is most innovative about the poem, from a formal point of view, is the way in which the conception has been *materialized*—in a manner that makes the physical layout, the spacing, and the typography not merely a representation of the poem but an integral aspect of the poem itself. The "paper intervenes"; the printed words are disposed variously on the page, sometimes in ideogrammatic fashion—so that central images or motifs are literally constellated (constellated literally) on the page (but the perceptions of readers differ widely on this point); and finally, the various motifs and themes that the poem develops are differentiated typographically: in terms of their importance (as Mallarmé indicates in the Preface), in terms of their location in the poem, and as a representation of the sometimes far-flung syntactical connections that the poem, with its absence of punctuation, makes or allows us to entertain.

All of this is sufficiently striking, even one hundred years later, and one can easily understand the astonishment of a Valéry when the poem was first presented to him by its author:

> It seemed to me that I was looking at the form and pattern of a thought, placed for the first time in finite space. Here space itself truly spoke, dreamed, and gave birth to temporal forms. Expectancy, doubt, consternation, all were *visible things*. . . . There amid murmurs, insinuations, visual thunder, a whole spiritual tempest carried page by page to the extremes of thought, to a point of ineffable rupture—there the marvel took place; there on the very paper some indescribable scintillation of final stars trembled infinitely pure in an inter-conscious void; and there on the same void with them, like some new form of matter arranged in systems or masses or trailing lines, coexisted the Word! I was struck dumb by this unprecedented arrangement. It was as if a new asterism had

proffered itself in the heavens; as if a constellation had at last assumed a meaning. Was I not witnessing an event of universal importance, and was it not, in some measure, an ideal enactment of the Creation of Language that was being presented to me on this table at the last minute, by this individual, this rash explorer, this mild and simple man who was so unaffectedly noble and charming by nature? ("On 'A Throw of the Dice,'" 309–310)

"*He has undertaken*, I thought, *finally to raise a printed page to the power of the midnight sky*"—this was Valéry's response after receiving the proofs of the Lahure edition, not long before Mallarmé's death (312).

One can too easily fetishize the physical properties of the poem, however, and if it were not for the greatness of Mallarmé's poetic conception, if it were not for the sheer power of his phrasing and for the way in which the ideational and the plastic aspects of the work are integrated, the typography, the spacing, the disposition of the words on the page—none of this would sustain our interest for very long. Is it possible to abstract that conception from the welter of phenomena presented by the poem? One might say that the very difficulty of doing so is at the root of the experience of *Un Coup de Dés*, and I am inclined to agree with Malcolm Bowie that we should resist the various efforts that have been made to rationalize or allegorize the poem according to some sort of totalizing interpretive grid (see *Mallarmé and the Art of Being Difficult*, 115–145); the poem incorporates contingency at the same time that it attempts to come to terms with it philosophically. But neither should it be regarded as aleatory, and I would suggest that the basic conception or "guiding thread" running through the poem (the "fil conducteur" of the Preface)—as given in the title and dispersed through the

work itself—is the old problem for Mallarmé of how to establish meaning in an essentially meaningless universe—that is, in a universe from which the gods have disappeared, with the result that meaning cannot be transcendentally conferred. Mallarmé's most explicit forerunner in this regard is certainly Pascal, and the basic motif or metaphor of the dice-throw hearkens back to Pascal's Wager. Whereas for Pascal, however, the purpose of the Wager is precisely to close off the abyss, for Mallarmé the drop into the abyss, or, in the poet's own metaphor, the shipwreck on the shoals of meaninglessness or contingency, is in one sense inevitable and in another a necessary prelude to transcendence of another kind. The Mallarméan Wager annuls nothing; chance (as the poet renders it within the terms of the dice-throw metaphor) remains forever in effect; and "Nothing will have taken place but the Place . . . Except perhaps a Constellation." The method of presentation has changed radically, but the underlying thought is not really so different from what it had been in the constellation sonnets that Mallarmé grouped together as *Plusieurs Sonnets*. On the one hand there are the hideous Pascalian spaces, but on the other, there is a secret concurrence between human creativity and the constellations of the night sky. If one wants to pose this in Hegelian terms, one might say that humanity, striving for the Absolute, is shipwrecked on the shoals of contingency, and that any attempt that is launched on the Absolute must pass through those infinitely self-generating shoals. Consequently (to bring the concluding and opening lines of the poem into conjunction), although "All thought emits a throw of the dice," "A throw of the dice will never abolish chance." What is allegorized in *Un Coup de Dés*—again, insofar as the poem can be seen as an allegory—is the ebb and flow of humanity's continual struggle to seize hold of the Absolute: the Master-Seaman's confrontation with the oceanic abyss, the Poet's confrontation with the white page, the Philosopher's with the Void, and Everyman's with the "wrecks and errors" (to borrow Ezra Pound's phrase) of experience.

In discussing *Un Coup de Dés* in detail, I shall refer to each of the double-page spreads as a folio, and although each double-page spread constitutes a single page of the University of California Press edition I shall indicate whether a particular passage in question occupies a verso or recto page in the standard Pléiade edition. The poem in its entirety contains eleven such folios or double-page spreads, and with the French text *en face*, runs from pages 124 to 145 in the California edition.

The central phrase, "Un Coup de Dés jamais n'abolira le hasard," functions both as a title and as a "dominant motif" that will be dispersed over much of the poem's course. Printed in thirty-point bold capital letters (in the California edition), the phrase begins on the right-hand side of the first folio, continues on the right-hand side of the second folio (preceded by white space), resumes on the fifth, and concludes on the ninth, interacting, in the process of its unfolding, with various other "adjacent" motifs. Note that Mallarmé has reversed the normal word order of the phrase, so that "jamais" comes before "n'abolira." "Jamais" can mean both "never" and "ever," and thus, as the central phrase unfolds, a wavering effect is created that English is unable to capture, since it is obliged to indicate the negative immediately.

Below "jamais," at the bottom of the second folio, a second, parenthetical motif, "Quand bien même lancé dans des circonstances / éternelles / du fond d'un naufrage," appears in twelve-point capitals. It is immediately followed, at the top of the left-hand side of the next page, by the word "Soit," also in twelve-point capitals—and this allows us to read "Soit" both as a new syntactical beginning and as a continuation from "naufrage." ("Though it be" in the translation attempts to capture the possibility of this doubled effect.) A word about the shipwreck motif that is introduced at the bottom of the second folio: it can be found already in "Brise Marine" and also in two late sonnets, "Salut" and "A la nue accablante tu." In all three poems it seems to coincide with a kind of ecstatic transcendence or letting-go that is associated, in turn, with the breaking of received forms and with the intersection of time and eternity. The "eternal circumstances" of the passage in *Un Coup de Dés* could be considered a catachresis, since, strictly speaking, circumstances belong to time rather than to eternity, but what Mallarmé is interested in conveying, I believe, is precisely that intersection. From the standpoint of temporality, or chance, the individual, subject to the Lucretian collision of atoms, is "thrown," as Heidegger would say (I have translated "lancé" as "launched" in order to convey the metaphysical parallelism connecting the dice and the ship), into the world of contingency. One can picture the Master (seaman or poet), from the wreckage of experience, of phenomena, attempting, as by a leap of faith, to create an ordered world of some kind; such an attempt, however, must itself be governed by contingency. This particular set of dice, it has often been noted, should be seen as black with white points, reflecting the night's starred sky.

"Soit," at the top left of the third folio, is in twelve-point capitals, as we noted, and this is also true of "Le Maître" at the top of the fourth folio, of "Rien n'aura eu lieu que le lieu" on the tenth, and, finally, of

"Excepté peut-être une constellation" on the eleventh and last folio. The body text of the poem, beginning with "que" at the top of the third folio, is ten-point roman type; but the reader should note that the first letter of "Abîme" is capitalized, as is the case with "Nombre" and "Esprit" on the fourth folio and "Fiançailles" on the fifth.

In the constellation of images that the poet presents on the third folio, wave is to wing is to sail. "Soit" can have the force of the Genesis "Let there be"; but what is immediately invoked is the Abyss, which can be thought of both in metaphysical terms and as the trough of a cresting wave. I believe that the conception Mallarmé is developing in these lines, vague and oceanic as they are, has something to do with a simultaneity of creativity and destruction, such that the confrontation with the Abyss is fructative also of plenitude. Being and nothingness meet at the site of the wave, which is both crest and trough, reaching up desperately and despairingly ("désespérément" has both of these senses) only to fall back down again (I have rendered the French "plane" as the same verb in English in order to capture "plain," the old-fashioned verb for "lament," as a homonym). In its imaged ascent the wave is also a wing, Mallarmé's great symbol of a heroic enterprise that is always doomed in advance, and a sail that shrouds the gaping maw of the wrecked vessel. The sail ("la voile") is homonymically connected to the *veil* ("le voile") that will figure so prominently on the fifth folio, and the homonym has the force here of emphasizing the nothingness that all being covers. Homonymic resonances will play an important role throughout *Un Coup de Dés*, as we shall see, much as they do in the *Poésies* in general. A number of critics have seen this double-page spread ideogrammatically as the Big Dipper, and this possibility connects us to the cosmic imagery of the "Sonnet en-*yx*" from *Plusieurs Sonnets*.

The layout of the fourth folio, with its alignment of left- and right-hand side passages (verso and recto in the original), poses syntactical problems of a different order from any we have seen thus far, in that it requires us to read not only from top to bottom on a given side of the page but also from left to right on the entire double-page spread. The ebb and flow of the text, constituting an internal mimesis of the waves or of the sunken vessel listing to starboard and larboard, poses difficulties of reading that are themselves related to the problem of contingency or chance that the poem as a whole addresses. To some extent, however, in the counterpoint of left- and right-hand passages, the latter seem to function as a further predication of the former.

As previously noted, "Le Maître" at the top of the fourth folio is connected to "Soit" at the top of the third by the fact that both phrases are in twelve-point capital letters. Reading back, then, we can say that the Master has either come into existence or into focus, and either in the midst of the metaphorical shipwreck or in its aftermath. We should recall that the "Master," as Mallarmé develops that conception in the *Poésies*, fully becomes himself only after death; the sonnet on Poe, for example, begins: "As to Himself at last eternity changes him"; and the same conception seems at least partly to hold for *Un Coup de Dés*, in that the Master, "beyond ancient reckonings," beyond everything that concerned him in his own time, has arisen ("surgi") from the conflagration that has consumed him or is now consuming him. The temporal confusion seems once again to mark the intersection of time and eternity.

In line with this temporal confusion there is a curious doubleness in the image that is presented of the Master. He is simultaneously shaking the dice and brandishing his fist—or, in other words, choosing (or following) a destiny, on the one hand, and cursing the fates, on the other, in the manner, perhaps, of a Vanni Fucci in the circle of the wrathful in Hell. In a sense we are confronted by the ancient problem of the One and the Many on this folio. Man, ruled by contingency, seeks to grasp hold of the Absolute. One existential choice would be to throw the dice, take the leap of faith, in the hope that by this action of choosing or accepting "the unique Number which cannot / be another" one becomes whole, a Spirit who (again note the capitalization of "Nombre" and "Esprit"), out of the "storm" of experience, "fold[s] back [or heals] division [or multiplicity] and passes proudly on," ("Nombre" conjoins within itself "nom" and "ombre," and so the unique number or name that might emerge from the ocean of experience is already shadowed, as it were, by death.) Another choice would be to reject choice—that is, existence—in its entirety; but since chance cannot be abolished, such a refusal would itself amount to a casting of the dice. The possibility of such a refusal, however, leading to the image of the corpse, generates the metaphysical possibility of an alternative destiny, one that the arm brandishing its refusal "withholds" and that will forever remain a "secret." The hesitation between being and nothingness is as much given in the metaphorical ebb and flow of the waves as any hesitation between alternative conditions of being would be; thus, man is inevitably "shipwrecked," a being "without vessel / no matter / where" he might be. "Nef," according to the Littré dictionary, is a poetic synonym for "navire" and thus has the meaning of *ship*, but Mallarmé doubtlessly chose it because it also means the *nave* of a church and therefore emphasizes the sense in which "ship-

wrecked" man is without supports, including those provided by religion. I take "où" to be connected to "n'importe," but it may be that Mallarmé separates it from the phrase in order to evoke the homonym "ou" and connect it to "vaine." In any event, the folio concludes with a condensed evocation of the *vanitas vanitatum*, the emptiness of human being.

At the top of the fifth folio the image of the clenched fist returns. The adverb "ancestralement" can give the sense of "from ancient time" or "like his ancestors"—so that the Master (insofar as the imagery refers us back to the previous folio), stands on the threshold of that which will gather him back to his ancestors or, already dead, lies supine on the ocean floor like his ancestors. Whether recently dead or long since dead, dead "from ancient time," the Master becomes one with ancient time, merges with it in the way that Gautier, the Master of "Toast Funèbre," merges with ancient death at the end of that poem. Indeed, death is so strong a presence in the fifth folio that it threatens to nullify all distinctions: the Master merges with the ancestor, the father with the child whom he leaves as a legacy to his own disappearance ("legs en la disparition"), the old man with the sea. Confined to the left-hand side of the page, the text seems to form a cresting wave that threatens to spill over on or smash the right-hand side, where the single word "n'abolira," in thirty-point bold capitals, sits like a rock at the bottom. We cannot parse out all of the distinctions because the "ulterior immemorial demon" is intent on wiping them out. This loss of distinction, this merging, neutering, and reduction of all of experience—ironically intoned as the capitalized "Nuptials" ("Fiançailles") at the bottom of the left-hand side of the page—can lead to madness ("folie"), because if the world is perceived without its "veil of illusion" every gesture becomes a phantom.

In the ancestral struggle, which, at the same time, is the struggle of the ancestor, the sea is both generative and destructive; it is that through which the ancestor (or old man) comes into existence but it is also that which threatens to overwhelm his existence. "La mer" is also, significantly, "la mère," the ancient mother who through or against the old man "tempts an idle chance"—the two coming together in a chance collision of sperm and egg that is at once acceded to and refused by the figure whose clenched hand is imaged at the top of the page. The latent sexual conjunction, as manifested homonymically by the presence of "la mère" in "la mer," is celebrated—in the ghoulishly capitalized "Nuptials" ("Fiançailles") which actually fall into the gutter in the two-page spread of the French edition, by the lifting of the "veil of illusion" ("le voile d'illusion")—which had already been prepared for homonymically by the sail ("la voile") of folio three. The syntax is doubled, however, so that when the veil is thrown back ("rejailli"), what springs back ("rejailli") is the haunting of those "Nuptials"—as if to say that humankind cannot bear very much reality.

Framing the sixth folio, at the upper left (about one third of the page down) and lower right (about two-thirds down), in twelve-point italic capitals, is the phrase "comme si." The sixth, seventh, and eighth folios, forming an embedded movement of sorts, are set off from the previous pages—*as if* by the "simple insinuation" of folio six—by being primarily in eleven-point italics. One is reminded of Hans Vaihinger's book, *The Philosophy of 'As If'* (1920), in which the question of reality is bracketed and the fictions we propose to ourselves are taken seriously on their own terms. In any event, we are now in the realm of art, a realm in which the imagination might dredge from its own depths *something*, however tenu-

ous, that can be held up against an abyss that, on the previous folio, threatened to smother all human distinctions and to become the only reality. That which "flutters / about the abyss" ("voltige / autour du gouffre") is, as we learn on folio seven, a mere feather, but in the feather/pen conjunction of *plume* (which Mallarmé also exploits in the "Ouverture Ancienne" of *Hérodiade* and elsewhere), it is one that simultaneously "cradles the virgin trace [or sign]" of poetry. A symbolic chain of associated images emerges from the white foam that, riding the crest of a wave, is about to disappear into the "whirlpool of hilarity and horror" ("tourbillon d'hilarité et d'horreur"): the white foam (the virgin trace or sign) is simultaneously the poet's pen and the feather that a Hamlet will wear in his black toque as he confronts the meaning of the universe. One is reminded, as so often in *Un Coup de Dés*, of the Pascal of the *Pensées*: "Man is but a reed, the most feeble thing in nature, but he is a thinking reed. The entire universe need not arm itself to crush him. A vapor, a drop of water suffices to kill him. But, if the universe were to crush him, man would still be more noble than that which killed him, because he knows that he dies and the advantage which the universe has over him; the universe knows nothing of this."

Folios six through eight of the poem constitute, as we have said, an embedded movement in italics pertaining to the realm of art; and, interestingly, as the unpublished Lahure edition clearly shows, Mallarmé marked most of the *f*'s on the proofs of these pages, striking out the printed letter and substituting a flowing handwritten *f* of his own. Either he simply wanted the letter struck properly, as La Charité argues (see *The Dynamics of Space*, 45–46), or, as I follow a number of scholars in urging, he wanted the printer to substitute the florin *f* (*f*), a more fluid, flowery *f*, for the regular italic letter. In any event, the present edition follows the Mitsou Ronat text in substituting the florin *f* on these pages and also on the lower right-hand side of folio nine, where the embedded movement is resumed. Cohn suggests that the special *f* represents "a fool's feather, as in the *folie* that introduced the whole 'mad,' airy, italicized section" (*Mallarmé's Masterwork*, 79). Certainly the feather/pen motif is central to the material that the poet is developing in the embedded movement; and whether this is merely fortuitous or an encoded feature of Mallarmé's special relationship to the English language, it is interesting that in the translation the entire section culminates in the alliterated *f*'s of "Falls the feather."

In the seventh folio there is a play of black-on-white that connects the whiteness of the feather and the blackness of the "midnight toque"—which can be seen both as an enveloping wave and as Hamlet's cap—to the night sky studded with stars. The florin *f* might be seen from this point of view as a hieroglyph for the curved feather in Hamlet's cap—as in the Romantic painting by Eugène Delacroix. The fragility and ephemerality of the feather (which, being also a pen, is a metonym for poetry itself) is *immobilized* by the blackness of the sky and stiffens, on the cosmic plane, into a constellation—much as the dying swan of Mallarmé's great sonnet "Le vierge, le vivace et le bel aujourd'hui" stiffens into the constellation Cygnus. In the way in which these images are conjoined—and however they are ultimately parsed—there is a deep ambivalence, a tragic laughter, and a mixture of hope and despair. The feather/pen motif (and all that it implies) must remain in a solitary and, therefore, unactualized condition unless it is willing to be enveloped or to undergo dissolution—unless, as Hegel says in the "Unhappy Consciousness" section of the *Phenomenology of Mind*, it "comes upon the grave of its own life"; insofar as it is able to do so, however, it becomes the feather in the cap of a Hamlet, the "bitter prince of the reef," who stands as an emblem of the heroic capacity to confront the abyss. Yet this, too, is an oversimplification because the lightning flash—or flash of enlightenment ("foudre")—that Hamlet experiences (I am borrowing from the interpretation of St. Aubyn here [see *Stéphane Mallarmé*, 136]) is ambivalently linked to his "small virile reason" ("sa petite raison virile"), which, heroic though it may be, is ultimately, of course, futile.

"Virile," at the bottom of the seventh folio, preserves its etymological meaning of "pertaining to man," and in the eighth folio (which, as Bernard Weinberg notes, follows from the seventh as a kind of enjambment [see *The Limits of Symbolism*, 286]) a strong masculine-feminine opposition comes into play. At the same time that Hamlet, the heroic prince who was also the protagonist of Mallarmé's closet drama *Igitur*, typifies that sense of existential crisis that leads (occidental) man (understood either generically or as the male of the species) to question the meaning of existence, he also stands for the "masculine," civilizing urge to impose a "limit on infinity" ("une borne à l'infini"), to become the lord of a "manor" in which to take refuge, to crown himself with "the lucid and lordly crest" ("la lucide et seigneuriale aigrette"), which has proudly been constructed from the "plume" of the previous folio. The problem, however, is that the manor, previously thought solid ("un roc"), turns out to be "false" and is "immediately / evaporated in mist" ("tout de suite / évaporé en brumes"), while for his part the hero turns out to be an anxious, expiatory adolescent ("soucieux / expiatoire et pubère"), atoning (as Freud

271

might have observed) for the internal drama driving him on. This is perhaps an enactment of Sartre's drama of the inauthentic *en-soi* (or in-itself) *avant la lettre.*

The figure who exposes the erstwhile hero for what he is (together with the civilization, or attempt at civilization, for which he stands) is his feminine antitype, the Siren, whose forked tail slapping foam at the rock brings down the manor that "imposed / a limit on infinity." We last met with the Siren in two poems from the *Poésies*, "Salut" and "A la nue accablante tu," published in 1893 and 1895 respectively, very close in time to *Un Coup de Dés*. In "Salut" the Siren clearly represents the temptation of the body, of animal existence, of that which threatens to waylay the poet-Odysseus from his epic task of imposing order on the otherwise vague and amorphous dream. (Mallarmé will pun on "vague" in the tenth folio, a term that in the masculine means "vague" and in the feminine "wave.") As Weinberg notes, the twisting of the Siren is associated with words such as "tourbillon" and "enroulée"—and hence with the whirlpool of Charybdis and, by antithesis, the rock of Scylla (*The Limits of Symbolism*, 291–292). In "A la nue accablante tu," which brings together many of the motifs that will later be developed in *Un Coup de Dés*, the Siren, figured in the foam and in the aftermath of the "shipwreck" of theology, of any human claim on the Absolute, seems to represent both the demise of the dream and the reduction of reality to something altogether arbitrary and untotalizable, the mere play of phenomena.

In the meantime, at the top right-hand side of folio eight, in twelve-point bold italic capitals, the word "si" appears, both as part of the phrase "que si" (which is parallel to the framing "comme si" of folio six and which makes the verbs "scintille" and

"ombrage" of folio eight conditional rather than indicative) and as the first word of a sentence that will emerge on folio nine: "Si c'était le nombre ce serait le hasard." The words of that sentence appear in twelve-point bold italic capitals, except for "le hasard," which, as part of the poem's dominant motif, "Un Coup de Dés jamais n'abolira le hasard" and complet-ing that motif, is in thirty-point bold roman capitals. (There is some question about whether the "Si" of folio 8 and the phrases "C'était le nombre" and "Ce serait" of folio 9 should be in bold or in roman type. The Pléiade edition has all of this material in roman, while the Ronat text, which we generally follow, has only the "Si" in bold. The unpublished Lahure proofs are unclear on this point, but since the "Si" leads into the phrases of folio 9, wisdom would seem to dictate that the typography remain consistent, in any event; and so in this instance we depart from the Ronat text by using bold type for the entire passage.) The ninth folio, containing six typographical levels, is certainly the most complexly contrapuntal in the poem. The parenthetical or subsidiary material on the left-hand side of the page is in eight-point italics; the phrases "existât-il," "commençât-il et cessât-il," "se chiffrât-il," and "illuminât-il" on the right-hand side of the page are in twelve-point roman capitals; the material subsid-iary to those phrases is in eight-point lowercase roman; and finally, the passage beginning "Choit / la plume" at the bottom of the right-hand side of the page is in eleven-point roman italics.

On the ninth folio, then, we return to the purely metaphysical concerns that Mallarmé is addressing in the poem: the problem of "number," the problem of chance or contingency (which is itself given by the fact that there is number—if we think of the ancient pre-Socratic problem of the One and the Many), the problem of what the American poet George Oppen expresses as the "shipwreck of the singular" (in a great poem entitled "Of Being Numerous," which might, indeed, have been influenced by *Un Coup de Dés*). The metaphysical elaborations on the dominant and adjacent motifs that have now come to fruition require little commentary at this point, but there are a number of ambiguities in the French that should be noted. First of all, by placing the phrase "que si" on the previous folio, Mallarmé produces both a conditional clause and an indicative sentence in "C'était le nombre," while in English one would have to insert "were" to render the former and "was" to render the latter possibility. Secondly, in the capitalized subjunctive phrases beginning with "existât-il" on the right-hand side of the page, "il" can be both masculine and neuter; this is important because the potentialities being expressed in those phrases, in addition to referring to the ambiguous "number," could refer to the Master himself—in other words to the individual (perhaps the poet) who struggles against contingency—and also to the poem that is coming into existence in the context of that struggle, indeed to *Un Coup de Dés* itself. Both of these possibilities are given, and it is precisely here on the ninth folio—which, with the phrase "le hasard," marks the completion of the poem's dominant motif—that the poem arrives at its highest moment of self-reflexivity. Everything that follows from this moment—everything placed after the thirty-point bold capital letters of "le hasard"—is part of the poem's denouement; and indeed, placed immediately below that phrase, in the eleven-point italics that return us to the embedded movement pertaining to art, the feather/pen of the *plume* constellation finally falls, having now achieved its destiny, to be buried "in the original spray / whence formerly its delirium sprang up to a peak."

And with the burying of the feather/pen, as the poem comes to a completion on folios ten and eleven, it will be as if nothing had taken place but the place itself—except perhaps a constellation.

In light of the allusion to Hamlet on folio seven, with all that is signified thereby, the falling of the feather is reminiscent of the prince's utterance in Act V of Shakespeare's play: "There is special providence in the fall of a sparrow" (5.2.220)—an utterance that itself echoes two equally famous lines that occur slightly earlier in the same scene: "There's a divinity that shapes our ends, / Rough-hew them how we will" (10–11). But with the substitution of chance for providence or divinity, all events, all results, are nullified; everything is put into question, including, of course, the meaning of man, who is that being who insists on meaning. This is the point that is reached in the denouement of folios ten and eleven, dominated as they are by a sentence, in twelve-point capitals, that first reduces the possibility of meaning to a tautology ("nothing will have taken place but the place") and then reluctantly allows for an ambivalent affirmation ("except perhaps a constellation"). That affirmation (if we can refer to it as such) is again reminiscent of the constellation sonnets of *Plusieurs Sonnets*: both the aforementioned Swan sonnet and the "Sonnet en-*yx*" ("Ses purs ongles très haut dédiant leur onyx"), in which the constellation in question is the Big Dipper, as it also is in *Un Coup de Dés*.

The tenth and eleventh folios have a simplicity—relative to the rest of the poem, of course—that is reflected in the typography. In addition to the sentence in twelve-point capitals, each of the capitalized words is modified or elaborated upon by text in ten-point lowercase type. Perhaps the most interesting word on the left-hand side of folio ten is "l'évènement." The editors of the Pléiade edition silently emend the accent of the second *e* from a grave to an acute accent ("l'événement"), no doubt assuming that Mallarmé's intended word-choice was what English would translate as "event." It is clear from the manuscripts and from the Lahure edition, however, that Mallarmé wanted the grave accent—and the reason, perhaps, as Weinberg suggests, is that he was combining "l'événement" ("event") and "l'avènement" ("advent") (see *The Limits of Symbolism*, 302). In any event, the portmanteau word that is thereby created seems to concretize very precisely the ambivalent wavering that the sentence in capital letters expresses: between an *advent* (or *coming*) that has religious or quasi-religious overtones and an *event* (or *happening*) the significance of which is nullified by the loss of a transcendental horizon.

Beginning with the starkly capitalized "Rien" on the left-hand side of folio ten, this penultimate page confronts not only the potential nullity of human existence but the tendency of humanity to turn nothing into something: that is, to found a "perdition" out of a fiction or lie. The "ordinary elevation [that] pours out absence" is both the crest and trough of the wave and the afflatus of the poet, which, though it confronts nothingness, must be said (from a certain despairing point of view) to partake of nothingness as much as any other act. The word "perdition" in French refers to the sinking or distress of ships, and in both English and French it is also, of course, a hell that is peopled by those who are *lost*; etymologically, it is a lostness, a forgetting, a nothing that has been made into something. The Mallarméan critique of religion is in part a demystification of a fiction or lie ("mensonge"), but—as in the portmanteau word "l'évènent," which hovers between an *event* that would otherwise be swallowed up or dissolved and an *advent* that consolidates a moment of real signifi-

cance—there is a deep ambivalence here, a shuttling between hope and despair. "Vague" in French, as we noted earlier, means "vague" and "empty" in the masculine and "wave" in the feminine, and the metaphor created by the homonym at the bottom of the folio suggests that in addition to the *vagueness* "in which all reality dissolves" (that is, in which all boundaries are lost), there is an ebb and flow in the thought itself between the possibility and the loss of reality.

This wavering, or *enantiodromia* (to borrow a term Jung takes from Heraclitus for the shuttling between opposites), is contained in the language of the eleventh and final folio as a shuttling between a concretely physical vocabulary (especially the technical vocabulary of seafaring) and a religious vocabulary. The phrase "à l'altitude," for example, which, significantly, is placed at the top of the left-hand side of the page, can be translated "at the height," "at the altitude," or, as I do here, "on high." Similarly, in "aussi loin qu'un endroit / fusionne avec au delà"— a phrase that cuts across the gutter of the French edition, thereby miming the very process of spanning or fusing that its words conceptualize—the "beyond" that is evoked can be either the physical realm of the stars or something more fully transcendental. The technical language of seafaring is given in the *obliquity* and *declivity*, terms respectively denoting the angle between the planes of the earth's equator and orbit and the deviation from the horizontal.

The Septentrion is the seven stars of the Dipper that point to the North Star, and the physical layout of the text on this folio forms a hieroglyph of the Dipper. The Dipper, in Mallarmé's poetry, as we noted in regard to the "Sonnet en-*yx*" and other poems, functions essentially as a symbolic container for the ineffable, in the play of microcosm against macrocosm that links poetry to the stars. (In the

"Sonnet en-*yx*," "the Master has gone to draw tears from the Styx" with the ghostly "ptyx," the ineffable container that is then connected to the "septuor," the seven stars of the Dipper.)   The problem of finding a container is the problem of fixing in place a reality that would otherwise dissolve; without that container, "Nothing will have taken place but the place"; and thus, the problem of finding a container, as *Un Coup de Dés* reaches its terminus, is the problem of the poetic process itself. The lines after the capitalized "une constellation" express the ambivalence that Mallarmé so often articulates in relation to an eternity that is locked into place; the phrase "cold from forgetfulness and desuetude" reminds us of "the useless exile of the Swan," locked into the constellation Cygnus in "Le vierge, le vivace et le bel aujourd'hui." Moreover, there will be no "total account in the making"; there is no way of summing everything up or making sense of it all. Nevertheless, even though "All Thought emits a Throw of the Dice," in the beautifully lyrical concluding passage of the poem, a passage in which a string of participles connects the rolling of the dice to the poet's meditations, Mallarmé's long vigil arrives at a shining moment "before coming to a halt / at some terminus that sanctifies it."

BIBLIOGRAPHY

PRIMARY SOURCES

Mallarmé, Stéphane. *Correspondance de Stéphane Mallarmé.* 3 vols. Ed. Henri Mondor and Jean-Pierre Richard. Paris: Gallimard, 1959–1969.

————. *Mallarmé.* Trans. Anthony Hartley. Harmondsworth: Penguin Books Ltd., 1965.

————. *Les Noces d'Hérodiade, Mystère.* Ed. Gardner Davies. Paris: Gallimard, 1959.

————. *Œuvres Complètes de Stéphane Mallarmé.* Ed. Carl Paul Barbier and Charles Gordon Millan. Paris: Flammarion, 1983.

————. *Œuvres Complètes de Stéphane Mallarmé.* Ed. Henri Mondor and G. Jean-Aubry. Paris: Gallimard, 1951.

————. *Selected Letters of Stéphane Mallarmé.* Ed. Rosemary Lloyd. Chicago: University of Chicago Press, 1988.

————. *Selected Poetry and Prose.* Ed. Mary Ann Caws. New York: New Directions, 1982.

————. *Selected Prose Poems, Essays, and Letters.* Ed. Bradford Cook. Baltimore: The Johns Hopkins University Press, 1956.

————. *Un Coup de Dés Jamais N'Abolira le Hasard.* Ed. Mitsou Ronat. Paris: Change/Errant/d'Atelier, 1980.

SECONDARY SOURCES

Austin, L. J. "'Le Principal Pilier': Mallarmé, Victor Hugo et Richard Wagner." *Revue d'Histoire Littéraire de la France* (April-June 1951): 154–180.

————. "Mallarmé, Huysmans et la 'Prose pour des Esseintes.'" *Revue d'Histoire Littéraire de la France*, 54:2 (April-June 1954): 173–175.

Ayda, Adile. *Le Drame Intérieur de Mallarmé.* Istanbul: Edition La Turquie Moderne, 1955.

Benjamin, Walter. *Illuminations.* Trans. Harry Zohn. New York: Schocken Books, 1969.

Berg, R.-J. "'Le Pitre Châtié' I et II, ou l'Intertextualité Problematique." *Nineteenth-Century French Studies*, 15, no. 4 (Summer 1987): 376–384.

Bersani, Leo. *The Death of Stéphane Mallarmé.* Cambridge: Cambridge University Press, 1982.

Bishop, Lloyd. "Musset's First Sonnet: A Semiotic Analysis." *Romanic Review* 74 (1983): 455–480.

Bowie, Malcolm. *Mallarmé and the Art of Being Difficult.* Cambridge: Cambridge University Press, 1978.

Burt, Ellen. "Mallarmé's 'Sonnet en-*yx*': The Ambiguities of Speculation." *Yale French Studies* 54 (1977): 55–82.

Cellier, Léon. *Mallarmé et la Morte Qui Parle.* Paris: Presses Universitaires de France, 1950.

Chesters, Graham. "A Political Reading of Baudelaire's 'L'Artiste Inconnu' ('Le Guignon')." *Modern Language Review* 79 (1984): 64–76.

Chisholm, A. R. *Mallarmé's "Grand Oeuvre."* Manchester: Manchester University Press, 1962.

———. "Mallarmé: 'Ses purs ongles.'" *French Studies* 6 (1952): 230–234.

———. "Mallarmé: 'Quand l'ombre menaça.'" *French Studies* 15 (1961): 146–149.

———. "Mallarmé's Vasco Sonnet." *French Studies* 20 (1966): 139–143.

Cohn, Robert Greer. *Mallarmé's Masterwork: New Findings.* The Hague: Mouton, 1966.

———. *Mallarmé's 'Un coup de dés': An Exegesis.* New Haven: Yale French Studies, 1949.

———. *Mallarmé's Prose Poems: A Critical Study.* Cambridge: Cambridge University Press, 1987.

———. *Toward the Poems of Mallarmé.* Berkeley: University of California Press, 1980.

Cornell, Kenneth. *The Symbolist Movement.* New Haven: Yale University Press, 1951.

Crow, Christine. "'Le Silence au Vol de Cygne': Baudelaire, Mallarmé, Valéry and the Flight of the Swan." In *Baudelaire, Mallarmé, Valéry: New Essays in Honour of Lloyd Austin.* Ed. Malcolm Bowie, Alison Fairlie, and Alison Finch. Cambridge: Cambridge University Press, 1982, 1–23.

Davies, Gardner. *Mallarmé et le Drame Solaire.* Paris: Librairie José Corti, 1959.

———. "Mallarmé's *Petit Air I.*" In *Baudelaire, Mallarmé, Valéry: New Essays in Honour of Lloyd Austin.* Ed. Malcolm Bowie, Alison Fairlie, and Alison Finch. Cambridge: Cambridge University Press, 1982, 158–180.

———. "Stéphane Mallarmé: Fifty Years of Research," *French Studies* 1, no.1 (January 1947): 1–26.

de Man, Paul. *Blindness and Insight: Essays in the Rhetoric of Contemporary Criticism.* 2d ed. Minneapolis: University of Minnesota Press, 1983.

———. "Lyrical Voice in Contemporary Theory." In *Lyric Poetry: Beyond New Criticism.* Ed. Chaviva Hosek and Patricia Parker. Ithaca: Cornell University Press, 1985.

———. "Poetic Nothingness: On a Hermetic Sonnet by Mallarmé." In *Critical Writings: 1953–1978.* Minneapolis: University of Minnesota Press, 1989.

Derrida, Jacques. *Acts of Literature.* Ed. Derek Attridge. New York and London: Routledge, 1992.

Finch, Alison. "'Réminiscence' and the Development of Mallarmé's Prose Poems." In *Baudelaire, Mallarmé, Valéry: New Essays in Honour of Lloyd Austin.* Ed. Malcolm Bowie, Alison Fairlie, and Alison Finch. Cambridge: Cambridge University Press, 1982. 202–221.

Fletcher, Angus. *Allegory: The Theory of a Symbolic Mode.* Ithaca and London: Cornell University Press, 1964.

Fowlie, Wallace. *Mallarmé.* Chicago: University of Chicago Press, 1970.

Franklin, Ursula. *An Anatomy of Poesis: The Prose Poems of Mallarmé.* Chapel Hill: North Carolina Studies in the Romance Languages and Literatures, 1976.

Fry, Paul. *The Poet's Calling in the English Ode.* New Haven and London: Yale University Press, 1980.

Gill, Austin. *The Early Mallarmé.* 2 vols. Oxford: The Clarendon Press, 1986.

———. "From 'Quand l'Ombre menaça' to 'Au seul souçi de voyager': Mallarmé's Debt to Chateaubriand." *Modern Language Review* 50 (1955): 414–432.

———. *Mallarmé's Poem* "La chevelure vol d'une flamme." Glasgow: University of Glasgow, 1971.

Goodkin, Richard. *Around Proust.* Princeton: Princeton University Press, 1991.

———. *The Symbolist Home and the Tragic Home: Mallarmé and Oedipus.* Amsterdam: John Benjamins, 1984.

———. "Zeno's Paradox: Mallarmé, Valéry, and the Symbolist 'Movement.'" *Yale French Studies* 74 (1988): 133–156.

Gordon, Rae Beth. *Ornament, Fantasy, and Desire in Nineteenth-Century French Literature.* Princeton: Princeton University Press, 1992.

Hambly, Peter. "Cinq Sonnets de Mallarmé." *Essays in French Literature* 22 (November 1985): 21–49.

Hegel, G.W.F. *Aesthetics: Lectures on Fine Art.* Trans. T. M. Knox. 2 vols. Oxford: The Clarendon Press, 1975.

Heidegger, Martin. *Early Greek Thinking.* Trans. D. F. Krell and F. A. Capuzzi. New York: Harper and Row, 1975.

Houston, John Porter. *Patterns of Thought in Rimbaud and Mallarmé.* Lexington, KY: French Forum Publishers, 1986.

Johnson, Barbara. *The Critical Difference: Essays in the Contemporary Rhetoric of Reading.* Baltimore: The Johns Hopkins University Press, 1985.

Kravis, Judy. *The Prose of Mallarmé.* Cambridge: Cambridge University Press, 1976.

La Charité, Virginia A. *The Dynamics of Space: Mallarmé's Un Coup de Dés Jamais N'Abolira le Hasard.* Lexington, KY: French Forum Publishers, 1987.

Langan, Janine D. *Hegel and Mallarmé.* Lanham, MD: University Press of America, 1986.

Lawler, James R. *The Language of French Symbolism.* Princeton: Princeton University Press, 1969.

———. "Mallarmé's 'La Gloire.'" *Writing in a Modern Temper: Essays on French Literature and Thought in Honour of Henri Peyre.* Ed. Mary Ann Caws. Stanford French and Italian Studies 33 (1984): 136–145.

———. "Three Sonnets." *Yale French Studies* 54 (1977): 83–95.

LeSage, Laurent. *The Rhumb Line of Symbolism: French Poets from Sainte-Beuve to Valéry.* University Park: Penn State University Press, 1978.

Lestringant, Frank. "Rémanence du Blanc: A Propos d'une Réminiscence Hugolienne dans L'Œuvre de Mallarmé." *Revue d'Histoire Littéraire de la France* 81 (1981): 64–74.

Lloyd, Rosemary. *Mallarmé: Poésies.* London, 1984.

Marvick, Louis Wirth. *Mallarmé and the Sublime.* Albany: State University of New York Press, 1986.

Mauron, Charles. *Introduction to the Psycho-analysis of Mallarmé.* Trans. Archibald Henderson, Jr., and Will L. McClendon. Berkeley and Los Angeles: University of California Press, 1963.

Michaud, Guy. *Mallarmé.* Trans. Marie Collins and Bertha Humez. New York: New York University Press, 1965.

Mondor, Henri. *Eugène Lefébure, sa vie, ses lettres à Mallarmé.* Paris: Gallimard, 1951.

———. *Vie de Mallarmé.* Paris: Gallimard, 1941.

Morel, Jacques. "Le 'Sortilège Bu' et la Pentecôte: Note sur le 'Tombeau d'Edgar Poe.'" *Revue d'Histoire Littéraire de la France* 83, no. 3 (1983): 459–461.

Morris, D. Hampton, ed. *Stéphane Mallarmé: Twentieth-Century Criticism (1972-1979).* University, MS: Romance Monographs, Inc., 1989.

Newton, Joy, and Ann Prescott. "Mallarmé's Clown: A Study of 'Le Pitre Châtié.'" *Romance Quarterly* 30, no. 4 (1983): 435–440.

Noulet, Émilie. *Vingt Poèmes de Stéphane Mallarmé*. Geneva: Droz, 1967.

Olds, Marshall C. *Desire Seeking Expression: Mallarmé's "Prose pour des Esseintes."* Lexington, KY: French Forum Publishers, 1983.

Poulet, Georges. *The Interior Distance*. Trans. Elliott Coleman. Baltimore: The Johns Hopkins University Press, 1959.

————. *The Metamorphoses of the Circle*. Trans. Carley Dawson and Elliott Coleman. Baltimore: The Johns Hopkins University Press, 1966.

Quennell, Peter. *Baudelaire and the Symbolists*. Port Washington: Kennikat, 1970.

Rand, Harry. *Manet's Contemplation at the Gare Saint-Lazare*. Berkeley and London: University of California Press, 1987.

Richard, Jean-Pierre. *L'Univers Imaginaire de Mallarmé*. Paris: Editions du Seuil, 1961.

Riffaterre, Michael. "On the Prose Poem's Formal Features." In *The Prose Poem in France: Theory and Practice*. Ed. Mary Ann Caws and Hermine Riffaterre. New York: Columbia University Press, 1983, 117–132.

————. "Prosopopeia." *Yale French Studies* 69 (1985): 107–123.

————. *The Semiotics of Poetry*. Bloomington: Indiana University Press, 1978.

St. Aubyn, F. C. *Stéphane Mallarmé*. Boston: Twayne Publishers, 1989.

Sartre, Jean-Paul. *Mallarmé, or the Poet of Nothingness*. Trans. Ernest Sturm. University Park: Penn State University Press, 1988.

Sonnenfeld, Albert. *Order and Adventure in French Post-Romantic Poetry*. New York: Oxford University Press, 1976.

Souffrin-le-Breton, Eileen. "The Young Mallarmé and the Boucher Revival." In *Baudelaire, Mallarmé, Valéry: New Essays in Honour of Lloyd Austin*. Ed. Malcolm Bowie, Alison Fairlie, and Alison Finch. Cambridge: Cambridge University Press, 1982, 283–313.

Steiner, George. *After Babel: Aspects of Language and Translation*. London: Oxford University Press, 1975.

Stierle, Karlheinz. "Position and Negation in Mallarmé's 'Prose pour des Esseintes.'" *Yale French Studies* 54 (1978).

Sugano, Marian Zwerling. *The Poetics of the Occasion: Mallarmé and the Poetry of Circumstance*. Stanford: Stanford University Press, 1992.

Thibaudet, Albert. *La Poésie de Stéphane Mallarmé*. Paris: Gallimard, 1926.

Valéry, Paul. *The Art of Poetry.* Trans. Denise Folliot. Vol. 7, *The Collected Works of Paul Valéry*, ed. Jackson Mathews. Princeton: Princeton University Press, 1958.

———. "On 'A Throw of the Dice.'" *Leonardo, Poe, Mallarmé.* Trans. Malcolm Cowley and James R. Lawler. Vol. 8, *The Collected Works of Paul Valéry*, ed. Jackson Mathews. Princeton: Princeton University Press, 1972.

Weinberg, Bernard. *The Limits of Symbolism: Studies of Five Modern French Poets.* Chicago: University of Chicago Press, 1966.

Wolf, Mary Ellen. *Eros Under Glass: Psychoanalysis and Mallarmé's Hérodiade.* Columbus: Ohio State University Press, 1987.